Creating Books for the Young
in the New South Africa

Creating Books for the Young in the New South Africa

Essays on Authors and Illustrators of Children's and Young Adult Literature

Edited by
BARBARA A. LEHMAN, JAY HEALE,
ANNE HILL, THOMAS VAN DER WALT
and MAGDEL VORSTER

Foreword by Elwyn Jenkins
Afterword by Beverley Naidoo

McFarland & Company, Inc., Publishers
Jefferson, North Carolina

"The 'Dual Realities' of Niki Daly: Dreaming Himself into Someone Else's Skin" appeared in different form in *Sankofa: A Journal of African Children's and Young Adult Literature* 11 (2012): 6–15 and is reprinted with permission.

"Chris van Wyk: A Man Intent on Sharing Africa with Africa's Children" by Jay Heale uses extracts from Chris van Wyk, *Shirley, Goodness and Mercy— A Childhood Memoir* (Johannesburg: Picador Africa, 2004) with permission from Pan Macmillan.

"Breaking New Ground with Reviva Schermbrucker" appeared in different form in *Bookbird* 49.1 (2011): 9–16 and is reprinted by permission.

LIBRARY OF CONGRESS CATALOGUING-IN-PUBLICATION DATA

Creating books for the young in the new South Africa : essays on authors and illustrators of children's and young adult literature / edited by Barbara A. Lehman, Jay Heale, Anne Hill, Thomas van der Walt and Magdel Vorster ; foreword by Elwyn Jenkins ; afterword by Beverley Naidoo.

    p.   cm.

Includes bibliographical references and index.

ISBN 978-0-7864-7551-3 (softcover : acid free paper) ∞
ISBN 978-1-4766-1716-9 (ebook)

1. Children's literature, South African—History and criticism. 2. Young adult literature, South African—History and criticism. 3. Children—Books and reading—South Africa. 4. Illustrators—South Africa. 5. South Africa—In literature. I. Lehman, Barbara A., editor. II. Heale, Jay, editor. III. Hill, Anne, editor. IV. Van der Walt, Thomas, editor. V. Vorster, Magdel, editor.

PR9363.9.C74 2014
820.9'92820968—dc23   2014031517

BRITISH LIBRARY CATALOGUING DATA ARE AVAILABLE

© 2014 Barbara A. Lehman, Jay Heale, Anne Hill, Thomas van der Walt and Magdel Vorster. All rights reserved

No part of this book may be reproduced or transmitted in any form or by any means, electronic or mechanical, including photocopying or recording, or by any information storage and retrieval system, without permission in writing from the publisher.

On the cover: open book, trees, and house on a hill © 2014 iStock/Thinkstock

Printed in the United States of America

McFarland & Company, Inc., Publishers
  Box 611, Jefferson, North Carolina 28640
  www.mcfarlandpub.com

To all those who work on behalf of
the young readers of South Africa

Table of Contents

Foreword (Elwyn Jenkins) — 1

Preface — 5

PART 1. TRANSITION MOVERS

Introduction — 9

Lesley Beake: Quality in Diversity
  JAY HEALE — 12

Alida Bothma: From Her Palette of Inspiration to Her Montage of Expression
  MAGDEL VORSTER — 21

Paddy Bouma: Precise Pure Art at Work in the Books of Africa
  JAY HEALE — 31

The Writing of Dianne Case: Making Choices and Facing Consequences
  LISA KIMBLE *and* BARBARA A. LEHMAN — 38

The "Dual Realities" of Niki Daly: Dreaming Himself into Someone Else's Skin
  BARBARA A. LEHMAN — 47

Native, Gone Wandering: Dianne Hofmeyr as Constant Explorer
  ERIN F. REILLY-SANDERS *and* ANDRÉS A. MONTAÑÉS-LLERAS — 55

Sindiwe Magona: Writing Oneself Out of Poverty
  TANYA BARBEN — 64

Linda Rode: Bookmaker of the Imagination
  MARIANNE VAN LOGGERENBERG — 73

Marita van der Vyver: Fairy Tales and Feminism
  MARITHA SNYMAN — 82

Smelling Ferdinand's Flowers: Marjorie van Heerden's Journey
    MAGDEL VORSTER   91

Chris van Wyk: A Man Intent on Sharing Africa with Africa's Children
    JAY HEALE   101

PART 2. WRITERS AND ARTISTS OF THE NEW SOUTH AFRICA

Introduction   109

Inside the Books: The Life and Work of Jude Daly
    BETTIE PARSONS BARGER   112

On a Journey with Leon de Villiers
    MAGDEL VORSTER   120

Piet Grobler's Little Bird Told Me
    MAGDEL VORSTER   128

Wendy Hartmann: The Hidden Heroine
    JAY HEALE   137

Jaco Jacobs Brings the Circus to Town
    MAGDEL VORSTER   145

Ingrid Mennen: Always in Africa
    TANYA BARBEN   155

Gcina Mhlophe: Imbira Player
    GENEVIEVE HART   164

An Odyssey Through Fantasy: Fiona Moodie's Long Journey Home
    ANNE HILL   173

Martie Preller: Empowering Readers Through Stories
    MARITHA SNYMAN   182

Changing the Colors of South Africa: Post-Apartheid Illustrations of Elizabeth Pulles
    ERIN F. REILLY-SANDERS   190

Joan Rankin: Illustrator by Surprise
    JAY HEALE   199

Listening to Others: Jenny Robson's Books for Young South Africans
    JUDITH INGGS   207

Breaking New Ground with Reviva Schermbrucker RUTH STONE *and* BARBARA A. LEHMAN	216
Dianne Stewart: Writer with a Sense of Purpose JAY HEALE	226
Ann Walton: Families and Fables ANNE HILL	234

PART 3. NOTEWORTHY NEW TALENT

Introduction	241
Kagiso Lesego Molope: The Caged Bird Flies and Sings RAJENDRA CHETTY	243
Nokuthula K. Msimang: The Gentle Gender Warrior ROBIN MALAN	250
Sally Partridge: Transitions from Outside In and Inside Out ANNE HILL	259

Afterword (Beverley Naidoo)	267
Appendix: Literary Awards and Prizes	271
Bibliography	274
About the Contributors	289
Index	292

Foreword

Elwyn Jenkins

In Peter Slingsby's youth novel *Jedro's Bane* (2002), a seer tells Koot, a young Khoisan freedom fighter of the early nineteenth century, "*Ta-rau/ka* is the turn-around, the time when the world changes so that it will never be the same again. Some are chosen to lead others through the changes" (86). Later the grandfather of Koot's modern descendant, Jedro, tells him about the advent of democracy in South Africa in 1994, already beyond the memory of a modern youngster, saying, "You're young, you can't remember that day, just a few years ago, when the world turned around yet again—*ta-rau/ka*—and we became free at last. Koot fought for that, it's the memory of people like Koot that brings hope when people are not free" (134).

While it may at first seem inappropriate that a collection of essays on children's and youth literature should take as its mainspring a political anniversary, the effect of 1994 on South African children's and youth literature, and the significance of the date in the history of the literature and its associated scholarship, deserve considered attention.

The imposition of apartheid after 1948 brought to an end the happy, inconsequential neocolonial literature that South African white children had until then enjoyed. After a while a new, edgy literature emerged, increasingly urgent in the responsibility that its young characters bore to "lead others through the changes." Writers and illustrators took young readers through the change, conveying the anxiety and euphoria of those amazing days when adults looked to the younger generation in the hope that they would put their liberation to the service of the nation. Perhaps today some of that momentum has been lost, as the dull statistics of social commentators may suggest, but creative writers and illustrators deal with the imagination and the spirit, not merely social history; they are heirs to the country's ancient traditions of storytelling, with their laughter, fantasy, and the conflict between good and evil; they carry the memory of Koot and his successors; and their works bring hope to people who are not yet free, whether they be young South Africans still struggling to rise above poverty, poor education and unemployment, or the comity of young people around the world.

While bibliographers had long worked on recording and classifying South African children's and youth literature, as they continue to do with distinction, in the 1980s an interest emerged among scholars in interpreting patterns in the literature. Carl Lohann did ground-breaking work on Afrikaans literature, and Andrée-Jeanne Tötemeyer courageously identified racism in stories and illustrations, even questioning the ideology underlying the retelling of indigenous folktales. My book *Children of the Sun: Selected Writers and Themes in South African Children's Literature* (1993) attempted discursive studies of what I saw as some of the most significant themes in books written in English.

Marguerite Poland's books in the style of San and African folktales were attracting a lot of interest and winning prizes, but were controversial because of questions over the reading age required, and misunderstood by critics who thought she was simply retelling folktales when in fact she was creating a new genre of intensely South African stories that drew on the country's literary traditions for a new generation. To understand where she stood, I went back to examine the strong tradition of retelling of folktales in translation in South Africa, moving on to the equally strong tradition of stories about talking animals, which drew more on English models. Before looking at the spate of books with a new environmental conservation theme that were appearing, I once more went back to their predecessors, puzzling on the early predominance of books set in the open spaces of the Karoo and the bushveld. That led me to considering the history of prescribing South African books in schools. In short, the history of South African books in English was revealed as an intimate but hitherto unnoticed documentation of how English-speaking white people had gradually cut their ties with the motherland and become South African. Regarding the interpretation of their history and the history of the country, there was one obvious author to read: Jenny Seed, whose innovative liberal historical fiction I felt had received less attention than it deserved. From there it was a small step to the young adult novels that were engaging with contemporary social developments in the country.

An unexpected finding was how many recent books presented alternative versions of masculinity to the stereotype of macho boys common to most stories of the nineteenth and first half of the twentieth centuries. Here were boys who were gentle, sensitive, clumsy, or scared.

Children of the Sun was published in South Africa by Ravan Press, whose directors accepted it because they had a strong interest in publishing radical and revisionist works that questioned the norms of the apartheid state. The book was awarded an Honourable Mention for the Noma Award for Publishing in Africa on the same grounds.

Writing *Children of the Sun*, and the reception that the book received, indicated what more research and criticism were waiting to be undertaken. What was needed was *contextualizing*. Modern South African English children's and youth books did not exist in a vacuum: they must have had a history, and they existed within a wider literary context both in South Africa and internationally. These concerns formed the subject of my next two books (Jenkins 2002; 2006).

They were published in the United States because South African publishers anticipated (correctly) too small a readership in South Africa. This overseas exposure reflected a growing international interest in the South African literature, but because they were published abroad they received limited exposure at home. However, my last book of essays, *Seedlings: English Children's Reading and Writers in South Africa* (2012), readily found a local publisher, thanks to the growing serious attention to South African children's and youth books in all languages that the country has seen in the last twenty years.

The status of children's literature in recent years was given a boost by the publication of two books, J.A. Kruger's *Kinderkeur* (1991), a study of awards and their winning authors and illustrators, and the landmark work on Afrikaans children's and youth literature, *Van Patrys-hulle tot Hanne Hoekom* (Wybenga and Snyman 2005). The encouragingly high profile of the literature in educated circles is sustained by serious informed commentary on authors and illustrators at conferences that include overseas delegates, by the International Board on Books for Young People and Bookchat newsletters, and by booklets such as the invaluable ones by Jay Heale. Agencies of the public exposure that the literature enjoys include awards for authors and illustrators, skilled book reviewers in newspapers and magazines, the work of librarians, the projects of various non-governmental organizations that promote reading and book distribution, and the efforts of publishers and book dealers. Above all, the originality and excellence of the books and their illustrators are their own guarantee of their success both at home and abroad.

South African children's and youth literature still needs more serious academic attention. There have been a few postgraduate theses, but in the absence of academic departments dedicated to the subject they will continue to be scarce. While articles on a reasonable number of South African authors of youth literature have been included in various local and international reference books, they are scattered and short. Lengthier articles in academic journals are still relatively scarce. This makes the present collection very welcome for bringing together in one volume serious studies of currently active illustrators and writers in English and Afrikaans.

When I wrote *Children of the Sun* I cast my bread upon the waters. It had an exciting reception, some of it critical. Since then, it has had its imitators and plagiarists. Some of its lines of investigation have proved dead ends, while others have proved open-ended and fruitful, both for me and, I hope, for others. Many of the authors and illustrators discussed in the following essays, and many of the contributors, have emerged since 1994. Creative artists need courage and perseverance, and they need the support of enthusiastic audiences. I trust that this book will oblige.

Elwyn Jenkins is an emeritus professor in the Department of English Studies at the University of South Africa. He is an honorary life vice president of the English Academy of Southern Africa and an honorary life member of the South African Institute of Race Relations, and has received awards for his academic and professional achievements and his contributions to education and society in South Africa.

Preface

South African children's and youth literature has a long history and a well-established publishing program, and its standing in the international literature context is highly regarded. South Africa is the most prolific publisher of children's books in Africa, produces arguably the highest quality of literature from the continent, its leading authors and illustrators are published internationally (e.g., Niki Daly, Lesley Beake, Dianne Hofmeyr, Joan Rankin, Paddy Bouma, Fiona Moodie, Gcina Mhlophe, Piet Grobler, and Marjorie van Heerden), and it has a strong presence in the International Board on Books for Young People (IBBY) (e.g., as twice-winner of the IBBY-Asahi Reading Promotion Award, South African jurors on the Hans Christian Andersen Award panel, and hosting an IBBY World Congress). Its themes and traditions, while certainly unique, resonate well within the larger world of children's literature. Internationally, its literature is solidly grounded in African myth and archetypes, and may be the literary cradle of much literature for the world as a whole. In particular, the African diaspora in the United States and elsewhere have stories rooted in these oral traditions. (See for example, Yenika-Agbaw, Lowery, and Henderson 2013.) In addition, American audiences will recognize specific echoes of their own historical issues as well as current topics that are relevant for today's young people everywhere. This is the context from which a collection of profiles and critical analyses of the work of South African authors and illustrators of literature for young people in the last twenty years emerges.

Literature for children and young adults in South Africa has a respected scholarly legacy with critics such as Elwyn Jenkins (professor emeritus of English), Jay Heale (children's book reviewer and author), Thomas van der Walt (professor and scholar of Afrikaans youth literature), Judith Inggs (professor of children's literature and translation), and Andrée-Jeanne Tötemeyer (Southern Africa children's literature scholar). Their work has chronicled well the history and growth of children's literature in South Africa in titles such as *Children of the Sun: Selected Writers and Themes in South African Children's Literature* (Jenkins 1993), *Adamastor* (Heale 2004), *The Racial Element in Afrikaans Children's and Youth Literature* (Tötemeyer 1984), and *Van Patrys-hulle tot Hanna Hoekom: 'n Gids tot die Afrikaanse Kinder- en Jeugboek* (A Guide to the Afrikaans Children's and Young Adult Books, Wybenga and Snyman

2005). From the earliest literature that featured exclusively white protagonists (usually boys) with blacks only as secondary characters (if included at all), sometimes as childhood companions, South African children's literature evolved to include such benchmark titles as Ann Harries' *The Sound of the Gora* (1980), Beverley Naidoo's (1985) *Journey to Jo'burg*, and John Miles' *Stanley Bekker en die Boikot* (Stanley Bekker and the Boycott, 1980)—all of which were banned by the Nationalist government—*A Message in the Wind* by Chris van Wyk (1982), Niki Daly's (1985) *Not So Fast Songololo*, the first full color picture book to feature a black urban South African child protagonist, and Maretha Maartens' *Die Inkvoël* (*The Ink Bird* 1987). Today South African youth literature—both in English and Afrikaans—encompasses all issues that relate to contemporary lives, including HIV/AIDS, neighborhood violence, and homelessness, in addition to the more mundane topics of peer relationships and parental approval.

In order to better understand this current literature, an overview of South Africa's political history of the past seven decades needs to be held in mind. In 1948, laws that separated South Africans into racial classifications and affected all aspects of life established the legal basis for what is known as "apartheid." However, by the 1980s, the country had become isolated from the rest of the world, and this way of life had become unsustainable as more and more South Africans of all ethnicities joined the struggle against apartheid. (In this book, the South African spelling of "coloured" as an ethnic group has been retained.) In 1986, South Africa's hated Pass Laws (requiring every black South African to carry a pass book or risk immediate imprisonment) and the Mixed Marriages Act (forbidding marriage between differing racial groups) were repealed. When F. W. de Klerk became state president in 1989, the process of removing all further apartheid-inspired laws—such as the Separate Amenities and the Group Areas Acts—commenced. In 1990, Nelson Mandela was released from prison, and the ban on political parties opposed to the apartheid regime—including the African National Congress (ANC)—was lifted. Negotiations started that paved the way for South Africa's first democratic election in 1994 and its new Constitution.

The country's emerging political liberation also increased freedom in the children's literary arena, with the first international symposium on children's literature in the country being held in 1987. Titled "Towards Understanding," this conference attracted 550 people to the University of the Western Cape (near Cape Town), and more books for young English-speaking readers were published that year than any other year between 1985 and 1994. (Children's books for Afrikaans readers, on the other hand, remained popular throughout this time period.) An outgrowth of the event, the South African Children's Book Forum (SACBF) was formed in 1988 and was admitted as the national section of IBBY in 1992 (renamed as IBBY SA in 2005).

Much has changed in South African literature for children since the 1994 election that brought Nelson Mandela to the country's presidency. A field that was dominated by all white and mostly female writers and illustrators has diversified and added many new voices in the last twenty years. Their work, along with updates about the ongoing work of previously established creators of books for young people, deserves attention and is the focus of this book. Our purpose is to raise global awareness of, interest in, and knowledge about the current status of this important body of literature. We intend the book to be a valuable resource for scholars, teacher educators, teachers and librarians and to stimulate greater use of the literature in South Africa, the U.S., and around the world. By adding to the scholarship about a specific area of international children's literature—South African—this book aims to enhance the study of children's literature as a whole. At the same time, we do not claim to be the final word in this area of scholarship, but adding to the body of knowledge in the ongoing line of research.

Profiles of the work of twenty-nine authors and illustrators are featured in this collection. While the group is not exhaustive, we based our selection upon the following criteria: while some individuals were well-known and published before 1994, all would continue to be major contributors of works since then, with a special emphasis on important creators who have emerged in the last twenty years; at least some of their writing, if first published in other languages, should be available in English, since the audience for this book is international; their work should recognizably reflect the South African context in its character and generally be acknowledged as high quality. Of course, these considerations—and overall length restrictions for the book—necessarily mean that some names have been omitted and create a rather limited view of the contribution of authors (particularly those writing only in Afrikaans, such as George Weideman, Barrie Hough, Francois Bloemhof, Carina Diederiks, Maretha Maartens, and Willem van der Walt, for whom the readership and market remain vital in South Africa) whose work is extremely important in the broader perspective of South African children's literature as a whole. In addition, the number of black writers for young readers is growing steadily, but very few so far are writing in languages other than English. Some significant creators whose work from pre-1994 has been widely explored elsewhere (for example, Marguerite Poland and Beverley Naidoo) are not the primary focus of this collection.

Finally, we also recognize that authors and illustrators are only part of the creative endeavor that results in high quality literature for young readers. Editors, art directors, book designers, publishers, and organizations dedicated to the importance of books and developing a culture of reading also play a vital role. We would be remiss not to acknowledge their contributions, even though we cannot feature them in this book. One additional point that needs to be noted is the effects of publishing costs in South Africa and how the route to viability for many authors has been via the education market in textbooks (although this outlet has suffered with the loss of government funding after 1994). Thus, much literature by accomplished authors and illustrators appears in "reader" format used for pedagogical purposes.

The book is organized into three sections that typify the authors and illustrators we have selected for the twenty-year span of its coverage, 1994–2014. The first section, "Transition Movers," represents a group of authors and illustrators who were already well-published before 1994 but have continued to produce new work since then. We view these individuals as leading the way in the transition between the old and new regimes in ways both subtle and overt and whose work continues to be emulated today. Our aim is to bring readers up to date with their output. The second—and largest—group, "Writers and Artists of the New South Africa," primarily developed and gained recognition since the government transition in 1994. These are creators whose careers are well-established and on-going. The final group, "Noteworthy New Talent," comprises a relatively small group of more recent arrivals who demonstrate promise of significant future acclaim. Their productivity to date may be limited, but it has already attained recognition in South Africa and even internationally.

Our focus in this book—and what we have tried to convey in the essays—is a critical analysis of each individual's major works. Each author or illustrator is profiled through a thematic lens that intends to capture insights about the person's style and unique qualities. As such, the profiles are designed to be more literary and artistic in approach, not primarily biographical. Certainly, each analysis is the contributor's perspective on the illustrator's or author's work and not the only perspective that could be taken. In addition, not every title by a writer or artist will be mentioned necessarily, but the ones that are most significant to the overall thesis being portrayed. The individual contributors (and whose biographies can be found at the back of the book) were carefully selected and recruited for their expertise on South African children's and young adult literature and represent perspectives from both South Africa and the United States. Because this book of essays is a product of so many persons (and to whom we are enormously grateful and indebted), readers will quickly recognize that the profiles reflect the different voices of the contributors. We believe this collaboration and diversity are strengths of the book as a whole and appropriately signify the strength in diversity of South Africa itself and the appeal of its literature abroad. We hope you will enjoy immersing yourself in this sampling of the richness of South African children's and youth literature and will see its relevance for your lives, wherever you are in the world.

Part 1. Transition Movers

Introduction

Children's literature does not sit easily inside imposed categories. However, it is fair to say that these authors and illustrators were already in action before 1994 and have continued creating work for many years after. So, yes, they helped South African children's literature move several steps further.

LESLEY BEAKE	SINDIWE MAGONA
ALIDA BOTHMA	LINDA RODE
PADDY BOUMA	MARITA VAN DER VYVER
DIANNE CASE	MARJORIE VAN HEERDEN
NIKI DALY	CHRIS VAN WYK
DIANNE HOFMEYR	

For too long, local children's stories were dainty versions of African animal tales or copies of European fairytales or adventures transposed into a slightly African setting—often in a derivative style that might be described as EBISA or "Enid Blyton in South Africa." Afrikaans children's literature led the way into more realistic writing. The requirements of a bilingual country (under the Nationalist Party) encouraged many writers of impressive quality. Marita van der Vyver followed such authors as Freda Linde, Maretha Maartens and Rona Rupert, and was already producing award-winning children's novels by 1991: *Tien vir 'n Vriend* (1987) and *Eenkantkind* (1991). Soon van der Vyver was redefining the role of the mother in local children's literature.

Lesley Beake, Dianne Case and Dianne Hofmeyr were writing in English at the same time, all three with an early focus on underprivileged children: *The Strollers* (Beake 1987) about street children in Cape Town, *Love, David* (Case 1987) set among the tin shanties of the Cape Flats, *A Red Kite in a Pale Sky* (Hofmeyr 1990) about flooded valleys in Natal (now called KwaZulu-Natal).

Illustration moved as printing technology improved. Alida Bothma was illustrating as early as 1974 (*Wat Maak Jy Hektor?* by Rona Rupert) and created a personalized style of torn-paper collage with added line and color. Niki Daly (for *Fly, Eagle, Fly!* written by Christopher Gregorowski 1982) and Marjorie van Heerden (*A Tiger Took Me to the Circus* 1986) both had to work with only black and one other color for economic reasons, and were required in those days to supply their own color separations. But four-color printing became increasingly available in the 1990s.

The "Towards Understanding" symposium held in 1987 was one of the milestones in South African children's literature. The outside world became more aware of the books being created—and South African book creators themselves were enthused by the publicity and growing approval. It was very much a multi-racial (and multi-lingual) event held with over 500 delegates during times when the state regarded such happenings warily.

Sindiwe Magona and Chris van Wyk had hauled themselves out of the repressive years of the "Bantu education" prescribed by government to become writers in New York and Johannesburg respectively. Paddy Bouma became one of those illustrators who trained other illustrators. Meanwhile many of those included in this group achieved publication abroad: Lesley Beake, Niki Daly, Sindiwe Magona, Paddy Bouma, Marjorie van Heerden, Dianne Hofmeyr among them.

Under the apartheid laws of "separate development" South Africans were discouraged and prevented from meeting people from differing ethnic groups. These barriers could be bypassed in the world of books. South African authors and illustrators were already allowing young white readers to make friends with black South Africans and to travel through pictures and text to restricted parts of the country. Under the wing of the independent publisher David Philip, Niki Daly set up Songololo Books, the stated mission of which was "to play a major role in introducing children to one another's culture through stories of city and rural life, African fantasy and other aspects which make Africa exciting and different" (pers. comm.). He and others ignored the notion that differences between people are more important than their commonalities. Instead, they created bridges.

The big money came from having a book accepted as a "prescribed" text for study in class—and such books had to comply with political restrictions and strict moral standards. Nevertheless, publishers were beginning to risk publishing books that dared to represent opposing views. Ravan Press was one of these, and Chris van Wyk worked for some while with them, though often there was no financial support for the children's books they wanted to create. *Two Dogs and Freedom* (from Ravan in 1986) was a collection of children's writing from an apartheid, poverty-stricken world. The "new South Africa" was thought of in terms of "a big house and to [*sic*] dogs and freedom" according to 8-year-old Moagi from the Open School in Soweto (*Collected Writings* 1986, 54–55). That possibility was still some years away.

Cut off from many cultural contacts by the sanctions imposed by many nations of the world, South African children encountered mostly the mass-market books from overseas. Libraries stocked up on the popularity of Enid Blyton, the Hardy Boys, and Roald Dahl—and the outrageous quality of Dahl was a welcome antidote to the imposed correctness of much local publishing. The picture books that sold best tended to be rather old-fashioned, Disneyfied cute normality. South African parents weren't ready yet for imaginative, atmospheric artwork—even though the children might have been.

But South African authors and illustrators worked at creating the solid foundation of what could be increasingly described as a South African children's literature: stories and picture books growing out of the country as it was (often to its shame) and as it might be. Fantasy and escapist adventure could come from overseas. Only indigenous book creators could capture the reality of urban squalor, homeless children, the longing for education, frustration—all contrasted by the magnificent scenery of South African mountains, coastlines, desert and game reserves. Children could look at a book and say, "Hey! I've been there!" or even "That's where I live."

Somehow, against the odds, South Africa built up an awareness of what its children's literature should be doing and a determination to strive for quality. When South Africa was admitted to IBBY membership in 1992, it had books of which it could be proud to take their place among subsequent IBBY Honour List nominations from around the world.

Lesley Beake: Quality in Diversity

Jay Heale

Lesley Beake's first book, *Detained at Her Majesty's Pleasure, The Journal of Peter David Hadden*, was published by Tafelberg in 1986. Among those books on display at the 1987 symposium was Lesley Beake's *The Strollers* which won the Young Africa Award. So Lesley started her published writing in a time of increasing change towards a better future at the southern tip of Africa. Her books continually offer insight and hope. For example, her youth novel *Song of Be* "... gives you a picture of how years of oppression destroyed people in Namibia and how the promise of independence brings hope back into their lives" (Anon. in *Upbeat* 1992).

The year of the democratic elections, 1994, is the setting to *Jakey* where the first page of text says, "the story of me, Jake September, and of what happened to us all in the month before we had the first real elections in South Africa. It was a terrible month. There was nearly a war" (1). Two decades after that stunning election year South Africans can breathe a sigh of relief that no child now in primary or secondary school has known apartheid. It is a word from history, though many of its effects are still evident, particularly in the unequal educational opportunities. The historical setting needs to be kept in mind, because Lesley Beake is one of those who have contributed towards a wider and wiser youth literature in this country.

Her first completed book was *Rainbow*, which she started writing when she was nine years old, at the same time as she started her first magazine:

> She showed me a magazine she had produced at eight or nine, called *Puppery Magazine*. She laughs as [she] relates how she has used this childhood production at workshops to demonstrate all the "ten flaws ... usually demonstrated in a first manuscript: no obvious quality control; not finished on time; written with the aim of money (because it was sixpence); illustrated by the author (don't do that); not planned properly; not adequately researched; over ambitious; under funded; filled with drivel; and encouraged by family" [MacRobert 2010, 106].

So the urge to write both books and magazines was part of Lesley's life as a girl in Edinburgh, Scotland. The family moved to South Africa in 1966 and Lesley almost immediately set out on her own, first at Rhodes University where she studied primary teaching and then in an Eastern Cape farming district, which saw the beginning of her love affair with the land and light of South Africa. Towards the end of *Merino* the old farmer plays the Pearl Fishers by Bizet on his gramophone.

> The strange thing was that when the music started, the springbok [outside the farmhouse window] lifted their heads as though they were listening and then they started to leap and spring in that way that they have. As though they were dancing to the music. As though they understood how beautiful it was [133].

She also taught in what was then the Transkei, revisited in *Grandfather Remembers*; the winelands of the Western Cape; Northern Natal, now part of KwaZulu-Natal province and well captured in *Café Thunderball*; East Griqualand in the Northern Cape Province and the setting for *A Cageful of Butterflies*; and Natal South Coast. Namibia (previously South-West Africa) inspired *Tjojo and the Wild Horses*, *Song of Be*, *Rough Luck*, *Waiting for Rain* and more. This movement, and the ensuing cross–Karoo journeys, gave her a real identification with and love for many different aspects of the landscape—all of which have appeared in her stories. Landscape is always the beginning, she says. And often personal memories are part of that including the fluorescence under the sand at Knoetzie on the south-east coast, which Catuba awakens at the end of *Detained at Her Majesty's Pleasure: The Journal of Peter David Hadden* as "The green light flickered under his feet and fireflies flashed around his head" (78).

Marriage and a move to England and then the Persian Gulf state of Qatar caused a diversion into second-language English teaching working with adults at an industrial area in the desert, and a keen enjoyment and deeper understanding of both the beauty of the English language and its difficulties. On her return to South Africa, she combined her teaching and language interests into a full-time writing career.

It is intriguing to note that *Detained at Her Majesty's Pleasure* provides a number of links sustained in her subsequent work and life: a fascination with Place, an acute awareness of Time, and an informed respect for diverse people.

Sense of Place

Although this profile is focused on children's literature, it is relevant when considering Lesley Beake's writing to note that she has been the editor of and main contributor to three magazines: *Reflections,* the in-flight magazine of Air Malawi, the national airline of the southern African country Malawi and another beloved landscape, and two glossy travel magazines that she devised and published with colleagues: *Savanna,* focusing on southern Africa travel, and *Winescape,* on the Cape Winelands. She also contributed as a writer and broadcaster to *Woman's World* on SABC radio for five years with a monthly column on travel and a "Letter from Namibia," which was broadcast during the run-up to independence there. All this demanded much travel and increasing knowledge of places around southern Africa.

Three excerpts demonstrate Beake's "sense of landscape" pieces. They could only have been written by someone who had stood in those places and breathed in the atmosphere:

> Before, there was a kraal in the mountains of northern Natal, where the frost lay white in the winter and the sun dreamed slow in the summer [*A Cageful of Butterflies*, Introduction, n.p.].

> The Parade[1] was a feast for the eyes. In the bright sunlight the stalls were dazzling. Best of all were the cloth stalls. Crimson and blue, yellow and green, orange of an orange-ness that hurt the eyes. And striped over them were contrasting braids and ribbons until every colour was mixed with every other colour and you had to go away and look at something else [*The Strollers*, 33].

> Except in the spring, when the veld flowers are out, Laaiplek[2] is clean and empty and grey. The wind whips down, blowing the rubbish away, and the smell is of the sea and of fish. The sky is big on the West Coast—like a high, pale roof over our heads [*Jakey*, 11].

Awareness of Time

Two of Lesley Beake's youth novels are set in time past: *Traveller* in 1824 onwards, and *Detained at Her Majesty's Pleasure* in 1849 onwards, both of them happening in the peninsula that stretches south from Table Mountain. One novel is set in the future: *Remembering Green* which takes place on a Table Mountain surrounded by water because global warming has caused the sea to rise up over the city of Cape Town at the foot of the mountain.

> Now the hot sea glitters where the city was and, just over the water, so near that it pulls my heart, is Africa—where I come from [16].

In this book (and in its intended sequels and the yet unpublished *Hap*) Lesley shows her understanding and love of Africa itself, old and potent and lasting in ways many of us may never understand. Time long past also features in a short story, "The Three Sisters of Three Sisters" (1991, 76), which has three modern girls finding themselves swept by a time-jump into the dinosaur-filled steamy air in the Karoo some 200 million years ago.

Merino is a set of historical episodes following linked characters from mostly the early Cape of 1789 to the British settlers arriving on the eastern coast in 1820 and the general trek of Dutch-speaking farmers, Boers, even further north in 1836, a combination of places and times. Through the whole book, the background theme is the development of the Merino sheep industry in South Africa.

The bulk of Beake's writing is set in the South Africa of the twentieth or twenty-first centuries. With most of the longer works, she is precise about the placing in time, aware that this country has changed a great deal over the near thirty years in which she has been writing, as has the publishing industry itself. *A Cageful of Butterflies* tells us that the boy Mponyane lived and died in northern Natal fifteen years ago. That places the story in 1974, twenty years before apartheid officially came to an end. *Jakey* is deliberately set in that year of the democratic elections that closed apartheid, 1994. *Home Now*, a picture book, carries a note at the end to explain that the story takes place as a result of the effect of the HIV/AIDs epidemic.[3]

Respect for People

Place and time are vital in all the stories that Lesley Beake has created about the San (Bushmen) because she is writing to counter the prevalent stereotypes. They live in a combination of traditional life and the twenty-first century. Neither way of life is functional in the very hard place where they find themselves. But the tired clichés are long-gone. There are around 90,000 San people who are now trying to adapt to an even harsher environment than they had before. So there are modern San students, dressed in jeans and T-shirts who use mobile phones and computers just like anyone else, and Lesley has run a number of workshops for them. This is the background to *Song of Be*, which is set in the newly independent Namibia on the farm of an impoverished white family.

> We see them [San] living on farms, collaborating with the police or film-makers, or working for the Namibian government as election officials. The most detailed and up-to-date is that in Lesley Beake's *Song of Be*, which is a remarkably imaginative feat. The narrator is a young San woman who works with her mother on the farm of a white man in Namibia. Her inner strength is emphasized by the contrast with the farmer's wife, who is driven mad by life on the farm and commits suicide. As the story of Be's life and that of her parents emerges, many aspects of the lives of modern San are covered. Beake emphasizes her own interest in the present-day San by including a note at the end entitled "The future," in which

she says that the Ju/'hoan people are going back to the land with new skills [Wagener 1996, 286–287].

The Ju/'hoan are a San community who are more fully described in *Waiting for Rain* co-written by Lesley Beake and Dr. Megan Biesele, anthropologist and linguist, whose regular work in the Kalahari, particularly with the Ju/'hoansi people, enhanced knowledge of their language. Lesley worked alongside Megan for many years on the Village Schools Project which aims to provide mother-tongue education for the first three years. The slim book combines one week in the life of a twelve-year-old San boy, with snippets of background information, and finally a folktale about the rain and the stars—until the first blessed, long-awaited, overdue drops of wetness gladden their hearts.

There is a modern San girl named Bau in both the very simple *Bau and the Baobab Tree* and the adventure story *Rough Luck*. The first is a book for early readers combining number awareness with the visual clues provided by animal spoor (tracks). The second has a white girl lost in the Kalahari desert in Namibia and helped to survive by the tracking and food-finding skills of modern San.

Lesley Beake shows sensitive understanding of the San people as a cultural community, particularly the Ju/'hoansi, and also of individual relationships within the San and between representative characters and people from very different cultural backgrounds.

She does the same with other paired characters: the escaped white Peter David Hadden and the freed black slave Catuba in *Detained at Her Majesty's Pleasure*; the deaf and dumb boy Mponyane and the bullied white farm boy Frank in *A Cageful of Butterflies*; the mourning, coloured boy Jakey and the shy, fearful, white boy in *Jakey*.

Body of Work

"Literature flourishes best when it is half a trade and half an art" (138). So said Jorge Luis Borges, way back in 1926. This seems a fair summary of Lesley Beake's contribution to youth literature.

Lesley's writing for young readers comes in two fairly distinct categories: shorter, easier stories (often part of a reading series) which have been commissioned, and which therefore have a defined readership ability, length, format; and longer stories for more mature readers which have been dreamed up, researched and written from the author's personal choice. Or as she puts it herself: "thick and thin books."

The literacy situation in Africa calls for realistic solutions. Millions of children need "thin" books—because they lack the ability to cope with reading anything else, because the education system cannot afford anything thicker, because the readers lack the intellectual stamina required by "thick" books. But those few in good schools with enough understanding need well-written "thick" books to feed their literary stamina, their knowledge of Africa, their awareness of the politics behind our society. Lesley Beake is not what one would call a political writer, but she listens to the voices of the children of Africa.

It is a publishing necessity in South Africa to create books that will sell as educational material. So a number of series have been created, particularly for early readers in English, and often designed for pupils using English as a second or third language. Lesley Beake's answer to this is to ensure that even a stapled booklet inside a series should still be as good as she can make it. She has stated firmly: "Children's books are important books for important people and ought to be thought of as such. Most especially by the people who aim to write them" (Beake 1993, 24).

She was the commissioning editor of Zebra Books (published by Kagiso in 1995–1996), bringing in Ann Walton as art director of the series. It was decided from the outset that all the stories offered must be clearly placed in Africa. Kagiso was bought by Maskew Miller Longman and the Zebra Books were incorporated into an even more far-reaching reading scheme (also dreamed up by Lesley Beake) to be called Stars of Africa (1998–2003). These junior readers were originally conceived as factual and fiction stories, fully African in content, and covering the whole primary age range. In fact, they ceased before reaching the top two primary years.

Beake also contributed fifteen titles to the Rainbow Reading series published by Cambridge University Press SA (2008–2009). Often her longer novels had to be set aside while these commissioned works were created, but it did not result in any lessening of quality for either.

"I know well that only the rarest kind of best in anything can be good enough for the young," wrote the poet Walter de la Mare. Lesley would agree. Everything she writes is created with care and love and when necessary, which is often, detailed research. The visual and historical details in *The Bead Book* and *Traveller* are equally carefully composed. One is part of the Stars of Africa series for young primary readers; the other an intricate novel of the relationship between a teenage would-be painter and a blind man. Both have a place in the history of our country and both are full of colorful, visual interest.

Style and Passion

Don't even try to separate the two! Lesley writes with intensity and a poetic feeling for the impact of words no matter for what age group she is writing. A book is an artistic creation—linked with her skills in painting, sadly long neglected, needlework and beading. She listens to music, particularly while writing, and her car radio is permanently tuned to Fine Music Radio, a community radio station based in Cape Town which dispenses quality classical and jazz music 24/7.

The Strollers, Beake's best-selling book (now past its twenty-fifth reprint) was the only South African title chosen for inclusion in the international publication *1001 Children's Books You Must Read before You Grow Up*. It has always been well reviewed: "Lesley Beake's *The Strollers*, a shrewd, well-written book full of humour, compassion and understanding" (Bennett 1996, 84). Reviews also provide evidence of the versatility of her writing. This first concerns a "thin" book: the other two are thicker.

> *Finding Dad.* This is almost more of a situation than a story but it reads with heart-aching reality. Son lives with divorced Mum, then: "One day, Dad died. Somebody phoned Mom and told her. Now Dad was really gone. My dad-space was gone too." But an understanding grandmother takes the boy back into the memory space that was his father. What quietly reassuring psychology! *Finding Dad* is a deep and moving piece of writing [Heale 2009].
>
> *Traveller.* This well-written and enjoyable historical novel shows Lesley Beake at her best. It is based on the diaries of a blinded ex-lieutenant of the Royal Navy, James Holman. Traff, a young man, is given the task of leading James on a journey to Cape Point—of being his "eyes." Traff's development from child to man, the central theme, is handled with realism and sensitivity [Astwood 1989].
>
> *Song of Be.* A story of love, courage and dignity, *Song of Be* is one of the most significant youth novels to come out of South Africa. It is written with polished, poetic style and deep insight of the genuine people who live in this part of Africa. The poignancy of the struggle is captured with compassion: "The scent of sweetness on the air and the soft, grey dust before our footsteps were blown out" [Heale 1991].

Another "thin" book is *The Message* which is "hidden" inside the Rainbow Reading series of themed, age-related boxes. It tells in simple, echoing prose the story of a political exile forced to leave home. In anyone's world, particularly in our African setting, this carries anguish. The kindness of an uncle supplies education from which comes progress in the form of attending university in a foreign land. Then, flying home, he watches the countryside below him changing from urban wealth to rural survival in the place that he knows as home.

Lesley Beake is an acknowledged author of stirring quality. She has been awarded the Percy FitzPatrick Award twice, in 1988 for *The Strollers*, and for *A Cageful of Butterflies* in 1990; the M-Net Prize for *A Cageful of Butterflies* in 1991; *Song of Be* was listed as a Notable Children's Book and as a Best Book for Young Adults by the American Library Association in 1994; and she was nominated for the Astrid Lindgren Memorial Award and by South Africa for the Hans Christian Andersen Award in 2004. Beake has received many other awards and nominations.

In collaboration with Sindiwe Magona and Gcina Mhlophe, in January 2012 Lesley launched the Children's Book Network to link many existing literacy and literature organizations, and to intensify the effort "to bring books to children and children to books" (Beake 2012, 1). Teaching writing through workshops is already one of the CBN main activities.

For any intelligent reader there will be a tightening of the throat when meeting the handicapped friendship of Mponyane and Frank in *A Cageful of Butterflies*, or the hesitant meeting of Sieta and the baby elephant in *Home Now*, or the acclamation given to Nelson Mandela in *Jakey*. Lesley can have you admiring, amazed or reaching for tissues as the occasion demands. As she has put it herself: "There is a fear in words. No ... I think I mean a power ... in them. They can destroy or they can make good" (James Holman speaking to Traff in *Traveller*, 48).

When she fulfilled a commission from the *Sunday Times*, visiting twenty-six primary schools all over South Africa and conducting writing workshops with the children, the resulting stories were published as *My Story, Our Stories* by no less a body than the Parliament of the Republic of South Africa. That is no small accolade in a country where there is no national award for youth literature.

Notes

1. "The Parade" refers to the Grand Parade, once Cape Town's main marketplace.
2. Laaiplek is a small fishing town on the mouth of the Berg River, on South Africa's western coast.
3. HIV was first diagnosed in South Africa in 1982. The most rapid increase in South Africa's HIV prevalence took place between 1993 and 2000. In 2001 the HIV prevalence rate among pregnant women was 24.8 percent (HIVSA).

Children's Books

Beake, Lesley. 1986. *Detained at Her Majesty's Pleasure: The Journal of Peter David Hadden*. Cape Town, SA: Tafelberg.
_____. 1987. *The Strollers*. Cape Town, SA: Maskew Miller Longman.
_____. 1989. *Merino*. Illustrated by Ann Walton. Cape Town, SA: Maskew Miller Longman.
_____. 1989. *A Cageful of Butterflies*. Cape Town, SA: Maskew Miller Longman.
_____. 1989. *Rainbow*. Cape Town, SA: Maskew Miller Longman.
_____. 1989. *Traveller*. Cape Town, SA: Maskew Miller Longman.
_____. 1990. *Serena's Story*. Cape Town, SA: Maskew Miller Longman.

———. 1990. *Tjojo and the Wild Horses*. Cape Town: De Jager-HAUM.
———. 1991. *Song of Be*. Cape Town, SA: Maskew Miller Longman.
———. 1991. "The Three Sisters of Three Sisters." In *Storyland*, compiled by Jay Heale, 76–82. Cape Town, SA: Tafelberg.
———. 1992. *Bau and the Baobab Tree*. Illustrated by Ann Walton. Cape Town, SA: Tafelberg.
———. 1993. *Café Thunderball*. Cape Town: De Jager-HAUM.
———. 1997. *Jakey*. Cape Town, SA: Tafelberg.
———. 2003. *Grandfather Remembers*. Cape Town, SA: Maskew Miller Longman.
———. 2003. *One Dark, Dark night*. Illustrated by Paddy Bouma. Johannesburg, SA: READ.
———. 2005. *The Bead Book*. Illustrated by Jiggs Snaddon-Wood and Jean Fullalove. Cape Town, SA: Maskew Miller Longman.
———. 2006. *Home Now*. Illustrated by Karin Littlewood. London: Frances Lincoln.
———. 2009. *My Story, Our Stories*. Cape Town, SA: Parliament of the Republic of South Africa.
———. 2009. *Finding Dad*. Rainbow Reading Level 4. Cape Town, SA: Cambridge University Press.
———. 2009. *The Message*. Rainbow Reading Level 5. Cape Town, SA: Cambridge University Press.
———. 2009. *Remembering Green*. London: Frances Lincoln.
———. 2009. *Rough Luck*. Illustrated by Alzette Prince. London: Hodder Education.
Beake, Lesley, and Megan Biesele. 2002. *Waiting for Rain: The Story of a Kalahari Village*. Illustrated by Jiggs Snaddon-Wood. Cape Town, SA: Maskew Miller Longman.
Heale, Jay. 1991. *Storyland*. Illustrated by Joan Rankin. Cape Town, SA: Tafelberg.

Alida Bothma: From Her Palette of Inspiration to Her Montage of Expression

Magdel Vorster

Alida Bothma, artist and illustrator, finds inspiration from "many things that stir my heart. Things like nature, my love for the African continent and all its cultures, human vulnerability, and my relationship with God" (*South African Artlife* 2013, n.p.), as well as from music, and the stories and poems she brings to life visually in her illustrations.

Bothma was born in Pretoria in 1953. After completing her schooling in Pretoria, she studied in Cape Town at the Cape Technikon's School of Art and Design, graduating with a diploma in Graphic Design with distinction in 1973. She started working as an illustrator at an advertising agency in Cape Town until she was asked to illustrate her first children's book cover. In 1974 the publisher, Tafelberg, commissioned her to do the cover for *Die Eerste Keer* (The First Time) by Rona Rupert, well-known and respected South African children's book author who published thirty-five books between the 1970s and mid–1990s. A cover for another Rupert manuscript, *Wat Maak Jy Hektor?* (What Are You Doing, Hektor?), soon followed, marking the beginning of her involvement in children's book illustration (Slippers 2012). The book was restricted to black and white, so Alida made pen and ink drawings. She immediately received another Rona Rupert manuscript, *Luister, Lefa* (Listen, Lefa), which she illustrated in pencil.

Since then Alida Bothma has proved to be a versatile artist, working in a wide range of media and techniques. She is known for her paintings as well as her children's book illustrations. International recognition came in 1979 when some of her watercolor paintings were included in an international Aquarelle (Watercolor) exhibition in Germany in 1979. To date her work has been exhibited in Japan, Belgium, Canada, Italy, the Slovak Republic, Iran and India, and, including covers, she has illustrated more than 200 books (Bothma 2013).

Alida's style is difficult to categorize. It varies from realistic to humoristic, to graphic, to stylized. It has been described as varying from stylized and simple, to sophisticated "children's art" drawings with shadows and scribbles, to illustrations where she exhibits an individualistic and unique form of freedom in line and texture. The essence of her illustrations is captured by the use of simplified realism. The expressive characteristics of her illustrations, however, often are manifested through her very clever handling of form, color and portraying an object realistically or with exaggeration. By combining her intuition for the experimental with brilliant drawing skills, she is capable of creating rich textures with washes of watercolor that lift out otherwise vague, visual images (Fairer-Wessels and Wessels 2007).

She is always led by the atmosphere of the manuscript and whether a light and humoristic, mysterious or serious message needs to be complemented. The atmosphere then dictates the style of the illustrations as well as technique to be used. She feels that illustrations inside the book should focus on specific details of the story or theme, sometimes allowing for more than one style in one book, while the cover should portray the subject and atmosphere of the book as a whole (Cilliers 1988). She prefers to work in a combination of pencil, charcoal, watercolor, colored ink, acrylic, oil, collage and pastel and freely experiments with various techniques to obtain the necessary texture, mood and atmosphere (Wybenga and Snyman 2005).

Human Vulnerability

After Alida illustrated *Wat Maak Jy Hektor?*, another twelve titles by Rona Rupert followed. They made a good team. Emotion and sensuousness are very present in Rupert's work, as she often creates less perfect characters, who have either a physical disability, or are going through an emotionally difficult time. Alida has perfectly complemented these stories with her expressionist illustrations.

Strong elements of figurative abstraction exist on different levels in Alida's work. In Rupert's *All Everest's Birds*, originally published in Afrikaans as *Al Everest se Voëls* and translated into English by Christopher Gregorowski, she uniquely creates the visually impaired boy, Everest, by the expressive use of mixed media techniques with newspaper as a collage element together with pastel and conté pencil (Fairer-Wessels and Wessels 2007). She has developed and made very much her own the method of collage with added line and color. She uses it here to indicate the blurred vision of the boy (Heale 1994). Combining collage with pastel or pencil cleverly ensures that the reader does not focus on the scraps of paper for what they are, but sees them as part of the composition.

Alida's partnering with Elsabe Steenberg proved to be very successful as well. In *Someday the Blue Bird,* translated from the original Afrikaans, *Eendag die Blou Voël,* Alida uses soft watercolors and crayons, mostly hues of yellow and blue, with fine line drawings in ink to show the blurring flight of birds and the air around them (Heale 1994). In this book on the battle between good and evil, good is portrayed by the blue bird and evil by the dusty and poisonous yellow cat, bad-mouthing everybody (Wybenga and Snyman 2005). In *The Wishful Walnut,* translated from the original Afrikaans, *Die Boom Wat Wou Loop,* the little walnut tree is the main character who wishes he could walk, and Alida uses soft watercolors and ink here as well. *Katie Colly Wobbles,* again translated from the Afrikaans *Kariena Karyn,* is in mixed media. Alida works with crayons and pastels on background monoprints, done in oil, to add texture. During the day her imagination takes Katie to games she plays with trees, fish, birds and flowers in the garden, but at night her fear of the dark takes over.

Alida is gifted in seeing the world through the eyes of a child, sharing their imaginary worlds to allow her to interpret and portray texts to appeal to them. She has had three daughters, and having always worked from home, stayed in touch with their interests. She also believes that by staying involved in the lives of children through illustrating for them, she has kept the child inside her alive. Alida has won the Afrikaans Taal en Kultuurvereniging (ATKV), translated as Afrikaans Language and Culture Association award for illustrations, which is significant since the award is selected by children.

Alida's latest alliance is with Wendy Maartens in two books published by LAPA Publishers. In *Princess Sparrow* and *Three Cheers for Tyron* Alida again had the opportunity to illustrate stories dealing with important issues, namely divorce and child abuse. In *Princess Sparrow* Dinah watches the sparrows with fascination and notices that they never argue like Mom and Dad. Dinah sometimes puts feathers in her hair and pretends that she is Princess Sparrow, allowing her to fly away to magical places where parents stay together. Wendy Maartens' *Three Cheers for Tyron,* is a sensitive story based on child abuse. Tyron starts to stutter after his uncle comes to stay in their guest room. He cannot speak to anyone about what is happening, because the words get stuck in his throat. In both these books Alida again uses monotype prints as background, adding to the atmosphere as the story moves between sad and happier. Cold blues and purples are used on pages where Princess Sparrow or Tyron are obviously struggling with loneliness and not being able to share their burden.

Alida also illustrated a number of educational or school books. In the Maskew Miller Longman (now Pearson) *Stars of Africa* series of readers,

Grandpa Makes a Toy by Irene Lewis carries a message about the value of elderly people in our families and communities (South African Artlife 2013). In another title in this series of readers, *No Thank You!* by Tertia Morris, family relationships are explored when Tambo's mother brings home her new baby and Tambo is very skeptical about the new sibling. The Afrikaans equivalent for these readers are *Rimpelstories* published by Maskew Miller Longman: Kagiso. Although publishers impose more restrictions on the illustrations of educational books, and illustrations are done in a more strictly realistic style, Alida manages to create atmospheric pictures so that these illustrations often match the depth of the illustrations in her trade books.

The African Continent and Its Cultures

Alida also cares deeply for Africa and its variety of cultures. In *Tintinyane, the Girl Who Sang Like a Magic Bird*, written by Corlia Fourie, the torn paper shapes become rocks and monsters and huge brown wings (Heale 1994). Alida's dramatic and evocative illustrations, here with an ethnic flair, support and complement Fourie's fairy tale with a twist (Le Roux 1991). This supposedly traditional fantasy combined with African folklore, tells the story of a girl, Tintinyane, whose voice is as beautiful as a magical songbird. Tintinyane lives with her father and three brothers, sharing her talent by singing unconditionally for everyone, until she is captured by a monster, Ngorongorui, and kept in the jungle. Ngorongorui tries to force her to sing for him, but she hides her voice in a nutshell hanging around her neck (Barker 1991). Then in this supposedly traditional fantasy combined with African folklore, the victim saves herself after her brothers failed to do so, singing her way back to freedom and her family. The moral of the story here is that everyone in the end is responsible for his or her own salvation: "Rooikappie nou slimmer Sprokies-heldinne te passief, sê feministe" (Red Riding Hood now cleverer, fairy story heroines too passive, say feminists) (Die Burger 1991). This book was originally published in Afrikaans as *Die Meisie Wat Soos 'n Bottervoël Sing*.

More folklore from this duo soon followed. *Die Wit Vlinder* (The White Butterfly), only published in Afrikaans, is a volume of three fantasy stories. In the first story, "Die Reënmaker" (The Rain Maker), the main character is a disabled boy who has to find three magical objects to break a long drought. This story contains elements of Khoi folklore. The Khoi are a historical division of the Khoisan ethnic group, the native people of southwestern Africa, and closely related to the Bushmen or San. In the title story a boy and a girl are looking for a white butterfly. In order to get advice from a wise woman, they need to help three people. The third story, "Swart Ster, Wonderster"

(Black Star, Wonder Star), has a burnt-out star looking for light. Magic realism plays a role in all three stories, and as in so many of the books in which Alida has been involved, the main characters are disabled, scarred or outsiders. Marina Le Roux (1993a) describes the illustrations as stylish and typical of Bothma's work, showing similarities to those of *Tintinyane, the Girl Who Sang Like a Magic Bird*, especially the collage effects with the impressionistic use of color and white accents. Leentjie Theron (1993) comments on how strongly the illustrations resonate with the atmosphere portrayed through all three stories. Here they add another dimension, and the written tales would be a lot less meaningful on their own. Alida also illustrated *Torit of the Strong Right Arm* by Cecily van Straten, one of South Africa's well-known authors of African stories. Le Roux (1993b) described Alida's black and white illustrations here as perfectly portraying the magic of Cicely's legend.

Monsters, Heroes and Sultan's Daughters: Cape Malay Folk Tales was compiled by Valerie Stillwell, and according to Le Roux (1990) partially contributed to a definite need in the market. However, the grey and sometimes ordinary pictures did not meet expectations of what is promised by the rich and mystical Eastern tales. *Stories South of the Sun* (Rode et al.) and *Storytime* (Heale) are two more read-aloud collections of indigenous South African stories. *Stories South of the Sun* offers twenty-eight read aloud stories, reflecting the multi-faceted southern African society. Alida and ten other illustrators were responsible for the vivid color illustrations. *Stories South of the Sun* was also published in Afrikaans, isiZulu, Sesotho and Tswana. In *Storytime*, Alida again used torn pieces of scrap paper with detailed line to illustrate the collection of stories and poems (Heale 1994).

Drawing inspiration from the different cultures of Africa was also necessary in some educational books Alida illustrated. *Special Days* is one of the titles in Nasou Via Afrika's literacy series, Story Street. In this volume, written by Izak de Vries, Alida lavishly illustrated the celebrations of the different cultures in South Africa, seen through the eyes of the photographer, Cameron Cameraman. Examples of these special days are Chinese New Year, Eid-ul-Fitr, Christmas, Divali, and Pesach (De Vries 2013). In a literacy program, Little Library Literacy Readers, published by Cambridge University Press (n.d.), *The Little Lost Goat* (Jesperson, Sonto et al.) is one of the titles developed to respond to a need for high-quality, indigenous books. Xolani loves animals, but he is not allowed one of his own. One day he meets a lost goat and tries to find a home for it. Illustrations in *Every Precious Drop*, written by Nomthandazo Sikhakhane for Cambridge Reading Routes, show Alida's dedication to detail in her presentation of African village people and their traditional costume.

Nature and the Environment

Two titles fairly established as modern classics in the Afrikaans children's book collection are *Goue Lint My Storie Begint* (This Golden Ribbon Unties My Story) and *Goue Fluit My Storie Is Uit* (This Golden Flute Concludes My Story). Alida illustrated both. *Goue Lint My Storie Begint,* by Linda Rode, is a collection of internationally well known as well as indigenous South African fantasy and folk tales and rhymes. The illustrations with "Blouvalk kry sy jokkie" in *Goue Fluit, My Storie Is Uit,* also by Linda Rode, are good examples of how Alida utilizes various graphic possibilities to develop her technical skills (Fairer-Wessels and Wessels 2007), with a mixture of collage, acrylic, pastel, ink and crayons. Unlike *Goue Lint My Storie Begint, Goue Fluit My Storie Is Uit* is aimed at an older, self-reading group, so the illustrations are designed with this audience in mind and required much research (Brand 1988). This title contains thirty-five illustrations in color as well as many black pen sketches. The main focus of all material included in this collection is traditional Afrikaans folklore, inspired by its European heritage (Le Roux 1988).

Although Alida prefers to work from her imagination or memory and not from a model or nature, and also prefers to often include the impossible, she had to portray historical likenesses in *Goue Fluit My Storie Is Uit* (Vermaak and Snyman 2004). She carefully researched lifestyle patterns during the 1800s to dress her characters and portray their day to day lives. In an illustration for the story, "Antjie Somers," featuring a well known Cape Town church, she cleverly presents the church as the three dimensional focal point, while the houses in the street leading to it, are shown flat.

More examples of Alida's dedication to portraying historical likenesses are found in *Steweltjies na Wonderland* (Little Boots to Wonderland), a collection of poems by Hester Heese, compiled by Charles Fryer and published posthumously. Alida focused on personalizing the collection to be of specific significance to Hester Heese's family. She took care to add detail to resemble scenes from Hester Heese's life. The book has a Capetonian atmosphere, a Cape Dutch homestead illustrates the first poem, leaves are from oak trees, and grandchildren have features similar to Heese's grandchildren after Alida carefully researched photographs (Norval 2000). Alida used the book, *Herfsblaar Gooi 'n Kaapse Draai: Hester Heese, Skrywer en Mens* (Autumn Leaves in the Cape: Hester Heese, Author and Person) compiled by Carl Lohann (1991) as the main source for her research. A poem titled "Ouma se huis" (Grandma's House) is cleverly portrayed by a Hansel and Gretel–type house just as Alida remembers Hester Heese's house in Jonkershoek, Stellenbosch (Norval 2000). Jay Heale (1994) notes the same accuracy in detail in a review of *Nobody's Cat* written by Jenny Seed and illustrated by Alida, when he remarks on the paint and ink line-drawing that includes a row of old Port Elizabeth houses in one of the background scenes of the book.

Alida loves to illustrate literature collections and poetry volumes. *Woordreise* (Word Journeys), compiled by Adinda Vermaak, is a collection of 450 poems by 150 poets that took more than two years to illustrate. Even though *Woordreise* was set up to adhere to the guidelines of outcome-based education,[1] Alida had free rein to interpret the manuscript and choose the poems she wanted to illustrate. The result was around eighty realistic as well as abstract illustrations in different sizes and done in pencil, acrylic, collage and mixed media. Alida's aim was for readers to do their own interpreting (Greyling 2004). In illustrating poems there is always room for the illustrator's own interpretation, and Alida particularly likes the fact that the various poems in one manuscript can be so different, allowing her to explore a variety of styles (Retief 2011). Alida's art is in fact often inspired by the written word, and especially poetry.

Rymreise (Rhyme Journeys), also compiled by Adinda Vermaak is aimed at attracting younger children to reading poetry. Alida especially enjoyed the bigger illustrations at the start of each theme. Written text often forms part of Alida's art, as in the chapter titled "Noah's Ark." She also often uses her own lettering in her paintings and has done many chapter titles in collections (Retief 2011). As computer design was not part of the curriculum when Alida was at the Technikon, she still appreciates hand-lettering. In *Rymreise,* all the chapter titles are by hand. In *Woordreise* the chapter title, "Bitterbessie Dagbreek," is an example of Alida's hand lettering as part of the illustration, here of a poem by one of South Africa's famous poets, Ingrid Jonker. In another poem by Johann de Lange in the same collection, she uses handwritten words as part of the picture, forming the water horizon from which the moon is rising.

Relationship with God

When examining Alida's contemporary art, it is obvious that she often draws inspiration from her relationship with God. Inspiration for her paintings is often a piece of scripture. She then incorporates the text—the scripture, a Biblical command, or just a word—in the final picture. She feels that artwork should invite people to think about what they see in it (Bothma 2013).

Her illustrations in *Bible for Children*, written by Louise Smit, have been described as collectible art. Creating new pictures from very familiar images in her mind proved a challenge to Alida, but she managed to add humor and imagination in her illustrations (Van Zyl 2002). Next to Miriam, hiding behind the reeds at the bank of the Nile, the reader finds a black Dachshund. The parrot on Noah's shoulder and a cat purring at his legs while he is looking at the plans for the Ark with his wife add humor and familiarity as well as an invitation for discussion to the young reader or observer. In *Vrede op Aarde* (Peace on Earth), a Christmas collection of stories and poems compiled by Linda Rode, some of Alida's illustrations are reminiscent of traditional Christmas cards, while others are more typical children's book pictures where she again makes use of mixed media.

An Awarded Artist

Alida Bothma is an esteemed artist and a leading children's book illustrator in South Africa, who has won numerous awards. In 1983–1984 Alida won the Katrine Harries Award for *All Everest's Birds* and *Die Aarde Moet Vry Wees* by Pieter W. Grobbelaar (Fairer-Wessels and Wessels 2007). In 1986 Tafelberg Publishers won the C.P. Hoogenhout award for *Goue Lint My Storie Begint*, beautifully illustrated by Alida. The award went to the publishers rather than the compiler and illustrator, because the idea for the book originated with the publisher ("Nog 'n wenner vir Tafelberg" 1986). In 1988 however, Alida won the M.E.R. award for children's literature for her illustrations in *Goue Fluit My Storie Is Uit*.

Alida won the ATKV award for illustrators twice. In 1993 she won it for *Kariena Karyn* (1992) by Elsabe Steenberg and in 1999 for *Steweltjies na Wonderland* by Hester Heese. In 1996 the ATKV award for illustrations went to *Stippe Stappe Stories* by Steenberg, in which Alida was one of the illustrators (Wybenga and Snyman 2005). On an international level Alida was awarded a merit award at the NOMA Concours for illustrations for *Die Wit Vlinder* (The White Butterfly) in 1994 (Nikita 2008). In 2005 Alida was again awarded the bronze medal and a runner up award for a few selected illustrations in *Woordreise* (Retief 2011).

Alida Bothma has been and still is generously contributing to South Africa's children's book history. No doubt her palette is far from exhausted, and the many different ways in which she is gifted to visualize and portray various texts will continue to enhance South African children's literature in years to come.

Note

1. Outcome-based education concentrates on student-centered learning methods that focus on empirically measuring student performance. It requires students to demonstrate that they have learned required skills and content.

Children's Books

De Vries, Izak. 2003. *Special Days*. Illustrated by Alida Bothma. Cape Town, SA: Nasou Via Afrika.
———. 1990. *Die Meisie Wat Soos 'n Bottervoël Sing/Tintinyane, The Girl Who Sang Like a Magic Bird*. Illustrated by Alida Bothma. Cape Town, SA: Human & Rousseau.
———. 1993. *Die Wit Vlinder*. Illustrated by Alida Bothma. Cape Town, SA: Tafelberg.
Fryer, Charles and Hester Heese. 1998. *Steweltjies na Wonderland: 'n Keur Uit Haar Kinderverse*. Illustrated by Alida Bothma. Cape Town, SA: Tafelberg.
Grobbelaar, Pieter W. 1984. *Die Aarde Moet Vry Wees*. Illustrated by Alida Bothma. Pretoria, SA: Daan Retief.
Heale, Jay. 1987. *Storytime*. Cape Town, SA: Tafelberg.
Jesperson, Amand, Sivo Sonto, et al. n.d. *The Little Lost Goat*. Illustrated by Alida Bothma. Cape Town, SA: Cambridge University Press.
Lewis, Irene. 2001. *Grandpa Makes a Toy*. Illustrated by Alida Bothma. Cape Town, SA: Maskew Miller Longman.
Maartens, Wendy. 2009. *Princess Sparrow*. Illustrated by Alida Bothma. Pretoria, SA: LAPA.
———. 2009. *Three Cheers for Tyron*. Illustrated by Alida Bothma. Pretoria, SA: LAPA.
Morris, Tertia. 2001. *No Thank You!* Illustrated by Alida Bothma. Cape Town, SA: Maskew Miller Longman.
Rode, Linda. 1985. *Goue Lint My Storie Begint*. Illustrated by Alida Bothma. Cape Town, SA: Tafelberg.
———. 1988. *Goue Fluit My Storie Is Uit*. Illustrated by Alida Bothma. Cape Town, SA: Tafelberg.
———. 1990. *Vrede op Aarde*. Illustrated by Alida Bothma. Cape Town, SA: Tafelberg.
Rode, Linda, Christel Bodenstein, and Hans Bodenstein. 1993. *Stories South of the Sun*. Illustrated by Alida Bothma. Cape Town, SA: Tafelberg.
Rupert, Rona. 1974. *Die Eerste Keer*. Illustrated by Alida Bothma. Cape Town, SA: Human & Rousseau.
———. 1974. *Wat Maak Jy Hektor?* Illustrated by Alida Bothma. Cape Town, SA: Human & Rousseau.
———. 1976. *Luister, Lefa*. Illustrated by Alida Bothma. Cape Town, SA: Human & Rousseau.
———. 1984. *Al Everest se Voëls/All Everest's Birds* (1984). Illustrated by Alida Bothma. Cape Town, SA: Human & Rousseau.
Seed, Jenny. 1990. *Nobody's Cat*. Illustrated by Alida Bothma. Cape Town, SA: Human & Rousseau.
Sikhakhane, Nomthandazo. N.d. *Every Precious Drop*. Illustrated by Alida Bothma. Cape Town, SA: Cambridge University Press.
Smit, Louise. 1982. *Bible for Children*. Illustrated by Alida Bothma. Cape Town, SA: Tafelberg.
Sonto, Sive, Caroline Mjindi, and Brian Prehn. 1996. *The Little Lost Goat*. Illustrated by Alida Bothma. Cape Town, SA: Cambridge University Press.
Steenberg, Elsabe. 1985. *Eendag die Blou Voël*. Illustrated by Alida Bothma. Pretoria, SA: HAUM Literary.
———. 1986. *Someday the Blue Bird*. Illustrated by Alida Bothma. Pretoria, SA: HAUM Literary.
———. 1989. *Die Boom Wat Wou Loop/The Wishful Walnut*. Illustrated by Alida Bothma. Pretoria, SA: Haum Literary.
———. 1992. *Kariena Karyn/Katie Colly Wobbles*. Illustrated by Alida Bothma. Pretoria, SA: Van Schaik.
———. 1995. *Stippe Stappe Stories*. Cape Town, SA: J L van Schaik Publishers.

Stillwell, Valerie. 1989. *Monsters, Heroes and Sultan's Daughters: Cape Malay Folk Tales*. Illustrated by Alida Bothma. Cape Town, SA: Human & Rousseau.

Van Straten, Cicely. 1992. *Torit of the Strong Right Arm*. Illustrated by Alida Bothma. Cape Town, SA: Human & Rousseau.

Vermaak, Adinda, Keith De Wet, and Lorenda Olivier. 2004. *Woordreise*. Illustrated by Alida Bothma. Cape Town, SA: Nasou Via Afrika.

Vermaak, Adinda, and Pieter Strauss. 2010. *Rymreise*. Illustrated by Alida Bothma. Cape Town, SA: Nasou Via Afrika.

Paddy Bouma: Precise Pure Art at Work in the Books of Africa

Jay Heale

Two major exhibitions of South African children's books have been held in the past thirty years. In 1986, the South African National Gallery presented a range of indigenous illustrated children's books. Then in 2004, and arranged to coincide with the 29th IBBY World Congress being hosted in Cape Town, the National Library of South Africa presented a historically-based exhibition of South African children's books under the title *Amandla ebali: The Power of the Story*. The 1986 exhibition was accompanied by the publication of a bilingual (in Afrikaans and English) collection of articles on youth literature, entitled *Doer-Land-y: Far Far Away*. In this, Raymond van Niekerk (1986), Director of the South African National Gallery, wrote: "Illustrated in this exhibition are important facets of South African publishing history as well as cultural and literary history" (1).

While one welcomes such an endorsement, it is disappointing that such bodies as our national library and art gallery have each, respectively, only once placed our indigenous youth literature on display in thirty years. Just how important is children's literature in this country? Sufficiently enough, anyway, for Stellenbosch University to maintain a degree course in illustration. Illustrators do not appear out of mid-air; they need guidance and encouragement. One of their long-standing teachers of illustration has been Paddy Bouma.

International author/illustrator Niki Daly (who also taught at Stellenbosch, in their Graphic Art course) commented recently that writers and illustrators of children's books are having a hard time. But he considered what they provided as: "...part of an 'essential service'—that is, providing children with good books, which I do believe is essential to the development of a curious and vital mind" (Daly 2013). Indeed, good books are essential to the development of a curious and vital mind. Good books so often need good illustrations. Paddy has contributed both illustrations and illustrators.

The Illustrator in Action

Paddy Niehaus was born in Cape Town. She had an eye problem when young and was taught at home by her mother for three years, during which time books were her companions and friends. Lewis Carroll's *Alice in Wonderland* was one of her favorites, especially the verses—though in an edition illustrated by Philip Gough, which Bouma (pers. comm.) says "were not so frightening as John Tenniel." She also loved a collection of Afrikaans poems (Paddy is bilingual) illustrated by the great Katrine Harries with line drawings which are often loosely sketched, like a first rough impression. In due course, she would also acknowledge the influence of such artists as Maurice Sendak, Beatrix Potter, Ron Brooks, Helen Oxenbury and John Burningham.

She studied at the Michaelis School of Fine Art at the University of Cape Town, obtaining a B.A. degree in 1967. Her first passion was for lithography, and she was awarded a scholarship to study this at the École Nationale Supérieure des Beaux-Arts in Paris the following year. Then she hurried home to marry architect Raymond Bouma. So started in 1971, a long career as a part-time lecturer in Lithography and Illustration at the Department of Visual Arts in Stellenbosch University. Her love for lithography seemed, as her two children grew up, a little somber, so she switched her main focus to book illustration which could be far more cheerful.

Three light, cheerful picture books published in South Africa were followed by a commission to provide illustrations for *Are We Nearly There?* by Louis Baum, which earned Paddy a commendation for the Kate Greenaway Medal in 1986. The Bodley Head liked her work, and she wrote and illustrated for them four stories about a stuffed hippo called Bertie.

> In these, the toy became an extension of the child, doing all the naughty things with dental floss and toothpaste which his owner, Thomas, would like to have done. Or perhaps he did, and Bertie takes the blame? [Heale 1994, 6].

She also illustrated two picture books by the well-known American author Carol Carrick, published by Clarion in New York. Of these, *Valentine* has sold over 70,000 copies—Paddy's "best seller" after Nelson Mandela's *Long Walk to Freedom* abridged by Chris van Wyk—and it's still in print.

According to Sally Howes, owner/publisher at Watermark Publishing, "Along with Niki Daly, Katrine Harries and a handful of others, Paddy is part of the illustrating aristocracy in South Africa" (pers. comm.). Howes asks

Paddy to illustrate only the exceptional stories that come her way. These stories are used in basal reading schemes as supplementary readers and as library books in schools across Africa. They are concerned with children's experiences of issues related to HIV and AIDS, so the subject matter is mostly serious and often sad. "In each case Paddy has brought poignancy and credibility to the characters and their experiences, which brings the story itself alive, and helps to hide the 'wagging finger' which often ruins series of this sort," according to Sally. Her next comments are quoted verbatim:

> There are four aspects of Paddy's work that stand out for me as a publisher working with her as an illustrator:
> - Empathy: Paddy treats each character as if she knows them—an individual, alive and believable. We are drawn into an emotional engagement with the characters, particularly in the quieter and sadder parts of a story, without any hint of sentimentality. In the book *Simon's Story* by Glynis Clacherty, about a child coming to terms with his mother's death, it is the illustrations that bring us to tears, that make the raw pain of the story inescapable.
> - Figure drawing: Sadly many of our South African children's book illustrators do not have a background in figure drawing or fine art. This leaves us often with unconvincing, or worse, cutesy or generic people, serving as little more than eye candy. The expressive and emotional character of Paddy's illustrations derive from her careful and confident rendering of the human form. It is never enough to guess. In a story about Beethoven losing his hearing, *When Bad Things Happen* by Jenny Robson, Paddy apparently had her husband sit for her at the piano so that she could properly capture the moment (the requisite look of frustration and dismay probably entirely genuine), and as a result we have a man who, despite being dressed in Viennese clothes from the 1800s, expresses anguish that is palpable and even familiar.
> - Research and detail: In conversation with Paddy during the time she was working on the Mandela book, *Long Walk to Freedom*, I was struck by how much research she does, of all sorts, before she puts pencil to paper. In the story *Tido's Bag*, by Bridget Krone, it wasn't enough to guess at a funeral, Paddy attended a funeral in the local township to make sure she had the details right.
> - Considering all aspects of page design: Paddy's work on the book extends beyond the pictures themselves. She happily advises on typography, layout and aspects of the cover. The story, art and page design must work in tandem, and Paddy engages with all three [Howes pers. comm.].

Equally praise-worthy from the figure drawing aspect has been Paddy's work for *The Best Meal Ever* by Sindiwe Magona. This is a potentially heart-rending story of a black South African family with absolutely no food in the house. So the eldest sibling, Siziwe, cooks up a meal by boiling water and making excuses until all her brothers and sisters are asleep. After which, there is a happy ending! Paddy provides honesty and compassion in her accompanying artwork. The book was included in the prestigious White Ravens list of the International Youth Library in Munich.

After a workload involving HIV/AIDs and dire poverty, one can hardly blame Paddy for branching off sideways and producing *The Mouseboat,* a delicious and light-hearted picture storybook about a mouse family having a boating holiday on a French river. Many echoes here of Bouma family holidays in France. This book was shortlisted for the MER Prize for Illustration in 2009.

Then came the commission (from Macmillan) to provide the accompanying illustrations for Chris van Wyk's version for young readers of Nelson Mandela's autobiography, *Long Walk to Freedom.* There is, naturally, a growing bibliography around Nelson Mandela starting with his own autobiography *Long Walk to Freedom.* Unfortunately, the number of books about the former president for primary level readers remains small. Yet *Nelson Mandela: Long Walk to Freedom* is of outstanding quality. As reviewed in December 2009 and listed as one of the best ten local children's books of the year: "The time will come when the crinkled, smiling old man with white hair is not with us any longer. This book will last and will carry the right sort of message to our future generations" (Heale 2009, 9). Paddy's artwork, which took her nearly a year to complete, is evocative and striking. First came the ultra-careful research Howes refers to above. Not only did Mandela himself have to look as accurately correct as possible at different stages of his life, but the background details of Eastern Cape countryside, of school and Fort Hare University, and of the twenty-six draining years on Robben Island as a prisoner, all also had to be checked. The artwork is collectively impressive, and the spread showing littered bodies in the haze of war after the 1960 Sharpville "massacre" is an immensely powerful painting. Quite rightly, Paddy regards this book as "the crowning piece of her career" (Bouma 2013, n.p.).

Contributions to the World of Children's Books in South Africa

Over a period of thirty-five years (1971 to 2006) Paddy Bouma was a lecturer at the University of Stellenbosch. With careful precision, she could explain to her students just what it was that made an illustration come alive, or not. Watching Paddy in action on a discussion panel for illustrators, Sally Howes noted how she was "gentle with her criticism and generous with her encouragement."

One of her students, Vian Oelofsen, now an increasingly successful illustrator, had this to say:

Paddy Bouma was my lecturer when I did a post grad degree in illustration during 1997/98. Her work on children's books and lithographs was instrumental in me deciding to jump headlong into a career of working in children's illustration. As a lecturer she was caring and fair. She taught through guidance and was never restrictive in her style of teaching; always open to new ideas and pushing boundaries when it came to exploring concepts in art, not just children's books [pers. comm.].

So she has provided a guiding voice behind a generation of emerging illustrators in South Africa. Many of them employ a style very different from Paddy's own, often more in line with contemporary graphic novels and comic art. It is not often realized that Paddy herself made contributions to the world of "comics," supplying graphic strip material for four editions of *Bitterkomix* from 1999 to 2002, a ground-breaking alternative publication that originated at Stellenbosch University. Through the years, she encouraged her students to keep pace with new approaches to illustration from the rest of the world.

Paddy Bouma has not shut herself away in her studio. She has maintained an active and involved membership in many children's book organizations: the Writers and Illustrators Group, the South African Children's Book Forum (now IBBY SA), and particularly as Co-Regional Adviser for the South African branch of the Society for Children's Book Writers & Illustrators (SCBWI). Together with fellow illustrator Marjorie van Heerden, Paddy has been involved both in plotting the strategic direction and in the more day to day bureaucracy of the SCBWI. She chaired a panel discussion of illustrators during the 29th IBBY World Congress in 2004 in Cape Town.

Paddy is an accomplished illustrator, a respected teacher and an active promoter of children's books in South Africa.

Illustration as Art

The surroundings in which an artist chooses to live can surely not be ignored. Paddy Bouma is precise and relaxed. In the same style, her home is precise, trim, welcoming. Outside, the garden looks half wild, deliberately dramatic (a location which has delighted many film directors). Paddy and her husband Raymond prefer deciduous trees, as they do not block out the sunshine in winter—the light which is such an important factor in her illustrative work. Look for the skillfully placed lamp in *The Best Meal Ever* and *Long Walk to Freedom*. So often her characters are suffused with a glow of light from a hidden source.

Her style has remained realistic, and she is one of the few South African artists who can capture the facial expressions of black South Africans with style and character. These are real people, full of life and humor. Not a hint of the caricature which used to creep in to local publications in the early twentieth century. She continued using pencil line and watercolor for many years, though now mostly watercolor inks which are closer to the original color when printed. Paddy has produced only one book, a reader published by Maskew Miller Longman, with computer assistance (and even more assistance from one of her students), and isn't quite sure why she hasn't done more. But for the illustrations to *Long Walk to Freedom*, she returned firmly to her tried and tested method of in-depth research and painstaking watercolors, making the atmosphere sad or joyous as the moment requires. Much to Paddy's disappointment, she never managed to meet former president Mandela. Though she made application to the Mandela Foundation, he had reached the point in his life when he was retired from public engagements.

This did not stop Paddy from creating one more, small and light-hearted tribute to South Africa's "Madiba" in her illustrations for Chris van Wyk's story "Mr Hare Meets Mr Mandela" in the *Storytime* collection published by *Sunday Times* and Nal'ibali (Times Media Education 2013) In this, the great "Mr Hare" of the African forest finds a two-hundred rand note. He is unable to read, but he can recognize Mandela's face, so he sets out to give the note back to the person it belongs to. And there we see a smiling "Mr Mandela," wearing a typically bright-colored Mandela shirt, bending low to accept the money from "Mr Hare." (Except that along the way, it seems to have changed color and value!)

There is more "illustration as art" in her illustrations (amongst those of other artists) for the *Children of God Storybook Bible* retold by Archbishop Emeritus Desmond Tutu. Paddy provided the illustrations for the chapters on "The Ten Commandments" and "Jesus is Born." The latter is certainly the kind of picture which could be framed and hung in a child's room with advantage.

> As pictures, they are beautiful. Almost every one of them. As illustrations, they are hugely successful—thoroughly researched, skilfully executed, and widely enjoyed. Her illustrations are rooted in her proficiency as a fine artist, and I think this enhances the reader's engagement with the story and enjoyment of the book, where often a more "arty" style of illustration alienates a reader, especially in a book market as conventional as our own [Sally Howes, pers. comm.].

All of which is strange when we consider that Paddy never considered illustration as a career for a long time. She was trained as a painter and printmaker, and for some time she was quite simply an artist. When the opportunity came to illustrate a book which excited her, it proved to be "such hard work, so poorly paid and so badly printed that I decided not to be an illustrator after all!" (pers. comm.)

It was in the collaboration with author Louis Baum for his emotive book

Are We Nearly There? (published in the U.S. as *One More Time*) that Paddy found her sensitive feel for true art could play an important role in illustration. Cathy Woodward (1987), a contributor to *School Library Journal*, described Paddy's ability to capture a wide range of emotions in her pictures, saying: "a delicately watercolored yet richly shaded panorama of scenes of father and son embellish the tender but dynamic relationship" (76).

She always hopes that her illustrative art will make a difference to the reader, perhaps offering a new perspective on life, perhaps enabling someone to say, "This confirms what I have always sensed, but could not have put into words." Pictures can say so much more than words. In addition, her books have been translated into Afrikaans, many African languages including isiZulu and Swahili, French for Francophone Africa, as well as Danish and Korean.

In Paddy Bouma's own words: "All my life, books have been my friends and mentors. I hope to be able to give back something of what I have received" (pers. comm.).

CHILDREN'S BOOKS

Baum, Louis. 1986. *Are We Nearly There?* Illustrated by Paddy Bouma. London: The Bodley Head. (Also published as *One More Time* by Morrow, New York, 1986.)
Bouma, Paddy. 1987. *Bertie at the Dentist's*. London: The Bodley Head.
_____. 1987. *Bertie Visits Granny*. London: The Bodley Head.
_____. 1988. *Bertie and the Hamsters*. London: The Bodley Head.
_____. 1988. *Bertie in the Bag*. London: The Bodley Head.
_____. 1999. "The Guilty Bystander 1 & 2" and "The Invisible People." In *Bitterkomix 9*, 15–19. Stellenbosch, SA: University of Stellenbosch.
_____. 2000. "The Guilty Bystander" and "The Art Room." In *Bitterkomix 10*, 26–29. Stellenbosch, SA: University of Stellenbosch.
_____. 2001. "Survivor's Tale." In *Bitterkomix 11*, 32–33. Stellenbosch, SA: University of Stellenbosch.
_____. 2002. "Evolution." In *Bitterkomix 12*, 39–41. Stellenbosch, SA: University of Stellenbosch.
_____. 2008. *The Mouseboat*. Cape Town, SA: Tafelberg.
Carrick, Carol. 1995. *Valentine*. Illustrated by Paddy Bouma. New York: Clarion Books.
Clacherty, Glynis. 2004. *Simon's Story*. Illustrated by Paddy Bouma. London: Heinemann.
Krone, Bridget. 2004. *Tido's Bag*. Illustrated by Paddy Bouma. London: Heinemann.
Magona, Sindiwe. 2006. *The Best Meal Ever!* Illustrated by Paddy Bouma. Cape Town, SA: Tafelberg.
Mandela, Nelson. 2009. *Nelson Mandela: Long Walk to Freedom*. Abridged by Chris van Wyk. Illustrated by Paddy Bouma. London: Macmillan.
Robson, Jenny. 2007. *When Bad Things Happen*. Illustrated by Paddy Bouma. Pietermaritzburg, SA: Shuter and Shooter.
Tutu, Desmond. 2010. *Children of God, Storybook Bible*. Various illustrators. Cape Town, SA: Lux Verbi.
Van Wyk, Chris. 2013. "Mr Hare Meets Mr Mandela." Illustrated by Paddy Bouma. In *Storytime*, 95–108. Johannesburg, South Africa: Times Media Education.

The Writing of Dianne Case: Making Choices and Facing Consequences

Lisa Kimble *and* Barbara A. Lehman

Dianne Case is a children's and young adult author who writes about life in coloured communities in South Africa. The characters from these communities reflect the experiences and offer the authentic voices of previously oppressed persons, which is vital to include in children's books because it is a way for children today to discover the history of their country through each character's unique story. Case's work also stands out because children's literature in South Africa traditionally revolved around white characters' experiences while the experiences of coloured characters were stereotypical or omitted altogether. Case crafts her characters to truly portray the sentiments that many coloureds felt before and after apartheid, all while placing her characters in a realistic and usually historical setting.

Under apartheid, "any mixture of blood established someone as coloured," while those who were purely one race or another were categorized as whites and blacks (Posel, 2001). In South Africa, the term "coloured" is how citizens of mixed races self-identify. Since coloureds make up 9.0% of the total South African population according to the 2011 National Census of South Africa, it is crucial that youths are exposed to literature by coloured authors like Dianne Case, since authors of color are few in number in South Africa relative to the overall population. Case's work, however, has much to offer for students of any race, nationality, or background, because her books tend to create empathy in readers and offer a glimpse of what life was and in some respects still is for many people in South Africa.In many of Case's books, a theme of choices and consequences is present, especially in *Love, David*, *92 Queens Road*, and *Katy of Sky Road*. Making choices and facing the consequences of these choices is a theme that is universal and is extremely relevant for children and young adults.

Early Biography

Dianne Case grew up during the apartheid era, became familiar with the harsh realities of this system implemented by the government firsthand, and was faced with many difficult choices of her own. Case explained that she chose to be educated, and with this education came the responsibility of passing along knowledge to others through her work. Choosing to write about her personal experiences resulted in genuine work that is representative of how many South African citizens have lived or still are living today. Although Case's suburb of Wynberg was not chosen as one in which the forced removals occurred, Dianne's childhood was still negatively affected by apartheid.

Case's father was an Indian from Durban, a city of the east coast of South Africa that is home to many Indians, while Dianne's mother was classified as coloured. Under apartheid, whites, of course, were at the top of the racial hierarchy with Indians coming in second, followed by coloureds, with blacks being at the very bottom. For Case's Indian father to marry her coloured mother caused a controversy, resulting in her father getting disowned by his own family. Not only that, but many of Dianne's mother's family were re-classified as white, so Case and her immediate family could not freely associate with members of her mother's family. As a result, Case grew up with the absence of her grandparents and other relatives and confessed that she felt alone. When she was still a child, her mother became ill, and she was basically left by herself, without a familial community to step in and care for her. Another vivid memory of apartheid that still haunts Dianne is that one day she accompanied her father to the beach. His arthritis was really bothering him and it was obvious to Case that he was in pain, yet the benches were reserved for whites only. There were no whites even sitting on the benches, and while her father did not comment and silently suffered through his pain, Case was thoroughly aware of this great injustice, and it stuck with her.

Personal Choices of Dianne Case

Although much has changed since apartheid ended, Case revealed that many coloureds "feel that they've been marginalized by the new government" (pers. comm.). In order to give back to the coloured communities, Case frequently goes into townships and visits schools to work with children, which again, ties the theme of choices and consequences present in her work to her real life. By working with non-white school children, she may influence how children see themselves since she is a living role model that authors of color can get an education and have shared with the world.

When wealthier schools ask Case to come and talk to children or to sign books, Case will take the money from the fee she charges in order to buy books to donate to schools in townships that may lack high quality literature that is culturally relevant. Dianne explained that the coloured townships have high crime rates, even in comparison to black townships. She believes that some young people have lost respect for the older generation and that turning to gangs and drugs is quite common, in part, because of poverty. Children may see her success and realize that there are other paths out there besides the ones that lead to violence.

Despite the hardships that Case suffered as a child, Dianne had many positive experiences in her younger days, including ones with books. Case described books as being "magical" and recalled in an article written for *The Times* (Sophy 2012) that she felt a "sense of freedom" when she learned to read because she could use her imagination to envision whole new worlds. This is a gift Case wishes to share with underprivileged youth, many of whom choose to escape by using drugs such as crystal meth, commonly referred to as "tik" in South Africa.

Early Success

Dianne Case started her career as a writer when she needed extra money to supplement the salary she earned as a bookkeeper. She submitted pieces to the local newspaper and won cash prizes. Somehow, she found the time to work while supporting three children while her husband was away and while working full time. Encouraged by her success, Case penned *Albatross Winter*, which was her first novel that focuses on the lives of coloured fishermen who live and work along the west coast of South Africa north of Cape Town. For this work, Case was awarded first place in the Young Africa Competition. She attributed her success after that to the fact that there were so few coloured writers writing stories about coloured communities. Case called herself a "curiosity" to other racial groups since whites, blacks, and coloureds "lived essentially separate existences," according to Case.

Love, David: Facing the Consequences of Poor Choices

Case's next novel, titled *Love, David* is regarded as a classic South African novel. This popular book has sold over three million copies, which is a feat considering how difficult it is to get published in South Africa, a country that

Case believes does not have a strong book buying culture. *Love, David* is commonly used in South African schools, and it became available in North America when Lodestar books published it. *Love, David* presents issues with which children in South Africa can still identify today. The story is set in a township of the area known as the Cape Flats—a large flat, sandy stretch connecting the Cape Peninsula in the west with the wine region and mountains of Stellenbosch to the east—where most of the residents removed from Cape Town under the Group Areas Act were relocated. These more established townships have exploded into vast informal shanty settlements with a huge influx of persons of color from rural areas seeking work in the metropolitan region. The story, told from young Anna's point of view, is about the struggles of a family living in such circumstances. The focus is on her older half-brother, David, who gets involved with a theft ring and is punished severely by his stepfather. David runs away to live with the gang and eventually is sent to do time in a reform school. Anna loves her brother in spite of his faults, and he treats her kindly, also. Anna mourns his absence at the end, but there is hope and compassion underlying the plot's bitter realities.

Case was nominated in 1987 to be Woman of the Year in the newspaper, *Star,* a daily tabloid based in Johannesburg. Her nomination occurred because of her realistic portrayal of street children in *Love, David*. In South Africa, it is common for children to live on the street and fend for themselves because, like David, they have decided to run away from home. Others are orphaned by parents who have died of HIV/AIDS, which affects a significant number of South Africans. By telling the story of street children, Case provides a mirror story for underprivileged children who may have lived on the street or who have friends who have run away.

The theme of choice and consequences is present throughout the novel. By reading *Love, David* readers will come to understand that David may have made some terrible choices, but the circumstances he was faced with impacted some of his decisions. David left home because he clashed with his stepfather who clearly had a drinking problem and became violent when he consumed alcohol. Readers will likely tend to feel sympathetic towards David because he does have many good qualities. He chose to rescue a drowning dog that he named Stumpy and cared for this dog diligently. David also developed a deep bond with his sister Anna and was a generous and loving brother. When asked how he was going to spend the money he earned selling drugs, David said he was going to use part of the money to buy clothes for his sisters.

However, the tension between David and Dadda escalated as the story progressed. When Dadda kicked David's dog several times, David could no longer tolerate living under the same roof as his stepfather. Since David did not get too far in school, he chose to join a gang in order to earn some easy money. David got caught with *dagga* (marijuana) and ended up having to face the consequences of his poor choices when he got caught. When David was sent to a reform school, Dadda considered it a blessing because, "He could have grown up to do worse before being caught out" (105). Dadda went on to say that if David continued on his destructive path, that he could have ended up a murderer.

Love, David carries a powerful message for readers everywhere without being didactic—one should consider choices carefully because actions cannot always be made freely without any repercussions. Even if David did not end up in a reform school, a consequence would have been that he could not see his dear sister Anna very often. This theme will strike a chord with students from a wide variety of backgrounds because many readers can relate to the problems David faces in the story. Poverty, a lack of education, abuse within a family, tensions between family members, living in a non-traditional family, and unemployment are certainly problems that occur worldwide.

92 Queens Road: Choosing Whether or Not to Emigrate

Like David, Kathy of Dianne Case's novel *92 Queens Road* (winner of both the Young Africa Award and the Percy FitzPatrick Award) must also make a big decision. Set in the 1960s during the apartheid era, Kathy and her family are affected by the brutality of the forced removals when Dolores's Aunty Sal and Uncle Herbie have to leave their home in Cape Town after living there for their entire married life. This change causes a great burden for the couple, who have no choice but to live with their daughter, who is described in the book as being "unkind." After watching Herbie fall into a deep depression, and die "an angry and defeated man," Dolores becomes bitter about how coloureds do not even have a say in their own government (141). Dolores suffers a terrible loss later on in the story when she, Kathy, and Bertha are exiting a bus, which is segregated with "whites downstairs" and "non-whites upstairs." Dolores loses her balance when the white conductor impatiently signals the driver to move too soon. The accident causes the pregnant Dolores to lose her baby. Uncle Reggie, who married Dolores earlier in the novel, has seen different parts of the world, and he knows that in other locations people of color and whites are considered equals. Kathy and her mother Bertha also have to make a choice about what to do. To stay in South Africa means that they are not truly citizens in their own country because they are denied many rights that whites have, such as voting. To move overseas means they would have to leave many of their friends and family members behind and start all over again. For

Kathy, this is not a path she is willing to take. Instead, Kathy and Bertha choose to stay, hoping that their country will eventually change.

Emigrating to another country or remaining in South Africa was a choice that needed to be considered carefully, as there were many consequences but also some advantages to each decision. Those like Kathy and her mother who stayed, hoping that the situation would change, suffered the hardship of not being able to vote until South Africa's first truly democratic election in 1994. This meant that decades passed before the apartheid government disbanded, so Kathy and other children her age would have faced many injustices in their childhoods, as adolescents, and as adults. Kathy's mother would have lived under a racist regime for most of her life, while some who chose to stay in South Africa would have died without ever being granted the right to vote, sit downstairs on a bus, or freely roam a public beach.

Many of those who left South Africa like Dolores and Uncle Reg, left for good. They established themselves in other countries and some renounced their South African citizenship. To stay in another country and never return to South Africa meant giving the up the life one had always known. Many who left were immersed in new cultures, very different from the culture of the coloured communities in South Africa. In some cases, their absences tore what would have been close-knit families apart. Case noted that her family members who moved to Canada did not return to South Africa to live, even after apartheid ended.

Katy of Sky Road: Struggling to Make Choices

Interestingly, not all of Case's work takes place under the rule of the old South African government. Case's latest book, *Katy of Sky Road*, co-written with Yvonne Hart, is set in contemporary South Africa. Katy, a coloured teenager, lives with her father, Hector, and her Auntie Rose in a coloured community. In this coming of age story, Katy must choose either to live life the way she wants or to obey her father and live up to his expectations of her, which include pursuing ballroom dancing as her deceased mother once did. Hector also expects Katy to attend as many church functions as possible and eventually start dating Wesley, whom Hector thinks is a fine, young man. Katy feels that she should please her father, but when she tries to obey his strict rules and do things his way, she ends up unfulfilled. Katy believes that Hector will disapprove of her dancing to "hip hop" music and of her spending time with Ricardo, a talented hip hop dancer. Katy begins to sneak out with her friends and lies to Hector while trying to cope with Wesley who is becoming more and more jealous of Katy and Ricardo's friendship. Because of his strong opinions, Katy does not feel that she can tell Hector what is really going on and is torn between the two worlds. Throughout all of this, there is the underlying problem of drugs that affects members of the coloured community and eventually even Katy's own friends. Case said that there is prevalent use of crystal meth and that it is "impossible to overcome." Often it is diluted with rat poison and chlorine to increase its profitability.

Katy ends up in a dangerous situation when Wesley lures her into his car and drives her to a building full of used appliances. It is then that Katy discovers Wesley is selling "tik" and has a drug problem himself. Wesley tries to get Katy to kiss him, but when she resists his advances, he becomes violent with her, and Katy narrowly escapes the area after encountering some potentially dangerous men. It is Ricardo who comes to her rescue, and Hector realizes that he has been wrong about Wesley. Upon meeting Brenda, Ricardo's mother, Hector eases up on Katy and gives her permission to dance in the hip hop competition with Ricardo.

Katy of Sky Road easily relates to readers across many countries because it covers topics such as addiction, jealously, and deceit. Many young adults will be likely to identify with strict parents whom they feel do not understand them. South African teenagers will be able to relate to Katy's perspective about the new South Africa since they, too, have not experienced the old ways. Katy believes that the South African government is doing its best to treat citizens of all colors fairly and equally, but Hector feels that the government has forgotten the coloureds and that while under apartheid he was too black, now he isn't black enough to receive any benefits from the new order. This is a hot topic in South Africa because many citizens, regardless of race, are faced with the choice of whether or not they accept the new government. Hector chooses to reject both the old and new governments and consequently does not fully embrace the new South Africa since he feels as though coloureds are still not adequately represented. Katy, choosing to dismiss Hector, makes the choice to live without the baggage passed down from the older generations. She feels that the old ways she has heard about are gone.

Hector also experiences consequences related to the choices he has made. By choosing not to trust Katy and by trying too hard to control her, he ends up stifling who Katy really is by forcing her to conform to his ways. The consequence is that Katy feels as though she must lie to Hector in order to live her life the way she wants to.

Throughout the novel Katy suffers the consequences of Hector's past actions. Katy has horrible nightmares, which are suppressed memories of her parents fighting, and involve the circumstances of her mother's death. Because of Hector's former drinking problem and after reading some notes written to Hector by Katy's late mother, Katy is led to believe that Hector may have been responsible for her mother's death. Since he used to be an alcoholic, Katy begins to question Hector's role in her mother's death and his overall character in general.

Like David in *Love, David*, Wesley must face the repercussions of his choice to become a gang member who uses and deals "tik." Wesley clearly has a crush on Katy and really wants her to feel the same way. While taking crystal meth, Wesley harms Katy and readers are led to believe that he may have raped her if she did not escape when she did. For Wesley, the consequence is that he almost loses Katy as a friend forever. He also has to deal with the consequences of breaking the law. Zeke, too, pays the price for his addiction to "tik." He ends up hospitalized and nearly dies from taking too many drugs.

Positive Choices of Dianne Case

Although Dianne currently focuses on visiting schools in townships to discuss her work, in the past she volunteered at Pollsmoor Prison where she taught a writing workshop to adults and adolescents. She also started her own publishing company called Kwagga. Under Kwagga, Case published *What a Gentleman!*, a colorful picture book in which the life and some accomplishments of Nelson Mandela are celebrated. Case hopes to inspire children by Mandela's example because throughout his life Mandela has continually made choices that benefited South Africa as a whole nation, rather than just a specific group of people. Through the eyes of many people around the world, Nelson Mandela is seen as a role model, but Case chooses to stress his positive personal choices rather than his political choices to children. In this picture book, Mandela is depicted exercising, helping families, and tending a small garden.

Case has two novels currently being considered by her publisher. One of the novels is a follow up to *Katy of Sky Road* tentatively titled *Oh, Katy!*, which picks up where *Katy of Sky Road* leaves off. The second novel is called *The Rules* and focuses on a set of boy/girl twins who are shuffled back and forth and live as practicing Muslims with their mother and attend church as Christians when they are with their father

Work by authors like Dianne Case is crucial to incorporate into young readers' experiences with books because they will have opportunities to read books portraying children of color. Some South African children are still not able to see themselves in books or do not have access to books in their native languages. Young South African readers need authors like Dianne Case to tell their stories, while children from around the world (and even in South Africa) can benefit from getting a glimpse into other cultures and can relate to the themes of choice and consequence, love, survival, and justice.

Children's Books

Case, Dianne. 1983. *Albatross Winter*. Cape Town, SA: Maskew Miller Longman.
———. 1985. *Love, David*. Cape Town, SA: Maskew Miller Longman.
———. 1991. *92 Queens Road*. Cape Town, SA: Maskew Miller Longman.
———. 1997. *What a Gentleman!* Illus. Joanne Harvey. Cape Town, SA: Kwagga.
Case, Dianne, and Yvonne Hart. 2007. *Katy of Sky Road*. Cape Town, SA: Maskew Miller Longman.

The "Dual Realities" of Niki Daly: Dreaming Himself into Someone Else's Skin

Barbara A. Lehman

Niki Daly, distinguished South African author-illustrator of children's books, says he is "fascinated by the dual reality children have when playing games" (Khorana 2002, 73), a playful spirit that he captures well in his books. The term "dual reality" aptly characterizes Daly's own life and work as well. He is a man with a name that sometimes is mistaken for a woman's, an African with European roots, a white South African who depicts the lives of black South Africans in many of his most beloved picture books, an accomplished artist who also writes with style, and a creator of books who also is a musician and performer. This profile explores the manifestations of dual realities in picture books that he has both written and illustrated since returning to South Africa in 1979.

"Child of Apartheid" and Agent of Change

Born Nikolaas, Niki describes himself as a "child of apartheid" (Daly 2002, 36), with Irish, English, and Afrikaans roots. His early primary contacts with blacks were two women hired as domestic workers for his family and who opened his world to the Xhosa language, songs, stories, and dance. Both women were named Miriam, and when Daly returned to South Africa, he reconnected with the one who still lived in the historically black township of Gugulethu outside Cape Town. She called him her "white son" (38) when he visited her home. In a nation in which skin color at that time was *the* defining classification, Daly came to regard his as more restrictive than helpful, particularly when some critics implied that he "ought to stay in my skin" (39).

"Dreaming myself into someone else's skin" (Daly n.d., 1) was something he had always done to escape a working class childhood; hence, as a writer and illustrator, "jumping out of your skin" (Daly 2002, 39) in the final decade of apartheid quite naturally led him to the creation of *Not So Fast Songololo*, the first full-color picture book published in South Africa depicting an urban black child protagonist (Heale 2004).The illustrations exhibit what can be regarded as his signature style until 2000—pen and ink with watercolor— while the story about a small boy and his *gogo* (grandmother) emerged from seeing two similar people walking down a city street, which sparked his own childhood memory of going to a shoe store with his grandmother to buy new shoes (Daly 2002, 39). Thus, it was a universal story at the same time that it was a groundbreaking publication under the apartheid regime when many books were banned for unsanctioned racial depictions.

Several years later, in *Papa Lucky's Shadow*, Daly set a story about non-white characters in an urban area like the Cape Town community of District Six that was home to many mixed-race families before their forced removal under the apartheid Group Areas Act. Again, it was an actual street image that sparked this story about Papa Lucky, the sidewalk dancer (Daly 1996, 95), whose granddaughter became his dancing "shadow." As in *Songololo*, Daly featured a warm relationship between a grandparent and child that takes place in a public venue.

Another book that visually echoes *Songololo* also was inspired by a public scene (Dossier 2004), this time a South African seaside in *The Boy on the Beach*. Although written before the end of apartheid, this beach is fully integrated, and the story features a black family enjoying a day there just like many other families of all ethnicities. After splashing in the waves with his parents, the young boy Joe sets off to explore other areas of the beach on his own. Before long, he is engrossed in imaginary play until he realizes that he is lost and is eventually rescued by a (white) lifeguard and returned safely to his parents, exemplifying the duality of children's lives between reality and fantasy.

The Jamela books follow Jamela from early childhood in *Jamela's Dress* to middle childhood in *A Song for Jamela*. Jamela's early interest in dressing up and pretending to be an African queen morphs into her thrill at meeting the "Afro-Idols" TV celebrity Miss Chaka Chaka in Aunt Beauty's hair salon. In addition, the first two books are clearly set in a traditionally black township, while the last three are set in a multiracial urban neighborhood, where Jamela moves with her mother and grandmother in *Where's Jamela?* Significantly, Daly locates Jamela in his then house in the Mowbray area of Cape Town (Daly 2007), another area from which "coloureds" had been removed during the apartheid Group Areas Act and where Niki also had lived as a child. With this subtle gesture, Daly, a "child of apartheid," symbolically reverses apartheid in his own work by bringing a child of the new democratic South Africa into his home.

Daly freely admits that he is a white writer-illustrator interpreting black lives in many of his most noteworthy books (Daly 2002). Certainly, this critique is a valid consideration regarding anyone writing or illustrating as an ethnic outsider in any setting, and readers must question whether the writer-illustrator "got it right." It is of particular concern as yet another possible manifestation of Whiteness and privilege and the assumption that white writers may appropriate any stories they wish. However, Daly strongly resists the creative "apartheid" of staying within one's own cultural or ethnic borders. In his speech at the International Reading Association convention in Toronto, Canada, in 2007, Daly stated, "whenever it's suggested that writers should stay within cultural borderlines, or stay in their own skin or sex, I feel the chill of apartheid mentality that would have us separated and suspicious of our amazing ability, as humans, to empathise with one another" (3). This ability to imagine himself in another person's "skin" also translates into his deep understanding of children and their concerns and interests.

Political and Personal

While Daly's work is undoubtedly political, it is not issue-driven, and much of it is about the personal. Relationships are primary in all the books discussed above, and they form major themes in several others. For example, *My Dad, Old Bob's Brown Bear,* and *Once Upon a Time* depict both the joys and challenges of close family and community relationships. *My Dad*, based on Daly's own childhood experience, relates the poignancy and pain of living with an alcoholic parent. The father's playfulness, musical talent, and skillful woodwork, which are all traits his son admires, are not enough to overcome the devastating effects his excessive drinking has on the family. Although the story has a hopeful ending and Daly dedicates the book to his father, in real life the outcome of their relationship was not so positive because his father committed suicide in 1984 (Daly 1996, 90).

From the boy Niki to an elderly image of himself in *Old Bob's Brown Bear,* Emma's grandfather, Old Bob (who bears a strong resemblance to an older Niki Daly), receives a birthday teddy bear from Gran (who resembles Niki's wife, the illustrator Jude Daly) because he had never received a stuffed toy as a boy. However, as Emma instinctively knows, it takes a child to teach an old man how to love a teddy bear properly. The love between a grandparent and his grandchild is symbolized by how the teddy comes to remind the grandfather of the child he loves and the child he once was in this tender story of the duality of childhood and old age.

Once Upon a Time expands the theme of family relationships by including a pivotal cross-racial friendship between a young girl and her elderly neighbor. Sarie dreads reading aloud in school because her classmates ridicule her when she stutters and stammers over the words. Ou Missus ("old lady," an Afrikaans term for a white Afrikaans woman), Sarie's neighbor, spends Sunday afternoons with Sarie in an ancient broken-down car, telling stories about her youth and reading from a dusty volume discovered in the car's back seat. Repeated readings of the "once upon a time" story about a "beautiful girl and two ugly stepsisters" bring Sarie's dream of succeeding as a reader to fruition and make her a good friend with her classmate Emile when Sarie includes Emile in her after school make-believe adventure with Ou Missus. More explicitly than in *Old Bob*, *Once Upon a Time* provides a strong sense of place in a South African setting, with scenes of the Little Karoo's rocky outcroppings and veld (grassy scrub) landscape and earth tone colors. Sarie's parents labor on a sheep farm, and Sarie, Emile, and their classmates look like they could be coloured children, as do many rural farm children in that area, who are descendants of the original Khoisan inhabitants and European settlers. In addition, the school principal's name, Miss November, suggests a traditional coloured surname. However, Sarie's dilemma is one with which children universally will identify.

Daly notes that "traditionally African children are encouraged to be part of a community that depends more on group efforts than individual interests" (Daly 2007). This philosophy of *Ubuntu*, or interconnectedness, emphasizes that individuals are only fully realized through their community and its greater good. Ubuntu is beautifully exemplified in *Zanzibar Road*, a story in five brief chapters about Mama Jumbo, an elephant, who encounters a friendly community on Zanzibar Road where she decides to live. She is helped in building her house out of a pile of scraps by Juju, the monkey, and all the other animal neighbors. When she becomes lonely living by herself, she takes in Little Chico, a small and apparently homeless chicken, and in the end they celebrate his birthday with all their neighbors. The illustrations depict a vibrant, diverse (as symbolized by the different animals), and culturally rich community that goes about daily life, making do with what they have, supporting and celebrating each other. These themes continue in the sequel, *Next Stop—Zanzibar Road!* in which the same cast of characters, led by Mama Jumbo, mutually solve routine challenges, hence exemplifying Daly's vision of the new South Africa.

Childhood Innocence and Experience

As a writer and illustrator, Daly captures a perspective of children with many universal applications. He says, "As a child, I knew no innocent children"

(Daly 1996, 78) and asserts that "childhood innocence" is a myth invented by adults; instead, he imbues "the children who inhabit [his] books with pluck rather than sunshine" (78). Indeed his fictional characters get into scrapes even when they do not mean to be naughty, such as Jamela in every one of the books about her. The entire premise of *Pretty Salma* is the cautionary tale of a young girl who is told by her grandmother to go straight to the market and back again without talking to strangers—a "Little Red Riding Hood" variant vividly set in Ghana. Of course, Salma, who is based on a real-life girl whom Daly saw passing his house every day on the way to school and taking a dangerous route along the railway tracks (Daly 2007), forgets Granny's warning and is tricked by the conniving Mr. Dog. However, unlike the European tradition of Red Riding Hood and her grandmother being saved by a woodcutter, Salma uses her wits to devise a plan with her grandfather to save Granny.

Along with the view of childhood exemplified by Jamela and Salma, Daly delivers a message to children to strive for their dreams and to "strut your stuff!" (Daly 1996, 95). Just as Sarie perseveres with encouragement from Ou Missus to perfect her reading, pursuing a dream is a central theme in *Ruby Sings the Blues*. When Ruby's loud voice gets her into trouble with everyone and their reactions give her the blues, two neighbors—a sax player and a jazz singer—help Ruby turn her loud voice into an asset by teaching her how to *sing* the blues, and Ruby becomes the star of her school concert.

Absurdity and comedy—two attributes that often appeal to children—are hallmarks of *Mama, Papa, and Baby Joe*. This story came about after a visit to New York City (Daly 1996, 92) and features a mishmash of human, animal, and storybook characters, artists Andy Warhol and Pablo Picasso, Charlie Chaplin, and Daly's own likeness on the back cover. The zany illustrations portray multilayered, overlapping bridges; a wild assortment of vehicles, some with rooftop giant likenesses of doughnuts or sausages; bawdy characters, including Mama in a very short, low-cut dress and Papa in a tanktop; silly headgear, such as a woman balancing a cocktail on her head; tongue-in-cheek shop signs, such as A. Tooth, Dentist; and chaotic street scenes, with cars, buses, bicyclists, shopping carts, and the odd snail or polka-dotted dinosaur. While all the drivers appear to be seated on the left (as in the United States), the Pick 'n Pay store's name is borrowed from a South African chain grocery market. Other global touches are the many African animals represented, the black woman in ethnic dress and braids, and the women wearing a Muslim hijab. Although this title was not a sales success in the United States—a disappointment to Daly—it may convey a theme, as noted by fellow South African illustrator Piet Grobler at the 2010 International Board on Books for Young People Congress, that such a diverse assortment of characters is "normal" or what is expected in a typical day.

"Stage and Page"

Daly's dynamic approach to art shines through the pages of his books in several ways. First, he dramatically changed his illustration style when he returned to South Africa from a static to a very active, even exuberant and exaggerated artistic mode. He says he first learned to capture movement and action from studying comics as a child, and he "will even make use of comic drawing devices, such as speed lines ... I also show my support characters interacting with the central action through their body language" (Lehman 2007, n.p.)—much like actors on a stage. He characterizes himself as a drawer more than a painter, and he is pleased that "[t]hese days ... it feels as though I am dancing with my pen" (pers. comm.). This dancing is especially evident in his drawings of the leaping, splashing, jumping *Boy on the Beach*, with water and sand flying; the blurred whirls of Papa Lucky's sidewalk dancing; the frantic chicken-chasing in *What's Cooking, Jamela?*; and the frenetic activity in *Mama, Papa, and Baby Joe*.

Along with this change in style, Daly's choice of media has continued to evolve. As noted earlier, he was known for his watercolor technique—accompanied by brush, pen, pencil, and even felt pen—in all his work before 2000. Starting in 2001 with *What's Cooking, Jamela?* he began to create with digital techniques, such as scanned pencil and Corel PhotoPaint, which have been employed in *Ruby Sings the Blues, Pretty Salma, Zanzibar Road, A Song for Jamela, The Herd Boy* (discussed later in this profile), and *Next Stop—Zanzibar Road!* At the same time, Daly also continued to use traditional media in *Old Bob's Brown Bear, Once Upon a Time, Where's Jamela?,* and *Happy Birthday, Jamela!* According to his website (nikidaly.wordpress.com), in 2013 he planned to return to some "old friends"—materials that he hadn't used as much in recent years, but which indicates Daly's continuing development as an artist who resists being classified with one style.

In addition, Daly's fascination with entertainment, drama, and music and his drawing talent—what he terms "stage and page" (2007)—are evident in the guitar-playing, rock n' roll-singing dad in *My Dad*; the sidewalk dancing Papa Lucky; Ruby's blues singing; and Miss Chaka Chaka's song for Jamela on "Afro-Idols." Jamela's dramatic imagination carries her away, as she pretends to be an African queen with Mama's dress material (in *Jamela's Dress*), and she stars as Mary in the school Nativity play (in *What's Cooking, Jamela?*). Sarie regains her self-confidence by dramatizing the Cinderella story with Ou Missus in *Once Upon a Time*. In addition, the central story of *Bravo, Zan Angelo!* focuses on the Renaissance street theater form, *commedia dell'arte*, of Venice. Young Angelo longs to be a clown and cleverly finds a way to insert himself in a performance of his grandfather's acting troupe, where he steals the show with his red rooster costume and loud cock-a-doodle-doos. That stage-lover's delight in costumes and fashion is exhibited through Jamela's character—her party dress and "princess shoes" in *Jamela's Dress* and *Happy Birthday, Jamela!* — and Miss Chaka Chaka's glamorous clothes in *A Song for Jamela*; the sparkling evening dress Ou Missus gives Sarie when she calls her "My princess!"; Pretty Salma's special go-to-market outfit; Mama Jumbo's "jazzy dress and her 'Flippy-floppy, flappy-slippy, this-way-that-way pompom' hat" (in *Next Stop—Zanzibar Road?*, 2) and the lush costumes of *Bravo, Zan Angelo!* In each of these ways, Daly uses the page as his stage and unites his skill with both.

"Out of My Skin" and into a "Rainbow" Nation

In the end, Niki Daly's comfort within the "skin" of his own dual realities enables him to transcend the polarities that so often accompany considerations of gender, class, race, culture, and nationality. When asked by Michael Thorne (2006) about South Africans' dependency "on Europe and the USA for our cultural stimulus at the expense of indigenous talent," Daly questioned that premise: "Who and what defines what is South African?...Our South African-ness should be no more than the soil in which great ideas germinate." More recently, he reflected, "I don't like to think of myself as being African or European when I do books. I get involved in different themes and backgrounds, yes, but I always feel myself in them....The thing is to *own* or *claim* one's material—otherwise one is writing as an outsider which undermines one's confidence" (pers. comm.).

Daly's skill at merging his diverse roots is borne out by his work, which reflects both European and African influences, as seen in the Italian-set *Bravo, Zan Angelo!* and the West African retelling of the European Little Red Riding Hood tale, *Pretty Salma*. Perhaps, Daly's most complete marriage of these traditions appears in *Why the Sun and Moon Live in the Sky*. Daly has "playfully interwoven" his retelling of a creation myth of the Ibibio people of southeastern Nigeria "with artistic images from the Renaissance, a time when new science challenged old myths" (jacket flap). Daly's version also retains a traditional ending: "This is my story, which I have related, if it be sweet, or if it be not sweet—take some elsewhere and let some come back to me" (n.p.). The dossier for Daly's 2004 nomination for the Hans Christian Andersen award describes this title as "the conquering of cultural apartheid" and states that "Niki felt sufficiently liberated to celebrate his European and African influences" (9, 9). One of Daly's first publications after the 1994 election, *Why the Sun and Moon* captures "the sense of relief [he felt] from the shame of the past and a freedom to explore [his] full potential as a South African artist" (Daly 1996, 98).

In *The Herd Boy*, Daly celebrates South Africa's changes over the previous two decades by envisioning a chance encounter between a young shepherd in a rural Eastern Cape Province setting and a distinguished-looking elderly gentleman, who strongly resembles Nelson Mandela. That Mandela was a herd boy himself as a child in a similar setting who rose to become the first black president of South Africa tells all children that anyone who demonstrates responsibility can aspire to be a leader in the new country. This may be the true magic of the "rainbow."

Overall, then, while Daly's work often is imbued with both overt and subtle South African images and diverse characters, he clearly asserts that he does not want it to be defined by race and politics. Rather, he strongly believes in the power of books to heal, and even stories set in poverty to offer hope to readers who may be facing their own challenges. Daly has devoted much of his personal time and energy since returning to South Africa to promoting and developing the work of black South African writers and illustrators. In addition, he understands the tension of a white writer interpreting black lives, but he is not deterred by that critique of his work. Instead, his message is to not be restricted by such categories. By dreaming himself into someone else's skin, Daly models the freedom to go below skin-deep differences. In the end, this ability to empathize and identify with others may be Niki Daly's most important reality and his vision of the true "rainbow nation."

CHILDREN'S BOOKS

Daly, Niki. 1985. *Not So Fast Songololo.* London: Gollancz.
———. 1991. *Mama, Papa, and Baby Joe.* New York: Viking.
———. 1992. *Papa Lucky's Shadow.* Bethany, MO: Fitzgerald.
———. 1995. *My Dad.* New York: McElderry.
———. 1995. *Why the Sun and Moon Live in the Sky.* New York: Lothrop.
———. 1998. *Bravo, Zan Angelo!* New York: Farrar, Straus & Giroux.
———. 1999. *The Boy on the Beach.* New York: McElderry.
———. 1999. *Jamela's Dress.* New York: Farrar, Straus & Giroux.
———. 2001. *Old Bob's Brown Bear.* New York: Farrar, Straus & Giroux.
———. 2001. *What's Cooking, Jamela?* London: Frances Lincoln.
———. 2003. *Once Upon a Time.* London: Frances Lincoln.
———. 2004. *Where's Jamela?* New York: Farrar, Straus & Giroux.
———. 2005. *Ruby Sings the Blues.* New York: Bloomsbury.
———. 2006. *Happy Birthday, Jamela!* New York: Farrar, Straus & Giroux.
———. 2006. *Pretty Salma: A Little Red Riding Hood Story from Africa.* New York: Clarion.
———. 2006. *Zanzibar Road.* Johannesburg, SA: Giraffe.
———. 2009. *A Song for Jamela.* London: Frances Lincoln.
———. 2012. *The Herd Boy.* Grand Rapids, MI: Eerdmans.
———. 2012. *Next Stop—Zanzibar Road!* New York: Clarion.

This essay is adapted from a version first published in 2012 in *Sankofa: A Journal of African Children's and Young Adult Literature* 11: 6–15.

Native, Gone Wandering: Dianne Hofmeyr as Constant Explorer

ERIN F. REILLY-SANDERS *and*
ANDRÉS A. MONTAÑÉS-LLERAS

The idea of exploration, as a process of discovery and self-discovery, of renewal and innovation, is very appropriate to describe the "new energy" (Hofmeyr 2008, 116) that characterizes contemporary South African children's literature since the late 1980s: a literature that not only explores what it means to be South African today, particularly after the end of apartheid, but also transcends national borders and explores universal human experiences.

A prolific South African author now living in England, Dianne Hofmeyr easily fits the role of the constant explorer. Not only has she traveled extensively across the African continent and many places around the world—an explorer in a literal sense—but she also delves through her writing into multiple literary forms, content, and themes. From difficult issues like HIV/AIDS and abortion to mystical places obscured by the past, and unfathomable oceans filled with whale-song, Hofmeyr's work demonstrates that she has the courage to leave the safety of the shore behind and explore different lands and territories.

Growing Up an Explorer

Dianne Hofmeyr was born just a few miles south of Cape Town, South Africa, where she grew up surrounded by the Hottentots-Holland Mountains on one side and the Atlantic Ocean on the other. The youngest of three sisters, Hofmeyr spent countless hours at the beach reading mostly American and British authors, through whose work she discovered the excitement and joy of literature: "I read all the *Secret Seven* (Blyton 1949) and *Famous Five* (Blyton 1942) books and wanted to be like George.... English children seemed to have much more fun than South African children" (pers. comm.). Other favorites included historical novels like R. D. Blackmore's *Lorna Doone* (1869), *The Diary of Anne Frank* (Frank 1952), and any book with out-going, strong female characters, like *Little Women* (Alcott 1868) or *Anne of Green Gables* (Montgomery 1908).

As did most authors and artists of her generation, Hofmeyr grew up in a country divided by apartheid. Like many youth in the white middle class, however, she was not really aware of the injustice and privilege that surrounded her until much later, when she was attending college with the intention of becoming a teacher: "I think it was only at university that I became challenged by it. But in retrospect I was too used to being the 'good child' to play an active role in the 'struggle' even though I can remember being traumatized by the death of Steve Biko [a black consciousness activist killed in police custody]. I felt very ineffectual" (Hofmeyr n.d.a). While some of Hofmeyr's novels and short stories are set during the last years of apartheid and address the social and political issues of the time, her work is more clearly defined by a strong sense of place that can be traced to her childhood.

Hofmeyr's father was a draughtsman and stargazer, and taught her early on to be aware of her surroundings. Though she remembers being a solitary child, she was also in tune with the textures, colors, and sounds of nature (Hofmeyr n.d.a). This type of connection with the South African landscape is a central element in many of her books, where space is not only described in a very sensual manner but also becomes a symbol of the spiritual and psychological experience of the characters. She writes (pers. comm.) about her novel *Fish Notes and Star Songs*, "I was influenced a lot by reading Bachelard's *The Poetics of Space*. I recall my own childhood of hiding under a desk with a blanket across the opening, which allowed me to become anything I wanted. By retreating into a dark space my imagination was free."

One of Hofmeyr's most vivid memories is driving with her family to Victoria Falls on the border of Zimbabwe and Zambia in their old 1937 DeSoto (a car curiously named after a famous Spanish explorer). From that moment on she has never stopped traveling, visiting such diverse places as Tunisia, Vietnam, and Russia, among many others. Hofmeyr describes herself as an archaeologist, always taking pictures, writing notes, and collecting artifacts that might lead her to a story (Hofmeyr n.d.a). Even when she is writing about places that she has never visited before, she makes an effort to put together images and maps in order to present the reader with a convincing image of the world of the story (pers. comm.).

Hofmeyr always comes back—both in person and through her writing—not only to her home in South Africa but to the African continent in general. As she points out, when asked about the strong sense of place that can be appreciated in most of her books, "without a firm idea of setting, I can't write. It's quite odd how my stories all seem to draw on Africa" (pers. comm.). Her profound connection with the landscape and history of her country, however, is accompanied by broad exploration of literary forms, content, and themes that take her beyond national borders and traditional depictions of South African experience. This unique perspective positions her as a significant contemporary South African author of children's literature.

Exploring with Forms

Though she does not intentionally look for imagery or metaphors when she is writing, Hofmeyr is very conscious of the expressive possibilities of language: "At school I loved poetry and the lilt of certain passages of prose. I grew up quite observant and still see patterns and color connections in objects that outwardly have no relationship" (pers. comm.). The detailed description of settings, objects, and characters; the careful use of adjectives and figurative language; and even the rhythm of the prose, distinguish most of Hofmeyr's works. Regardless of genre, these techniques can be found from more reflective and literary books like *Fish Notes and Star Songs* to her historical-adventure novels *Eye of the Moon* and *Eye of the Sun,* where her particular use of language and attention to detail is able to bring the world of ancient Egypt to life.

Even in a book like *Blue Train to the Moon*, where the protagonist-narrator is a teenage girl living in contemporary Johannesburg, it is possible to recognize Hofmeyr's particular style: "I lifted up a fine transparent-white delicately ridged nautilus shell. I felt all of these things inside me. Most of all I felt brittle, as brittle as the shell that snapped loudly between my fingers as I held it" (17). Though the reader hears Sylvie's voice, her description of the shell is essentially lyrical, paying special attention to both textures and colors, much like Hofmeyr did when she was a child. Furthermore, the image of the brittle shell becomes a metaphor of the emotional state of the character and the confusion and insecurity she is feeling, providing the reader with an effective and affective poetic image.

While novel length books allow Hofmeyr the opportunity to explore extensively the expressive possibilities of language, it is in her picture books where the careful use of language and attention to rhythm are most evident. As she acknowledges: "In a picture book every word must be meaningful and in the right place. There's no room for redundancy. It's closest to poetry than anything else" (pers. comm.). In books, for example, like *The Faraway Island* or *Do the Whales Still Sing?* her evocative description of the sea is able to capture the sound and mystery of the ocean.

Hofmeyr's experimentation with form is not restricted to the lyrical quality of her prose or her use of figurative language alone. Especially in her novels, she pays particular attention to the construction of convincing and evocative narrative voices. While all her narrators share a similar tone and indulge in visual and often lyrical descriptions, Hofmeyr manages to capture the distinctive voice of each of her protagonists. These include contemporary teenagers like Sylvie or Daniel, the character-narrator in *Boikie, You Better Believe It*, but also people who lived thousands of years ago like Isikara, the narrator in *Eye of the Moon*. Even when she resorts to a third person narration, as in novels like *When Whales Go Free* and *The Waterbearer*, she still balances the careful description of settings, characters, and events with a detailed exploration of her protagonists' inner lives and particular experiences, keeping the child's perspective at the center of her work.

Her most complex book in terms of narrative voices, however, is *Fish Notes and Star Songs*. This novel tells the story of four children—Vanessa (Fish), Jonah, Rebecca, and Sweet—who find a mysterious cave on the coast of South Africa and travel into the past in a mystical journey of self-discovery. While most of the chapters are narrated by Vanessa (who not only holds the dominant perspective but seems to be the fictional author of the book), these are alternated with sections in which the other characters take up the narrative voice in order to share their own experiences with the reader:

> Inside it was dark as the forest on a rainy day. In the middle, the trunk of the huge tree spread its branches everywhere.
>
> I listened at the edge of this dark green place. I felt the sea shuddering under the earth even though the sea was far below. And I heard the leaves of the tree whisper my name.
>
> I stood like a shadow at the edge of this place and the girl didn't see me [93].

In contrast to other novels in which the reader follows the perspective of just one character, this multiplicity of narrative voices invites the reader to assume different positions and compare alternative points of view, generating a rich experience. As Hofmeyr points out: "Jonah's story told through Fish's eyes might have been too sentimental and the same goes for [Jonah]. I think it's far more powerful for him to tell the reader why he doesn't speak rather than Fish interpreting the reason" (pers. comm.). This interplay of narrative voices responds to an intention to capture and portray the struggles and voices of her characters, an effort that is in turn informed by her own experience and knowledge.

On a different level, Hofmeyr is also constantly breaking the conventions of the different literary genres by mixing elements of realistic and historical fiction with a little bit of magic. In *The Waterbearer,* for example, the main character, Maji, has the mysterious ability to find water in the middle of the desert: "It was the spirit of your ancestors that helped you guard your father's grave. It was their spirit that helped you fight the poison of the arrow. Then at the Kapsuku rapids they helped you save the boat" (77). Hofmeyr, however, does not define her books as fantasy, preferring instead the term "magical realism" (pers. comm.). The fantastical elements in her stories, like Maji's connection with water or Vanessa's travel into the past in *Fish Notes and Star Songs*, are not in this sense just plot devices but symbols of the spiritual and psychological journey of the characters.

Dianne is able to write for different audiences and age ranges, moving from simple picture books like *The Magic Bojabi Tree* (pers. comm.) to formally complex texts that deal with controversial and more mature issues, like her short stories "The Magic Man" and "The Face of a Killer." Hofmeyr's experimentation with form is finally related to a broad exploration of South African reality, history, and culture that is expressed also in the content and themes of her books.

Exploring Different Content

Just as she explores different literary forms and narrative perspectives through her writing, Hofmeyr's books for young readers investigate multiple settings, characters, and subjects, often connected with her own experience as traveler. Despite living in England for over fifteen years, all of her books take place in various locations in Africa, including Zimbabwe, Egypt, Botswana, and Madagascar, and almost half take place in South Africa itself. While some places are only vaguely situated, other locations are described in detail like the suburbs of Johannesburg in *Boikie, You Better Believe It* or the journey of Isikara and Tuthmosis through the Nile in *Eye of the Moon*.

Time even proves to be no barrier to Hofmeyr's sense of exploration. Her writing dips back in history as far as 3000 BCE with *The Star-Bearer*, and has visited 1350 BCE in *Eye of the Moon*, sixteenth century AD in *The Faraway Island*, 1630 in "Where the Dark Ocean Rolls" and 1912 in *When Whales Go Free*. Several of her picture books have a timeless feel, likely because both time and place are difficult to explain in the short poetic text. On the other hand, many of her social issues books and short stories are contemporary to when they were written.

Stemming from a sense of place and an interest in the poetic description of places and feelings, Hofmeyr's inspiration often comes from particular visual images. She comments, for example, in relation to *The Waterbearer*: "I have a memory of standing with my father beneath the conical tower of the Great Zimbabwe Ruins at the age of five, but the real inspiration for *The Waterbearer* came when I was about twenty and was sitting at the stone ruins with the full moon flooding the valley below, listening to drumbeats vibrating through the darkness" (Hofmeyr n.d.b). Other books come from images and stories that she found in the newspaper, like *Eye of the Moon* and *Eye of the Sun*, inspired by the image of "three royal mummies who'd been purposefully damaged" (pers. comm.), "The Face of a Killer" (2001), inspired by a photo of the Oklahoma bomber (2010), or *Fish Notes and Star Songs*, which begins with a powerful description of a photograph documenting the return of the remains of Sara Baartman—a Khoikhoi woman who was put on exhibition in Europe in the early 1800s—to South Africa in 2002.

Like a true explorer, Hofmeyr has had the courage to leave the shore behind and visit different—even unfamiliar to her—places and stories. The subjects of Hofymer's writing fall into four general areas: social issues, ecology and the ocean, folklore, and adventure.

Many of her early books examine various social issues affecting South Africans that are often valuable for older youth and teens as they approach an adult understanding of their cultural topography. *A Sudden Summer* attempted to address the forced relocations of coloured South Africans (people of mixed ancestry, often the indigenous Khoisan and European) from the whites-only Cape Town area. Inspired by the Natal Floods of 1987, *A Red Kite in a Pale Sky* takes a look at poverty in South Africa and the resulting disadvantages coping with natural disasters. *Blue Train to the Moon* presents a sympathetic portrayal of AIDS at a time when fear and prejudice surround the rapid spread of the disease, and *Boikie, you Better Believe It* looks at the possibilities of peace and violence with protests at the end of apartheid. Hofmeyr's short stories for use in tenth and eleventh grade classrooms investigate even heftier subjects than these early novels—"The Magic Man" powerfully deals with grief and abortion through the metaphor of speech, and "Face of a Killer" considers the violence resulting from war and terrorism.

These texts could represent Hofmeyr's growing awareness of social issues in the wider spaces of South Africa as she explores beyond the limited world of her early years. The growing protests of the 1970s and 1980s similarly expanded the consciousness of some white South Africans to the inequities faced by coloured and black people. Hofmeyr's books demonstrate a subtle understanding of these issues but typically avoid direct confrontation with them, which Hofmeyr (pers. comm.) says is a deliberate choice. In comparison to other contemporary authors who addressed these issues in a more overt manner, Hofmeyr's writing can serve as a reminder that, along with the activists who make headlines, a body of sympathetic and supportive citizens is also an important instigator of change.

Although related to social issues, Hofmeyr's books that focus on the ocean often take a strong stance on ecology. *When Whales Go Free* and "Where the Dark Ocean Rolls" portray a historical view of whaling and trade, respectively, while *Do the Whales Still Sing?* presents a similar ecological message in a timeless picture book format. In *The Faraway Island* a solitary sailor transforms a barren and deserted island into a lush and exuberant landscape that comes to life through Jude Daly's beautiful illustrations. Hofmeyr (pers. comm.) feels that "we are part of a fragile ecology." In her descriptions of animals, ecosystems, landscapes, and cultures, she asks that her readers take a close look at the world, perhaps from a different perspective than they are used to. She says, "I want children to get some sense of [the world around them] whether it's through writing about frogs or whales or stars."

Although she is still concerned with social and ecological issues, Hofmeyr's most recent works move away from direct investigation of these topics. She comments, "Athol Fugard was once quoted as saying that the huge relief of leaving the 'struggle' years behind was that he could turn away from writing about it and was free to explore other dimensions and new dynamics" (2008, 116). Hofmeyr herself explores subjects like folklore and adventure after moving away from South Africa in the mid-1990s. *The Stone: A Persian Legend of the Magi, The Star-Bearer: A Creation Myth from Ancient Egypt, The Faraway Island*, and *The Magic Bojabi Tree* retell traditional tales from different locations, while *Fish Notes and Star Songs* weaves together the spiritual beliefs of the Khoikhoi people with a sense of both realism and adventure.

As Hofmeyr has worked on streamlining her prose for younger audiences, her subjects have progressed from social issue books with a sense of adventure like *A Red Kite in a Pale Sky* to historical quest stories like *The Waterbearer* and *Eye of the Moon*, and most recently to contemporary adventure in Hofmyer's newest series, Oliver Strange. Jay Heale (2012) describes this series: "A rip-roaring junior Indiana Jones.... Plenty of genuine Africa around the fast-moving action adventure." These stories often contain elements of survival in the raw African outdoors, heightened by the tension of escaping from dangerous human enemies. The characters become explorers of ancient tombs, mysterious oases, and the lush African wilderness, from jungles and deserts to the magical coastal landscapes of Hofmeyr's own childhood.

Investigating Theme as Exploration

While Hofmeyr explores a variety of subjects through her work, there are also recurrent themes and motifs in her books. While some of her books treat religion as a subject—in particular *Boikie, The Stone*, and *The Star-Bearer*—her other writing seems to transcend religion and present spirituality as a theme. The universe extending beyond the surface of things in almost a magical sense runs through several books. Hofmeyr sees Maji's world in *The Waterbearer* as "imbued with the way things might have been in an earlier time in Africa. I was drawing on a world of sangomas [traditional healers] and truth-sayers and a belief in the hyena as a witch or bearer of evil" (pers. comm.). These books seem to show that cultural beliefs in this realm go beyond the dismissive term "magic." Hofmeyr (pers. comm.) comments with regard to *Fish Notes and Star Songs*, "the reader has to be more trusting of the 'magic' because the heroine, Fish, actually transforms. Or does she? Is this just a dream? Or does she truly enter another world? ... Can someone of another culture go into the San world to draw out her own inner strength?" Through suggesting open-ended questions within her prose, Hofmeyr sets up the opportunity for readers to embark on their own exploration beyond what is typically considered scientific reality.

In addition, many of Hofmeyr's characters are introverted and shy, like she was when she was young: "We lived in a small village and there weren't that many young people about" (pers. comm.). Characters like Eric in *When Whales Go Free* and Laurence in *A Red Kite in a Pale Sky*, for example, focus on their environments and personal feelings. Hofmeyr's later works also include characters who are at least initially on their own, like Fish in *Fish Notes and Star Songs* and Oliver Strange, but more often end up finding connection with peers over the course of the story. The young woman in "The Magic Man" creates an unlikely bond with a street performer when she overcomes her inability to talk about the past in response to his muteness—"she had shared her story with him and he had understood" (71).

The Rewards of Exploration

Because there is also the possibility of appropriation and subjugation of places, events, and even ideas that belong to multiple people, the idea of author as explorer raises some concerns about the authenticity of a work of literature. The perspective of the explorer suggests a particular way of engaging with a place—a view that is closely investigated but still mediated by one's primary discourses, culture, imaginative and empathetic abilities, and personal history. Hofmeyr (pers. comm.) comments: "I take on board that I'm white and privileged and that one must tread carefully lest one 'steals' something that's not yours, just like Sara Baartman was stolen by the curious."

In Hofmeyr's work, one can see some of the attributes of an explorer—her sense of observation focuses on visual images, history, and imagined possibilities. However, when asking questions of authenticity such as "What is the author's status relative to the culture being depicted?" (Lehman, Freeman, and Scharer 2010, 120), an author like Hofmeyr has the advantages of being widely traveled and globally aware. Due to these experiences, Hofmeyr's writing translates her awe of other cultures into respect; demonstrates sympathy towards characters who may come from different places, literal and figurative, but still share internal connections; and uses the many perspectives of her exploration (a technique recommended by Adichie 2009; Lakshaman 2009) to avoid "treating the subject matter as strange, exotic, or foreign" (Lehman, Freeman, and Scharer, 120).

Hofmeyr's desire to learn about and imagine other places, times, and possibilities is immediately apparent in almost all her work. At the same time, an air of mystery at embarking into the unknown leaves Hofmeyr's readers with a vibrant sense of exploration, widening and expanding their own limits.

CHILDREN'S BOOKS

Hofmeyr, Dianne. 1987. *A Sudden Summer.* Cape Town, SA: Tafelberg.
____. 1988. *When Whales Go Free.* Cape Town, SA: Tafelberg.
____. 1990. *A Red Kite in a Pale Sky.* Cape Town, SA: Tafelberg.
____. 1991. "Where the Dark Ocean Rolls." In *Storyland: An Exploration of Southern Africa in Story Form.* Edited by Jay Heale, 100–105. Cape Town, SA: Tafelberg.
____. 1993. *Blue Train to the Moon.* Cape Town, SA: Maskew Miller Longman.
____. 1993. *Boikie, You Better Believe It.* Cape Town, SA: Tafelberg.
____. 1995. *Do the Whales Still Sing?* New York: Dial Books for Young Readers.
____. 1995. "The Magic Man." In *Crossing Over: New Writing for a New South Africa.* Edited by Linda Rode and G. J. Gerwel, 68–72. Cape Town, SA: Kwela Books.
____. 1998. *The Stone: A Persian Legend of the Magi.* Cape Town, SA: The Inkman.
____. 2001. "Face of a Killer." In *In the Rapids: New South African Stories,* edited by Linda Rode and G. J. Gerwel, 32–36. Cape Town, SA: Kwela Books.
____. 2001. *The Star-bearer: A Creation Myth from Ancient Egypt.* Cape Town, SA: The Inkman.
____. 2003. *The Waterbearer.* London: Hodder.
____. 2005. *Fish Notes and Star Songs.* London: Simon & Schuster.
____. 2008. *The Faraway Island.* London: Frances Lincoln.
____. 2009. *Eye of the Sun.* London: Simon & Schuster.

Sindiwe Magona: Writing Oneself Out of Poverty

Tanya Barben

The scars left by centuries of colonialism, dispossession, oppression and racial segregation have cut deeply into the souls of black South Africans—and some white ones too. The writer of this essay is very conscious of the heavy responsibility she bears in writing about someone who has been the receiving end of so much discrimination. How can she (white, middle-class) give a balanced—even insightful—assessment of Sindiwe Magona, a strong, feisty and resourceful woman who has never allowed the multiple adversities that she has faced deter her from fulfilling her destiny as a writer, a healer of psychological wounds, an inspirational speaker, a leader and an educator?

Virginia Woolf famously declared that in order to be able to write, a woman should have a room of her own and £500 per year. Michel de Montaigne, in his essay "Of Solitude," suggests that we should "reserve a backshop, wholly our own and entirely free, wherein to settle our true liberty, our principal solitude and retreat" (1970, 83). These rooms represent not only the physical space but also the contemplative or mental space that free time, uncluttered by the distractions of family and household, financial insecurity and societal pressures, permits. Sindiwe Magona has not been so fortunate: for many years she had neither a room of her own, whether at the back of a shop or not, and no £500. She has, however, become one of South Africa's most noted storytellers and writers, and is celebrated as the author of insightfully honest autobiographies and powerful works of fiction, nonfiction, drama and poetry. Her literary and personal successes belie her humble beginnings.

The societal pressures that encumbered her were threefold, yet intermeshed: she was black in apartheid South Africa, poor (with little other than her own devices to pull herself out of poverty), and a woman trapped within the confines of an extremely patriarchal environment. On reflection, she has recognized that "many, many people have directly or indirectly contributed to who I am today ... more people have been kinder to me than I deserve. And for that I am truly grateful" (Magona 2006, 53).

Born in the rural Transkei, now South Africa's Eastern Cape Province, she spent the first four years of her life surrounded by a family and a wider community who took an active interest in her development. She was fortunate to be nurtured by loving parents who, though themselves uneducated, saw that in education their children could find a way out of poverty, and it is they who had the greatest influence on her life. From her father she "got a deep sense of belongingness and of the meaning and importance of family." From her mother came "some stubborn streak" that made her instinctive response that of "'if someone gives you a lemon, then make lemonade'" (Magona 2006, 53). She has described her childhood in the Transkei in her autobiographical writings, the first of which was *To My Children's Children* thus, "childhood, by its very nature, is a magic-filled world, egocentric, wonderfully carefree and innocent. Mine was all these things and more" (4). She goes on to say:

> It was in such a warm human environment that I spent the first five years of my life. I had much attention, much discipline, much loving, much play, much work; in short, total immersion into a group where my own place in it was clearly defined.... I was happy, I was loved. And my world felt safe and secure [7].

Move to Cape Town

These halcyon days ended somewhat in her fourth year when, because of circumstances beyond their control, the family moved to Cape Town. The excitement of being plucked away from her rural home faded among the tin shacks, poverty, police raids, and the harsh realities of strict segregation introduced by the National Party from 1948, that characterized life in Blaauvlei Location (an area outside Cape Town designated for black occupation). Despite these circumstances, her happiness was undiminished, was—if anything—added to, by her first (and subsequent) days at school. The inadequacies of Bantu Education[1] were compensated with a growing ability to read and the generosity of a neighbor who recognized in the young girl a precocity and hunger to read (pers. comm.) who brought to Magona children's books and magazines from her employer's home. Her mother would excuse her from doing housework if she were reading; although initially she opportunistically took advantage of this, her appetite grew. She feasted on English magazines such as *Beano, School Friend, Girls' Crystal, Look and Learn,* American comics about Mickey Mouse and Donald Duck , the adventures of the Famous Five and other Enid Blyton characters, Lucy Maud Montgomery's *Anne of Green Gables* (1908), Mary Lennox in her secret garden (1911) and *Little Lord Fauntleroy* by Frances

Hodgson Burnett (1886), and countless others. Sarah Nuttall (1994) surmises that, based on their autobiographies, for black writers like Magona,

> reading is mainly undertaken to acquire formal education or political knowledge. It is not the imagination which is stressed but a useful reading or knowledge; reading can provide inspiration but it is mainly for social knowledge rather than escape, a means through which identity is achieved and confirmed [86–87].

This contradicts Magona's own account of how she became "hooked on books" and assumes that the habit of ludic reading acquired in childhood is not carried into adulthood. Magona is a committed reader—she believes that reading and writing are the conjoined twins of culture and that one cannot become a writer if one is not a reader. She reads widely for many reasons and the reading foundation that was laid in childhood—when a world of wonder and imagination lies open before one—remains, and has become part of her very being. Hans Christian Andersen's *Eventyr*,² in particular, has stayed with her, speaks to her, and she returns to it. "These are made-up stories—which is what stories are—they are adaptable, we can twist them, bend them, fold them, lay them flat" (pers. comm.).

The Lure of Storytelling

Her life has been vividly portrayed in her own autobiographical writings and short stories based on her own experiences (written during the twenty years that she spent working at the United Nations). These describe her life in rural Transkei and Blaauvlei out of which the family was moved in 1960 and resettled in Nyanga West (now known as Guguletu), a township some nine miles out of Cape Town: her sojourn at boarding school; her early pregnancy and marriage which temporarily interrupted her education; her husband's desertion of her and their children (including an unborn son); her struggle to support her family as a single parent in any way she could; her work as a domestic servant; pursuing a career as a teacher deeply conscious of the inequality of her salary as compared with her male counterparts (and even more so with males from other racial groups); and her continuing efforts to improve her educational status, which ultimately enabled her to go to the United States to pursue a postgraduate education. The vicissitudes that she had to face and the nature of her childhood left her with "a wonderfully resilient sense of worth ... one of the strongest weapons in the war of survival" that awaited her in adulthood (Magona 1992, 19). Her life was beset with troubles, but she was able to bring her children out of South Africa at a time when the education of black youth had virtually ground to a halt.

Looking back Magona is astonished that she became so wise so young. She endowed herself with tremendous self-esteem. She also knew that she did not want another child after she reached the age of thirty. No one was going to die and leave her a fortune, and she needed to get herself better fitted for a better job. That is when she embarked on correspondence education (distance learning). After that she never paused, and strode forward in the world to take advantage of any opportunity that came her way.

She has been the subject of many dissertations, published interviews, and countless academic articles and works of criticism. She has written an outstanding biography of the former Anglican Archbishop of Cape Town, Njongonkulu Ndungane, *From Island to Bishopscourt*, as well as, jointly, a couple of Xhosa language textbooks for English speakers. She is particularly celebrated for her novels, namely, *Mother to Mother*, based on the 1993 mob murder of U.S. Fulbright scholar, Amy Biehl, in Guguletu, and *Beauty's Gift*. The latter is considered one the best books to describe how HIV/AIDS affects the lives of (mostly) black women in South Africa. Both books have been turned into stage performances, while *Beauty's Gift* has also become a musical.

She realized in the years prior to her retirement from the United Nations where she had worked in the organization, primarily with the Department of Public Information's anti-apartheid radio unit (Shober 2013), that if she wished to remain independent she would have to find a new career. She had known since she was seventeen that she had always wanted to write a book (Magona 2009). It was then that she began writing about herself, very conscious that this was something that very few black South African women undertook. Maya Angelou's *I Know Why the Caged Bird Sings* strengthened her determination that writing about her life was something that she could do (Chiavetta 2004).

She is recognized as a skilled storyteller. She practiced this gift of orality while living in New York—and has captivated and beguiled her audiences, both young and old, for years. Storytelling was something that came naturally to her: in a way it enabled her to get back to her roots as it was an essential part of the culture in which she matured. A.C. Jordan (1973) the great South African literary scholar, has this to say about the significance of the folktale in Xhosa culture:

> It will be noted that most of the factors that constitute the subject matter of the great human literature are to be found in rudimentary form in these tales: courage and resourcefulness; love and readiness to sacrifice for one's loved ones; the vindictiveness of despised love; the power and influence of beauty; conflict of duties....; retribution for upsetting the moral and social order; the triumph of brain over brawn; the triumph of good over evil [13].

These tales, or *iintsomi*, are "an essential and integral part of the socialization among ama–Xhosa" (Magona 1990, 6); "the seven deadly sins are covered in our *iintsomi* to inculcate standards of *ubuntu*- how to live amongst others" (pers. comm.). That road map is there, and today, when she types away she is following that tradition. She knows that not every one reads, so storytelling bridges the gap between audience and reader. This is something she manipulates, encouraging members of the audience who ask for more to read. Her storytelling performances and interactions with her audiences are awe-inspiring. They are done with great passion, and with a reverence and acknowledgement of (and to) the role of women in all traditional societies, in which they pass on their knowledge of culture to their descendants.

Writing for Children

What is, perhaps, less well known about her is her creative output as a writer of books for children. Initially she feared that that this was something she could not do, for she thought she was unable to put herself in the skin of a child, not having been one for such a long time (pers. comm.). Being able to write successfully in this genre is particularly gratifying for someone who had previously said:

> I would love to write for children, but I am scared! I keep thinking it must be very difficult to write for children. I would like to do this, and I'm thinking about it. I really would like to do this, it's one of the things I really would like to do [Magona, Attwell, Harlow and Attwell 1994, 292].

This wish has been fulfilled many times over; she has had many titles published by, among others, Nasou/Via Afrika and Oxford University Press. Some of her books, written first in Xhosa or English, have also been translated into Afrikaans. Creative writing had always been something with which she toyed, but she had not contemplated writing for the younger reader until a well-known American children's writer asked her if she had ever thought of writing children's books, since her descriptions of events and people in her autobiographies were so good. Magona regrets that she cannot recall the name of this author as their chance meeting was a very significant moment in her life. The author commented, further, that an incident in Magona's autobiographies reminded her of the folktale "Stone Soup," a classic tale of a hearty soup conjured up in a poverty-stricken environment. This inspired Magona (Schateman 2007) and out of that conversation came *The Best Meal Ever*. It was chosen by Jay Heale and Lona Gericke as one of the eight South African picture books to appear in the International Federation of Library Associations/International Board on Books for Young People compilation, *The World Through Picture Books: Librarians' Favourite Books from Their Country* (Everall and Quiñones 2012). Heale described it in his 2006 *Bookchat* review as a read-aloud picture-book story—and a theme that connects immediately with every young listener. Hunger! Siziwe is looking after her four younger brothers and sisters in Guguletu, with both parents away. There is no food in the house—nothing. In desperation she heats up a pot of water, and adds salt and pepper, stirring and stirring until the younger ones gradually fall asleep as they wait. Then Siziwe falls to her knees and prays: "Thank you, Father in Heaven, for the gift of hope. This was the best meal ever! But, Lord, can you send us a different one, tomorrow?" And then—because the hopes and prayers of children need to be answered—a knock on the door. There is their kind and generous neighbour, back from holiday, with food and money. This is the extended family of Africa—and author Sindiwe Magona, born in what was Transkei, knows it well [n.p.].

Her own approach to *The Best Meal Ever* and her writing for children in general is articulated in a an interview with Kim Morton (2009) of Room to Read:

South African writer Dr Sindiwe Magona thinks African children need more stories about naughty girls and boys that can cook. And she should know! She's been voted as one of the Top 100 Best African writers and ...Top 10 Best African Women writers. She's written over 100 children's books in all 11 of South Africa's official languages. Dr Magona believes that if you want children to read, you must write exciting books, wild stories, fables, and mysteries [n.p.].

Perhaps this is why she enjoys writing series (doffing her hat to all the series she read as a child). She believes that they help to get children reading for as they read they grow with the characters. A series offers incremental action which is age appropriate, and the readers can visualize the changes taking place in the characters, for these are changes with which they can identify as they are developing themselves (pers. comm.).

Her first children's book, however, was *Life is a Hard But Beautiful Thing* published in English and Xhosa two years after her return to South Africa. It was written as a reader for seventh graders. It dealt with the very real and chilling problem of teen suicide. Since then she has written over one hundred stories for children, in Xhosa or English, on her own or in collaboration with other authors, among them Tracy Blues and the equally superbly talented Gcina Mhlophe. In fact, just before *The Best Meal Ever* was published, "Gcina Mhlophe asked me to join her writing a series for Oxford University Press. Of the twenty-four books she had agreed to do, grades 1–3, she got so busy, touring and other engagements, she did seven and I did seventeen. There was no going back after that; I was convinced I am a children's writer" (pers. comm.).

Her stories for children, like her writing for adults, are written—whether in Xhosa or English—in the mellifluous cadences and melodious lilt and rhythms of her mother tongue. She writes in either of the two languages—as the stories come. Every story has in it a gentle lesson from which its reader or listener can learn. One of them is the delightful *Paragon the Perfect Piglet* whose lesson is that one should be discerning about what one wishes for, while *Amalungiselelo* (*Preparations*) tells of a family's preparations for celebrating their father's very special birthday on February 29 and teaches the complexities of the calendar. *ULizeka Wazikhethela* (*Lizeka's choice*) tells of Lizeka's shopping expedition with her father to buy a dress for her. She finds nothing she likes and ends up (much happier) choosing books which her father buys for her. *Betty's Braids*, written together with Tracy Blues and Gcina Mhlophe, takes a wry look at a little girl's desire to have braids, despite her mother's disapproval. When her misguided aunt gives her the chance to have her wish fulfilled she realizes that the braiding process is very painful and that braids are not so wonderful after all.

Andersen's Duckling

She returned once more to Andersen's much-loved fairy tales, rewriting the story of the ugly duckling in an African setting and giving it a quintessentially African twist,

> the swan who had been an ugly duckling never forgot his past. He remembered how unloved and miserable he had felt when others were unkind to him. So he always treated everyone kindly and, in return, he was loved by all [28].

Jay Heale awarded the book a recommendation in the 2010 *Bookchat* and described it as a "sensitive retelling of the Andersen story we all love, set in an African vlei [shallow lake] with suitable wildlife. Evocative, detailed artwork [by Natalie Hinrichsen]. What a delight for our young readers."

Magona has been working with and writing for a U.S.—based international organization called Room to Read, whose goal is to improve literacy and gender equality in education. Its particular focus is the development of literacy skills and the habit of reading among primary school children, and the supports for girls to complete their secondary school education. Magona sits on the organization's selection committee and has served as a judge for its writing competitions. *Nkanishe, the Stubborn One*, published by Room to Read, is a perfect vehicle for explaining the need for self-discipline and the need to follow societal laws. It tells of a quiet, untroubled rural existence in which everyone lives according to a set of rules which they know very well and happily obey. Nkanishe is the exception, she is never able to follow any rule, even that of her mother-in-law who enjoins her not to collect wood in a particular forest on a Sunday. Accompanied by her children and dog, she disappears into the forest and was never seen again, for,

> when the forest gods saw that the woman came to fetch wood on a Sunday, they decided to teach her a lesson. From the village with its law-abiding people, they banished her to the moon ... where you can see her in her long skirt, a bundle of wood on her head, a baby on her back, a little boy beside her, and a tired-looking dog limping behind them [22–23].

Giving Birth to Young Writers

Magona's interest in writing is not inward-looking. She has done much to encourage fledgling writers, has run many workshops with them, and thus has "given birth" to other children's writers (pers. comm.). Particularly gratifying is the fact that someone from one of her workshops, who had not written anything before, won first prize a few years ago in the competition sponsored by Maskew Miller Longman (a leading publisher of educational material in South Africa and in sub–Saharan Africa generally).

Her latest venture has been as a writer-in-residence at the University of the Western Cape. Together with noted poet and author, Antjie Krog, and academic Meg Van der Merwe, she has participated in UWC Creates, the University of the Western Cape's Creative Writing Initiative, which encourages diversity and hybridity in the work of student writers, lecturers, as well as renowned Xhosa, Afrikaans and English poets and authors. She is particularly proud that out of this project twenty-four funded children's books will be published later this year, and that around twelve young people still at university will be able to add to their résumés the fact that they are published authors (pers. comm.).

Magona keeps on writing for children. Following the success of the Ndungane biography, she has been asked to write more books in that genre, but for the middle-school child. She has written a three-volume collection of Xhosa nursery rhymes, and poems for the very young to the middle-school-age child. She has self-published the first volume of nursery rhymes (for the very young) with assistance from the National Library of South Africa's Centre for the Book, but has not yet found a publisher for the next two volumes of poetry. She would like to reconstruct Andersen's "The Emperor Has No Clothes," for stories like this speak a lot of truth in life today; they said something to her when she was young, and say something to her now. She also would like to turn her hand to writing for young adults, for this cohort faces so many problems and insecurities, not least of which are high youth unemployment and the inadequacies of school education in South Africa.

Conclusion: Leaving Footprints

Magona has not deviated from the path she took to write herself out of poverty, and has been joined on the way by many younger companions. She feels that people write about what they know and there are many stories bubbling up inside South Africans waiting to force themselves out. For her, the act of writing is therapeutic, it enables her to bring to herself and her readers some healing sense of closure. She has said that she writes to "leave footprints" (Magona 2007, 132). There is no doubt that her work has created pathways for many readers, writers and literary critics to tread. Strangely enough, although much attention has been given to Magona's novels, plays and autobiographical writings, her output for children has received no substantial critical consideration. This writing for young readers, which differs vastly from her other work, is a rich area for future research.

Notes

1. A system of school education for blacks introduced in 1953 that was considered a pillar of apartheid. It was designed to provide black schoolchildren with a comparatively inferior education, but considered by the authorities to be suitable for their "culture" and future role as laborers in white society.

2. Collections of Andersen's fairy stories published by C.A. Reitzel (Denmark) between 1835 and 1841 and subsequently frequently translated into English by various writers.

Children's Books

Blues, Tracy, and Sindiwe Magona. 2008. *Paragon the Perfect Piglet*. Cape Town, SA: Oxford University Press.

Blues, Tracy, Sindiwe Magona, and Gcina Mhlophe. 2007. *Betty's Braids*. Cape Town, SA: Oxford University Press.

Magona, Sindiwe. 1990. *To My Children's Children*. Cape Town, SA: David Philip.

_____. 1991. *Living, Loving and Lying Awake at Night*. 1991. Cape Town, SA: David Philip.

_____. 1992. *Forced to Grow*. Cape Town, SA: David Philip.

_____. 1998. *Mother to Mother*. Boston: Beacon.

_____. 2005. *Life Is a Hard But Beautiful Thing*. Mthatha, SA: Juta Gariep.

_____. 2005. *ULizekaWazikhethela*. Cape Town, SA: Oxford University Press.

_____. 2006. *The Best Meal Ever*. Cape Town, SA: Tafelberg.

_____. 2008. *Beauty's Gift*. Cape Town, SA: NB Publishers.

_____. 2008. *Nkanishe, the Stubborn One*. San Francisco, CA: Room to Read.

_____. 2009. *Amalungiselelo*. Cape Town, SA: Via Afrika/Nasou.

_____. 2010. *The Ugly Duckling*. Auckland Park, SA: Jacana.

_____. 2011. *From Island to Bishopscourt*. Cape Town, SA: David Philip.

Linda Rode:
Bookmaker of the Imagination

Marianne van Loggerenberg

Linda Rode's name and persona form an integral part of the history of South African children's literature before and after 1994. She has become a definite figure of transformation in this genre and has made a continuous contribution to the inheritance and availability of Afrikaans literature for children. She might be described as an almost invisible main character, always working behind the scenes improving and recreating the meaning of an existing story either taken from another language or taken from the oral tradition. She has a unique ability to take readers deeper into the realm of the story, exposing the true nature of a tale. She has the gift to understand the theme and essence of stories, and she uses this gift to transform the essence of the stories into Afrikaans. She has contributed to the richness of Afrikaans literature for children on so many different levels, applying her unique sense for discovering beauty and meaning in stories from all over the world, including traditional African folktales.

Linda Rode has done this by means of translating a vast number of original German, English and Dutch children's stories into Afrikaans. These translations include picture books, first chapter books, fairytales, folktales and youth literature. She started her translating journey in 1970, when she translated some of Grimm's fairy tales into Afrikaans, as picture books (Wybenga and Snyman 2005). According to Uca Eiselen, Linda Rode translates creatively into Afrikaans while her translations stay true to the unique voice of the author (in Wybenga and Snyman 2005). Linda feels that translation requires a strict adherence to the source text but she never translates slavishly. She does allow for differences in idiomatic expressions for different shades of meaning, and for different emotive qualities. A "faithful" translation is not necessarily an authentic reading experience in the target language (pers. comm.).

As a frame for analysis of Rode's work, story titles from her collection *In the Never-Ever Wood* are used metaphorically in the following discussion.

"The Little House in the Far-far Hills": Remembering the Old Traditional Tale

There are many variations of this story in other languages, based on the old English children's tale "The House on the Hill" (Rode 2009). The theme of this story is that a wide world, to be explored by different individuals, exists out there. Exploration starts in the imagination of the explorer. Linda Rode's road of exploration began on a quiet farm in the Little Karoo (Rode 2011). She was born on July 3, 1937 in Ladismith, a small town in the Western Cape Province (Breuer 2013). This town nestles at the foot of the Klein Swartberg mountain range in the Klein Karoo.

Growing up, she would sit and read by lamp- or candlelight with her family each night, until when she was ten years old, electricity was introduced to the farm (Rode 2011). It was her father who told her the tales of *Jackal and Wolf* in front of their Welcome Dover wood stove in the kitchen on winter evenings, and during thunderstorms her mother would cover the mirrors to keep the lightning out (Rode 2011). She loved the old traditional tales her father told her, because they were infused with an earthiness and a farm-like aura (pers. comm.).

She spent most of her childhood outside, with her father in the veld and sometimes riding his trusty white horse, Ben. This lifestyle was conducive to her interest in myths, fables, folklore, and stories in general (Rode 2013). She attended a farm school, where a single teacher taught from grade one to grade seven in one classroom, until she was twelve years old (Rode 2011).

After finishing school in Riversdal in 1954, she obtained a Bachelor of Arts degree as well as a teacher's diploma from Stellenbosch University. After four years of teaching, she returned to Stellenbosch to complete an Honors degree in German in 1963 (pers. comm.). Besides teaching German in different high schools, she also taught Afrikaans for two years at a German semi-private school in KwaZulu-Natal and became part of the German community there. She is still an avid reader of German literature (pers. comm.).

"Over the Hills to the Faraway Sea": Entering the First Layer of the Imagination

The origin of this story is an old English nursery rhyme which Linda used as an inspiration in combination with the traditional tale, "Tom the Playful Piper," to write a story in a South African setting (Rode 2009). The theme of this story is how one boy's gift of melody, combined with imagination, has the power to create an adventure for others who are willing to follow his invitation. Growing up on a farm gave Linda the opportunity to experience the invitation of her own imagination. As an only child of elderly parents, Linda was never lonely (Rode 2011). Her playmates, as a child growing up in the Little Karoo, were the daughters of her father's right-hand man on the farm and they had beautiful names: Nankies, Soen, Toesie, Klein-Toet, Sielja, Mietjie (pers. comm.). They were always at hand with a story to tell (Rode 2009). Together they played imaginative games—shop-bought toys were scarce—under the Blue-Gum trees (pers. comm.). They roamed the koppies (Karoo hills) together and gathered wood in the late afternoons for the open fire and for their small black Dover stove (pers. comm.). As constant companions they had tea-parties with no fancy toy tea-sets. For cups and saucers they used round and flat stones. They told each other folk rhymes or riddles, but were particularly good at telling ghost or folk stories, of which the one of the water woman that waits in the pool among the bulrushes is an example (Rode 2011). Those magical experiences, firmly rooted in nature, were the starting point of her lifelong enchantment with myths and folk and fairy tales and stories of all kinds.

"The Buried Treasure": Unfolding the Wisdom of Stories

This is a story of Russian/Moldovian origin (Rode 2009), depicting the theme of working together as brothers to harvest the true meaning of their father's last words. Their father set the example and set them free to discover their own treasures. In an essay on "Re-imagining the Possibilities," Lester (2000) says that literature is the royal road that enables us to enter the realm of the imaginative. It is the words and often images of physically small texts that turn out to be capable of filling the minds of generations of young readers with experiences, emotions and the mental furniture and tools necessary for thinking about themselves and the world they inhabit (Reynolds 2007). The farm school library of her childhood consisted of a single slim, two door cupboard of humble proportions, containing well-thumbed selections from the Greek and Germanic myths, the fables of Aesop and the fairy tales of Hans Christian Anderson and the Brothers Grimm (Rode 2009). These books transported her to be forever caught into the world of folklore and fantasy (Rode 2011).

There were old favorites with a strict Victorian countenance inside these library books. These included Hesba Stretton's (1867) *Jessica's First Prayer*, other delightful classics like the "What Katy Did" series by Susan Coolidge (1872), Laura Ingalls Wilder's (1935) *Little House on the Prairie* and still others like *Black Beauty* by Anna Sewell (1877) and Harriet Beecher Stowe's (1852) *Uncle Tom's Cabin*. There were also books by early Afrikaans writers like C.J. Langenhoven, Andries Albertus Pienaar (Sangiro) and Maria Elizabeth Rothman (M.E.R) (Rode 2011). According to Spufford (2003) there are times when a particular book, like a seed crystal, drops into our minds exactly when we are ready for it. Thus the germination of stories finds a home in the life of a reader.

Linda compiled *Sonroepertjies* (Calling the Sun), an anthology of read aloud poetry and rhymes for very young children, written by various South African authors in 1988. A few years later, she translated Graeme Kent's version of *Aesop's Fables*, illustrated by Tessa Hamilton, into Afrikaans. In the same year she selected and rewrote *Tick Tock Story Clock*, illustrated by Cora Coetzee. This was published in Afrikaans and English simultaneously. Many stories in this collection originated a long time ago, courtesy of Linda's earlier storyteller friends. One of the stories in this collection was told to her by her father as a riddle, designed to test the problem solving powers of the listener (Rode 1992).

"What the World Looks Like": Discovering the Other

This story is a free adaptation of an anonymous verse titled "The World," published in 1927 in *Fun and Thought for Little Folk: Home University Series* (Rode 2009). Linda read this as a child, when her mother, a farm school teacher, exposed her to this series of books (pers. comm.). Quintero (2009) quoted the following from Mary C. Bateson's (2004) book, *Willing to Learn, Passages of Personal Discovery*: "You do not even know that you 'have' a culture until you encounter other ways of thinking and behaving... Today we are challenged... to think more inclusively about other cultures and species, about the biosphere as a whole, to be unafraid as we make new meanings" (27).

According to Linda, it was the magic in those early books, the otherworldliness that appealed to her, the sense of reaching out to other worlds—worlds of the imagination in the first place, but also to reach other geographical worlds and cultures. These were boundary-crossing texts: books leaning towards metaphor, allegory and magical realism that captured her attention (pers. comm.).

In 1985, Tafelberg published *Goue Lint My Storie Begint* (This Golden Ribbon Begins My Story), a compilation of international and indigenous fairy tales, folk tales and rhymes, retold by various South African authors, brought together by Linda and illustrated by Alida Bothma. Tafelberg received the

C.P. Hoogenhout award (given every other year) for this publication. A facsimile edition of *Goue Lint My Storie Begint* was published in 2001.

Three years later, a follow up compilation by Linda and again illustrated by Alida Bothma, titled *Goue Fluit My Storie Is Uit* (This Golden Flute Concludes My Story) was published. In 1989, this title was awarded the M.E.R. prize for the best children or youth publication that was published in the previous year by NB Publishers (Wybenga and Snyman 2005). Linda also compiled *Vrede op Aarde* (Peace on Earth), a compilation of South African related Christmas stories, written by various South African authors and illustrated by Alida Bothma. This publication follows the trail of a true South African celebration of Christmas.

"The Sun's Children": Exposing the True Nature of a Story

In a story of Nama/Damara[1] origin, previously recorded by W.H.I. Bleek and Lucy Lloyd in a version in which the sun inhabited the earth in the shape of a man, the sun's children tossed this man into the sky, and the sun became round and lost its human shape (Rode 2009). The theme of this story is that even though the sun lost its human shape and found rest high above the sky, the sun's children still live on the earth and when the sun slides down it reveals the end of the day. Much as she loves stories from far-off regions, the ones situated in the South African veld and farm life (though their earliest source, Reynard the Fox, hails from overseas) struck a special chord in her heart (pers. comm.).

Stories South of the Sun was published in English and Afrikaans simultaneously. This is a compilation of indigenous tales, written and illustrated by a variety of South African authors and illustrators. This compilation encompasses a cross-cultural selection of stories. The stories reflect the multi-faceted southern African society (NB Publishers 2009). Linda co-compiled this title with Christel and Hans Bodenstein. She also translated some of the stories that were originally written in English into Afrikaans. *Stories South of the Sun* is also available in Sesotho as *Dipale tsa ka Borwa ho Letsatsi* and in isiXhosa as *Amabali maTshona kweLanga*. The English-language title won the Percy FitzPatrick Award for children's literature in 1993 (NB Publishers 2009).

Linda (pers. comm.) thoroughly enjoyed translating and reworking the manuscript that was published as *Uit die Hart van die Vuur* (From the Heart of the Fire) in 2005. This is a treasury of twenty-one largely unknown African stories and fables collected by a German missionary, Julius Oelke, during his service in what is now known as Tanzania, containing folklore recorded early in the twentieth century (pers. comm.).

Another important title is *Madiba Magic* compiled by Nelson Mandela. It comprises a collection of Nelson Mandela's favorite fairytales, also available in Afrikaans and the Nguni languages. Linda was the consulting editor for this publication and she translated some of the stories into Afrikaans.

"Words Can Take Root Too": Connecting the Core of Young Voices

This story is an adaptation of a story of Greek origin where the truth is always revealed in the end (Rode 2009). According to John Henry Newman (Sedgwick 2011), literature stands to man as science does to nature. Youth feel the changes in a society first and most directly, and they usually deal with them first as well (Bentley 2000). Since Nelson Mandela was released from prison in 1992, everything in South Africa, including the settings, characters, plots, themes, authors, points of view, and tones of young adult novels have changed (Bentley 2000).

Linda also co-compiled and co-edited *Another Kind of One Nation: Young South African Writing 1* with Hans Bodenstein. This volume is a collection of short prose, and graphic works written by young South Africans. "The writing was selected from entries submitted by high schools from all over the country and reflects a broad spectrum of insights and experiences. Together these pieces give the reader a true insight in the world of South Africa just after the first democratic elections in the country" (Rode and Bodenstein 1994, foreword n.p.). The second volume, titled *I, A Living Arrow: Young South African Writing 2,* was compiled and edited by the same team four years later. "This anthology was written by children from diverse race, class, and language backgrounds in secondary schools from all over South Africa, in rural as well as urban areas. It offers a snapshot of children's concerns through short stories, poetry and musings" (foreword n.p.). The editors dedicated this volume to those young people who dared to tell the truth. The third and final volume was again compiled and edited by Linda and Hans and titled, *Up the Down Escalator: Young South African Writing 3*. This volume offers an open-eyed view of reality as experienced by young people in 2000. "Without sparing the reader, they raise their views on the rapidly changing social, moral and political fabric of their country. It is an 'open book' for every young person and interested adult; a journey through the fantasies and perspectives of young South Africans at the beginning of the twenty-first century" (forward n.p.). Volume 2 and Volume 3 were published in English and in Afrikaans.

"I Wish I Wish I Wish": Moving Towards Freedom of Choice

This is an adaptation of an original French fairy tale, by Charles Perrault (Rode 2009), depicting the theme of how choice can influence reality, and not necessarily the opportunity of a granted wish. The ability to cross a boundary lies in the heart of every individual that dares to choose and act in line with what they believe to be the truth. In 1995, Linda compiled *Crossing Over*, the first volume of stories for a new South Africa, with Jakes Gerwel. *Crossing Over* is a collection of twenty-six short stories written by established as well as new South African authors. Writers were invited to contribute stories dealing with some kind of crossing over. All contributors were required to give insight into the world of young people entering adulthood amidst the wide-ranging changes in South Africa after 1994. According to Gerwel, the aim of this publication was to challenge writing and reading in South Africa, to play its part in the process of healing required for the miracle of transition to become a permanent reality (Rode and Gerwel 1995). Another compilation by Rode and Gerwel, *In the Rapids: Stories for a New South Africa*, followed later, in 2001. The individuality of the different voices and the strong human condition around the lives of young South Africans are specifically noticeable in this volume. Both titles were simultaneously published in English and Afrikaans.

"The Magic Palm Tree": It All Came Together Under One Magical Roof

This story of Ghanaian origin, retold and translated by various storytellers lends itself to being renewed with sounds and flavors of other languages and countries (Rode 2009). The retelling by Linda is the concluding story in *In the Never-Ever Wood*. The theme of this retelling is that a negative spell can be broken by true love with true intentions and nothing in life is set in stone. *In the Never-Ever Wood* is Linda's most influential publication to date and was selected for the International Board on Books for Young People (IBBY) Honour List in 2011 (IBBY 2013). According to Linda, this publication is a good example of what her role in the field of children's books in South Africa comprises. In her own words, "this is a gathering and retelling of classic children's stories and folklore from different parts of the world, with a fair amount of innovation and originality thrown into the bargain, combined with some research about the sources of these stories" (Rode 2011, n.p.). To trace the roots of a story to its earliest printed source, she uses all possible sources, such as libraries, the internet, etc. to track the oldest form available (pers. comm.). This publication was awarded the Alba Bouwer Prize in 2010 (Heale 2013).

Linda edited the Afrikaans edition herself, since editing and assessing Afrikaans manuscripts has been a major part for many years of her freelance services to different publishing houses (Rode 2011). She collaborated with Fiona Moodie, the illustrator, who created exquisite etchings, and Elsa Silke, who translated the text so sensitively and delightfully into English. For Linda, this was an exhilarating experience of give and take and she sometimes had to change the text slightly to accommodate something in Fiona's illustration, while Fiona at times had to adapt her illustration because it didn't reflect certain aspects as verbalized in the text (pers. comm.). It received the M.E.R. prize in 2010 for the best illustrated South African children's book (NB Publishers 2009). In 2012, it also received The Exclusive Books International Board on Books for Young People (South Africa) (IBBY SA) award (Heale 2013).

Linda believes that every story has its own rhythm and this is something that should ideally be reflected in the retelling, especially in an anthology of diverse stories and origins like *In the Never-Ever Wood*, where the key is to maintain a similar stylistic approach (pers. comm.). She has included sixty stories from around the world in this volume and rewrote certain stories to reflect the African continent. According to Scheepers (2010), readers will be surprised by the poetic way an African tale can be told. Linda has the unique ability to draw her readers or listeners right into the imaginative heart of a story, transporting them into a bright new world of real possibilities.

"As Much As I Love Salt": Exploring Elements of Truth to Escape Through the Heart of the Reader

This retelling of a particular story of Indian origin, known in many languages in different variations (Rode 2009), depicts the theme of the hidden meaning of truth which is not as obvious as it seems at first. Ross (2011) wrote that exploring is not necessarily about finding places that you never knew existed. Exploring is also about connecting different places of existence and uncovering the true value of your discovery. It is also a way to find an alternative route to move an unknown world closer to becoming known and understood. Fairy tales and myths are especially valuable literature experiences for children, because they help to stretch the imagination (Uchima 2007). For this reason Linda can be described as an invaluable explorer of stories and tales. By her way of collecting fairytales and folktales from around the world, she travels wide and far within the realm of the imagination and then breaks through the boundaries of language, rewriting the stories into a renewed reality. Sedgwick (2011) asserts that "writing is, among other things, the place where we can help ourselves cope with the dark parts of our living" (61). As bookmaker, Linda speaks to her readers on so many levels across all age groups. She has the ability to create more light through each level of understanding that unfolds in the minds and hearts of each reader who becomes an interpreter engaging deeply with the books that she has created. Thus reading also becomes a place where we can learn to cope with the dark parts of our living. "The sky is not the limit if you have books—books suggest a sky full of holes with an even brighter world beyond into which you can escape whenever you want" (Rode 2011, n.p.).

Note

1. Two Namibian cultural groups.

Children's Books

Kent, Greame. 1992. *Fabels van Esopus.* Illustrated by Tessa Hamilton. Translated by Linda Rode. Cape Town, SA: Human & Rousseau.

Letterie, Martine, and Betty Sluyzer. 2010. *My HAT Storiewoordeboek: vir Voorlees en Self lees.* Illustrated by Paula Gerritsen. Translated by Linda Rode. Cape Town, SA: Pearson Education.

Mandela, Nelson. 2002. *Madiba Magic: Nelson Mandela's Favourite Stories for Children.* Cape Town, SA: Tafelberg.

Oelke, Julius. 2005. *Uit die Hart van die Vuur.* Translated and reworked by Linda Rode. Cape Town, SA: Tafelberg.

Rode, Linda. 1985. *Goue Lint My Storie Begint.* Illustrated by Alida Bothma. Cape Town, SA: Tafelberg.

———. 1988. *Goue Fluit My Storie Is Uit.* Illustrated by Alida Bothma. Cape Town, SA: Tafelberg.

———. 1988. *Sonroepertjies.* Illustrated by Lorrain Roodt. Cape Town, SA: Tafelberg.

———. 1990. *Vrede op Aarde.* Illustrated by Alida Bothma. Cape Town, SA: Tafelberg.

———. 1992. *Tick Tock, Story Clock: Timeless Tales for Wide-awake Kids.* Illustrated by Cora Coetzee. Cape Town, SA: Tafelberg.

———. 2009. *In the Never-Ever Wood.* Illustrated by Fiona Moodie. Translated by Elsa Silke. Cape Town, SA: Tafelberg.

Rode, Linda, Christel Bodenstein, and Hans Bodenstein. 1993. *Stories South of the Sun.* Cape Town, SA: Tafelberg.

Rode, Linda, and Hans Bodenstein. 1994. *Another Kind of One Nation: Young South African Writing 1.* Cape Town, SA: Kwela.

———. 1998. *I, A Living Arrow: Young South African Writing 2.* Cape Town, SA: Kwela.

———. 2000. *Up the Down Escalator: Young South African Writing 3.* Cape Town, SA: Kwela.

Rode, Linda, and Jakes Gerwel. 1995. *Crossing Over: Stories for a New South Africa Volume 1.* Cape Town, SA: Kwela.

———. 2001. *In the Rapids: Stories for a New South Africa Volume 2.* Cape Town, SA: Kwela.

Marita van der Vyver: Fairy Tales and Feminism

Maritha Snyman

Marita van der Vyver is often associated with fairy tales. She retold and translated into Afrikaans Grimm's fairy tales twice: first in 1984, when she was still an unknown writer, and again in 2010.The first translation was reprinted in 2006. It is understandable that her first novel for adults, *Entertaining Angels* used fairy tales abundantly as intertexts. A literal translation of the Afrikaans title *Griet Skryf 'n Sprokie* is not accidently "Gretel Writes a Fairy Tale."

The name Griet is linked to Van der Vyver herself. Van Coller (2006) indicates that Van der Vyver is also called "Grietjie." This book took the Afrikaans literary world by storm. It has already been reprinted more than seven times, and won three major literary prizes in 1993: the yearly prize of the Afrikaans Language and Cultural Association (ATKV) for prose, the M-Net prize for prose and the Eugene Marais prize for young up-and-coming authors in Afrikaans. It has been translated into twelve languages, and had the conservative Afrikaans-speaking society gasping for breath. It was the first time that a woman wrote openly about eroticism and sex in a book of fiction. In the chauvinist Afrikaans society of that time it was acceptable for men to discuss and portray sexuality, but not for women. Van der Vyver was quickly referred to as the Afrikaans Erica Jong.

In an interview after the publication of *Entertaining Angels*, Marita van der Vyver said: "Gretel was the one fairy tale character who did not wait for a man to save her ... she saved herself and Hansel as well" (my translation) (Terreblanche 1991, 12). This book and her response to this book contain the essence of Van der Vyver's work for children: a fascination with the transformational nature of fairy tales, and life, from the perspective of a "confused feminist" (Terreblanche 1991, 12).

In *Die Mooiste Sprokies van Grimm* she retold and translated a selection of her own favorite Grimm tales. In the preface to this book she writes about the role of fairy tales: "Like one draws up a pail of cool water from a well, fairy tales surface as part of the consciousness of mankind since time began and can still today quench the deepest thirst of man" (my translation). Her works display a love-hate relationship with fairy tales—"on the one hand they are wonderful things and on the other hand ... they are full of lies that create passive heroines" (my translation) (Terreblanche 1991, 12).

Van der Vyver, who started writing when she was twelve, obtained a Master's degree in journalism with a dissertation about the increasing role of women in the Afrikaans press. Her life and work exhibit a view of womanhood and family life that does not conform to the views of the conservative Afrikaans establishment. Her personal life reflects aspects of the characters and plots in her work. Being down and out after a divorce and a miscarriage, she met and married a Frenchman and went to live in the South of France with her extended family. Her ties with South Africa and Afrikaans are, however, very strong, and she visits the country as often as possible.

She wrote four youth novels of which three have only been published in Afrikaans: *Van Jou Jas* (Of Your Coat), *Tien vir 'n Vriend* (Ten for a Friend) and *Eenkantkind* (Aside Child) . *Eenkantkind* was awarded the ATKV youth book prize for thirteen- to fifteen-year-olds in 1992. *Dinge van 'n Kind* (*Childish Things*) is regarded by most critics as a coming of age novel suitable for young people and adults (Le Roux 1994). Van der Vyver does not agree and professes that it is written for adults. Her best-known youth novel, *The Hidden Life of Hanna Why*, was published simultaneously in Afrikaans and English. This novel was awarded the Sanlam prize for youth literature (gold), has been prescribed in schools, and has been adapted as a successful Afrikaans film. She also published two picture books, one for each of her two children: *Olinosters op die Dak;* English *Rhinocephants on the Roof* for Daniël, and *Mia's Mom* for Mia. Both were translated from the Afrikaans. *Mia's Mom* was awarded the prestigious MER prize. She wrote three picture books for educational publishers that are not translated in English: *Boomklim* (Climbing Trees), *Die Simpel Dinge Wat Mens Mis* (The Simple Things One Misses) and *Hy Bly My Broer* (He Remains My Brother).

Feminism and Family Structures

Although the traditional family consisting of parents—a father and mother—and children living in a semblance of harmony has long been accepted as the norm in the Western world (Berger 2002; Cheal 2008), major social, economic and demographic changes in the course of the last thirty years changed this (Cheal 2008). The ideology of the core family is particularly criticized by feminists (Newman and Grauerholz 2002) who see family life as one of the primary causes of the oppression of women in a patriarchal and chauvinistic society. There is, however, not only one school of feminism. Steele and Kidd (2001) refer to "many different feminisms" (66). Although most feminists criticize the traditional view of a family, it is mainly men's control over women in the traditional view of families that they warn against (Abbott, Walace and Tyler 2005).

The Afrikaans family in South Africa was traditionally a strict patriarchal entity based on biblical norms. Because the clash between Afrikaaner nationalism and a democratic dispensation was the focal point in the 1970s and 1980s, feminism did not feature high on the Afrikaans woman's agenda. Consequently, the traditional family structure and defined gender roles were depicted in most Afrikaans children's and youth books (Van der Walt in Wybenga and Snyman 2005) until the 1980s. It was only when the political transformation was taking off that concrete changes were seen in mainstream Afrikaans children's and youth literature.

Van der Vyver was one of the first writers for children whose work exhibited a more honest depiction of women and family life. Being herself a "confused feminist" she says that "she writes exclusively for women [because] she has been reading stories about men for ages" (my translation) (Terreblance 1991, 12). She feels that women must be able to say "no" and must not be scared to take a stand against the expectation of husbands and fathers (Leuvennink 1992). Her first three youth novels, published between 1982 and 1991, are part of a new generation of Afrikaans youth novels (Van der Walt in Wybenga and Snyman 2005) that depict the changing face of family life and the consequent changes it brought to the lives of women and children. Family life in *Van Jou Jas, Tien vir 'n Vriend* and *Eenkantkind* is broken, eccentric and dysfunctional—not at all the ideal families that were the norm for Afrikaans books. The women characters in these books are not, as radical feminists would argue, caught up in marriages from which they cannot escape. They are not good housewives in service of their husbands (Steele and Kidd 2001). In sharp contrast, the grandmother in *Eenkantkind*, for instance, cannot be bothered by domestic chores (Van der Walt and Nieman 2009). The only exception is the mother in *Eenkantkind* who feels she cannot escape her husband's violence and her financial dependence. It becomes the task of the other strong women in the novel to change this.

The typical female character in Van der Vyver's work is strong, resourceful and in control of her life. A good example is the mother in Van der Vyver's second picture book, *Mia's Mom*. Mia the rabbit's mom is not like any other mom. She is a witch, a sorcerer and a good fairy. She can talk to anybody and can fly on a carpet. Mia and her friends believe this for certain because Mia's mom tells them that in stories all things are possible: "Everything that happens in a story also happens with the one who tells the story" (n.p.)

An article, titled "The Representation of Masculinity in Afrikaans Picture Books for Children" (my translation) (Loubser 2009), points out that Van der Vyver's first picture book, *Rhinocephants on the Roof*, can be categorized as "subversive" in its representation of masculinity in Afrikaans picture books. The male character, Daniel's grandfather, is independent, active and competitive. These traditional "male" characteristics are, however, balanced by his creativity. Although the grandmother is caring like a traditional woman, she is also assertive and active. She shouts at the monsters and chases them away. Daniel's grandparents encourage him to see the "soft" side of the monsters. He caresses the soft body of the "bobberilla" and acknowledges that the monster is also "soft and warm" (25). The depiction of the monsters as caricatures, the humor in the words and the warm and playful illustrations create a cozy space filled with love. It is in this space that the story of a little boy's fear is told, in direct opposition to the hegemonic view of masculinity that men are always brave and fearless (Loubser 2009).

Childish Things, often referred to as the first crossover book in Afrikaans (Van der Walt and Nieman 2011), does not, however, fall so easily into the pattern described above. The book caused and still causes controversy. Some reviewers were not impressed by this book and called it boring (Gouws 1994) and "hardly unique" (Allan 1996). Others write positively about it (Van Coller 1994), but the merits of this book have not yet been adequately discussed.

The story is about Mart Vermaak who, as an adult, writes letters from London to herself as a child who grew up in South Africa in the 1970s. There is no question that Van der Vyver successfully captures the zeitgeist of that time period. "What can you say about the seventies—except to wish you hadn't been there? The sixties produced hippies and sex, the eighties yuppies and *money*. But the seventies? Disposable fashion, disposable dances, disposable music. And disposable lives in the warm country where I grew up," writes Mart (5). Set against this background, shy, serious Mart has to confront *various moral dilemmas* when she meets the almost embarrassingly extroverted Dalena. She discovers rebellion and becomes initiated into a world of sex, love, pregnancy and loss. She gains political awareness: "I thought all countries were like ours," says Mart, the narrator. "I thought everybody lived the way we do here" (34).

Mart's initiation takes place during the traumatic times of the Soweto revolt against Afrikaans in schools in 1976 and the war on the border of Angola that eventually would change the South African political landscape. The binding and determining factors in this initiation novel are the space and context. "It is a novel about rebellious female teenagers who are struggling to adapt in this chauvinistic time of rules and regulations determined by men and the church (and for men and the church). It is a world of Afrikaans men devoted to rugby, barbecue, hunting and sex. Violence, as portrayed in war on the border, where many young men lost their lives, is part of the culture" (my translation) (Van der Walt and Nieman 2009, 160–161). Van der Vyver's chauvinistic men in this novel are archetypes who always place their own needs first—sexual needs included.

Similar to the chauvinistic and violent space in which she finds herself, Mart's personal life is disrupted by her father's unilateral decision to venture into a business. This forces her to leave behind her beloved Cape and her sympathetic mother and to go and stay in a hostel (Van Coller 1994). These circumstances shape Mart's coming of age. Taking into account that Van der Vyver explicitly states that she did write this book for young people, Van der Walt and Nieman (2009) contend that Van der Vyver's novel targets the youth of the 1970s she knew so well. She was after all an insider of that time.

The postmodern family is "diverse, fluid, [a place where] family relations are contested and undecided" (Cheal 2008, 43).Van der Vyver's work depicts a variety of family concepts characterized by choice, freedom, diversity, ambivalence and fluidity. This is nowhere more pertinent than in her last youth novel *The Hidden Life of Hanna Why*. This title is described by Rode in her commendation for awarding the Sanlam prize (gold) to this book as "a youth book written with compassion and humour, one that convincingly unmasks clichés -like the stepfather stepmother syndrome" (my translation) (Rode 2002).

The reader quickly gets drawn into Hanna's weird existence. Hanna's family consists of a mother, Mana (an eccentric artist), a half-brother, two stepbrothers and their father, Beyers (an actor). Her biological father is a gay fashion designer and her half-brother's father was a test tube baby—Mana's creative solution for a second child without wanting a man. Then Mana meets a man, Beyers, who gives her, because of a lack of financial resources, a huge potato and a bunch of parsley tied with a red ribbon as an engagement gift. There can be no doubt that Hanna's family is an extreme example of a diverse, postmodern family.

The central plot revolves around the long overdue honeymoon of Hanna's mother and stepfather. The whole family, including Hanna and her best friend, whom she wants to impress, her highly pregnant mother, and the rest leave to go and stay in an isolated house on a mountain. The unexpected arrival of her gay father and her stepfather's previous wife, an actress working in the United States, complicates matters that become more and more complex when the family is trapped in the house on the mountain after a torrential rain storm. Things get out of hand as Mana's labor starts. During this crisis masks tumble and family members learn to know who each one really is. The dramatic experiences unite this very strange family. Hanna, who is in the process of writing a book to escape from her family, realizes that her own family provides ample material for a book and that she need not escape from the family but can escape into it. *The Hidden Life of Hanna Why* is the result of this realization.

Van der Vyver's books don't idealize family life as universal, natural, warm, caring and safe, nor exhibit an aversion to it. They provide solutions for maintaining peace by successfully handling family members and problems in a diverse family: "We cannot choose our families, but our imagination can help us to learn to live with them" (my translation) (Rautenbach 2001, 72).

Fairy Tales and Transformation

The references to fairy tales in Van der Vyver's well-known and highly acclaimed *Entertaining Angels* is a precursor for quite a few of her works that would follow—especially her children's literature. It is the possibility of transformation in fairy tales that fascinates Van der Vyver. In a fairy tale a frog can become a prince and gold can be spun from straw. In fairy tales transformations can be literal or refer to an internal state or social status.

Transformation is also a reality in Van der Vyver's own life: "I underwent a metamorphosis," she says in an interview, "to a married woman with a patched family of four children, which includes a bad-tempered teenage son, two nine-year-old monster boys and an extremely busy baby daughter—in a chaotic, noisy rambling stone house" (my translation) (Rautenbach 2001, 72). This description echoes the family of Hanna and confirms Van Coller's view (2006) that many of her works contain autobiographical information.

Van der Vyver uses various transformational possibilities of fairy tales in some of her picture and youth books. References to specific fairy tales in a story allow the reader to investigate the role of the specific intertext in the story. Actions of a traditional fairy tale can be reworked into "new" actions in a new story: an adaptation of an existing fairy tale (Coetzer 2009). New fairy tale characters in new fantasy spaces can be created in a story that can be interpreted as a parody on or an imitation of a traditional fairy tale (Coetzer 2009). Propp (1975) listed thirty-one functions that characters in Russian fairy tales can fulfill. These were reduced by Zipes (2007) to eight, and because the functions will be used in the discussion to follow, they are listed and briefly explained below:

1. "The protagonist is confronted with an interdiction or prohibition that he or she violates in some way" [3];
2. "Departure or banishment of the protagonist who is either given a task or

assumes a task related to the interdiction and prohibition or to the desire for improvement and self-transformation" [3];
   3. "The protagonist encounters: (a) villain [...]"[4];
   4. "The endowed protagonist is tested and moves on to battle the villain or inimical forces" [4];
   5. "The peripety or sudden fall in the protagonist's fortunes is generally only a temporary setback" [4];
   6. "The protagonist makes use of gifts (and this includes magical agents and cunning) to achieve his or her goal" [4];
   7. "The villain is punished or the inimical forces are vanquished" [4];
   8. "The success of the protagonist usually leads to (a) marriage; (b) the acquisition of money; (c) survival and wisdom; or (d) any combination of the three" [4].

In her first picture book *Rhinocephants on the Roof*, Daniël goes to stay with his grandparents, but the bedroom in which he has to sleep becomes after dark a threatening space with monsters lurking in the shadows. Van der Vyver creates these monsters by fusing characteristics and names of real animals: rhinocephants (rhinoceros and elephant) and bobbarilla (baboon and gorilla). These fusions, beautifully represented by Piet Grobler's illustrations, become the villains that Daniël has to conquer (Function 3). In his battle (Function 4), Daniël inadvertently uses magical agents (Function 6) in the form of his grandfather and grandmother. They lead Daniël with sensible creativity to conquer the villains. Consequently, the threatening creatures are transformed and Daniël falls asleep with the newly acquired wisdom (Function 8) that boys may be scared but that fear can be overcome. The transformation of threat to fun in this book is aptly supported by creative word play, humor and illustrations.

In *Mia's Mother*, Mia's mother can transform herself into anything because stories and especially fantasy tales give her the power. Mia and her friends accompany Mia's mom on Aladdin's carpet for a fantasy trip to fairyland. Piet Grobler's illustrations play an exemplary role to capture these transformations. There are two types of illustrations: those that depict Mia, her mother, and friends and those that illustrate Mia's and her friends' thoughts about fairy tales. The children's illustrations are drawn in a childish fashion with crayons and are used to playfully touch on various issues such as the variety of languages, death, and good and evil. "With this book Marita van der Vyver and Piet Grobler succeed to take the reader to the fairyland where all is possible" (my translation) (De Beer 2006).

It is, however, *The Hidden Life of Hanna Why* in which all three strategies for integrating fairy tales into a text are used. Intertexts activated by references in *The Hidden Life of Hanna Why* are, among others, Cinderella, Sleeping Beauty, Snow White and the Seven Dwarfs, The Arabian Nights, Harry Potter,

Perdita and Pongo, the work of Stephan King, the film "Men in Black" and the biblical Noah.

The Hidden Life of Hanna Why can also be regarded as a parody and/or imitation of the traditional story of Cinderella. Hanna refers to herself as Cinderella: "I'm not really pretty, but not so bad-looking that you would mistake me for one of Cinderella's stepsisters"(10). Hanna resembles and contradicts Cinderella: Hanna has two stepbrothers (not sisters), her mother is alive and her father is a gay fashion designer who uses make up (while Cinderella's mother died and her father remarried); Hanna does not become a housemaid but she sleeps in a separate room; Hanna receives not a beautiful dress as Cinderella does, but an expensive black cashmere jersey from her father. Grimm's Cinderella is the foundation upon which the characters in *The Hidden Life of Hanna Why* are based.

Embedded in the story of *The Hidden Life of Hanna Why* are also stories that Hanna writes in her attempt to escape from the reality of her family life. Fabienne is the main character in Hanna's stories that feature her amazing teeth and perfect family. The fact that these stories serve as an escape from reality, is a reference to the story technique used in "The Arabian Nights." Sheherezade escapes from danger by telling 1001 stories to the sultan. Thus, *The Hidden Life of Hanna Why* also can be regarded as a parody and/or transformation of the traditional fairy tale.

Finally, *The Hidden Life of Hanna Why* can be interpreted as a new, modern fairy tale. Coetzer (2009) uses the fairy tale *Sleeping Beauty* for such an interpretation (Ashliman 1998–2013). When Hanna's family arrives at their holiday destination, it is compared to the arrival of "the poor prince" who arrives after a hundred years at Sleeping Beauty's rose-entwined castle. This interpretation can again be supported by Zipes's typology of functions (Coetzer 2009). Hanna's "interdiction or prohibition" (Function 1) is her reservation regarding her own capabilities and looks and her place in her bizarre family. This is depicted in the manner in which she withdraws into the imaginative world of Fabienne and her family. Hanna's "departure or banishment" (Function 2) is represented by the isolated holiday on the mountain. Her isolation grows with the heavy rain until the house becomes as difficult to penetrate as Sleeping Beauty's castle. The villain (Function 3) in *The Hidden Life of Hanna Why* can be connected to Hanna's fights with her step-brothers and the rain that keeps them stranded on the mountain. Hanna's victory over the villain (Function 4) is suggested by the fact that she no longer needs to escape into her imaginative world. She writes less and less about Fabienne and starts to make friends with her step-brothers. The miracle that is needed to save them (Function 5) takes on the form of a pilot in a helicopter who rescues her. Hanna uses her own natural gifts (language skills and her character) to survive the time on the mountain (Function 6). She gains new insights (Function 8) that complete her transformation. In contrast to her initial opposition to her mother's planned honeymoon, the end of the story resembles the well-known fairy tale ending: "and they lived happily ever after."

Van der Vyver's contribution to post-apartheid Afrikaans children's and youth literature is considerable. Her works, because of her intimate knowledge of the children for whom she writes and her skill in transferring this knowledge into amusing stories, resonate in her readers' minds and hearts. The world of Afrikaans children's and youth books needs more writers of her caliber.

Children's Books

Grimm, Jacob. 1984. *Die Volledige Sprokies van Grimm*. Translated by Marita van der Vyver. Cape Town, SA: Rubicon Publishers.
_____. 1984/2006. *Die Volledige Sprokies van Grimm*. Translated by Marita van der Vyver. Pretoria, SA: Protea Boekhuis.
_____. 2010. *Die Mooiste Sprokies van Grimm*. New selection translated and retold by Marita van der Vyver. Cape Town, SA: Human & Rousseau.
Van der Vyver, Marita. 1982. *Van jou Jas*. Cape Town, SA: Tafelberg.
_____. 1987. *Tien vir 'n Vriend*. Cape Town, SA: Tafelberg.
_____. 1991. *Eenkantkind*. Cape Town, SA: Tafelberg.
_____. 1992. *Griet Skryf 'n Sprokie*. Cape Town, SA: Tafelberg
_____. 1996. *Dinge van 'n Kind/Childish Things*. Cape Town, SA: Tafelberg.
_____. 1996. *Entertaining Angels*. London: Joseph.
_____. 1996. *Olinosters op die Dak/Rhinocephants on the Roof*. Cape Town, SA: Human & Rousseau.
_____. 2002. *Die ongelooflike Avonture van Hanna Hoekom*. Cape Town, SA: Tafelberg.
_____. 2002. *The Hidden Life of Hanna Why*. Cape Town, SA: Tafelberg.
_____. 2004. *Boomklim*. Cape Town, SA: Kagiso Education.
_____. 2004. *Die Simpel Dinge Wat Mens Mis*. Cape Town, SA: Kagiso Education.
_____. 2005. *Hy Bly My Broer*. Cape Town, SA: Maskew Miller Longman.
_____. 2005. *Mia se Ma/Mia's Mom*. Cape Town, SA: Human & Rousseau.

Smelling Ferdinand's Flowers: Marjorie van Heerden's Journey

Magdel Vorster

"When you're on a journey and the end keeps getting further and further away, then you realize that the real end is the journey." This quote by Karlfried Graf Durckheim comes up fairly regularly in the Van Heerden's house, and when lecturing, Marjorie van Heerden always emphasizes her journey as children's book writer and illustrator. The journey started when she was four and met Ferdinand the Bull, created by Munro Leaf, and is to date strewn with more than 120 of her own titles. Since 1983, books illustrated or written and illustrated by her have been translated into thirty-four languages and have been published all over Africa as well as the United States, Canada, the United Kingdom, Greece and Hong Kong.

A Traveler in the Making

Marjorie van Heerden was born in De Doorns in the Hex River Valley in South Africa's Western Cape Province and grew up on a farm in the valley. She used to watch her mother in their house and garden always creating pleasing pictures in everything she did. She is convinced she learned her sense of combining colors and placing objects and figures to create balanced pictures from her mother. Her father on the other hand was a great storyteller, and she learned a lot about timing and rhythm in storytelling from him. Marjorie's love for books and reading stem from those years when she remembers that her parents used to go to Cape Town and come back with books as gifts for her and her sister (Van Heerden 2005). One of these books was *The Story of Ferdinand*, by Munro Leaf (1936). Marjorie's fascination with the interaction between words and pictures was triggered by this classic book. Later in her journey as illustrator, she came across a quote by Maurice Sendak confirming this: "To me, illustrating means having a passionate affair with the words" (Cilliers 1988, 239).

She can still recall how she paged through *The Story of Ferdinand* and remembers that some of the pages showed far away scenes with big open spaces, while others had close-up figures that filled up the whole page. She knew that she wanted to create something similar. Marjorie is dyslectic, and it has always been easier for her to express herself through her drawings than through words (Van Heerden 2005). By interacting with an illustration's pleasing qualities and beauty, the reader can depart on a journey, escape into the picture, go beyond the limited borders of any familiar environments and world of reference and leave uncomfortable settings or spaces behind. With visual images aiding text, the story becomes real and the reader's mind is broadened (Van Heerden 2012c).

An Illustrator's Journey Takes Off

Marjorie's journey as children's book illustrator started after her daughter Alexia was born in 1977. She soon realized that she was now experiencing life through her daughter's eyes, became aware of how much an adult misses and embraced this newfound clarity in her work, always remaining sensually as aware as possible of the physical world around her while still using her imagination. Three years after Alexia, their son Markus was born. As mother, Marjorie found that she was never short of a supply of stories, and her children were her muses. Naturally they became the models for her drawings, just as later on some of her characters were inspired by her grandchildren. Her work embodied the words, thoughts, fears and joys of her children (Van Heerden 2005).

After Marjorie had illustrated three books by other authors, she wrote and illustrated *Die Een Groot Bruin Beer* (The One Big Brown Bear), published in Afrikaans only. In this book, based on an actual family outing to the Tygerberg Zoo near Cape Town, a little boy, Markus, takes his toy bear along on a visit to the zoo with his father. At the zoo Markus notices that all the animals, but the brown bear, have at least one mate, and he leaves his favorite toy with the brown bear as company. In *A Tiger Took Me to the Circus*, published in Afrikaans and English, Alexia is the main character. Alexia's cat changes into a tiger and takes her to the circus on his back. Alexia has a very busy and exciting day at the circus and at the end of the night is carried home by the ringmaster. The last picture of the book shows Alexia, fast asleep with her cat next to her. The only sign of the night's adventure is a red balloon floating in the room. These two books could only be printed in two colors, of which one had to be black.

In *Good Night, Grandpa*, a comforting, imaginative story in full color, Marcus cannot go to sleep, because he misses his grandfather who has recently died. Grandpa however visits him in a dream, and they go on a walk to collect all the stars that have fallen to earth. Marjorie published another picture book with Alexia as main character, *A New Bed for Alexia*, in which Alexia's bed is old and quite unstable. Her dad tries to fix it with his saw and soon the bed is a lot lower than he intended it to be. Alexia is however very happy about this, because no monster can now fit under her new bed.

Marjorie was now set on pursuing a career in children's literature and extensively researched the picture book genre. She soon discovered Maurice Sendak. In her lectures on illustrating, she still likes to quote Sendak, who said,

> A picture book is not what most people think it is—an easy thing, with a lot of pictures in it, to read to small children. For me, it is a damned difficult thing to do, like working in a complicated and challenging poetic form. It demands so much that you have to be on top of the situation all the time, finally to achieve something so simple and so put together—so seamless—that it looks as if you knocked it off in no time. One stitch showing and you've lost the game [Cilliers 1988, 235].

While they lived in Chicago from 1984 to 1985, during her husband's sabbatical, Marjorie met American children's book authors, illustrators and academics, and she attended conferences and study groups on children's literature. She acknowledges her experiences and exposure there as key in establishing her career as children's book illustrator (Parker, 2010). Back in Stellenbosch in South Africa, Marjorie started working towards organizing a conference similar to the one she attended in the U.S., and in 1987 it became a reality when the first International Children's Book Conference in South Africa, titled "Towards Understanding," was presented in South Africa with 550 local and international delegates attending. Joseph Schwartz, whose presentation Marjorie attended in the U.S., was one of the speakers, and Marjorie had the privilege to share her work with him, after which he analyzed and discussed insights with her. She is convinced that she learned more in that week than she might have done doing a university degree course.

Marjorie wrote and illustrated the "Peanutbutter" series, published in full color, shortly after she returned to South Africa. Big and green Peanutbutter is Alex's imaginary dragon friend. His name was inspired by the still fresh-in-their-minds peanut butter and jelly sandwiches with which the Van Heerdens were so familiar while living in the U.S. In the first book, *A Monster in the Garden*, Alex used peanut butter in a mouse trap and caught a monster's toe, who since then only ate peanut butter and jelly sandwiches. In the second book, *Old Enough*, Alex is old enough to go to the shop by himself, which he fortunately does not have to do, since Peanutbutter can go along unnoticed. In the third book, *Father Christmas Needs Help*, Alex and Peanutbutter help Santa when he has an accident. *A Monster in the Garden* also has been used as an example of early South African anti-racism picture books, because of its subtle anti-racism messages embedded in the illustrations (Van Heerden 2012a). Alex's best friend is Vincent, and through the illustrations it is obvious that the mothers are friends too. This regardless of the fact that Alex and his mother are not white. In the South Africa of 1987, different cultural groups portrayed as having the same interests, would not have been a common theme.

Down Newly Opened Roads

After the changes brought about with democracy and the official end of apartheid in 1994, the focus moved to education and literacy, which meant that many writers and illustrators became involved in writing and illustrating educational books as well as trying to still publish trade books. Many authors and illustrators also wanted to contribute to what became known as the African Renaissance of which education and basic literacy were fundamental keystones (Van Heerden, 2012a). For years Marjorie has been very active in promoting children's books by writing articles for specialist publications, giving talks, lectures and workshops. Her main focus has been to help address and support developments in the new democratic South Africa. She specifically aimed to promote child and adult literacy among the previously disadvantaged communities (Van Heerden 2013).

Her opportunity came when she wrote and illustrated twenty-one booklets for the Ntataise Trust. Ntataise, meaning "to lead a young child by the hand," is an independent nonprofit organization founded in South Africa in 1980 to help women in poor rural areas gain the knowledge and skills to establish early childhood development programs for children in their communities. Marjorie conceptualized and developed an original folding format for these low-cost readers, resulting in eight illustrated pages. These innovative easy-readers, designed for the specific needs of rural pre-school children, were available in English, isiZulu and Sesotho. Themes of these books related to the immediate context of the intended readers, while reinforcing early learning concepts such as space, numbers, counting, size and time, nature and animals, and social behavior and emotions (Steyn 1995).

Traveling the Learning Curve

Marjorie's next journey took her to Chautauqua, New York, in the United States in 1995 when she won a scholarship to attend a Highlights Foundation's Children's Book Writers Workshop. She spent a week with Ed Young, Caldecott winner, as mentor after which she completely changed her approach to her work. She attempted what she would never have done before, changed the media she used, changed the paper she had used for decades, and discovered a new energy and joy in her work.

The result of this new energy was the Bright Books Reading Series. In 1997 Nasou Publishers developed and published this brainchild of Marjorie in full color. These books looked completely different from any other educational books available at that time. The first set of eleven books contained thirty-six original stories aimed at grade one learners. In 1998, a second set, four books for grade two, followed, and in 1999 a third set aimed at grade three was published. These sets of readers were scientifically developed to suit the specific cultural and educational needs of the youth of the new democratic South Africa and covered the Foundation phase of the new South African school system (Van Heerden 2013). They were not only interesting stories, but the different scenarios, character descriptions and colorful illustrations were often humorous, which created an easy and light-hearted learning situation ("Range of pupil-centred books launched" 1998). Marjorie has managed to tell the stories in a way that the story and characters came first, while the lessons are unobtrusive and subtle to lead to learning through the fun of reading and enjoying the illustrations.

The Bright Books set created for grade one concentrates on the various development areas of young children and focused on carefully researched and chosen subjects including counting and basic math concepts, spatial awareness, shapes, opposites, and food groups. For the grade two set of four reader/activity books, Marjorie subtly focused on codes of social behavior, and in the single grade three volume she put the thematic focus on the development of individual creativity and self-initiative (Van Heerden 2013).

During this time she also published a few trade books, using her new technique of illustration. *The Zebra and the Baboon*, written by Thomas A. Nevin, tells the Venda story of how the zebra got his stripes and how the baboon ended up with no hair on his backside. Illustrations are done in strong oil pastels with the text in white on a black background.[1] This book was eventually published in five local languages.

Monde's Present, originally written by Alexia when she was six years old, was first published in five languages and eventually in all eleven official languages of South Africa. Again illustrations here are realistic and colorful, the use of bright oil pastels to portray movement and very often an expression of happiness, masterfully done. Facial expressions and everyday body language skillfully depict emotion and an enthusiasm for life in a unique way. This originality landed her an honorary mention for the Katrine Harries Award in 1997–1998 for *Monde's Present* (Fairer-Wessels 2007).

In switching between writing and illustrating books for educational purposes and trade books, Marjorie keeps inspired by a quote by Joseph Schwarcz: "Do not let us treat children's literature as a well-kept garden, thus robbing it of its nature as a windswept field." Roughly translated into Afrikaans, this quote is also the title of her chapter in the writing manual, *Die Afrikaanse Skryfgids*, compiled by Riana Scheepers and Leti Kleyn (Van Heerden 2012b).

Beyond Local Languages

From 1999 to 2003 Marjorie and her husband lived just outside Athens, Greece. This was a time to stop and smell the flowers. She was however almost immediately involved in the world of Greek children's literature. After her debut as eikonográfos (illustrator) and the thrill of seeing her name in Greek letters with *The Moon Story* by Voula Mastori, more commissions followed. Her involvement with the children's book world in Greece was secured when she became the regional advisor of the Greek branch of the International Society of Children's Book Writers and Illustrators. She got her new Greek colleagues together and organized an international symposium, titled "May the Myth be your Muse."

In illustrating *The Three Teapots* (Eliopoulos), Marjorie was again creating delightful green dragons, even though this time they spoke Greek. It tells the story of a little girl who, through clever tricks, wins the friendship of a dragon that keeps disguising himself to try to scare her away. She was also very fortunate to illustrate the Greek translation of Katherine Paterson's *The King's Equal*.

After having to rely on her memory because of very strict deadlines during her previous years in Johannesburg working on educational projects, Marjorie felt her senses being sharpened during this period. She became very aware of the impact of being attentive to the light source in an illustration, and she also started focusing on a sense of place by working in detail on the backgrounds of her illustrations. Her paper, pencils, crayons and paint became the vehicle taking her on journeys through each story she illustrated (Van Heerden 2003).

Years later Marjorie was commissioned to illustrate *Ears Hear* and *Numbers Do*. These two bilingual books (English and Mandarin) were written by Kathleen Ahrens and Chu-Ren Huang and published in Hong Kong.

The Fantastic Journey Ahead

Back in South Africa, in Gordon's Bay in the Western Cape, Marjorie started receiving exciting commissions based on her work in Greece. She began to do more fantasy stories.

A number of books in Marjorie's now established signature style, using many blues, purple and turquoise were published between 2004 and 2006. *Professor Fossilus en die Dinosourusse* (Professor Fossilus and the Dinosaurs) by Louise Smit and *Ek en My Monster* (My Monster and I) by Leon de Villiers were published in Afrikaans only. Leon de Villiers's tongue-in-cheek beginners manual for anyone who would like to keep domestic monsters was done in full color. Marjorie's very original illustrations of all the different species of monsters complement their hilarious names perfectly, and this book can be enjoyed by many different age groups on different levels (Brand 2005).

The Authentic, Unusually Alarming, Actual Factual Story Book, written and illustrated by Marjorie is everything (except "alarming") that the title promises. It is a collection of twelve delightful stories about real children in real situations. Marjorie's illustrations are again animated and humoristic, strongly contributing to the readability of the stories (Heale 2006).

Uncle James and the Delicious Monster is a story written by Nick Paul about family and imagination and monsters. Marjorie's son, Markus, now adult, was again the inspiration behind Uncle James. Jay Heale, well-known South African critic, reviewed it as a top read-aloud text, full of rhythm and patterns, fun, frolic and scary bits. He continues, saying that Marjorie's pictures play games with the delicious monster's leaves, portrayed as monster heads, and create real children as the heroes (Heale 2005). Furthermore, there is a strong likeness between Uncle James and Jacob at the bottom of the stairs in "A Wonderful Dream" in the storybook Bible, *Children of God*, by Archbishop Desmond Tutu. This is because of Marjorie's stylistic approach when drawing portraits. Paddy Bouma and Marjorie were the only two South African artists among the twenty artists illustrating Tutu's Bible.

Between 2009 and 2012, Marjorie was honored to illustrate the works of some of South Africa's best authors, such as the aforementioned Archbishop Desmond Tutu, André P. Brink and Antjie Krog, as well as a well-known story by C.J. Langenhoven, *Kootjie Totjie. Die Avonture van Alice in Wonderland* is André P. Brink's Afrikaans translation of Lewis Carroll's classic, and Marjorie's illustrations brilliantly revitalize the familiar story while maintaining a central character. Her Alice has the long golden hair like the original, but she has a fresh look of determination about her. Marjorie uses color spreads effectively, and her black-and-white drawings are magical, especially where precise-line is used (Heale 2012). *Sam, 'n Ware Verhaalvan 'n Dogtertjieen Haar Olifant* (Sam, a True Story of a Little Girl and Her Elephant) (Van der Veken) was translated from the Dutch into Afrikaans by Antjie Krog. The book is based on the true story of a girl traveling from China to France with her elephant.

A Rewarded Road

In 2005 Marjorie received the M.E.R. Prize in the illustrated children's literature category with author Wynand Louw for *Mr Humperdinck's Wonderful Whatsit* (Fairer-Wessels and Wessels 2007). This is a book filled with dwarves, fairies, and gargoyles, and surprises with talking bricks, heaps of garbage that can fly and talk, and man-eating giant rats. The author effortlessly succeeds in suspending the reader's disbelief in these characters and their adventures and the illustrations suggest rather than show exactly what is happening, cleverly activating the reader's imagination as most important asset. Marjorie's drawings provide glimpses of the many weird creatures in this magical adventure (Heale 2004).

Marjorie has always had an active imagination and making up stories comes naturally. Growing up on a farm, she made up stories with her sister and cousins and then acted them out, sometimes on horseback. She's always felt she could communicate with animals and remembers two animals specifically, her horse Billy Boy and a small duck. Animals taught Marjorie to believe in magic, and she is convinced that her contact with animals from a young age has influenced the way she draws animals in her children's books (Van Heerden 2005). In 2008 Marjorie again received the M.E.R. Prize for best illustrated children's book for *Nina and Little Duck*, written by Wendy Hartmann. The stories and rhymes in this picture book center around Nina and Simon and Little Duck. Nina and Simon play around the house and shop of the Rajahs and sometimes even in their garden. This garden is also the playground and home of Little Duck and her ducklings. In *Bertus Soek 'n Boek* (Bertus Looking for a Book) (2009), written by Jaco Jacobs, the librarian reminds the reader of the delightful Mrs. Rajah, as does the woman in C.J. Langenhoven's *Kootjie Totjie*. This is another example of Marjorie's stylistic approach to portraits.

In 2009, *Long Juju Man*, written by Ndedi Okorafor and illustrated by Marjorie, was the winning book for the Macmillan Writer's Prize for Africa, and in 2011 Marjorie won the W.B. Mkhize Award, given by the Usiba Writers' Guild, for *Uhambo Luka Lulama Olude*, the Zulu version of *Lulama's Long Way Home*, which she wrote and illustrated (Van Heerden 2013).The story of Lulama's journey, meeting animal friends along her way home, was published in all eleven official languages of South Africa as well as Portuguese. Marjorie won the M.E.R. Prize for illustrated children's books for the third time in 2012. This time she shared the honor as the illustrator of Alex D'Angelo's *Goblin Diaries: Apprenticed to the Red Witch*. This book is the diary of Ymaldris, the youngest of three goblin brothers, and Jay Heale describes this story as a superb magical adventure on the fringe of Hobbit country and one of the best fantasy stories to appear in local literature (Heale 2011).

Marjorie van Heerden has always felt that any creative artist, focusing on children as end users, implicitly accepts the responsibility of shaping young minds and that a picture book for a young child is one of the few art forms specifically designed with the child in mind (Van Heerden 2012c). It seems that since that day she met Ferdinand, sitting under his tree, she's travelled many places, smelled many flowers and through her illustrations has taken many children traveling and will continue to do so for a long time.

Note

1. Venda is now part of the Limpopo Province after it had been one of the self-governing homelands during the former government. People from Venda have their own language.

Children's Books

Ahrens, Kathleen, and Chu-Ren Huang. 2012. *Ears Hear*. Illustrated by Marjorie van Heerden. Hong Kong: Sun Ya.

———. 2012. *Numbers Do*. Illustrated by Marjorie van Heerden. Hong Kong: Sun Ya.

Brink, André P. 2010. *Die Avonture van Alice in Wonderland*. Illustrated by Marjorie van Heerden. Cape Town, SA: Human & Rousseau.

D'Angelo, Alex. 2011. *Goblin Diaries: Apprenticed to the Red Witch*. Illustrated by Marjorie van Heerden. Cape Town, SA: Tafelberg.

De Villiers, Leon. 2004. *Ek en My Monster*. Illustrated by Marjorie van Heerden. Pretoria, SA. LAPA.

Eliopoulos, Vangelis. 2000. *The Three Teapots*. Illustrated by Marjorie van Heerden. Athens, Greece: Patakis.

Hartmann, Wendy. 2007. *Nina and Little Duck*. Illustrated by Marjorie van Heerden. Cape Town, SA: Human & Rousseau.

Jacobs, Jaco. 2009. *Bertus Soek 'n Boek*. Illustrated by Marjorie van Heerden. Pretoria, SA: LAPA.

Langenhoven, Cornelis J. Revised edition 2009. *Kootjie Totjie*. Illustrated by Marjorie van Heerden. Pretoria, SA: Protea.

Louw, Wynand. 2004. *Mr Humperdinck's Wonderful Whatsit*. Illustrated by Marjorie van Heerden. Cape Town, SA: Human & Rousseau.

Mastori, Voula. 2000. *The Moon Story*. Illustrated by Marjorie van Heerden. Athens, Greece: Patakis.

Nevin, Thomas A. 1996. *The Zebra and the Baboon*. Illustrated by Marjorie van Heerden. Durbanville, SA: Garamond.

Okorafor, Nnedi. 2008. *Long Juju Man*. Illustrated by Marjorie van Heerden. London: MacMillan.

Paterson, Katherine. 2001. *The King's Equal*. Illustrated by Marjorie van Heerden. Athens, Greece: Patakis.

Paul, Nick. 2005. *Uncle James and the Delicious Monster*. Illustrated by Marjorie van Heerden. Cape Town, SA: Tafelberg.

Smit, Louise. 2004. *Professor Fossilus en die Dinosourusse*. Illustrated by Marjorie van Heerden. Cape Town, SA: Human & Rousseau.

Taylor, Ann. 1999. *Baby Dance*. Illustrated by Marjorie van Heerden. New York: Harper Collins.

Tutu, Desmond. 2010. *Children of God, Storybook Bible*. Cape Town, SA: Lux Verbi.
Van der Veken, Ingrid. 2012. *Sam 'n Ware Verhaal van 'n Dogtertjie en Haar Olifant*. Translated by Antjie Krog. Illustrated by Marjorie van Heerden. Pretoria, SA: LAPA.
Van Heerden, Marjorie. 1984. *Die Een Groot Bruin Beer*. Cape Town, SA: Human & Rousseau.
———. 1986. *A Tiger Took Me to the Circus*. Cape Town, SA: Human &Rousseau.
———. 1987. *Father Christmas Needs Help*. Cape Town, SA: Human & Rousseau.
———. 1987. *A Monster in the Garden*. Cape Town, SA: Human & Rousseau.
———. 1987. *Old Enough*. Cape Town, SA: Human & Rousseau.
———. 1990. *Good Night, Grandpa*. Cape Town, SA: Human &Rousseau.
———. 1992. *A New Bed for Alexia*. Cape Town, SA: Human & Rousseau.
———. 1997. *Monde's Present*. Durbanville, SA: Garamond.
———. 2006. *The Authentic, Unusually Alarming, Actual Factual Story Book*. Cape Town, SA: Human & Rousseau.
———. 2007. *Lulama's Long Way Home/UhamboLukaLulamaOlude*. Johannesburg, SA: Pan MacMillan.

Chris van Wyk: A Man Intent on Sharing Africa with Africa's Children

Jay Heale

The Cambridge History of South African Literature (Attwell and Attridge 2012) contains thirty-nine authoritative chapters in over eight hundred pages ranging from the early oral tradition of Africa to cultural criticism as recent as 2008. Chris van Wyk is mentioned five times in these august pages—even though they contain no chapter concerning South African children's literature.

Van Wyk is a South African poet, novelist, and past editor of *Staffrider*, one of the key publications in the Black Consciousness era—a time when nearly all published writing was being done by white South Africans. His collection of poetry, *It Is Time to Go Home*, was awarded the 1980 Olive Schreiner Prize by the English Academy of South Africa. He is the author of *The Year of the Tapeworm*, which Rita Barnard (2012) calls "a neglected novel ... uncannily predictive in its deep ambivalence about the political transition it records" (653).

Readers who want to meet Chris van Wyk should read *Shirley, Goodness & Mercy* and its companion piece *Eggs to Lay, Chickens to Hatch*. Through these entertaining anecdotes of boyhood and growing up in South Africa under apartheid, the reader will come to realize first how good a storyteller van Wyk is, and then how bitterly hard it was to be a thinker and writer in those days.

However, the reader will also discover (from those two books) two important and lasting beliefs of Chris van Wyk: that reading is highly important for young people, and also that he sees the importance of writing for young readers. That is what this essay is about.

The Writer in the Making

It may sound insulting to say that someone grew up in an under-privileged community. To many in South Africa, however, this is a proud boast. In spite of sub-standard education, Chris van Wyk always wanted to be a writer. This started with storytelling. When he was nine, he recalls, "Whenever my teacher left the classroom she would ask me to tell the class a story to keep them quiet" (Watson 2001, 729). This school was in Riverlea, a poor suburb about eight kilometers (five miles) west of Johannesburg, surrounded by dusty mine dumps, where he had his home until 2004.

Like many youngsters, he started to fall in love with new words. "Panoramic" was one of them, easily explained by the view from the top of the nearby mine dump. Other word discoveries included "alacrity" and "buoyant." Love of stories grew from the local *skinder* (gossip), from radio serials and plays, from stories told by his extended family. In *Eggs to Lay* Uncle Eddie tells a glorious tale of a gang of men who (according to his story) hoist a deep hole out on to the back of a truck; but the truck is parked on a slope, the hole falls off the truck and then the whole truck, crane and workmen also slip down the hole. "And that is the end of my story" (73). Not all of Chris's memories are fun. When he was twelve, a sadistic teacher gave him "one hundred cuts" (strokes with a cane). Corporal punishment was in favor in those days.

He also started keeping a diary, assuring himself that such an activity wasn't for "sissies" (weaklings) so long as you didn't say things like "Dear Diary" or dot your i's with little hearts. The embryo writer was starting to write, but there was an ongoing problem:

> I was born with a squint in my left eye. Before I'm a year old Ma, Dad and I are making monthly trips to St John's, the eye hospital near Baragwanath Hospital in Soweto where I was born. I have my first eye operation when I'm about nine months old, and, Ma says, the eye simply wandered back to the inner corner, where it preferred to stay [2004, 181].

Poor eyesight has given Chris problems all through his life. In boyhood his squint brought unfeeling laughter from other children at school. Childhood surgery damaged the eye muscles. Only in manhood did he meet an eye surgeon who took one look and said, "I can fix that." With a quiet smile, Chris tells how after he had finished the first set of ten stories about *Freedom Fighters*, Awareness Publishers swiftly commissioned a second set. Peering at the screen was slowing down the writing process. Publisher Michael Neu-Ner sent him a surprise present: a brand new large screen.

Reading Is Important

As a boy, Chris read everything he could put his hands on: comics (swapped regularly with his friends) such as *Richie Rich*, *Spider-man*, and *Superman*; series by Enid Blyton; "Franklin W. Dixon's"[1] the *Hardy Boys*;

newspapers; *One Hundred Great Lives* (author unknown); a dictionary; and discarded books from the rubbish dump. Confirmation comes from *Shirley, Goodness & Mercy*:

> This facility with language comes about through my voracious appetite for books and the written word. Teachers were forever encouraging us to read. Open books, they'd urge. You will discover places and people, whole worlds you never knew existed. And reading will give you knowledge, and knowledge will give you confidence to go into that big wide world waiting for you. You'll have power [54].

The power to write was the power to communicate. Chris served as editor of the influential magazine *Staffrider*. This is described by David Johnson (2012) as:

> Arguably the most significant of the "small magazines" [that] came after the Soweto uprising. *Staffrider*, which achieved distribution figures of 7,000, ran from 1978 to 1993 under the collective editorship of Mike Kirkwood and Mothobi Mutloatse, and later Chris van Wyk and Andries Oliphant, and published short stories, poems and photographs as well as essays and manifestoes on literature, culture and politics [830].

Chris hadn't thought much of poetry until he came across the writing of Stephen Spender (1965). The blunt directness of "My parents kept me from children who threw stones" made him sit up. Later, he was similarly stunned by Oswald Mtshali's *Sounds of a Cowhide Drum* (1971), read aloud by a teacher in school. Chris admits, "Until now I didn't even know one could write a poem about being black" (2004, 230). Only a few weeks later he talked with his friend Fhazel Johennesse about writing poetry themselves, and that's how Chris became a poet. Together, they started a magazine called *Wietie* (township slang for talk, to communicate, to exchange ideas). It contained poems, short stories and artwork. It lasted for two issues.

> About black consciousness: We are black, not carbon copies of white people. We reject the term 'non-white'; when we are forced, for whatever reason, to use the term 'Coloured' we make two little double quotes in the air.... We speak of Africa.... Our teachers had told us nothing about Africa and I hate them for it [2004, 281–282].

Information about the Leaders of South Africa

Chris is especially anxious that children should readily access the information he was denied as a boy concerning the history and people of South Africa. He emphasizes this in *Shirley, Goodness & Mercy*:

This is apartheid into its second decade, its second phase if you like, with Mandela, Sobukwe, Sisulu and others safely locked up, thousands in exile, and the white people smirking and prospering. But of all this I knew nothing... [12].

...I would have to wait until after I finish school to know about Africa. White people write our history books and as far as they're concerned, they are the only ones who make history. For the moment I don't know what's going on [215].

This lack of available knowledge concerning the major figures in the growth of South Africa resulted in Chris van Wyk creating the text for no fewer than thirty-one books (ten to each boxed set, plus a descriptive fold-out time-chart in Series 3) in the *Freedom Fighters* series (2003, 2006, 2010). These three boxed sets are perhaps the greatest gift from Chris van Wyk to young readers. They contain factual biographies of thirty "heroes" of South Africa's progress towards democratic freedom. Designed for primary school readers, and with clear, uncomplicated text, color photographs, glossary and key dates, each book is a miniature gem of the life, character and importance of such people as Albert Luthuli, Nelson Mandela, Ruth First, Robert Sobukwe, and (in the third series) Jacob Zuma.

The biography of Steve Biko is particularly effective. It opens with a word picture of a boy walking with books under his arm (much as Chris probably did), opposite a photo of a dirt road in a black township. Biko's ideas about being proud of being black became known as "black consciousness," the cause for which Chris himself had given many years of his life.

The extra book in Series 3 is called *The Road to Democracy 1652 to 1994*. This is beyond price. At last we have a clear, concise story of South Africa from the arrival of the first intrusive settlers until the 1994 democratic election. Printed on a long zigzag (accordion fold) strip of tough glazed card (which could be hung up as a classroom display) it contains factual text, old paintings or more modern photographs, captions and a central time-line stretching over twenty-eight pages. Chris van Wyk points out how, after the Anglo-Boer War of 1899–1902 "the British had promised 'equal laws and equal liberty' to all races if the Boers were defeated, but they did not keep this promise" (n. p.). So the struggle for equal rights began then, in 1902.

Freedom Fighters 3 has seventy-six pages per book (and a larger page size) compared to the forty-eight pages of Series 1. However, the book on Jacob Zuma has ninety-two pages and recaps relevant episodes of South African history, so it is a most useful history book in its own right. Chris takes the reader through the court cases involving Zuma in a lucid, logical manner. This is a black writer telling of black history for all young readers. Zuma's own story is, of course, not yet finished.

Many of the biographies are of black leaders whose lives are contemporaneous, so there is inevitable repetition in these books of key events and concepts such as the founding of the African National Congress (ANC; first called the South African Native National Congress, started in 1912) and the Freedom Charter drawn up in 1954. However, Chris looks for opportunities to make each book different. So the life of Thabo Mofutsanyana is preceded by coverage of Chief Moshoeshoe and the mountain kingdom of Lesotho. With Moses Kotane we learn about life as a rural cattle-herder and working in the mines.

The story of Ruth Mompati is even more interesting, for it provides coverage of those "struggle" times from a woman's point of view. Ruth too was a "wanted person," living in hiding and eventually arrested, then set free, after which (like so many others) she left the country and worked for the ANC in Tanzania and Russia, returning after twenty-eight years in exile. In 1996 she was appointed South Africa's ambassador to Switzerland. It must also be said that the picture research for all these books is particularly impressive.

When offered the chance to create a picture book text out of Nelson Mandela's autobiography, *Long Walk to Freedom* (1994), Chris was delighted. Most picture books have thirty-two pages, but there was so much to tell that the publishers (Macmillan) happily agreed to double the size. All the *Freedom Fighters* books are written objectively in the third person. In the *Freedom Fighters: Nelson Mandela* we read:

> Nelson Mandela was born on 18 July 1918. He lived in a tiny village near Umtata in the Transkei, now the Eastern Cape. When Nelson's father first saw his newborn son, he called him "Rolihlahla". This Xhosa name means "pulling the branch of a tree." It also means "troublemaker"! [5].

The *Long Walk to Freedom* abridged version gave Chris the chance to write from inside the character, using the first person (following Mandela's own autobiographic style):

> I was born into the Thembu tribe, one of many tribes that made up the Xhosa nation. I entered the world in the tiny village of Mvezo, in the beautiful Eastern Cape, on 18th July, 1918. My father was a Thembu chief, a leader of our people. He named me Rolihlahla, which in Xhosa means "troublemaker" [n.p.].

Of the many publications seeking to present Mandela for young readers, this is one of the most successful. *Nelson Mandela: Long Walk to Freedom*, illustrated by Paddy Bouma, is a reliable, entertaining and moving account of the man known in South Africa as "Madiba." It is also a beautiful book. Chris recalls (pers. comm.) how his first sight of Paddy Bouma's artwork brought tears to his eyes.

A Writer of Fiction for Young Readers

A Message in the Wind was the Adventure Africa Award winner, later renamed the Young Africa Award. As Richard Rive (South African short story writer and novelist) mentions in his generous Introduction, the book starts with everyday boys doing normal things and then becomes fantasy as they travel back three hundred years in time. But both parts of the book carry important subtextual messages. Vusi complains to himself, "Fourteen on my next birthday and I've never been to school like the other boys!" (2) Then he does go to school. His grandfather tells him how their ancestral tribe warred with one another. In his time jump, he finds the origin of this quarrel and learns "that men must forget their differences and live together" (66). "The message in the wind" is that literature belongs to all men and will be appreciated by all if it contains the essential messages of love and peace.

In *Eggs to Lay, Chickens to Hatch* Chris admits that *A Message in the Wind* is "not the best book I've ever written, and yet it remains one of my favourites" (3). During a school visit, Chris and his young audience pondered what time in the past they would choose to visit and what change they would make. One boy said, "I would go back to a time when my father was still alive ... and I would spend much more time with him than I did" (4). Chris van Wyk has this gift of turning make-believe storytelling into something that pushes us to think more deeply.

Written twelve years before apartheid would finally be removed from the statute books, *A Message in the Wind* carries the same message of living together in peace that Nelson Mandela brought with him out of twenty-seven years of imprisonment.

Other children's stories include *Petroleum and the Orphaned Ostrich*[2] and *Peppy 'n Them*. The former must take the prize for the most unusual title! "Petroleum" is a robot child made out of a petrol can and old table legs by an imaginative black South African dustman (trash collector). Told with typical van Wyk vigor and humor, Petroleum rides the ostrich to find its missing mother but ends up with a lady's hat instead. It's a clever progression from the wire-made vehicles that Chris must have played with as a boy. In the second title, Peppy is one of a gang of runaway boys in the crime-filled Johannesburg suburb of Hillbrow who end up trying to find the murderer of a friend before that person finds them. In a theme similar to Lesley Beake's *The Strollers* (1987), Chris shows sympathy for those with a life of petty crime.

Ouma Ruby's Secret is an intriguing picture book story. Its origin lies inside *Shirley, Goodness & Mercy* (70–74) where it is followed by a poem written some twenty years later. In outline, beloved Ouma Ruby ("Ouma" being Afrikaans for Granny) takes the boy Chris to a bookshop where he is allowed to choose two books. He does so, Ouma Ruby looks at them and approves, and they become his very own. He wants to thank her when her own birthday comes around, but having no money decides to write a loving, grateful letter. He does this and gives it to her, but she puts it aside for later. Chris's mother explains to him that Ouma Ruby can't read. That's some secret!

In creating the picture book version, a much younger reader was clearly envisaged. Instead of Chris choosing (with delight) two titles from the popular *Hardy Boys* series, in this account he chooses much easier books. In the illustration we see a cheese-eating mouse and very large text. The thank-you letter is also much shortened, and in the picture book Chris gets the chance to read this letter aloud to his grandmother.

The greater impact of the original anecdote is given fuller significance in *Shirley, Goodness & Mercy*. In his subsequent poem, Chris refers to Ouma Ruby's inability to read in these words:

> Although much later I learned that the black words
> on the white sheets that swept me across the seas
> to adventures in faraway lands were to Granny
> like coal strewn across a field of snow [76].

Most recently, Chris contributed a story to the collection of ten African stories entitled *Storytime* published by Times Media Education. In the story of "Mr Hare Meets Mr Mandela," "Mr Hare" finds a two hundred rand note. He can't read, but he can recognize the picture of Nelson Mandela. So he decides that as the note obviously belongs to Mr. Mandela, he'd better take it back to him. There is a lovely picture by Paddy Bouma of Mandela bowing low to "Mr Hare" and accepting the money. Unfortunately, because of Hare's inability to read, he has been steadily fleeced along the way. So what he hands over is not an orange 200 rand note, but a green ten rand[3] bill!

A Long Walk to Knowledge

During Chris van Wyk's lifetime, the African National Congress has grown into the major political party in South Africa. The ANC has been banned, opposed, unbanned and elected to government. Its leaders have been reviled, arrested, tortured, jailed (or exiled) and eventually have risen to positions of authority and power. Yet thanks to the Nationalist Party's stranglehold on the media, publishing and education, the one thing most citizens have *not* known is the story behind these people. Almost single-handedly, Chris has filled a gaping chasm in our youth literature.

In Chris van Wyk we have a man who fought his way through the inadequacies of the Bantu Education System (deliberately limited education for non-whites designed by the Nationalist Government), poor eyesight, restricted income, all the indignities of apartheid laws—and yet managed to fall in love with language, with books and with reading. At first, writing was for Chris van Wyk a weapon to use against state control, though he often used humor instead of bitter hatred. Now, he is concentrating on the need for young South African readers to have good stories and more knowledge of their own heroes.

Notes

1. "Franklin W. Dixon" is a pseudonym for Leslie McFarlane and the Stratemeyer Syndicate, authors of the series of adventure stories.
2. This title was published by Ravan Press, where Chris van Wyk worked as editor for a while. Ravan was an important publisher of dissident voices opposed to apartheid, and was established in 1972. Its name was created from the initial letters of the surnames of its founders: Peter Randall, Danie van Zyl and Beyers Naudé. Ravan Press published *The Mantis and the Moon* by Marguerite Poland in 1979, a work that remains one of the landmark books of South African children's literature.
3. The rand is South Africa's unit of currency.

Children's Books

Mandela, Nelson. 2009. *Nelson Mandela: Long Walk to Freedom*. Abridged by Chris van Wyk. Illustrated by Paddy Bouma. London: Macmillan Children's Books.
Van Wyk, Chris. 1979. *It Is Time to Go Home*. Johannesburg, SA: Ad Donker.
_____. 1982. *A Message in the Wind*. Introduction by Richard Rive. Illustrated by Peter Clarke. Cape Town, SA: Maskew Miller Longman.
_____. 1989. *Petroleum and the Orphaned Ostrich*. Johannesburg, SA: Ravan Press.
_____. 1991. *Peppy 'n Them*. Swaziland: Macmillan Boleswa.
_____. 1996. *The Year of the Tapeworm*. Johannesburg, SA: Ravan Press.
_____. 2004. *Shirley, Goodness & Mercy—A Childhood Memoir*. Johannesburg, SA: Picador Africa.
_____. 2003; 2006; 2010. *Learning African History: Freedom Fighters 1, 2, 3*. [Boxed sets]. Gallo Manor, SA: Awareness Publishing.
_____. 2006. *Ouma Ruby's Secret*. Illustrated by Anneliese Voigt-Peters. Johannesburg, SA: Pan Macmillan South Africa.
_____. 2010. *Eggs to Lay, Chickens to Hatch—A Memoir*. Johannesburg, SA: Picador Africa.
_____. 2013. "Mr Hare Meets Mr Mandela." Illustrated by Paddy Bouma. In *Storytime*, 95–108. Johannesburg, South Africa: Times Media Education.

We thank Chris van Wyk and Pan Macmillan for permission to reproduce extracts from *Shirley, Goodness & Mercy*.

Part 2. Writers and Artists of the New South Africa

Introduction

In 2007, in an article on South African children's literature, Beverley Naidoo wrote that South Africa needed a new generation of writers to reflect its diversity and concerns. While it is true that the South African children's literature author and illustrator corps still does not adequately represent all ethnic groups, the literature itself is definitely more representative and open to its diverse readers. Settings now more often reflect national arenas where more and less economically privileged situations or environments meet each other. Youth literature honestly reflected liberating as well as uncertain times right from the start of black majority rule in South Africa. As a character in *Don't Panic, Mechanic* (Robson 1989) remarks, "all the old rules are disappearing now. But nobody is making any new rules to take their place" (90). Some children's literature scholars regard *Charlie's House* by Reviva Schermbrucker and illustrated by Niki Daly (1989) as a turning point in the genre of children's picture books written and illustrated for the South African market. This period of renewal started by Daly with Songololo Books was now supported and expanded by a new generation of writers and illustrators whose work celebrates the power of creativity to overcome dire circumstances.

>JUDE DALY
>LEON DE VILLIERS
>PIET GROBLER
>WENDY HARTMANN
>JACO JACOBS
>INGRID MENNEN
>GCINA MHLOPHE
>FIONA MOODIE
>MARTIE PRELLER
>ELIZABETH PULLES
>JOAN RANKIN
>JENNY ROBSON
>REVIVA SCHERMBRUCKER
>DIANNE STEWART
>ANN WALTON

With the end of apartheid, South Africans faced national life with less separation and were hopeful for the newly coined phrase, "rainbow nation," to emerge from years of segregation and racial oppression. According to Jakes Gerwel in a foreword to *Crossing Over* (Gerwel and Rode 1995), this remarkable transition grabbed writers' and artists' imaginations. Liberating effects led to an awareness of others. The challenge for authors, not representative of all groups, however was to portray the other, the former outsiders as round and dynamic characters (Bentley and Midgley 2000).

Jenny Robson has always been against any stereotyping. She never deliberately drew attention to the ethnicity of her protagonists but rather revealed it through the names and dialogue, like colloquialisms and slang, she used. Mess, in *Mellow Yellow* (2002), could typically be categorized as a former outsider, but through this book, Robson moves him from anonymity to identity and self-respect. *Dark Waters*, published in 2007, is another perfect example of Robson's skill at portraying blurred spatial boundaries as diverse citizens began to live side by side.

Charlie's House (1989) is also said to have spearheaded the process to produce multi-lingual texts that addressed racism, ageism and sexism, and many of the authors and illustrators mentioned here became more involved in writing and illustrating for educational publishers as the market for trade books seemed to shrink. Library budgets were cut, and publishers concentrated more on publishing readers and school books. The resulting high quality readers impacted positively when considering that these books represented the first exposure to books for many children, according to Thomas van der Walt (pers. comm.).

Schermbrucker earned the label of never being "politically correct,"[1] an attribute much needed to drive South African children's literature to an all-encompassing national genre. Dianne Stewart's realistic stories demonstrate both the grief and joy of South African social history. In *Chasing the Wind* (1994) she deals with personal as well as emotional development. Nothing is sugar-coated as she explores topics like job losses and the lives of young orphans among others. Ingrid Mennen also feels strongly about writing books that include all children. She further wants books to be placed in a recognizably African context. *Ashraf of Africa* (1990), published in the United States as *Somewhere in Africa,* tells the story of Ashraf, who lives in Cape Town and visits the library, his jungle, regularly. There he reads about Africa, his continent, that is so different and so much more than a jungle filled with wild animals as is so often the picture recalled when Africa is mentioned. Years later, Mennen also wrote *A Wish This Big* (2011), a story written with the FIFA 2010 World Cup as backdrop, to carry the message of hope that in the "new" South Africa even the smallest dream can come true for its children. Gcina Mhlophe, one of South Africa's best known storytellers, declared that she aimed at inspiring young people to believe in themselves, that she used her stories to reinstitute pride in African cultures and history.

Critique of South Africa under apartheid with its conservative practices is also evident in a number of young adult novels published as science fiction. Alongside Jenny Robson's *The Denials of Kow-Ten* (1998) and *Savannah 2116 AD* (2004), Leon de Villiers's *Shorn* (2009) comments on the importance of change through exploring a different world. Martie Preller's *In the Reign of the Ilev* (2012) also has as its core message that even though a price must be paid for changes that take place, there is hope for new beginnings.

Likewise, illustrators play an important role in the reconciliation of the world of books with the world of South African children. In *Fynbos Fairies* (2007) Fiona Moodie used one of South Africa's natural floral heritages, namely Cape "fynbos,"[2] as backdrop for Antjie Krog's flower fairies. Jude Daly's landscapes and wide-open spaces always remind viewers of Africa. As illustrators were challenged to portray a unique South African identity in their pictures, authors aimed at telling real South African stories. This led to the birth of indigenous South African book characters. Martie Preller produced Balkie and Babalela, Niki Daly created Jamela, and along with Elizabeth Pulles's Lulama and Musa, Piet Grobler's Makwelane, and Joan Rankin's Sisi, they all became well-known and loved characters.

It is only fitting that while children's authors and illustrators were focused now on always reflecting diverse cultures, stories and settings, books would also be available in the eleven official languages of South Africa. Picture books, especially, are often published simultaneously in different languages. Fiona Moodie's Nandi from the Nguni folktale, *Nabulela* (1996), could therefore be read in Afrikaans and six other languages, successfully cross-pollinating South Africa's varied cultures. Thomas van der Walt feels that this could lead to the establishment of a national children's literature as the topics and content of these books should be acceptable to all language and cultural groups (pers. comm.).

Perhaps Ann Walton and Piet Grobler's *Here I Am* (1998) can be a metaphor for South African children's literature a decade or so into the twenty-first century, quite a few years after it was written. With the growing number of authors and illustrators, it seems South Africa can rightly claim an opportunity to be a more active player in the international arena of children's literature.

Notes

1. In South Africa the term "politically correct" has been coined to mean doing exactly what is expected by the establishment rather than just taking everyone into consideration.
2. "Fynbos," literally translated as "fine bush," refers to a floral kingdom of richly diverse, fine-textured species of flowers and grasses, an ecosystem which is unique to the Western Cape Province in South Africa.

Inside the Books: The Life and Work of Jude Daly

Bettie Parsons Barger

In a quiet studio off her bedroom, with a small window and skylights, Jude Daly sits at a wooden desk with a lamp. Her acrylic paints surround her, as she works on the paper that she has stretched herself, using a hairdryer to speed up the drying time of her thin layers of paint. Sometimes there is soft music playing in the background, but mostly she works in the quiet. For Daly, the solitude allows her to concentrate on the images she is creating.

To Everything There Is a Season: Biography

Jude Kenny was born on August 24, 1951, in London. Her father, a Merchant Navy Sea captain, took a job in civil service after Jude was born (pers. comm.). He found post-war London to be grey and depressing and looked for somewhere with a warmer climate and wide-open spaces. When Jude was eighteen months old, her family moved to Cape Town, South Africa. She was an active child in the small seaside village, "with a glorious beach," of Fish Hoek with her mother, father, older brother, and eventually, her grandfather. Daly described herself as "having ants in [her] pants" and was never one for sitting still for long (pers. comm.). She walked on the beach, sucking mint imperials with her grandfather, played cards, climbed trees, and learned how to do woodwork. When she was interested in reading, she delighted in poetry, Beatrix Potter's stories, and Enid Blyton's novels about Noddy.

Daly looked back on her "charmed" childhood from "a child's point of view, before becoming conscious of the worries and injustices of the world" (pers. comm.). It was not until later that she realized there was a "horrid, cruel, terrible world of apartheid so cleverly constructed that other than maids and delivery 'boys,' [she] had no contact with people with different coloured skins" (pers. comm.). She went on to reflect that even answering a question about what it was like growing up in South Africa "makes [her] skin crawl at the shame of it all. That alongside [her] secure, comfortable childhood, other children were living in dire, de-humanizing conditions for no other reason than their skin was not 'white'" (pers. comm.).

Jude began working on her graphic design degree at Cape Technical College where she met her future husband, Niki Daly. After a year, she left her program and moved to London. As Daly reflects on this decision, she thought it was a good thing because she "never mastered the art of being slick" (Kumar 2007, 42). Daly believes she might have lost her style had she learned other styles and techniques while in school (pers. comm.). Niki and Jude married in 1973 and had their first son, Joe, in 1979. When Joe was approximately eighteen months old, the Dalys moved back to Cape Town. Leo, the Dalys' second son, was born in 1982 (pers. comm.).

When her sons were school age, in 1990, Daly wanted to get back into art. She began working with papier mâché, sculpting animals and people before painting them. These were sold at markets and galleries. At this time, Niki was creating the children's book list, Songololo Books. He had several manuscripts around the house, and Jude asked to play around with one of them, as an exercise. She created a dummy book for the text, which Greenwillow Publishers in the United States picked up. *The Dove*, written by Dianne Stewart, was Daly's first illustrated picture book, beginning this new venture "almost by chance" (pers. comm.).

The Books

Since then, Daly has illustrated over eighteen picture books, three of which she is both author and illustrator. Daly believes her style is "fairly fixed" and that her art seems "to suit a certain genre of story" (pers. comm.). Many of her picture books illustrate myths, legends, or other types of folklore. One of the perks of illustrating someone else's texts is that they have themes that Daly claims she would never "dream up," although many have similar themes, those of kindness and fairness. Daly believes that her books should maintain a sense of wonder and "serve up the profound as simply as possible" (pers. comm.).

Daly likes texts that present a new challenge and feels that "one has to sort of fall in love with the story and feel so possessive about the text that one can't bear the idea of anyone else illustrating it." She believes that illustrators are "at risk of losing ownership of the work, their uniqueness," if they allow other influences to come between the story and the art (pers. comm.). That strong connection with the text is reflected in her art. Critics have reflected that Daly's detailed art matches Hofmeyr's bold text in *Do the Whales Still Sing?* and the mystical feel in Hofmeyr's *The Stone: A Persian Legend of the Magi* (*Publishers Weekly* 1995; Rosenberg 2008).

When Daly was asked to reflect on her role within South African children's literature, she was humble and gracious. Initially, she was reluctant to comment on this, saying that her knowledge was not vast enough to answer this question. Instead, she stated that she believed her job, as an author and illustrator, was to bring "dignity to the simplest of lives represented." She has seen the lack of local texts available to children addressed with more publications in the past few years. Now is the time to "open it up," to show children a wide range of cultures, countries, and stories, hoping to add "to the range of illustration available in local books" (pers. comm.). Daly's diversity of settings and content for her picture books reflect these beliefs.

Honors and Awards

Daly won the prestigious Katrine Harries Award for illustrations for her work in Hofmeyr's *The Stone* and also for the illustrations in Stewart's *The Gift of the Sun: A Tall Tale from South Africa* (Kumar 2007). She was won several other awards for her illustrations including: International Board on Books for Young People Illustrator Honour Book and a Smithsonian (U.S.A.) notable book, all for *The Gift of the Sun,* and *The Hungry Mind Review* (U.S.A) children's book of distinction for Stewart's *The Dove* (Kumar 2011). Daly's grace and humility show in her comment about winning the South African Katrine Harries Award twice: "Though I feel quite undeserving, I feel honored to have been awarded" (pers. comm.).

Artistic Process

Each of Daly's picture books, which have been described as both quietly and powerfully moving (Dickinson 2007; Heale 2008), takes her approximately eighteen months to complete. She begins with pencil sketches before creating a dummy book, where she designs every element, from layout to composition, on paper that is the actual size for the proposed book. Finally she begins the painting stage, sketching her illustrations before applying thin watery layers of acrylic paint (pers. comm.). Hofmeyr, for whom Daly has illustrated four picture books, reflected on Daly's work: "Jude Daly's illustrations, with her bird's eye view and ability to capture immense vistas in the limited space of a page, whether portraying the deserts of Persia, the rolling hills of Natal or the distant horizons of the Atlantic Ocean, have always had the landscape of Africa at their root" (2008, 118). In her comment, Hofmeyr identifies many of the elements that are present in Daly's illustrations.

Content

Frequently, the paintings in Daly's picture books include vast landscapes. Daly creates quiet, spacious pictures that seem almost empty (Heale 2008, 2009). These "expansive, extra-wide horizontal illustrations take in the whole sweep of the rather austere landscape yet retain an anchoring intimacy" (Parravano 1996, 83), showing how the characters are temporarily part of a large world (Hannavy 2006). Her images depict the wide-open spaces that her father was seeking when he moved the family to South Africa. Daly's landscapes have been described as simple and rolling (Connor 2010; Roback, Brown, Britton, & Zaleski 2001), showing lush, pastoral images (*Kirkus Review* 2006; *Publishers Weekly* 2000) that seem to dominate each illustration (Walkins 2006). These landscapes are consistently present in her work.

Even while illustrating a variety of countries, Daly makes great use of landscapes. *Chirchir Is Singing* (Cunnane) and *Lila and the Secret of Rain* (Conway) are both set in Kenya. *The Elephant's Pillow* (Roome) is set in China. *Inside the Books: Readers and Libraries Around the World* (Buzzeo) and *Let There Be Peace: Prayers from Around the World* (Brooks) depict diverse countries and cultures. *Fair, Brown and Trembling* is set in Ireland. Her native South Africa is the setting for *To Everything There Is a Season, Sivu's Six Wishes, The Gift of the Sun* (Stewart), *The Dove* (Stewart) and *Seb & Hamish. The Faraway Island* (Hofmeyr) depicts a Portuguese location. Ancient Egypt and Persia are the settings of Hofmeyr's *The Star-Bearer: A Creation Myth from Ancient Egypt* and *The Stone: A Persian Legend of the Magi. Way Up and Over Everything* (McGill) and *Imani's Music* (Williams) are set in the United States, dealing with issues of slavery. Her settings are varied, but all have landscapes as a focal point of the art (Boyd 2011).

One of the comments many critics note about Daly's representation of Africa in her illustrations is her genuine and realistic images. Heale (2000) described *The Gift of the Sun* as "superbly illustrated by Jude Daly with spacious, airy, glowing artwork which is full of accurate observations of genuine rural life in Africa presented with dignity and affection" (n.p.). *Sivu's Six Wishes* sets the ancient Taoist tale in contemporary Cape Town, showing a variety of realistic representations of South Africans (Rochman 2010). In *The Dove* Daly's illustrations "show American readers an unexotic Africa with children living lives not too different from their own" (Andrews 1993, 220). To

Everything There is a Season shows the universality of experiences families in South Africa share with other families around the world. Daly says, "I am pleased to think that I have had the opportunity to reflect South African and African lives in children's picture books, where up until fairly recently, this was not the case" (pers. comm.). Her realistic and honest portrayal of settings allows readers to gain a better understanding of the contexts of her picture books.

Style

Daly's style is often described as folk art (e.g., Connor 2010; Johnson and Giorgis 2001), which is uncommon in South African children's literature. Kiefer (2010) describes folk art as created by self-taught artists, like Daly. This type of art is often characterized by a simple design, with minimal use of perspective or realistic images. Folk artists pay careful attention to color, as Daly often does, using bright hues as elements of design, and detail with simplicity of style.

Many of Daly's reviewers comment on her simple style (Andrews 1993; *Publishers Weekly* 1995, 1996, 2004). Her figures are often stylized and willowy (Bloom 2001; Connor 2010; *Kirkus Review* 2001). They are almost fragile, similar to medieval portraiture (Bush, 2006; McDowell 2000); most of her small figures seem to be miniatures (*Kirkus Review* 2006, 2010; *Publishers Weekly* 2006; Walkins 2006).

With her vast landscapes and her diminutive figures, Daly also plays with scale and perspective, elements of design often found in folk art. One critic said of *The Gift of the Sun*, "Creatively tinkering with traditional perspective and scale, Daly's comically detailed, folk art-like pictures have the same playfulness as Stewart's storytelling" (*Publishers Weekly* 1996, 83). Her illustrations are sophisticated and spare at the very same time, which Mears (2000) believes could be challenging for some children.

Another element of folk art that Daly utilizes in her illustrations is color. Call (2001) said that *The Star-Bearer* is uplifted by Daly's use of jewel-toned colors, which have been described as luscious (Budin 2000; Decandido 2004; Zaleski, Roback, Brown, and Britton 2001). Daly's art in *Sivu's Six Wishes* is done in a rich, clear palette, which has been described as quietly stunning (Parravano 2011). For *The Gift of the Sun; Chirchir Is Singing; Fair, Brown, and Trembling; Thank You, Jackson;* and *To Everything There Is a Season* she uses soft colors (Freeman, Lehman, and Scharer 1998; *Kirkus Review* 2006; Lehman, Short, Son, and Kiefer 2007; McDowell 2000; Walkins 2006) for many of the backgrounds, to create a mood, while inserting bright colors as a focal point (Andrews 1993; Rochman 1995, 2000, 2010). She does the same in her set of concept books: *Animals*, *Bugs*, *Colours*, and *Opposites*. One reviewer said that the rich, warm colors in *The Dove* create a low-key mood (*Publishers Weekly* 1993, 79). In *The Tale of Paradise Lost* (Willard) her full-color illustrations are said to soften the violence of the story (*Publishers Weekly* 2004).

Daly also uses color to contrast different aspects of the story. For example, in *Lila and the Secret of Rain* she has blue skies and vivid colors in the beginning but moves to sepia tones when the village is in the drought. In *Let there be Peace* she has more color in the peaceful scenes than she does with the juxtaposed images of unsettledness. As Sivu makes more and more greedy wishes, the vibrant colors diminish in *Sivu's Six Wishes*. Again, she uses contrast in *Imani's Music* to make a point. "The sun-drenched colors depicting the African landscape where people and animals live in joyous harmony contrast sharply with the dark pallet used to depict the harsh realities of the slave ship's journey" (Saccardi 2002, 114). Her use of color helps convey moods. Scenes from *Way Up and Over Everything* look like dramatic tableaux, helping readers feel the emotions of sadness, despair, and hope as the story unfolds (Stevenson 2008). Others, like those in *The Gift of the Sun*, have an anchoring intimacy (Parravano 1996). Her illustrations in *To Everything There Is a Season* allow readers to be in quiet, optimistic contemplation (Bush 2006).

Format

Not only does she use color to create a feeling for a book, but she also uses eloquent design (Heale 2009). Her illustrations comprise a variety of layouts and perspectives to help the reader focus on the important elements (Freeman, Lehman, & Scharer 1998; Heale 2000; Stewig 2006). In most picture books, Daly makes use of panels to separate images—and often text—from one another. Daly said, "I like to keep the text out of my pictures!" (pers. comm.); therefore the majority of her illustrations are framed with plenty of white space for the text. "This design orientation makes the reader observe each illustration closely to interpret the connection to the words and to spot the tiny, cleverly inserted details" (*Kirkus Review* 2006, 129). Her pictures are suggestive, allowing readers to come to their own conclusions (Hannavy 2006; *Kirkus Review* 2010).

Intrigue

Many of her books also have images that extend the text. In *The Gift of the Sun,* the illustrations "extend the connections that are the heart of this funny story" (Rochman 1996, 145). In *The Stone*, the images suggest many struggles the travelers face that the text does not address. Each illustration in her concept books, like *Colours*, depicts a certain item in a specific color. These are combined on the last page, forming a complete image, allowing the reader to co-create a story. Also, in several of her picture books, Daly has objects hidden on every page. In *Imani's Music* (Saccardi 2002), Imani is hidden on almost every page, a whale in *Do the Whales Still Sing?*, the playful cat in *Fair Brown and Trembling*, and a doll in *To Everything There Is a Season*. These details pique the reader's attention.

Daly's illustrations provide readers with a "visual feast" (*Publishers Weekly* 2004). She uses bright colors contrasted with soft, earthy backgrounds to set the mood and elicit emotions. Paneled images help to focus readers. The varied perspectives ask the reader to pay careful attention to the illustrations, as do her "hidden" objects and her extensions of the text. Her art not only captures the reader's attention, but holds it as one turns each and every page. Her genuine representations of settings and vast landscapes create a very authentic feeling, allowing the reader to trust her illustration. Daly's gentleness and humility spill into each and every painting she creates.

In an article about South African illustrators, Diane Hofmeyr (2008) writes that the island in *The Faraway Island* is "transformed not just by the man but by Jude Daly's magical three-haired brush" (119). An element of magic characterizes all Daly's illustrations as she captivates readers from cover to cover.

Children's Books

Brooks, Jeremy. 2009. *Let There be Peace: Prayers from Around the World*. Illustrated by Jude Daly. London: Frances Lincoln.
Conway, David. 2007. *Lila and the Secret of Rain*. Illustrated by Jude Daly. London: Frances Lincoln.
Cunnane, Kelly. 2011. *Chirchir Is Singing*. Illustrated by Jude Daly. New York: Schwartz & Wade.
Daly, Jude. 2000. *Fair, Brown, & Trembling: An Irish Cinderella Story*. New York: Farrar, Straus & Giroux.
_____. 2006. *To Everything There Is a Season*. Grand Rapids, MI: Eerdmans Books for Young Readers.
_____. 2010. *Sivu's Six Wishes*. Grand Rapids, MI: Eerdmans Books for Young Readers.
_____. 2013. *Animals*. Cape Town, SA: Little Hands Trust.
_____. 2013. *Bugs*. Cape Town, SA: Little Hands Trust.
_____. 2013. *Colours*. Cape Town, SA: Little Hands Trust.
_____. 2013. *Opposites*. Cape Town, SA: Little Hands Trust.
_____. 2014. *Seb & Hamish*. Illustrated by Niki Daly. London: Frances Lincoln.
_____. 2015. *Thank You, Jackson*. Illustrated by Jude Daly. London: Frances Lincoln.
Hofmeyr, Dianne. 1995. *Do the Whales Still Sing?* Illustrated by Jude Daly. New York: Dial Books for Young Readers.

———. 1998. *The Stone: A Persian Legend of the Magi*. Illustrated by Jude Daly. New York: Farrar, Straus & Giroux.

———. 2001. *The Star-Bearer: A Creation Myth from Ancient Egypt*. Illustrated by Jude Daly. New York: Farrar, Straus & Giroux.

———. 2008. *The Faraway Island*. Illustrated by Jude Daly. London: Frances Lincoln.

McGill, Alice. 2008. *Way Up and Over Everything*. Illustrated by Jude Daly. New York: Houghton Mifflin.

Roome, Diana Reynolds. 2003. *The Elephant's Pillow*. Illustrated by Jude Daly. New York: Farrar, Straus & Giroux.

Stewart, Dianne. 1993. *The Dove*. Illustrated by Jude Daly. Cape Town, SA: Songololo Books.

———. 1996. *The Gift of the Sun: A Tall Tale from South Africa*. Illustrated by Jude Daly. London: Frances Lincoln.

Willard, Nancy. 2004. *The Tale of Paradise Lost*. Illustrated by Jude Daly. New York: Atheneum Books for Young Readers.

Williams, Sheron. 2002. *Imani's Music*. Illustrated by Jude Daly. New York: Atheneum Books for Young Readers.

On a Journey with Leon de Villiers

Magdel Vorster

In *Wat Doen Jy Daniel?* (What Are You Doing, Daniel?), a picture book by Leon de Villiers, a little boy lies on his back with his grandfather and inspects the world from a different angle. A new angle, a different perspective, is often the driving force behind Leon de Villiers's inspiration to write. He describes himself as a nomad. Writing for him is going on a journey through his own undiscovered inner self. He is never sure where exactly this journey will lead or end or how he will get to his destination, but each journey turns out as an enrichment in some way (Greyling 2004). In an interview with Ihette Jacobs (2007) he states that writing for him should stay a challenge and that he therefore has to come up with something new every time.

De Villiers admires the work of Michael Ende, Roald Dahl and J.R.R. Tolkien because they have written books that speak to their readers on different levels. He feels books should touch their readers intellectually as well as stimulate imagination and multiple emotions (Loots 2005). He also believes that children should be exposed to a wide variety of texts to be able to pursue their own uniqueness through what they read. Rather than demanding that children read, he maintains that they should be introduced to the wonder, danger, fun and challenges that different texts offer (Vermaak 2005).

De Villiers was born in 1960 in Pretoria. After finishing school he obtained a Bachelor of Arts degree, a Higher Education Diploma and an honors degree in political science at the University of Pretoria. After teaching for a couple of years, he started writing full time in 1993 (Wybenga and Snyman 2005).

Humor and Absurdity

Flights of imagination help De Villiers to stay nomadic, and all fiction involves imagination. It is believed that Francis Bacon said that imagination was a quality given to man to compensate him for what he was not, and regarding De Villiers could be extended to add compensation for where he could not be. Bacon presumably added to this that a sense of humor was given to man to console him for what he is (http://www.goodreads.com/quotes/tag/imagination?page=3).

Some of the best examples of humor in children's literature rely on the brilliant use of language to create the absurd, the surprising, the unexpected and the outrageous. In *Erik en die Kido-Dinges* (Erik and the Kidorary) the ten-year-old Erik and his pet spider Hairy are exchanged at the Kidorary (a place where parents can swap their children) for a better-behaved child. Erik has had to clean up after the dog as punishment and consequently wished he were part of a different family. De Villiers captures his young readers in the first sentence by using toilet humor, before he continues to keep them interested and amused with the unexpected and original. After the swap Erik ends up with parents who worry about everything and after he has had to live in a padded room and bathe with a safety belt among other strange and very comical safety measures, he, with the help of Hairy, manages to exchange his new parents for his real parents at the Parentary, another De Villiers creation. *Erik en die Kido-Dinges* is a very funny and fast easy-read for nine- to eleven-year-olds (Meiring 2004).

De Villiers displays a highly original sense of humor in a few of his titles where fantasy also plays a role. Almost all fantasy consists of elements of magic, which refers to something or somebody equipped of the supernatural to influence something particular or to cause a particular event (De Villiers 2012). For example, in *Elsie Soek 'n Strooihoed* (Elsie Wants a Straw Hat), the first picture book De Villiers wrote, Elsie is a cow and goes wandering through town to find a straw hat. She visits, among other places, a computer shop, a bookshop and a hardware shop. She walks past a butchery and is horrified when she realizes that no right-minded cow should enter a butchery. She finds a hat, but with no money, she returns to the farm sad and empty-handed. Her mood, however, is changed when she's given an old hat by the farm girl.

My Sussie se Tande (My Little Sister's Teeth) is another unique and funny picture book by De Villiers. Jannie's baby sister is teething, and she chews on anything she can find, even biting a hole right through her bed. Jannie flees up to the clouds with their family dog until the doctor arrives to extract his sister's teeth. De Villiers started this fantasy in reality with a real scenario, and elements of the supernatural add hilarious absurdities to be enjoyed by all age groups.

As children grow in language proficiency, words become a source of amusement and their sense of humor grows (Cairney 2009). In the beginners' manual for anyone interested in keeping domestic monsters, *Ek en My Monster* (My Monster and I), De Villiers takes full advantage of this aspect. Realistic writing contributes to the story's humor, and it would be hard for very young readers to discern between reality and fantasy. Marjorie van Heerden's highly original illustrations of all the monster species perfectly complement their names, which provide evidence of De Villiers's talent at word play and creating new words. They include names like "Libiese Boudus Enormous" (Libyan Enormous Bum), "Australiese Ouwtbek" (Australian Outback) and the "Toskaanse Terrorkotta" (Tuscan Terrorcotta). In this very tongue-in-cheek book, De Villiers also deals with feeding guides, hygiene of monsters, teaching monsters tricks, the relationship between monster and human owner, and the fear meter against which prospective monster owners can decide what they could handle (Brand 2005).

In *Die Klein Seuntjie en die Drake* (The Little Boy and the Dragons), De Villiers again displays his sense of humor through the use of language as well as the creation of absurd scenarios. A little boy is confronted by three big dragons. They block his way and try everything to scare him, but he stays calm and explains that he is on a mission to help his friend, Karpat, who has phoned him on his cell phone earlier. The little boy is portrayed as quite cheeky in the way he almost challenges the dragons, empowering young readers or listeners to be brave in facing scary situations while humor is maintained in the dialogue and complementary illustrations. Each page starts with dialogue from the boy, and he is then interrupted by the three dragons who from biggest to smallest make fun of him, each one elaborating on what the one before him said. The typography of this book is original and vivid. Each character's picture precedes his dialogue and the font size resembles the size of the character. De Villiers also has fun with synonyms in this book. He uses eight synonyms for "big," such as "huge, enormous, large, gigantic," etc., through this book, and they are all, appropriately, printed in capitals.

The little boy finally overpowers the dragons by soaking them with his water pistol and putting their flames out, but he then feels sorry for them and dries them with his handkerchief. On his way with his laser sword to aid his little dragon friend, Karpat, he receives another phone call from Karpat in which the dragon explains that he has freed himself by pulling his toe out of a drain, so no longer needs the little boy. The little boy's name is only revealed when he answers his phone at the end of the story, and the choice of Ivan is just another sign of this author's fine sense of humor and attention to detail as it alludes to Ivan the Dragonsmith, a familiar toy character from the recent past.

De Villiers showcases his love for nature and animals in the original and funny collection of animal stories, *Tales from the Marula Tree*. Every night at sunset a troop of baboons climbs to the top of the big Marula tree[1] from where they watch for the evening star to appear before starting the storytelling ritual of the night. A variety of fifteen stories, told by the elders of the troop, are presented on white paper, while the comments and requests for more stories by the baboon audience are done on blue to tie all the stories together until the end when Grootbek (Big Mouth) asks whether the moon felt like hearing a story. Stories are woven around topics like why kudu have spiraled horns, where buffalo lost their stripes, what happened when giraffes had a big fright, and where guinea fowl got their name. Emily Bornoff's sensitive illustrations, in particular of the baboons, perfectly complement the rich humor displayed throughout the stories.

Fantasy with Social Commentary

Fantasy, where the laws of nature can function differently or in a newly designed way, can help the author to move even further away from the reality with which the reader is familiar. An imaginary world of fantasy can in fact require childlike freedom of thought while still maintaining a more mature theme. The story, therefore, would communicate to readers on different levels, which De Villiers aims to achieve. Children would enjoy the fantasy for what it is, and adults or more mature readers would grasp and understand hidden social commentary. Thus, fantasy is often used by the author as a vessel for commentary on society (De Villiers 2012).

In *Droomoog Diepgrawer* (Dreamy Eyed Deep Digger), the main characters are reminiscent of meerkats or mongooses, but are explained by De Villiers to be "Erde," a made-up species of nocturnal creatures living underground. "Erde" is German for earth and also closely links to the Afrikaans word, "Aarde." The Deep Diggers family has to leave their colony after a naughty stunt by the triplets. They meet other Erd, each with their own characteristics and talents, as well as everyone's biggest enemy, Vreet (loosely translated as Guzzler), in their search for a new home. In detailed descriptions of each species' characteristics and with original narrative, De Villiers successfully manages to warn against stereotyping and short-sightedness without moralizing. One of the groups uses glow worms to light their underground tunnels and archive their life lessons through memory stones kept in a story hole. In his travels Dreamy Eyes comes across groups that question and others that invent new plans. With his natural tendency to plan and his courage when they are attacked by Vreet, Dreamy Eyes becomes the hero. He learns that those embracing renewal contribute towards a wider and better world by reinventing old truths through adding, exchanging and creatively applying new information. De Villiers won the Alba Bouwer Award for Children's Literature for *Droomoog Diepgrawer* in 2004 (Vorster 2004).

De Villiers debuted as an author with *Aliens en Engele* (Aliens and

Angels), a novel in which elements of fantasy again are used as tools towards social commentary. The main character, Pieter, is ten years old and lives with his divorced mother in an apartment. Pieter's imagination about the nine floors of the building being nine planets, and his adventures with Nebiekatneser, his very naughty pet brick, are repeatedly interrupted by reality. The story starts off in a light-hearted manner, but turns more serious when the reader realizes that Pieter is in fact suffering from emotional deprivation and that he is creating a world for his own survival, because his Mom, her new friend, his Dad, and his dad's new girlfriend seem like aliens to him. During the day he plays with Nebiekatneser and rides the elevator, or spaceship, past the other planets to get out at Neptune, where they live. He has one other friend in the building who lives one level above him on Pluto, Uncle Niel. Madeleine Roux's (1997) book review describes this novel as a jewel. She emphasizes that De Villiers's use of humor and imagination is evident in his knowledge of children and their ways of thinking.

Some children's and youth literature authorities strongly argue that young readers should not be underestimated or stereotyped. They believe that they deserve unpredictable and original books to stimulate further thinking and to encourage them to look at the world differently. De Villiers likes to write for these flexible readers who look at the familiar from a different angle, and *Groete van die Hiëna* (Greetings from the Hyena) is one of the best examples here. In this title, the main character, Roek Rykema, is confused. He is unhappy with himself and everyone around him. It feels as if his whole life is upside down, which then becomes the literal case when he lands in the Palace of Chaos. A journey through strange but parallel worlds, fantasies, and stories from his subconscious follows. In the unpredictability of life and the future, he has to find and interpret patterns of good and evil, weak and strong, and pretty and ugly for himself. He finally travels through the Garden of Order. Roek learns that chaos exists inside order, and he has to accept himself before he can be accepted by people around him. This learning process takes Roek through phases of self-pity, fear, aggression, and introspection until finally reaching self-acceptance. He is literally stripped, as he loses a piece of clothing in each chapter until he is naked and has only himself and the choices he has to make to face.

Groete van die Hiëna will not be enjoyed or even understood by all readers; it is especially aimed at those who are willing to be flexible, to be stretched and even disturbed by what they read. De Villiers brilliantly succeeds here in forcing his readers to think while being entertained (Vorster and Van der Walt 2000). One could conclude that, through this story, he is commenting on complicated family relationships and a teenager's fear of failure and difficulties around maintaining individuality among peer pressure. Chaos theory, the connection between chaos and creativity and the therapeutic value of stories are important subthemes in this novel. Marié Jacobs (2000) describes *Groete van die Hiena* as a reading adventure for the sophisticated teenage or mature reader who believes in the creative and healing power of words.

Social Commentary in Realistic Fiction

In addition to fantasy, De Villiers conveys social commentary in his realistic fiction, which accurately reflects life as it could be lived today and helps readers move forward to a clearer understanding of themselves and others. In *Die Pro* (The Pro) the main character is the seventeen-year-old Tiaan who is also the narrator. The main theme of the book is his processing of a best friend's death by drowning. His character develops from anger and denial to final acceptance and overcoming feelings of guilt, grief and egocentrism.

De Villiers weaves his story through letters from Tiaan to his deceased friend and his biology study notes. The heavy theme of the book is lightened by these humorous notes and Tiaan's budding relationship. Young readers will also be able to identify with and be drawn in by the portrayal of a narrow-minded school and church system, dysfunctional families and the lack of or weak communication between teenagers and their elders (Wybenga and Snyman 2005). Even though De Villiers says that he tries not to consciously moralize in his books (Jacobs 2007), it is clear that this book, like many of his others, carries a message. Barrie Hough (1997), former South African children's book author, says in a review that this is an honest book stripped of dishonest pretensions and that the theme here is, "Cowboys can and do cry" (16). De Villiers was awarded the M.E.R. prize as well as the Scheepers Prize for youth literature for *Die Pro* in 1998.

Social Commentary or Subversive Messages?

Children's literature has long included grave cultural issues or complex sociopolitical concerns and is increasingly discussing topics which had previously been ignored or even forbidden, pushing the boundaries in daring directions (Abate 2010). In *Wat Doen Jy Daniel?* (What Are You Doing, Daniel?), Daniel and his grandfather are lying on their backs in different rooms of the house to look at things from a different angle. They end up outside where they look at the clouds, the birds and the changing colors of the sky as the sun sets. De Vries (2008) praises De Villiers for the way in which this book challenges Afrikaans children to look at things from a different perspective.

According to him Afrikaans parents are reluctant to allow children to interpret outside the norm. He continues to then mention *Cheeky*, a translation from the Afrikaans (*Parmant*) also by De Villiers. Cheeky is a cute little crocodile and several other animals want to pet, hug or kiss him. Staying true to his name, however, each time he adamantly declares that his little body belongs to him and refuses. De Vries again states that "saying no" to adults is not the norm among traditional Afrikaans-speaking and even general South African circles. This story will empower children to say no when strangers or those familiar to them want to touch them in ways that make them feel uncomfortable. *Cheeky* was first only published in Afrikaans as *Parmant* and illustrated by Samantha van Riet. Subsequently it was translated into English, and a new version illustrated by Alzette Prins followed in English and Afrikaans.

In *Shorn*, a young adult novel originally published in Afrikaans as *Toko* and translated into English, De Villiers creates an alternative and primitive civilization where non-conformists are not tolerated (Fourie 2007). Although he wanted to establish an African atmosphere, his main aim was the establishment of a primitive society, and so used white characters in a typically black tribal environment (Jacobs 2007). *Shorn* could be classified as iconoclastic, and De Vries (2008) argues that De Villiers' subversive brain is clearly showcased here. Perhaps a clue to this is found in the book's dedication where De Villiers mentions those whose hands build (create) rather than break (destroy). Fanie Viljoen (2007) praises the way in which De Villiers succeeds in inventing a mystical new world by actually creating an old world.

In order to motivate the main characters' behavior, De Villiers uses different perspectives, including those of Shal, Toko's half-brother and enemy; Vasi, Toko's sister; Rako, Toko's cousin; and Toko himself. Through this De Villiers shows that people often act cruelly and aggressively because their lives have been destroyed by others, and in doing so a vicious circle is created (Jacobs 2007). This technique also contributes to building suspense and keeping readers interested (Viljoen 2007).

Toko is chosen to carry the water up the mountain where a number of young men, referred to as young lions, are gathered for an initiation ritual in which their heads are shaved and they are left to do whatever they want before they return to be considered mature men who could get married. No laws, morality or justice exist on this mountain, and it is therefore here that Shal awaits Toko, who has long stood out as an individual (Fourie 2007). Shal has orders from his father, the tribal leader, that Toko was not to return to the village again. In the scene on the mountain, De Villiers does not shy away from the violent, crude dialogue and actions expected from initiation candidates, and a strong line of suspense is built up through the various narrative perspectives. In the end it is through Toko, who goes against the laws of the elders with his wood carvings, that years of deceit and evil are revealed and a new freer era commences. Like the boys on the mountain who choose their new names when they become men, Toko, when at last accepted as a prominent figure of the future, chooses Tanako as his new name. Where his old name meant clay that could be molded and stamped on, his new name carries the meaning of the source of his creations, namely forest, holding in itself a promise of a fruitful future.

On the Road Again

In reply to a question about favorite moments while writing *Shorn*, De Villiers revealed that he loved experiencing a different world with distinctive characters and dialogue (Jacobs 2007). Together with his other books, clearly these new worlds and extraordinary characters created by him would keep a nomad on the road. Even though the tent or means of travel might stay the same at times, his readers can be guaranteed many new places still to be explored while familiar concepts might be shaken up to stimulate brand new ideas and beliefs.

Note

1. The Marula tree is indigenous to the woodlands of Southern Africa, the Sudano-Sahelian area of West Africa, and Madagascar.

Children's Books

De Villiers, Leon. 1996. *Aliens en Engele*. Cape Town, SA: Tafelberg
———. 1997. *Die Pro*. Cape Town, SA: Tafelberg.
———. 2000. *Groete van die Hiëna*. Cape Town, SA: Tafelberg.
———. 2001. *Elsie Soek 'n Strooihoed*. Illustrated by Nico Meyer. Pretori, SA: LAPA.
———. 2001. *Wat Doen Jy Daniel?* Illustrated by Annelie van der Vyver. Pretoria, SA: LAPA.
———. 2003. *Die Klein Seuntjie en die Drake*. Illustrated by Marriana Booyens. Pretoria: LAPA.
———. 2003. *Droomoog Diepgrawer*. Illustrated by Berco Wilsenach. Pretoria, SA: LAPA.
———. 2003. *Erik en die Kido-dinges*. Illustrated by Nicolene Louw. Pretoria, SA: LAPA.
———. 2003. *Parmant*. Illustrated by Samantha van Riet. Pretoria, SA: LAPA.
———. 2004. *Ek en My Monster*. Illustrated by Marjorie van Heerden. Pretoria, SA. LAPA.
———. 2004. *My Sussie se Tande!* Illustrated by Vian Oelofsen. Pretoria, SA: LAPA.
———. 2007. *Tales from the Marula Tree*. Illustrated by Emily Bornoff. Pretoria, SA: LAPA.
———. 2007. *Toko*. Pretoria, SA. LAPA.
———. 2009. *Shorn*. Translated by Elsa Silke. Pretoria, SA: LAPA.
———. 2011. *Cheeky*. Illustrated by Alzette Prins. Pretoria, SA: LAPA.

Piet Grobler's Little Bird Told Me

Magdel Vorster

In 2005 in an interview with a Dutch newspaper, Piet Grobler said: "There are almost always birds in my illustrations. They are my favorites in the animal kingdom. A bird is the ideal animal; it carries no baggage along, it sees so much more than any other animal" (Van Vlimmeren 2005, n.p.). He continued by saying that if there was something like reincarnation, he might have been a bird in a previous life. By giving his own interpretation of a specific culture, he, like a bird effortlessly crossing borders, manages to bring different cultures subtly together, making his work accessible to a worldwide audience, especially if translated into different languages (Gericke 2008).

Two examples of Grobler's books can serve as a metaphor for his work. In *Little Bird's ABC*, Grobler produces an onomatopoeical interpretation of the alphabet, using his favorite character, the bird (Authors Voices 2008). "G" is "Grrr!!" as a big bird snarls at a smaller one that has just pulled its tail. "M" for "Mmm" is followed by "N" for "Nice worm!" as the same colorful bird swallows his doomed victim. Grobler uses a rich variety of color and facial expressions in his line-and-watercolor art to ensure that this small square alphabet book will charm all ages. *The Rainbow Birds* provides wordless double-page spreads of a progression from a sad, colorless Africa with birds visible in a cage, through an addition of one color bird at a time through to glorious seven-color rainbow sunshine. By that time all the "rainbow children of God," as Archbishop Tutu (1993) called them, are dancing and happy.

Grobler does not set any boundaries to a child's imagination. He sees the picture book as a starting point for the child into the world of art, and picture books step across borders. Quoting Kveta Pacovska, he believes, "A book is the first art gallery through which a child walks," and he seeks to make this a memorable and enjoyable experience (Gericke 2008).

Grobler creates an aesthetic universe peopled with humans, animals, angels and monsters. The world in which he renders his brightly colored illustrations is a beguilingly light-hearted one without boundaries and prejudices (Authors Voices 2008). According to Grobler, his visual language borrows from folk and naive art while still leaning towards caricature and humor. He says he is naturally inclined towards lightheartedness, but a lyrical element is present as well. These qualities appeal to both children and adults (Slippers 2013). References to biblical history, classical fables and African folklore are integrated in the stories. Grobler has developed an unmistakable visual idiolect with his playful, humorous approach—the "Pietness," as enthusiasts of his art call it. He uses acrylics, gouache and pastel, but also watercolors and India ink on handmade paper or in combination with collage (Authors Voices 2008).

Staying in South African Skies

In *Makwelane and the Crocodile*, which tells a variation of the Little Red Riding Hood story, Grobler incorporates elements of South African Zulu culture through rich colorful illustrations in mixed media including impressive collage (Authors Voices 2008). When the crocodile beats Makwelane to her grandmother's hut, she does not notice anything, and the eyes of the hornbill, as part of Grobler's subtext in a tree above her head, are closed. Makwelane arrives in time to save her grandmother by throwing her calabash as well as her makwelane (her musical instrument) in the crocodile's mouth. Piet used acrylic paint on acrylic paper with photo collage for detail like eyes, the river, and some rocks and plants, and further detail was done in gouache (Bredenkamp 2006). Grobler's human characters here are very dark brown and dressed in bright colors against muted backgrounds of the browns, greens, and blues, establishing rural scenes (Lehman 2013).

The main message through *Mia's Mom*, written by Marita van der Vyver, one of South Africa's best-known Afrikaans authors, is the magic of storytelling. Even though the stories mentioned are familiar fairy tales originally from Europe, the power of the storyteller is emphasized as the strength of this book. Mia spreads magical stories about her mother among her friends, which are confirmed by her mother at her birthday party when she explains that everything that happens in a story also happens to the storyteller. Grobler uses clear, fine lines for the real characters and rough wax crayon for the fairytale (imaginary) characters. Marita van der Vyver praised Grobler's illustrations in *Mia's Mom*, for the way in which his illustrations helped tell her story (Brand 2005). Van der Vyver and Grobler received the Tienie Holloway Award in 1997, for *Rhinocephants on the roof*, Van der Vyver's first book for young children (Fairer-Wessels and Wessels 2007). In this book Daniel is at a sleepover with his grandparents and at bedtime hears strange scary noises. His imagination leads him to inventing and naming South African animal-derived monsters using word blends like rhinocephants, crocopotamus and baborilla. Grobler's imaginary, colorful illustrations again complement and enhance the story.

Heading North Across Africa

Grobler's bird extended its wings beyond South Africa to the African continent. After he had done a number of educational publications, he actively started illustrating in the cartoon style with naive elements in the 1990s. In *Here I Am*, written by Ann Walton, his style is mainly playful and stylized, with elements of humor. Piet's illustrations offer many examples of how he often portrays more than just supporting the narrative. A burning giraffe on the horizon where the sun sets in the savannah and a waitress in North Africa serving from open drawers in her thigh remind viewers of Salvador Dali's famous painting, "The Burning Giraffe" (Grobler 2004). In the savannah illustration the more informed reader will also find the three flying ducks as well as the ostrich burying his head in the sand. Grobler won the Noma Concours Silver medal for *Here I Am* in 1997 (Fairer-Wessels and Wessels 2007).

Commissioned by his Dutch publisher, Lemniscaat, Grobler in *Please Frog, Just One Sip*, adapted an Australian folk tale into an African setting. In this story, the very thirsty animals of the savannah use endearing tricks while attempting to get water from a selfish frog who drank all the river's water (Authors Voices 2008). The eels finally tickle Frog and the water gushes from his mouth when he breaks into laughter. Grobler's sublime watercolor illustrations on a light apricot background are vibrant and full of motion.

Beverley Naidoo enjoyed working with Grobler on an African version of Aesop's fables, in *Aesop's Fables*, especially when it came to exercising her creative license, lengthening the stories, writing the dialogue and incorporating African animals. She cleverly changed boars into warthogs and goats into klipspringers,[1] while still staying true to the underlying themes and messages of the original fables (Bosman 2011). Grobler's primitive, whimsical watercolor-and-pencil illustrations preserve the African theme and decorative borders set off each fable (*Kirkus Review* 2011).

The Magic Bojabi Tree by Dianne Hofmeyr is a re-telling of an old African tale. A group of very hungry animals stumble across a tree bearing wonderful fruit as good as mango, melon and pomegranate in one. Unfortunately this tree is guarded by a python who would not let anyone near the tree if they can't tell him the tree's name. Grobler's illustrations are scratchy, stylized and humorous, with small clever details on every page. The facial expressions of the animals are particular favorites as they are, in typical Grobler style, portrayed as grumpy, silly and playful rather than cute (Kumagai 2013).

Circling Above Europe

Even working with multicultural content, which flows naturally from his South African background, Grobler's European descent cannot be kept from his work. He feels picture books should lead their readers across borders, and in this regard he has a greater affinity for European illustration than for those of the British. He feels that European illustrators are more prone to experimentation and the abstract than the safer tendency of the British towards realism or interpretation (Nieuwoudt 2002).

Piet worked with Philip de Vos on De Vos's nonsense rhyme collections as well as a regular cartoon for a South African Afrikaans magazine, and he admits that illustration became synonymous with excitement and fun during these times. Illustrating *Carnival of the Animals*, inspired by Camille Saint-Saëns (a French composer) and written in Afrikaans and English by De Vos, stands out as a highlight of his career (Slippers 2013). His mostly brown, gold and blue etchings have been said to recall the work of Paul Klee (Authors Voices 2008). Using the hair-breadth lines of the etching plate, he produced a weird and wonderful array of animal-like people, such as two elegantly dancing elephants (Bentley 2004). This book received several awards, including the Prix Octogones de Chêne from The International Center for the Study of Children's Literature in France in 1999 (Authors Voices 2008).

Illustrations in *Die Spree met Foete* (The Frairy with Feckles), written by Annie M.G. Schmidt and translated into Afrikaans by Philip de Vos, are caricatures done in a sometimes grotesque style to complement Schmidt's eccentric sense of humor (Grobler 2004). In the title poem, a fairy with freckles is sent to the king and nervously introduces herself as a frairy with feckles to explain the title, which otherwise would have been "Die Fee met Sproete," translated as a "The Fairy with Freckles." The reader is already nudged towards what the enigmatic title entails on the flyleaf with Grobler's portrayal of the frairy with feckles in white on an ochre background (Bredenkamp 2006). Piet's illustrations in this volume confirm how strongly he feels that children should not be underestimated and that they should sometimes be intellectually challenged (Retief 2002).

Rooi-Kiri Wordt Verliefd (Red-Kiri Falls in Love) was written and illustrated by Piet Grobler and published by Lemniscaat, one of the oldest and most well-known children's book publishers in Holland. Rooi-Kiri is a little bird, and because it is spring, she desires to fall in love like everyone else. She, however, has no idea who her partner should be and visits different animals to try to find out. In the illustrations every option is visualized by Rooi-Kiri and none of them would work. In the end she discovers that the solution to her problem, another bird, has been under her nose all along (Pople 2008).

Little Mouse is Lida Dijkstra's version of the Friesian parable, sometimes titled "Mouse Bride." A little mouse is adopted by a hermit, and when the time comes for the little mouse to get married, they set out to find the strongest being on earth as bridegroom. Starting off with Sun and then being referred to Cloud, Wind and others, they eventually get to Mountain, who reveals that its crumbling force from the inside is a mouse, culminating then in a mouse wedding and the mouse couple, with their offspring, continuing to live with the hermit. In *School Library Journal,* Grobler's charming, stylized color illustrations are described as the highlight of this version of the folktale. It continues to say that the characters are expressively drawn, from Little Mouse's huge black eyes to the hermit's exuberant hair and wide smile, and the fauna and flora are also mentioned as subtly detailed (Gibson 2005). Grobler's birds are again ever present, and they help take the characters up to the sun and the clouds in the search for the strongest partner.

According to Piet, a sense of humor is one of the most important elements when illustrating iconic stories and when using and playing with caricatures, and humor infuses his particular style. Because of the nature of the stories selected by Marita van der Vyver for a collection of Grimm fairy tales published in Afrikaans as *Die Mooiste Sprokies van Grimm* (The Most Beautiful Grimm Fairy Tales), Grobler's main focus was to entertain, and it was unnecessary to add more layers and dimensions to already well-known and established stories (De Beer 2011). He did however create new worlds from established and well-known material. Rather than being frightened by some of the very scary and explicit fairy tales, children would escape into their own imaginary scenarios, triggered, for example, by Hansel offering a bone to the witch, while casually sitting on a branch with two birds (Pople 2010). Grobler embraces the different demands of texts on an illustrator. Sometimes it is simply as an illustration, but at other times his drawings play a much larger part in the telling of the tale and bringing the message of the story across. With the Grimm tales, the drawings were simply an extension of the stories. He however seldom fails to include his own thoughts as subtext or additional message and because of his distinctive and unique style, it never overshadows or obstructs the written story (De Beer 2011).

Ballade van de Dood (Ballad of Death) written by Koos Meinderts and Harrie Jekkers confirms Grobler's preference for European publishers that are more willing to publish books dealing with often taboo subjects. The Lion King has Death locked up in a glass dome, and a jolly life of parties and embracing everything dangerous follow. Life soon gets boring and becomes too crowded, so Grobler's Death, portrayed as a rabbit in a nursing uniform, is freed. There is a strong contrast between firm lively illustrations and the more subdued and darker images where death is discussed. One of the king's subjects, a big beaked bird, is introduced on the title page and is defined by a one-wheel foot, illustrating the dangers birds face when walking instead of flying, where they have the advantage of seeing more and going about without baggage.

A Visit to the East

Grobler's bird has also traveled to the East. In *Today Is My Day* (Ravishankar), the cheeky main character claims one day of the week for herself and everyone who comes close to intrude on her activities for this day, is punished (i.e. daddy becomes a twittering bird, grandma a cow, her teacher a multiplication sign). Grobler's little messenger bird here again has a one-wheel foot at the start of the book and two by the end of the story, another subtle message of dangers faced. Marina Le Roux (2004) describes Grobler's illustrations as surprising and sharp while not shocking or insulting, as well as humoristic while not vulgar.

Nowhere is Piet's versatility better illustrated than in *Doctor Me Di Cin* (2001) by Roberto Piumini and set in China. Prince Ma La Di is sick, and his father summons Doctor Me Di Cin. The doctor prescribes a dose of fresh air, but the young prince refuses to leave the palace. Every day the doctor returns to the palace empty-handed; instead of herbs for an herbal cure, he brings news of what he has seen in nature. Very soon the prince is so intrigued by these reports that he ventures outside with the doctor. Grobler's ink-and-watercolor illustrations include whimsical plants and birds drawn from Chinese folklore. Pictures assembled from pieces of torn paper represent images that the prince creates from his imagination and add a three-dimensional quality to some of the pages.

Aiming South Across New Borders

Grobler has to date illustrated two books by the Argentinian-born Mexican author, Jorge Luján. In *Sky Blue Accident*, a boy is riding his bicycle when he is distracted by a bird and crashes into the sky. This bird is not mentioned in the text; it acts like a totem-bird that seems to preside over the fantastic events through the short story. Pieces of the sky fall out, and the boy collects these pieces in his pocket. At school he offers a few pieces to his teacher, who then grows wings and flies out the window, accompanied by the bird. There is now a big hole in the sky, causing lost clouds to bump into each other. The children come to the rescue and paint the sky back, and when there is still a piece missing, the boy produces a few pieces of the real sky from his pocket to put the universe back in order. The last blue triangle, however, is handed to the boy by the totem-bird, confirming its importance. Maria Forte (2007) describes this book as clever and fanciful and remarks that the illustrations capture the whimsical nature of the story.

The first bird in their other book, *Colors!;Colores!*, is found with the first color mentioned—beige—where a seagull is sitting on a broken fence. This book is more than an introduction to colors. From the first of the single-stanza poems, where beige falls asleep on the sand, young readers are lifted out of the mundane to explore the world of color. The harmony of the words and images send the imagination flying on a magical rainbow of a ride, made all the more expansive by the apparent simplicity of both. Time passes signaled by the yellow disc of the sun, rolling through the daytime sky with a wave of birds, to night appearing, wearing her black gown. Grobler's broad swathes of watercolor blend to create a subtle spectrum for each hue, against which more defined details, like children, birds and trees are set (Coughlan 2008).

Touching Down in the United Kingdom

Since 1989, Grobler had lived in Stellenbosch in the Western Cape with his wife, Marietjie, and daughter, Catharina, until they moved to the United Kingdom, where he is currently a senior lecturer and course leader in illustration at the University of Worcester. Piet tragically lost his wife and ten-year-old daughter in a road accident near Pretoria while on holiday in South Africa in 2012 (Breuer 2013).

At the university, Piet is a member of the Worcester International Forum for Research in Children's Literature, and his research interests include multiculturalism in picture books and graphic novels (University of Worcester 2013). Grobler's brightly colored illustrations in *Fussy Freya* by Katherine Quarmby are good examples of the multicultural character of his work. These illustrations are, despite the obvious English setting of the story, brimming with African images, further emphasized because of Quarmby's choices of exotic food examples being African wildlife. His comic and eccentric pictures perfectly match the story.

Grobler's Bird Keeps Flying

Clear evidence of Piet Grobler's generosity and warm spirit abounds in his unstinting contributions (refusing any remuneration) for the first ever IBBY World Congress in Africa in 2004. He had initiated a series of seven workshops in which children from differing schools in the area of Stellenbosch (Western Cape Province) created and painted their own rainbow birds, each session concentrating on a different color. The result was a huge rainbow-colored display of birds. He repeated these workshops with children from schools in the Cape Flats (an under-privileged area outside Cape Town) and the resulting birds were used as an ever-moving rainbow display during the Congress in Cape Town.

Piet also designed the conference logo—another bird, this time with a chameleon-like tail—which was replicated in African beadwork, and an IBBY member was seen proudly wearing the earrings at the 2010 IBBY World Congress in Santiago, Spain. He provided the lustrous poster of animals cavorting past Table Mountain, with a slice of symbolic rainbow behind. They are led by a hare and a tortoise (both well-known in African traditional folklore), with a guinea-fowl, a book-balancing zebra, a giraffe in high heels and a cheerful crocodile. The zebra still adorns one of the pages of the international IBBY website. As if he hadn't yet done enough, he also created wine labels and greeting cards for the Congress.

Among numerous awards Grobler has received for his transformative artistic abilities in addition to the ones mentioned previously are the Bratislava (Slovakia) International Biennale for Illustration (BIB)'s Golden Apple award, the Peter Pan prize for translated work in Sweden, the Primo Alpi Apuane Award for illustration in Italy, and the Alberto Berlusconi Award in Argentina. In 2008 he was South Africa's candidate for the Hans Christian Andersen Award (Authors Voices 2008).

His work is accepted and popular worldwide, and he feels that this could be a result of his South African heritage and the influences of so many cultures (Pople 2010). He has always been interested in different cultures (Retief 2002), and his work captivates the reader through its symbiosis of European-style illustration and African folk art as it spans editorial design, picture books and installations (Authors Voices 2008). He strongly believes that there will always be room for more challenging and sophisticated illustrations (Pople 2010), and his work clearly supports this assertion.

Note

1. A species of small African antelope.

Children's Books

De Vos, Philip. 1998. *Carnival of the Animals*. Illustrated by Piet Grobler. Cape Town, SA: Human & Rousseau.
Dijkstra, Lida. 2004. *Little Mouse*. Illustrated by Piet Grobler. Honesdale, PA: Frontstreet.
Grobler, Piet. 1997. *The Rainbow Birds*. Cape Town, SA: Kagiso.
_____. 2002. *Please Frog, Just One Sip*! Honesdale, PA: Frontstreet.
_____. 2005. *Little Bird's ABC*. Honesdale, PA: Frontstreet.
_____. 2008. *Rooi Kiri Wordt Verliefd*. Rotterdam, Netherlands: Lemniscaat.
Hendriks, Maria. 2004. *Makwelane and the Crocodile*. Illustrated by Piet Grobler. Cape Town, SA: Human & Rousseau.
Hofmeyr, Dianne. 2013. *The Magic Bojabi Tree*. Illustrated by Piet Grobler. London: Frances Lincoln.
_____. 2013. *The Name of the Tree Is Bojabi*. Illustrated by Piet Grobler. Cape Town, SA: Human & Rousseau.
Luján, Jorge. 2008. *Colors!;Colores!* Illustrated by Piet Grobler. Toronto, Canada: Groundwood.
_____. 2006. *Sky Blue Accident/Accidente Celeste*. Illustrated by Piet Grobler. Translated by Elisa Amado. Toronto, Canada: Groundwood.
Meinderts, Koos and Harrie Jekkers. 2008. *Ballade van de Dood*. Rotterdam, Netherlands: Lemniscaat.
Naidoo, Beverley. 2011. *Aesop's Fables*. Illustrated by Piet Grobler. London: Frances Lincoln.
Piumini, Roberto. 2001. *Doctor Me Di Cin*. Illustrated by Piet Grobler. Rotterdam, Netherlands: Lemniscaat.
Quarmby, Katherine. 2008. *Fussy Freya*. Illustrated by Piet Grobler. London: Frances Lincoln.
Ravishankar, Anushka. 2003. *Today Is My Day*. Illustrated by Piet Grobler. Chennai, India: Tara Publishing.
Schmidt, Annie M.G. 2002. *Die Spree met Foete*. Translated by Philip de Vos. Illustrated by Piet Grobler. Cape Town, SA: Human & Rousseau.
Van der Vyver, Marita. 1996. *Rhinocephants on the Roof*. Illustrated by Piet Grobler. Cape Town, SA: Human & Rousseau.
_____. 2005. *Mia's Mom*. Illustrated by Piet Grobler. Cape Town, SA: Human & Rousseau.
_____. 2010. *Die Mooiste Sprokies van Grimm*. Illustrated by Piet Grobler. Cape Town: Human & Rousseau.
Walton, Ann. 1996. *Here I Am*. Illustrated by Piet Grobler. Cape Town, SA: JUTA.

Wendy Hartmann: The Hidden Heroine

Jay Heale

Back in 1986, Lydia Snyman (an Afrikaans specialist in children's books) wrote: "Yet when one is dealing with a text which falls into the category of children's literature, the recognition and study in literary circles of such a book as a work of art, are largely lacking—possibly or probably because this involves a further dimension, namely the child" (Snyman 1986, 47).

Wendy Hartmann never ignores this vital further dimension. She is the quietly industrious author of about forty South African children's books, and it is high time she was given the recognition she deserves. Such titles as *All the Magic in the World*, *Nina and Little Duck*, and *Just Sisi* have received international recognition, but it was the illustrators—respectively Niki Daly, Marjorie van Heerden and Joan Rankin—who were placed center stage. Time now to switch the spotlight onto the author.

Surprisingly, Wendy Hartmann is one of the few authors in South Africa striving to earn a full-time living out of writing for children. Unsurprisingly, she finds it mighty hard work. The inside of the car was her first study while she fulfilled her duties as Mom's Taxi for her two daughters. The rest of her writing she did at night. A study space in her home was created, and finally the garage was adapted as work place, for book storage and occasional meetings. Here she works with a computer, a scanner, a printer, Internet, a digital camera and a cell phone—and her faithful dog. "The rest is self-discipline and hard work" (pers. comm.).

South Africa has grown up with a European literary awareness. Certainly, the majority of children's books for many years came from Britain (with a few from the United States). So the legacies of such as Enid Blyton and Walt Disney remain. Young South African readers typically expect straightforward storytelling in fairly simple language, with pictures that verge towards the "cute 'n cuddly" style that sells well internationally. Yet in recent years, there has been an increasing call for more African relevance and less European blandness. Illustrations are becoming more imaginative and less photographic.

A good picture book creator today needs to have skill in at least three main areas:

- Ability to listen to the sound of language;
- Creativity to produce a strong storyline, with the adaptability to make changes if production or marketing require them;
- Willingness to work in a creative team.

It is fair to say that Wendy Hartmann seems a fine example of these three strengths in action together.

Sound Qualities of Language

Wendy is acutely aware of sounds. Water trickles continuously into rock-laid ponds reminiscent of a precise Japanese garden (though far more friendly and rural). The change of birdsong in her garden warns that a hawk is threatening. She listens to the sound and rhythm of words, and talks of the way that the turn of a page might indicate a comma pause, a new stage in a story or a moment of surprise. "Words, picture and storyline all have their own rhythms" (pers. comm).

Most of her writing is in simple, effective prose. Wendy seems uncertain about her ability to handle verse, though in fact her natural ear creates the kind of poetic text that is just what children love.

Here is part of *We're Having a Party!*:

> A party is announced. Now, who will come?
> "Mmmmm... I will come on my padded paws, with my terrible teeth and my very sharp claws."
> "Yesss! I will come, but late at night. I'll slither and slide and squeeze you tight."
> "And ... I will come at the crack of dawn, with my enormous mouth and sky high yawn" [n.p.].

Textual design has fun with such words as "terrible," "squeeze" and "yawn," while Alzette Prins' wide-spread pictures show the reader that it is Lion and Snake and Hippo who are preparing to come to the party. One small black boy realizes that they all want to eat him—so he also invites his father with his assegai (short spear or javelin), his brother with his hunting knife, his uncle with his spear. Thus he ends with two separate parties: the humans and the animals. Most satisfying. The storyline would have worked just as well in prose, but verse makes it even more fun to read aloud.

Consider this agreeable passage from Beatrix Potter's *Tom Kitten* (1907) as Joan Aiken (1982) describes it: "'The three Puddle Ducks came along the hard high road marching one behind the other ... pit pat paddle pat, pit pat waddle pat.' My daughter absolutely adored that sentence, it sent her into ecstasies of laughter every time. 'Read it again, Ma,' she'd cry, 'Read it *again* !'" (25).

A young listener can focus on desirable elements in the text itself—even before the illustrations are considered. So the text has to be of high quality as a starting point. Dorothy Butler (1980) makes this point firmly: "Illustration interacts with text, of course, but it is the story and its telling on which the book stands or falls. Make no mistake about this" (81).

Inside *Nina and Little Duck* Wendy offers prose and poetry, both of strong quality. Brief, read-aloud stories of a very normal small girl called Nina—who dresses up, tries conjuring tricks, plays with the ducks and ducklings, and has a loving mother—are sandwiched between snatches of lilting verse.

> One yellow duckling, all on its own.
> This duckling said: I think I should go home.
> Home, home, home.
> I think I should go home [n.p.].

Only a writer in full awareness of the effect of words would have thought of repeating those three words. (And what a vital word is "home" for every child.)

> Go north, go south.
> Go east, go west.
> Go anywhere.
> Our mom is best [n.p.].

Find a mother who wouldn't love reading that out loud. Find a child who wouldn't enjoy hearing it.

Strength of Story

Wendy does not only write picture book text. She has written a number of chapter books for younger solo readers. This is an important part of juvenile publishing in South Africa where many learners are studying in a language that is not their mother tongue.

In *Marshmallows, Monsters and Mice* the story is both powerful and playful. A girl suffers from a recurring nightmare and suggestions from various relatives do not help the situation. Wendy lightens this frightening theme with the girl's cat who has increasingly enjoyable dreams. Only Niki Daly, as commissioning editor of Songololo Books, would have dared to publish this finely written story. The publishing problem lay in the choice of illustrator: Tertia Kleinhans was adept at creating flying fears and assorted objects (slight echoes of Salvador Dali at times), but the bodies of her humans were not "pretty" and that, it seems, doomed a strongly imaginative picture book. Although most children seemed to enjoy it, South African book-buyers were not happy with the grotesque, and librarians (and parents) declared that young readers might be frightened, which (ironically) is exactly what the book was about!

One of her first international successes also came through Songololo Books, though this time the illustrator was Niki Daly himself. The Bodley Head snapped it up for their U.K. list, followed by Dutton in the U.S., and the South African edition from Songololo. *All the Magic in the World* is a reality story of ordinary children playing around the way that children do.

> Every Friday evening, Sonnie, Stefan, Anna, Chrissie, and Lena played in the street or in the yard. If it had rained, they made mud socks on their feet and paraded past the chickens, making silly noises [n.p.].

Watching them and clutching his tin of collected treasures is old Joseph, the odd-job man. They are riotous children, hanging like monkeys -all except Lena "who was teased because she stumbled on stairs." For her, specially, Joseph reveals the magic in a piece of string, of collected bottle-tops, and of a shell with the sound of the sea. "So you tell me where the magic is found" (n.p.). Full-page, magical Niki Daly paintings sweep across the endless horizon.

The Sun, the Moon and the Blanket of Night has the style of an African folktale, with the Sun showing off his power, the Moon warning that Night is on the way—and so to the balance of heat and dark, with everything in the world reassuringly in its place. Wendy Hartmann's simple, poetic storytelling does its job well, providing a strong starting point for the illustrator.

The interdependence of text and illustration is made clear by Shaun Tan (2013). On his website, he states: "I have to say that illustrations are for me the main 'texts' in my books, and although writing is often the starting point, it rather acts as a kind of scaffolding or binding that stitches everything together." Wendy builds "scaffolding" adroitly.

"Wendy Hartmann meets Joan Rankin" sounds like a television program; in fact, it was the beginning of a hugely productive succession of top quality picture books, as author and artist sparked ideas off each other. They "stitched everything together."

Why the three *Theo* books never hit the headlines is inexplicable. *Theo the Library Cat* led the trio, all written by Wendy Hartmann and illustrated by Joan Rankin. Stout covers, perfect-bound, full color on gloss paper, available in English and Afrikaans (from Lapa Publishers). Certainly, there was plenty about love of books and libraries! In *Theo the Library Cat*, there is a nasty, chilling old lady called Mrs. Pratt who locks all the cats (except Theo) inside her house where their duty is to keep her warm. The illustrations rank alongside Korky Paul's *Winnie-the-Witch* (Paul 1987) for vigor and inventiveness. *Theo and the Circus Act* and *Theo and the Cat Burglar* were equally inventive in their story-weaving and sheer delight. They should have become classics. Sadly, even a reprint in South Africa is unusual. Consider this final paragraph in *Theo the Library Cat*:

> Theo went back home to his mother and his brother and sister. He liked living right next to the library. Because ... he still wanted to read hundreds of books ... learn about a thousand things ... and of course ask a million and one questions [46, 48].

Wendy has written four short eerie stories aimed at an older readership though using a simple vocabulary and style: *The Key and the Casket, The Short Cut, Voices in the Dark,* and *The Black Dog*. All four were given a color cover and black and white line drawings inside by the artist Ian Lusted, who can masterfully depict both atmosphere and character. Of the four, which are all engagingly spooky, *The Black Dog* may be the best, with a strong plot concerning a teenager being led by a mysterious black dog to the cottage where an old lady is trapped under a fallen box. Yet the dog appears to have been run over that same morning. The other three link on to fear situations such as a graveyard, strange voices halfway up a mountain, and a severed hand. No specific places are named, but the illustrations clearly depict modern teenagers with jeans, tackies (sneakers), baseball caps, and camping gear on the mountain.

Though only forty-eight pages long and well supplied with line drawings by Robert Foote, *Dolphin Day* is probably Wendy's most ambitious longer book—setting aside the quartet of junior spooky stories. However, this book too was written with high interest, low vocabulary levels in mind. The story concerns a brother and sister, well created as individual characters, who try to combat intruding fishing boats in the bay that threaten the dolphins. The intention is much deeper: to inform young readers of the threat to our marine life and the wonder of dolphins themselves. Each pithy chapter takes the action a stage forward towards a strongly exciting climax in which the harbor police catch the baddies, and the friendliness of dolphins to humans is once more shown to be true. Environmental awareness carried on a wave of good storytelling; one feels that Wendy is herself deeply concerned with such matters.

Creative Teamwork

Storytelling in a picture book also can start jointly in the hands of author and illustrator. For example, many people know the classic picture book *Rosie's Walk* (1968) by Pat Hutchins. The text consists of only one sentence:

> Rosie the hen went for a walk across the yard around the pond over the haycock past the mill through the fence under the beehives and got back in time for dinner [n.p.].

That text is spread over twenty-seven pages, some of which carry no text at all, but the pictures follow the steady progress of Rosie who is totally unaware of the attempts by the fox to catch her. In artwork alone, the fox falls over a rake, tumbles into the pond, is buried in hay, covered with flour and chased away by bees.

Wendy Hartmann and Joan Rankin collaboratively use an identical formula in the opening (main) story of *Just Sisi*. Sisi the rabbit walks unconcerned through an African landscape where lurk troublesome goats, crocodile, lion and python. She delivers the eggs to Ma Tembo and then walks past all the dangers, which the young reader knows, are lying in wait, even if Sisi doesn't. Echoing the pattern of Pat Hutchins, Wendy's text doesn't waver "all the way home" while the most incredible things happen in the background!

Some of Wendy's most inspired work has been the result of creative teamwork, technological interaction, "a marriage of true minds"—call it what you will! *Nina and Little Duck*, *Just Sisi*, and another collection of *Sisi* stories (in production) have come from a quartet of skilled minds: writer Wendy Hartmann, illustrators Marjorie van Heerden and Joan Rankin, book designer Teresa Williams, and Aldré Lategan, publishing editor at Human & Rousseau. Internet technology has allowed author and artist to exchange ideas, push pictures around the page, rewriting if necessary, extending a picture if greater impact is required, checking overall balance. As Aldré Lategan described the process (pers. comm.), all four provided input, but such a successful result was unlikely to have happened without Wendy's own strong sense of design from the beginning. Email and Internet link offices together in a way that book creators could not enjoy perhaps as little as twenty years ago.

The Business of Being an Author

"I think," says Wendy, "I have been a quiet storyteller all my life, not a writer. I had no experience of writing, submitting or publishing, but I had to try…. It is important that the writer and the illustrator understand the whole process because a picture book is not just a story or illustrations. It is a marriage of both."

On the inspiration for her stories: "Many of my stories have a feeling underneath; something a child might be experiencing. It could be loneliness, sibling rivalry, failure or fear of certain things. You don't have to have experienced it all, but you could have friends who did" (pers. comm.).

Sometimes, Wendy's original story idea is about a child, but is transformed into an animal because animals are universally acceptable and make for better illustrations. *In a House, in a House* could have been quite a scary story if the characters had been humans, frightened by unpleasant smells and noises in the night. But characterized as a short-tempered home-loving mouse, with other animal friends, and visited finally by a trembling greyhound named Rosebud, the result is hugely funny.

So, in Wendy Hartmann we have a workaday author who has learned her craft, has supplied what is wanted by publishers (with the usual ABC, counting, concept books) but—which is far more important—has supplied what is appreciated and enjoyed by her young readers. She lives and works in the suburb of Cape Town, South Africa, called Table View, which (as would be expected) has a fine vista of Table Mountain.

Many of her books have been award-winners, though more often for the work of the illustrator. This doesn't seem to worry Wendy. For example, *One Sun Rises,* illustrated by Nicolaas Maritz, was a U.S. Parents' Choice for Best Illustration 1994. Awards which judge the book as a whole include: *All the Magic in the World* was selected for the White Ravens list of 1994 by the International Youth Library of Munich; *The Dinosaurs Are Back* was listed as an International Reading Association/Children's Book Council Children's Choice in 1998; *Just Sisi* was the Bookchat "Book of the Year" 2010.

She doesn't sit still. (Like most committed writers, she can't afford to.) Two tales of hers appear in the *Sunday Times Storytime* collection: one an explosive verse fun piece, "Ma Rosie's Pig," illustrated by Joan Rankin. In spare moments she paints or creates craftwork. Then she writes again, and more books are already in the production line. Meanwhile, Wendy believes in what she is doing: "Dare to dream and then do it" (pers. comm.).

South African publishing has often lagged behind world trends. Book buyers are probably hesitant and conservative. It is to the credit of such writers as Wendy Hartmann that picture books are coming alive—and with a South African relevance, which is something that is very special to South African readers.

Children's Books

Hartmann, Wendy. 1990. *Marshmallows, Monsters and Mice.* Illustrated by Tertia Kleinhans. Cape Town, SA: Songololo Books.

_____. 1993. *All the Magic in the World.* Illustrated by Niki Daly. London: The Bodley Head.
_____. 1994. *The Key and the Casket.* Illustrated by Ian Lusted. Cape Town, SA: Human & Rousseau.
_____. 1994. *One Sun Rises.* Illustrated by Nicolaas Maritz. New York: Dutton.
_____. 1994. *The Short Cut.* Illustrated by Ian Lusted. Cape Town, SA: Human & Rousseau.
_____. 1996. *The Dinosaurs Are Back.* Illustrated by Niki Daly. London: The Bodley Head.
_____. 1997. *The Black Dog.* Illustrated by Ian Lusted. Cape Town, SA: Human & Rousseau.
_____. 1997. *Voices in the Dark.* Illustrated by Ian Lusted. Cape Town, SA: Human & Rousseau.
_____. 2007. *Dolphin Day.* Illustrated by Robert Foote. Cape Town, South Africa: Human & Rousseau.
_____. 2007. *Nina and Little Duck.* Illustrated by Marjorie van Heerden. Cape Town, SA: Human & Rousseau.
_____. 2007. *Theo and the Cat Burglar.* Illustrated by Joan Rankin. Pretoria, SA: LAPA.
_____. 2007. *Theo and the Circus Act.* Illustrated by Joan Rankin. Pretoria, SA: LAPA.
_____. 2007. *Theo the Library Cat.* Illustrated by Joan Rankin. Pretoria, SA: LAPA.
_____. 2008. *We're Having a Party!* Illustrated by Alzette Prins. Cape Town, SA: Human & Rousseau.
_____. 2009. *The Sun, the Moon and the Blanket of Night.* Illustrated by Alzette Prins. Cape Town, SA: Songololo Books.
_____. 2009. *In a House, in a House.* Illustrated by Joan Rankin. Cape Town, SA: Human & Rousseau.
_____. 2010. *Just Sisi.* Illustrated by Joan Rankin. Cape Town, SA: Human & Rousseau.
_____. 2013. "Ma Rosie's Pig." Illustrated by Joan Rankin. In *Storytime*, 5–20. Johannesburg, SA: Times Media Education.

Jaco Jacobs Brings the Circus to Town

Magdel Vorster

Jaco Jacobs was born in 1980 in a small Karoo town, Carnarvon, in the Northern Cape Province, a semi-desert region of South Africa. Visits from the circus to their town stand out as a definite highlight in his childhood memories. When he was seven years old he was sure he was going to become a crocodile tamer in the circus. Years later he wanted to become a psychologist. He finished school in Carnarvon and then went to study communication science at the University of the Free State in Bloemfontein where he also did a post graduate degree in Afrikaans Dutch literature (Jacobs 2013).

Jacobs started writing in high school. He wrote short stories for magazines as well as competed in many writing competitions. He won numerous prizes, and in his final year of school he was awarded prizes in all three genres offered in a prestigious competition for new writers. He won the first prize for prose and poetry and the second prize for drama ("Vindingryke skrywer skitter" 1998). Jacobs juggles genres in the same way that he alternates between writing scary stories, funny stories and rhymes, realistic stories, teenage fiction, and factual books for a variety of age groups.

On the question about why he writes, Jacobs replies that he writes to entertain himself. By making up stories, he brightens up everyday life, adding color and flavor to mundane tasks and events, like the circus in those days while growing up brightened the quiet Carnarvon. He pitches the big circus tent in his head and allows the lions and clowns and acrobats to enter the arena and entertain him. His mind is then filled with stories and characters which he later shares with his readers when putting words to the fun he has experienced in his head.

Jaco Jacobs is an intelligent adult with the imagination of children of all ages. He is therefore especially skilled in writing from his young readers' perspective. He cleverly creates funny as well as scary characters like wardrobe monsters, pet elephants, zombies and even famous rock star grandmothers

(Fouche 2011). Jacobs believes children should read for their enjoyment, and therefore he aims to supply them with books that would have this specific effect.

The number of Afrikaans Taal en Kultuurvereniging (ATKV) awards that he has won so far, is proof of the fact that he knows exactly what his readers want, especially when taking into consideration that children are the judges for the ATKV awards ("Jaco Jacobs" 2008).

He has been called a phenomenon based on the sales of his books as well as the rate at which he is publishing and winning awards (Diedericks-Hugo 2011). Between 2004 and 2012 he has won fourteen ATKV as well as eight other awards, including three for translation and an honorary award by the South African national section of the International Board on Books for Young People (IBBY).

There Is No Circus Without Humor

Jacobs refers to clowns as the backbone of his circus. Like the clowns he likes to play around with funny ideas, ideas for stories, phrases, situations and characters that would make him laugh. Jacobs is a huge fan of Dr. Seuss and aims at achieving with his rhymes what Dr. Seuss did. The characters and stories of Dr. Seuss are all "over the top," and children love his odd, almost out of control humor. The rhymes of Dr. Seuss also always had a moral lesson, but it was well hidden in absurd situations and brilliant rhyme (Nieuwoudt 2007).

Trevor Cairney, who has extensively researched how children become literate, has found that humor has enormous benefits for early literacy learning. Stories that rely on word play, rhyme and the unexpected have been proven to amuse children and form one of Cairney's categories of humor in children's books (Cairney 2009).

Jacobs has published a number of nursery rhyme volumes, and the reader is often drawn to the catchy and original titles before opening the books. Titles include *Wurms met Tamatiesous en Ander Lawwe Rympies* (Worms with Ketchup and Other Silly Rhymes) and *My Boetie Dink Hy's Batman en Ander Rympies* (My Brother Thinks He's Batman and Other Rhymes). With *Wurms met Tamatiesous en Ander Lawwe Rympies* Jacobs has won the Alba Bouwer prize for Afrikaans children's literature and the C.P. Hoogenhout medal for the best original Afrikaans book for children between seven and twelve years of age.

"Meerkat," a rhyme in *Wurms met Tamatiesous en Ander Rympies* strongly reminds the reader of Dr Seuss. In "Meerkat," Jacobs rhymes:

> is 'n meerkat
> minder of méér kat
> of maar net 'n min-of-meer kat?
> eintlik lyk hy maar na min kat
> glad nie soos 'n miaau-en-spinkat
> waarom is hy dan 'n méérkat?
> of is hy dalk glad nie kat nie?
> ek verstaan 'n meerkat glad nie [n.p.].

Meer is Afrikaans for "more" and even though the rhyme and rhythm is lost in translation, the resemblance to Dr. Seuss still remains:

> is a meerkat
> less or more cat
> or just an almost cat?
> not at all like a meow or purr cat
> why is he then a meerkat?
> or is he maybe not at all cat?
> I do not understand a meerkat.

Humor helps children to engage with stories and at the same time the language that is used to create stories. For younger readers illustrations are added to support word play and the unexpected (Cairney 2009). In *Liewe Land, 'n Olifant* (My Goodness, an Elephant), illustrated by Maja Sereda, Sonja has lost hope of ever finding a pet that would please her whole family. Then, on a school trip to the zoo, she finds the perfect pet—playful, wrinkly, grey and big. In *Haasmoles* (Bunny Trouble), also illustrated by Maja Sereda, Simon is bored because it is raining and he is stuck inside the house. Suddenly, though, the house is filled with hopping bunnies, and the adventures start. Maja Sereda and Jacobs were both awarded an ATKV award for *Liewe Land, 'n Olifant* in 2009, and Jacobs was awarded an ATKV award for *Haasmoles* in 2012.

More conventional stories that use novel storylines and characterization to amuse, include *Bertie Blikbrein* (Bertie Tin Brain) and *Suzie se Superdoeper-Sjampoe* (Suzie's Super Duper Shampoo). Bertie Blikbrein's father is an inventor, and a tickling chair for when you fall asleep, color changing hair gel, and sandals that cut your toe nails are on the list of products he has invented. His latest however is a robot that can do math and tell jokes. The fun starts when Bertie steals this robot and takes it to school one day. Suzie in *Suzie se Superdoeper-Sjampoe* aspires to be a hairdresser one day, and when their grandparents come to stay, she and her brother mix up a shampoo from kitchen ingredients to then apply to their bald, sleeping grandfather's head with unexpected, hilarious results.

The Zackie Mostert series is a good example of how Jacobs creates the absurd, the surprising, the unexpected and the outrageous from conventional stories. In *Zackie Mostert en die Super-Aaklige Soen* (Zackie Mostert and the Super Awful Kiss) Zackie wants the part of the ugly troll in the school play, but is given the part of the singing fairy prince, just like the magic tricks at a magic show at school go wrong in another title of the series, *Zackie Mostert en die Ongelooflike Kulkunsie* (Zackie Mostert and the Unbelievable Magic Trick). Zackie Mostert compares to Horrid Henry, the key character of Francesca Simon's well known Horrid Henry series, illustrated by Tony Ross.

The four Professor Fungus books Jacobs has written so far add fantasy to often real and modern scenarios, to result in very funny stories. In *Professor Fungus en die Zombie-Tamaties* (Professor Fungus and the Zombie Tomatoes) Bennie and his twin sister Jenny love to visit their eccentric uncle and observe his latest inventions. This time they have to fight off zombie tomatoes when an experiment goes wrong and the fast growing vegetables show different side effects, like turning cannibalistic. The effects are most severe in tomatoes because they are not really vegetables.

Scared and Spellbound

Shock and fear are two more modes of entertainment present in a good circus. In most of the scary stories or thrillers of Jacobs, however, there is a safety net as you would find underneath the acrobats swinging from their bars high above the audience. The fire breathers are trained to do what they do. Jacobs knows that children enjoy being scared or given a fright. The secret lies in the balance between being scared and feeling safe. The *Bastian Blom* series is a good example.

Troetelgedrog (Pet Monster) was published by LAPA Publishers and was the first in the *Grille en Goeters* (Thrills and Stuff) series as well as Jacobs's first book published. *Troetelgedrog* is a modern and imaginative fantasy successfully addressing a context familiar to his readers (Diedericks-Hugo 2002). The *Grille en Goeters* series comprises five titles.

Pretpark (Amusement Park) was actually the first book Jacobs wrote, although not published until two years later. This story—which won an ATKV award, with Madame Zelda hypnotizing people with a magical stone and the kind Geena with her elephant Tantor—is a spellbinding and well-balanced book where three young children decide to investigate strange things happening at Zomna amusement park. It stimulates the reader's curiosity all through the story, and in the end when good overcomes evil, the otherwise almost sinister character is cancelled (Van Taak 2003).

Kas Vol Monsters (Wardrobe of Monsters) is another series of thrillers.

Like many other stories, this series started with a What-if game, Jacobs often plays with himself. What if the old wardrobe in your new house is the secret entrance to the castle of a group of monsters. These monsters are Kriewels (Thrills), a green hand without a body; Elvis, a flamboyant vampire; Toets (Test), a blonde mummy; Flaffie (Fluffy), a moody werewolf; and Frank, a tall, kind, slow-speaking monster (Jacobs 2013). What if questions to inspire some stories include: what if a vampire wants to send his grandmother a photograph but he is invisible in each picture? (Jacobs 2013) This very popular series comprises six titles.

Net Aliens Eet Spinasie (Only Aliens Eat Spinach) is a volume of short stories with humor similar to Roald Dahl's while being scary at different levels of intensity. Every story has a surprising end and themes are varied to intrigue different interests with male as well as female main characters (Venter 2005).

Virus is an apocalyptic teenage novel. A destructive virus is changing people into zombies, and is now attacking the home city of Jake, the main character. Jake is looking for his father and along the way meets a few interesting characters, all uniquely battling for survival. DJ Max, a radio presenter, comments on the dying chaotic world in the background. It's a fast story with many angles to keep readers engrossed. Jake is an aspiring cartoonist, and his black and white cartoons to process his emotions and experiences are one of the extra angles through which the reader can interpret the events. Daniel du Plessis is responsible for the cartoonlike illustrations in the book (Van der Walt 2010). *Virus* reminds readers of the films "Zombie Diaries" and "I Am Legend." With this book Jacobs leaves his readers with some philosophical questions to ponder (Schuurman 2009).

In 2010 and 2011 Jacobs won the ATKV award respectively for *Middernagfees* (Midnight Feast) and *Harlekyn* (Clown). In *Harlekyn* the main character suffers from coulrophobia, a fear of clowns. Even though he loves scary films and games, he is scared of clowns. His sister then buys him an antique clown doll, and strange things start to happen at home. *Harlekyn* was featured in a local newspaper serial for thirteen weeks before it was published in book format by Tafelberg in 2010 (Van Rooy 2009).

A Realistic Decoy

Jaco Jacobs also juggles plots, themes, settings and characters to reflect the world as his audience knows it. He writes realistic stories for all ages. *Slaaptyd, Matilda* (To Bed, Matilda) and *Madelief, Moenie!* (Madelief, Don't!) are both picture books with familiar commands or warnings from parents to children as titles. Bedtime routine becomes an adventure when Matilda takes her bath with a pirate, brushes her teeth with a dinosaur and has her glass of milk with a hairy wolf. Zunica Joao was responsible for the extraordinary illustrations. In *Madelief Moenie*, illustrated by Sebastien Quevauvilliers, princess Madelief, like Matilda, chooses adventure above convention. She is different from other princesses, and her antics at opposing adult rules will be enjoyed by all young readers.

Some of his earliest books for young readers include *Duskant die Doodlyn* (Just Before the Deadline), *Rugbypret* (Rugby Fun), *Krieketpret/Gevaarlike Lopies* (Cricket Fun/Dangerous Runs), and *Wiskunde Gee My Maagpyn* (Maths Gives Me a Tummy Ache). In each of these titles the setting and topic of the book are obvious. In some of his later titles however the theme of the book is not stated in the title. In *Borrels* (Bubbles) Jacobs in fact mixes fantasy into realism, when the new girl in Christo and Nelson's class turns out to be a mermaid.

Realistic novels for teenagers are not meant to be morality tales, but rather reflections of the life of adolescents and the challenges they face, and this is another aspect of writing where Jacobs succeeds. His characters in books for this target group are generally the same age as their readers. Vocabulary and dialogue are convincing to keep readers interested (Scheepers and Kleyn 2012). In the South African multicultural and multilingual context, modern Afrikaans teenagers often use slang and English phrases in their Afrikaans conversations. Because of this, Jacobs often uses English phrases or slang in dialogue. He believes the language young people use is part of their identity, so for the sake of authenticity teenage language is necessary when teenage characters are portrayed (Botha 2008).

In *Suurlemoen* (Lemon) the sixteen-year-old Tiaan, Zane, Liezl and Bongi are members of the band, Suurlemoen, competing in a rock band competition for schools. *Suurlemoen* is a contemporary novel with all the necessary ingredients, including romance, friendship and rock music, that would interest teenage readers. The layout of the book is another aspect that would capture the attention of young people. The book includes drawings, photographs and handwritten notes on post-its. These graphic elements, together with the first person narrative, create a personal and almost interactive approach. *Suurlemoen* received an honorary award by IBBY South Africa in 2008 (Odendaal 2008).

Jacobs also publishes using two female aliases, Tania Brink and Lize Roux. They could represent the bearded lady of the Jacobs circus. Tania Brink has so far published *Liefde Laat Jou Rice Krispies Anders Proe* (Love Changes the Taste of Your Rice Krispies), *Ouens Is Nie Pizzas Nie* (Guys Are Not Pizzas), *My Hart Is Vol Graffiti* (My Heart Is All Graffiti), *Al die Meisies Hou van Divan Louw* (All the Girls Love Divan Louw). Teenage girls are the target market of these books, so Jacobs's publisher thought it best to have him write these books using a female pseudonym.

Wearing the Lize Roux cloak, Jacobs has been publishing a very popular teen horse fiction series, titled *Stalmaats* (Stable Mates). It is a contemporary series, written in modern dialect with realistic scenarios to which teenagers comfortably relate. The main character, Anri, is part of a normal family with siblings that do not always get along. The author succeeds in building on and modernizing the series concept established in Afrikaans children's literature by Stella Blakemore and Theunis Krogh with their well-known boarding school series (Van den Heever 2006). To date fourteen titles have been published in this series.

Jacobs also has quite a few animals jumping through hoops or big cats being tamed when taking into account the number of factual books he has written. Titles like *How Wide Can a Hippo Open His Mouth?*, *How Many Teeth Does a Crocodile Have?* and *How High Can a Grasshopper Jump?* are three books where interesting facts about animals are presented to young readers in an original and fun way with colorful illustrations complementing humoristic text. He also wrote a number of Afrikaans as well as English readers for educational publishers as well as contributed to poetry and prose volumes prescribed for secondary schools. *Toulopers—Verse vir Tieners* (Tightrope Walkers—Poems for Teenagers) is a poetry volume, compiled by Jacobs with poems by himself and other well-known South African authors, including Fanie Viljoen, Francois Bloemhof, and Janie Oosthuizen. Formats vary from facebook, email and sms conversations to themes like teenage angst, emo's and self mutilation. Jacobs's poem, "My hart is 'n hamburger" (My Heart Is a Hamburger) deals with unrequited teenage love and the title poem, "Touloper" (Tightrope Walker) by Fanie Viljoen deals with the way in which a teenager focuses on walking the tightrope and balancing life when bombarded with being misunderstood and blamed by parents (Diedericks-Hugo 2011).

In 2007 Jacobs won the Maskew Miller Longman Literature Prize for Afrikaans with *Verneukpan*. Verneukpan is a large dry salt pan in the Northern Cape Province. Verneuk is Afrikaans for trick, cheat, mislead or swindle. In *Verneukpan* the main character Sean and a friend are on their way to a New Year's rave during their last holiday before their final year of school. The party was organized by a guy Sean met in a chatroom on the internet. Jacobs pulls out all the stops to set a realistic frame of reference for his target group, including alcohol and drugs. The storyline was, according to Susanne Harper (2008) in a newspaper review, probably influenced by the Spanish American film, "Y Tu Mama Tambien," and a quote from the film, "Life is like the surf, so give yourself away like the sea" (13), is included in the beginning of the book.

Jacobs knows young people, how they speak and their struggles, and without moralizing he explores their boundaries (Viljoen 2008).

The World Mimed into Afrikaans

The translation of books is an obvious way to replenish indigenous literature when dealing with a relatively small group of writers and readers. Young Afrikaans readers are given access to classic and international bestselling children's literature through translation of these books. Afrikaans subject literature consists mainly of translations and in some cases these texts are adapted to suit the South African environment (Wybenga and Snyman 2005).

Translators are sometimes referred to as invisible storytellers. In the context of a circus theme, they could also be referred to as mimes of the original. Jacobs has been responsible for a big portion of international children's literature available in Afrikaans in South Africa. To date he has translated more than 200 books from English into Afrikaans.

Translations include numerous board books, lift-the-flap books, and touch-and-feel books, originally produced by prominent publishers like Priddy Bicknell and Usborne. Emma Thomson's fairy Felicity is, thanks to Jacobs, well-known and loved by Afrikaans toddlers as Lili. Likewise Jan Fearnly's Martha is known as Miemie and Katherine Lodge's Mimi as Mandie.

Other familiar children's books he added to the Afrikaans children's literature collection, include four of Hergé's Tintin books and one of Terry Deary's popular Horrible Histories titles, namely *The Horrible History of the World* (2003) that was translated into *Die Gruwelike Geskiedenis van die Wêreld*. Knowing Jacobs's thrillers, it is clear why he was assigned the translation of Deary.

In 2009 Jacobs received the Elsabe Steenberg award for translated children's literature for translating Chris Riddell's *Ottoline and the Yellow Cat* into *Willemien en die Geel Kat* ("Gewilde kinderboeke word bekroon" 2009). With an intricate storyline, this book is appropriate for many age groups. It would be very successful as a read-aloud book, with enough detailed illustrations to entertain, while the amount of text would also not discourage beginner readers. *Willemien en die Geel Kat* was also awarded an IBBY Honour award as well as the South African Translators Institute (SATI) prize (Britz 2009). Thomas van der Walt (2009) commented that the judges for the SATI award were impressed with the way in which Jacobs succeeded in remaining true to the original source text while ensuring that the unique author's "voice" was honored and at the same time maintaining his familiar dry style of writing and humor. Jacobs especially enjoys translating youth fiction, because he feels he then has the opportunity to see how other authors work and to explore other techniques, which teaches him to read more accurately ("Jaco Jacobs ryg pryse in vir eie en vertaalwerk" 2009).

Jacobs also had the privilege to translate Niki Daly's *No More Kisses for Bernard* (2011), *Welcome to Zanzibar Road* (2006) and *Next Stop—Zanzibar Road!* (2012) into Afrikaans as *Moenie vir Bernard Soen Nie*, *Zanzibarstraat* and *Zanzibarstraat, Hier Kom Ons!* Jacobs succeeded brilliantly in mimicking Daly's clever use of playful sounds in his clever and colorful descriptions in *Zanzibarstraat, Hier Kom Ons!* "Flippy-floppy, flappy-slippy, this-way-that-way pompom hat" becomes "flip-flap-flop-oppiekop-diékant-daaikant-pompom-hoed."

Having published more than ninety books and translated more than two hundred titles in twelve years, Jaco Jacobs is one of South Africa's most successful children's book authors. He seems to have an instinctive feel for his readers' needs and likes and effortlessly switches between writing for different age groups. Jacobs is a ringmaster par excellence. He has cleverly stage-managed the performances of various acts and guided his audience through many entertaining experiences. He definitely has many more rabbits to yet pull out of his hat.

CHILDREN'S BOOKS

Brink, Tania. 2002. *Liefde Laat Jou Rice Krispies Anders Proe*. Pretoria, SA: LAPA.
_____. 2006. *Ouens Is Nie Pizzas Nie*. Pretoria, SA: LAPA.
_____. 2011. *My Hart Is Vol Graffiti*. Pretoria, SA: LAPA.
Daly, Niki. 2007. *Zanzibarstraat*. Translated by Jaco Jacobs. Pretoria, SA: LAPA.
_____. 2011. *Moenie vir Bernard Soen Nie*. Translated by Jaco Jacobs. Pretoria, SA: LAPA.
_____. 2012. *Zanzibarstraat, Hier Kom Ons!* Translated by Jaco Jacobs. Northlands, SA: Giraffe.
Deary, Terry. 2003. *Gruwelike Geskiedenis van die Wêreld*. Translated by Jaco Jacobs. Cape Town, SA: Human & Rousseau.
Fearnley, Jan. 2009. *Miemie in die Middel*. Translated by Jaco Jacobs. Pretoria, SA: LAPA.
Jacobs, Jaco. 2001. *Duskant die Doodlyn*. Pretoria, SA: LAPA.
_____. 2001. *Rugbypret*. Pretoria, SA: LAPA.
_____. 2001. *Troetelgedrog*. Pretoria, SA: LAPA.
_____. 2003. *Pretpark*. Cape Town, SA: Human & Rousseau.
_____. 2004. *Krieketpret/Gevaarlike Lopies*. Pretoria, SA: LAPA.
_____. 2004. *Wiskunde Gee M Maagpyn*. Pretoria, SA: LAPA.
_____. 2005. *Net Aliens Eet Spinasie*. Cape Town, SA: Human & Rousseau.
_____. 2005. *Wurms met Tamatiesous en Ander Lawwe Rympies*. Pretoria, SA: LAPA.
_____. 2007. *Suurlemoen*. Pretoria, SA: LAPA.
_____. 2007. *Verneukpan*. Cape Town, SA: Maskew Miller Longman.
_____. 2008. *Bertie Blikbrein*. Pretoria, SA: LAPA.
_____. 2008. *Borrels*. Pretoria, SA: LAPA.
_____. 2008. *How Wide Can a Hippo Open Its Mouth?* Pretoria, SA: LAPA.

———. 2008. *Liewe Land, 'n Olifant*. Pretoria, SA: LAPA.
———. 2008. *Suzie se Superdoeper-Sjampoe*. Pretoria, SA: LAPA.
———. 2009. *How Many Teeth Does a Crocodile Have?* Pretoria, SA: LAPA.
———. 2009. *Middernagfees*. Pretoria, SA: LAPA.
———. 2009. *Virus*. Pretoria, SA: LAPA.
———. 2010. *Harlekyn*. Cape Town, SA: Tafelberg.
———. 2010. *How High Can a Grasshopper Jump?* Pretoria, SA: LAPA.
———. 2010. *Madelief, Moenie!* Pretoria, SA: LAPA.
———. 2010. *My Boetie Dink Hy's Batman en Ander Rympies*. Pretoria, SA: LAPA.
———. 2010. *Zackie Mostert en die Ongelooflike Kulkunsie*. Pretoria, SA: LAPA.
———. 2010. *Zackie Mostert en die Super-Aaklige Soen*. Pretoria, SA: LAPA.
———. 2011. *Haasmoles*. Pretoria, SA: LAPA.
———. 2011. *Kas Vol Monsters*. Pretoria, SA: LAPA.
———. 2011. *Slaaptyd, Matilda*. Pretoria, SA: LAPA.
———. comp. 2011. *Toulopers—Verse vir Tieners*. Pretoria, SA: LAPA.
———. 2012. *Al die Meisies Hou van Divan Louw*. Pretoria, SA: LAPA.
———. 2012. *Bastian Blom en die Pratende Portret*. Pretoria, SA: LAPA.
———. 2012. *Professor Fungus en die Zombie-Tamaties*. Pretoria, SA: LAPA.
Lodge, Katherine. 2012. *Waar is Mandie*. Translated by Jaco Jacobs. Pretoria, SA: LAPA.
Riddell, Chris. 2008. *Willemien en die Geel Kat*. Translated by Jaco Jacobs. Pretoria, SA: LAPA.
Roux, Lise. 2011. *Stalmaats*. Pretoria, SA: LAPA.

Ingrid Mennen: Always in Africa

Tanya Barben

Ingrid Mennen lives in Cape Town, a city "at the very tip of the great African continent" (Mennen 1990, 8) where lions and elephants once roamed, and where zebras still graze not too far from its center. It is a vibrant, pulsating metropolis that is nestled against the bosom of Table Mountain and cradled in the arms of Devil's Peak to the east and Lion's Head and Signal Hill to the west. The country's colonial history began in the mid-seventeenth century with the establishment of a Dutch refreshment station on the shores of Table Bay. Since then it has been riven by social and economic inequalities, and policies of racial separation that encouraged among its diverse population mistrust and ignorance of each other, abuse and fear. This segregation became fully entrenched in the statute books when the National Party came into power in 1948.

Birth and Background

Mennen was born six years later and grew up in the rather protected environment so typical of many South African children of white (and in her case, Afrikaans-speaking) middle-class parentage. Her father was a professor of forestry at Stellenbosch University and later farmed avocados in the northeastern part of the country. Her mother, Rene Deetlefs, is an author of much-loved children's books. Mennen has commented that she was born between her mother's library and her father's vegetable garden. Her childhood memories are full of overlapping metaphors, of "seeds being placed in soil and seeds in a story" (Meyer 2013).

Her mother was an inspiration to her. She grabbed whatever opportunity she could to put pen to paper while she watched her children grow. She believed with Einstein that in order to develop their imagination children need to be exposed to fairy tales and folklore, myths and legends. Writing was quite clearly in Mennen's blood. She was thus introduced to the process of reading and writing and listening to stories at an early age, and recalls with enjoyment the vast array of books that she and her siblings were exposed to, both in their mother tongue and English: poetry and stories that connected them to the wider world as well as those rooted in their country's soil. She knew that she wanted to, had to, write. When she was just a youngster of nine one of her stories was published in *Die Jongspan*, a popular children's magazine in Afrikaans.

After graduating with a bachelor's degree from the University of Pretoria, she returned to the Cape Province to read for a postgraduate qualification in museology. She was employed in the cultural museum services of the Cape Province and was given the task of working in the Bo-Kaap Museum which was situated in an old house in a part of Cape Town reserved for members of the Cape Malay (or Muslim) community, many of whom were descended from slaves. These slaves had been brought to the Cape from the East Indies by the Dutch East India Company during the seventeenth and eighteenth and centuries when the Cape was ruled by the Company. The suburb was formerly known as the Malay Quarter, now Bo-Kaap, as it was located on the slopes of Signal Hill above the city of Cape Town (Kaapstad in Afrikaans). Mennen soaked up the heady, spice-filled, colorful atmosphere of her working environment and became acquainted with the quintessential cosmopolitanism of the city, exploring its streets and alleys during lunch breaks. These images were to remain with her, and were put to good use in *Ashraf of Africa*, which she wrote together with Niki Daly, prize-winning illustrator and author of South African children's books.

A Writing Life

During the 1980s the demands of a young family kept her occupied, yet the seeds of stories were germinating within her. With some temerity she submitted her writing to Human & Rousseau, a noted South African publisher. One of her stories was accepted. This was *'n Grot vir 'n Grootman / Barney Climbs a Mountain*, illustrated with sensitivity by Mel Todd, a gentle, domestic story, published in 1987 when her youngest child was a baby. It is about a boy who has to give up his bed when his grandmother comes to visit.

Todd introduced Mennen to an informal group of writers and illustrators with whom she attended a symposium, *Towards Understanding: Children's Literature for All Southern Africa's Children*, held in July 1987 at the University of the Western Cape, a university at the time designated for coloured persons.

This was an extremely exciting and eye-opening experience for Mennen and her group, as they felt that they were becoming a part of a far wider children's literature community. It was clear that the winds of change were blowing through the country for, undeterred by an increasingly oppressive state, millions of their compatriots were anticipating the coming of democracy and the end of apartheid. The main thrust of the symposium was to contribute towards the breaching of the barriers that separated South Africa's population by producing books with which all children, regardless of background, could identify.

Introducing Ashraf

Mennen, who did not yet consider herself a "real" author, felt that her attendance at the symposium represented a life-changing experience, a pivotal moment in her life. She participated in sessions with authors and illustrators and met individuals who were an inspiration to her. She had dreamed for years of being a writer, and she was able to sense the possibility of her dream becoming a reality. Sometime after the symposium Mennen was invited to participate in workshops for writers and illustrators led by Niki Daly, who is discussed in another essay in this book. During 1989–1990 Daly was the commissioning editor of Songololo Books, the children's book division of David Philip Publishers. Under his direction the Songololo imprint created ground-breaking picture books. All were rich in images of Africa and a local South African setting, and so Mennen saw her inclusion in these workshops as a great encouragement. Daly and his wife, Jude, became Mennen's lifelong friends and an inspiration for her. Out of the workshops came *Ashraf of Africa* illustrated by idiosyncratic South African artist, Nicolaas Maritz. Mennen (Meyer 2013) reminisces as follows:

> It was mainly Niki's work-shopping group that started me thinking that I wanted to write books that would include all our children. My eyes opened up to the closed lives we were living. I wanted my books to be placed in a recognizably African context—this was an epiphany. I began playing with words like "Ashraf" and "Africa"—and thought about what I wanted to say about our children to a wider audience. Playing with words was an activity that seemed to consume me. It enabled me to create a new world for myself beyond the domestic confines of privileged South African homes. Niki negotiated with Nicolaas to do the illustrations, and his work was a perfect complement to our joint venture. There is a sense of Africa in them, raw, untamed and exciting. Nicolaas's contribution our book was very important, while Niki was masterful in the way he ignited our creativity [n.p.].

Significantly, when Mennen was just starting to write stories about her continent, she recalled an incident in her childhood when a friend visiting from what is now Zimbabwe asked why there were no lions and elephants wandering around. This is exactly what she wanted to ask the friend about her own country.

Ashraf has been described by Elwyn Jenkins, scholar of South African children's literature, as "outstanding" (Jenkins 2006, 184). This gentle story, pitched at the younger child, tells the story of a boy who lives in a city in Africa, but not the Africa inhabited by wild animals that western readers imagine, or that Ashraf reads about—and sees only—in the book he has borrowed from the library. It is a city that Ashraf loves and knows well, a city that bathes in the heat of summer beneath an iconic mountain, one with a diverse citizenry and culture, both of which are captured in the seamless marriage between text and illustration. Ashraf criss-crosses the city, passing drummers and dancers, curio shops, flower and fruit sellers, in order to visit the library where he finds a jungle—of books—through which he can stalk for "something special. Something wild and untamed" (25). He chooses *not* a new book, but the old favorite that he has just returned. The sympathetic librarian, Mrs Mackenzie, re-issues it to him with a smile. There is much about *Ashraf of Africa* that is appealing. A heart-warming prominence is given to books, the library (and librarians) and to Ashraf's love of reading, a role-model for South Africans who are not considered great readers of books.

Ashraf of Africa was recently critiqued in an academic dissertation in which Ashraf is described as demonstrating "self-sufficiency" and "skill" while negotiating the bustling city, "buzzing with urban energy in the illustration," and "using books and his imagination to experience an exotic Africa of crocodiles and lions" (Thyssen 2012, 29). It was reviewed widely, and generally positively, in the United States and the United Kingdom. Celia Gibbs writes that "the authors attempt to confront the stereotype that Africans are the inhabitants of a rural never-never land" (Gibbs 1995, 55), while E.F. (1992) describes the book as an "enlightening look at a child in a distant place to whom many children will instantly find themselves connected" (193). A review in *Publishers Weekly* (1992) thinks it a "bit slight," but recognizes it as "an immediately appealing story at once universal and distinctly African" (n.p.). This is, of course, precisely what the authors and illustrator had in mind for the children of South Africa and the world. For the latter it would be "an enjoyable introduction to a faraway, multifaceted land" (*Publishers Weekly* 1992, n.p.). A contrary viewpoint is expressed by Raoul Granqvist (1997), who describes the book as having been "conceived outside Africa for Euro-American children" (24). This is quite clearly not the case. Granqvist comments on the fact that the librarian is a "'European'" (she might not be, despite her name), that

Ashraf's book choice is for "non-Africa, the Africa of the myth, and not for the world outside the library" (30). The contents of the curio shop that Ashraf passes are representative of "icons of conquest and oppression" (30) He sees in the book "unabashed cultural prejudices and stereotyping" (30), a controversial interpretation of a book whose purpose was to describe the authentic rhythms and character of inner-city Cape Town and which was coincidentally innovative in its move away from these prejudices and stereotyping.

Mennen, her co-creators and *Ashraf* have been vindicated and amply rewarded, for the book has, among other things, been exhibited internationally, translated into several languages, and in 2012 was chosen as one of the books to represent South Africa in the International Federation of Library Associations/IBBY compilation, *The World through Picture Books: Librarians' Favourite Books from Their Country* (Everall and Quiñones 2102).

Sky Creatures and a Small Boy

Mennen continued writing, this time for Juta which was publishing a series of books for young readers, but her full energies were spent on a story (initially conceptualized as a counting book) which developed into *One Round Moon and a Star for Me*. "When I put its opening words on paper I realised that I could be giving a poetic imagination to a black child—like that which you want any child to have but which had been denied—often—to our children. The words in the story flowed naturally from me" (pers. comm.). After submitting it to Songololo Books she heard from Daly that he had sat up all night working on the illustrations and was going to take the dummy book to the Bologna Book Fair. There the book was accepted by an international publishing house. This gave her a tremendous fillip—she could now write her name as an independent author—not just a co-author.

The story is set in the rural Transkei (now South Africa's Eastern Cape Province) among the Xhosa-speaking people. A small boy and his very expectant mother gaze up at the night sky and the moon as round as her pregnant belly. They watch as the boy's father seems to scoop a falling star into his milk bucket. The boy pleads with the moon to return to her empty hut. He celebrates the rising of the sun and enters his own hut where his mother is nursing a brand-new baby. The boy helps his aunt mark the hut to warn the menfolk that they cannot enter it until the *intake* (umbilical) cord drops off the baby's belly. Female friends and family bring meaningful gifts for the mother and infant. Then Papa arrives to look at the baby and recognizes in the infant Mama's ears and his own hands. The dark shadow of insecurity (usual with the arrival of a new sibling) spreads over the boy's heart. "Papa, are you really my papa too?" (15) he asks. His father takes his hands and assures him that he is his father too. "Your eyes are like Mama's eyes. You are your papa's child and you are your mama's child." (17). The boy lies in his father's arms, absolutely secure in his love and the promise of catching his own falling star.

One Round Moon was published in the United States by Orchard Books, in the United Kingdom by The Bodley Head, and in South Africa in Afrikaans, Xhosa and Zulu by Human & Rousseau. An English-language copy was published by Songololo Books in 1995. Niki Daly's illustrations are a superb companion to Mennen's text. It has been translated into many languages and praised unreservedly, both for its text and its illustrations. Stephen Del Vecchio (1994) has described it as "an example of a multicultural picture book at its best, combining the universal and the particular while not skimping on quality and emotion" (190). What is particularly pleasing is the way that Mennen celebrates Xhosa traditional practices relating to childbirth and the love between parent and child, and how Daly endorses breast-feeding, a fact that was noted in an article in the *Journal of Human Lactation* (Altshuler, 1995). The review that meant the most to Mennen appeared in the *New York Times Book Review*. In it Sarah Stein describes Mennen's writing as being "as smooth as ivory," praises "the synergy of author and artist" and adds that "the richness of this story arises in the marriage of author and artist" (Stein 1994, 18). The book was also taken up in an anthology, *Night, Night, Sleep Tight* published by The Bodley Head in 1998 and by Red Fox in 1999, along with the works of well-known authors, such as Shirley Hughes, and has been translated into many languages and published widely.

Drawn from Life

This was her last book for a while, not that she stopped writing—on scraps of paper, in journals and with a different motivation. Material to her identity and existence is her role as a wife and as a mother to three children, so it is not surprising that she was caught up in the routines of motherhood and domesticity. While thus occupied she studied English at the University of Cape Town to Honours level (post–Baccalaureate), passing all her courses cum laude. This gave her confidence a great lift, but in her mind she still could not consider herself an author. She was convinced that she was not a writer, that her books had been merely lucky breaks. Writing made her feel that she had a place in this world, where maybe she could mean something and make a contribution, even a small one. She took up her creative pen once more with *A Wish This Big*, reworked into the Afrikaans, *Soos 'n Wens So Groot*.

As is the case with all her books, this one was drawn from life, inspired by South Africa's hosting of the FIFA World Cup in 2010 and the building of Cape Town's magnificent, albeit controversial, football stadium in sight of Robben Island, South Africa's infamous prison in which the iconic Nelson Mandela and many other heroes of the country's liberation struggle had been incarcerated.

> I was struck by the impression that the stadium was like an island too. It had the shape of an island—that there were two islands: this super modern, nearly fantastic structure and this old-old island with its real history. They were both powerful symbols—contrasting, iconic—not only of the South African struggle for freedom, but the celebration of freedom [pers. comm.].

Evocatively illustrated by Katrin Coetzer, *A Wish This Big* tells of Rashied who lives, like Ashraf, in Cape Town. He has a warm, loving relationship with his grandfather, once a prisoner on Robben Island. His grandfather's stories are as good as any soccer ball. He tells Rashied how the game of soccer that he and his fellow prisoners played on the Island, or the soccer he practiced alone in his cell, made life tolerable, made them "forget that we were caught between the four walls of a prison. We felt part of the real world again, free like birds over the island. It filled us with hope" (19). None of the prisoners could ever imagine that one day a stadium would be built in Cape Town for all the people of South Africa.

Rashied longs for something round: not the moon, not the sun, not his bowl of breakfast porridge which reminds him of the Island. His Grandpa guesses that what he wants is a brand-new soccer ball. Grandpa reminds him that the game is not made by the ball but by the skills that come with practice, hard work and playing fair. Grandpa has a special gift for Rashied. From the back of his cupboard, he fetches the ball, now deflated, that he had played with on the Island. Together, they have it filled with air and polish it "till it shone, bright like hope" (25). All summer is spent practicing and playing. Sometimes the ball bounces right over the wall of Rashied's yard, and he imagines that he, too, is soaring over the wall into the wide open stadium where he and his friends are playing before thousands. Encapsulated in this story is the element of hope—and the sure knowledge that in the new South Africa even the smallest dreams can come true for its children.

Jay Heale, doyen of South African children's literature, recognized its excellence when he gave this title a 2011 Bookchat award:

> I have a wish as well. That this bright, bold, artistic, simple yet deep picture book could be put in front of everyone who does not understand what is meant by a truly South African children's literature, anyone who does not appreciate the word 'relevant,' everyone who wants to cling to the past instead of the future [Heale 2011, n.p.].

Mennen's love for and pride in South Africa, and Cape Town specifically, is palpable. The link between its past and future is very deftly interwoven in the story without being over-emphasized or saccharine-sweet.

Death, Independence and Earning Wings

Her most recent work is *Ben and the Whales: The Extraordinary Journey*, which was also published in Afrikaans as *Ben en die Walvisse: 'n Wonderlike Reis*. The book, like *A Wish This Big*, tells the story of intergenerational relationships between the chief protagonist, Ben, and his grandfather, and Ben and his father. It also describes the awe and wonder that is engendered in them by the humpback whales that visit the coast of South Africa every year in the southern winter and spring to breed and give birth. That is not all, however, for *Ben and the Whales* is also about death and its necessity as part of the cycle of life, about dealing with loss and becoming independent. *A Wish This Big* was accepted enthusiastically by the publishers, and proved to Mennen that she could stand on her own. *Ben and the Whales* opened new vistas and helped her deal with the loss that comes with the death of someone personally significant. She hoped that the book would make it easier for parents to talk to their children about death. While walking with his father on the same cliff path that he had strolled along with his grandfather, Ben is able to talk about his loss. His father tells him a story about birth and death among the whales, and about a calf that is called to the safety of the Southern Ocean by the song of the whales. He is strengthened by his father's story and the time he has spent with him... "for the first time ever he went home all by himself; and he felt as if he had wings, like one of those flying giants of the sea" (31). In this way Mennen has expressed what she so fervently believes: that stories make us strong, they give us an understanding of the world and bring us closer to independence and freedom. Stories, as has been said so often before, give us wings (Meyer 2013).

The illustrations are by Irene Berg, who is Mennen's elder daughter. Mennen has always been fortunate in her books' illustrators as they have drawn out from her writing images that have added considerably to it. Here, however, the mother-daughter partnership is especially fitting. Berg's beautifully detailed images (a tortoise on the foot path, a gannet on a rock, the companionable Basset Hound, the comfortable but empty chair) complement the text "just so."

There is another dimension to the illustrations in the form of Dorling-Kindersley-type endpapers packed with bits from Grandpa's scrapbook containing information about whales, including Ben's note to his grandfather:

"We are mammals. A whale is my favourite animal. Like you Grandpa," which appears on the front pastedown.

Mennen's merit as an author—she now accepts that that is what she is—has been acknowledged nationally in the best possible way. Not only was *Ben and the Whales* awarded the Bookchat Book of the Year for 2012, but in 2013 it also received South Africa's prestigious M.E.R. Prize for the best illustrated children's book, ages 0 to 8.

CHILDREN'S BOOKS

Mennen, Ingrid. 1987. *Barney Climbs a Mountain/'n Grot vir 'n Grootman*. Cape Town, SA: Human & Rousseau.

———. 1994. *One Round Moon and a Star for Me*. Illustrated by Niki Daly. London: The Bodley Head. New York: Orchard Books.

———. 2012. *Ben and the Whales: An Extraordinary Journey*. Illustrated by Irene Berg. Cape Town, SA: Tafelberg.

Mennen, Ingrid and Katrin Coetzer. 2011. *A Wish This Big*. Cape Town, SA: Tafelberg.

Mennen, Ingrid and Niki Daly. 1990. *Ashraf of Africa*. Illustrated by Nicolaas Maritz. Cape Town, SA: Songololo Books.

———. 1992. *Somewhere in Africa*. Illustrated by Nicolaas Maritz. New York: Dutton. London: The Bodley Head.

———. 1998. *Night, Night, Sleep Tight*. London: The Bodley Head.

Gcina Mhlophe: Imbira Player

Genevieve Hart

The warning at the outset was "writing about Gcina Mhlophe will be trying to distil stardust" (Heale pers. comm.). The warning referred to the challenge of capturing Mhlophe's multifaceted gifts on paper. But it could also be hinting at the risks of writing about a South African celebrity—a national "treasure." Her many awards and honorary degrees attest to her stellar standing in theatrical and literary landscapes.[1] She has spoken for Africa on platforms throughout the world—as in her "Invitation to Africa" presentation at the 2002 IBBY Congress in Basel, Switzerland, which reportedly did much to persuade people to attend the first IBBY Congress in Africa, held in Cape Town in 2004 (Heale pers. comm.).

Her web site describes her as a "well-known South African freedom fighter, activist, actor, storyteller, poet, playwright, director and author." She is all these things and far more—Oboe's (2007) label "oral artist" (61) might fit best her blending of poetry, drama, storytelling and song. This essay will show the impossibility of containing her under any label. In 1994, on being accused of being "all over the place," she replies:

> Yes I do different things, and they complement each other. It doesn't bother me at all that I'm in storytelling. A play that hasn't got a good story is never a good play. A song that hasn't a good story is not a song. The story is mother of everything. Even a poem needs to have an essence, the story, from which to start [Solberg 1996, 33].

Her career certainly has coherence. In her gentle poem, "In the Company of Words" (*Love Child* 9), she tells us of her love affair with *words*. And perhaps it is her love of words that weaves the threads of her various art forms together into such a solid fabric. To her, they are a source of both power and solace. She uses her agility with words to celebrate, praise, protest, entertain—and to reflect.

Another cohering thread in her career is her concern for children. Today, with scores of children's books under her name and with her various school literacy projects, she might well be described as a children's author, dramatist and activist. In the early 1990s, after carving out a successful career in local and international theater, she decided to devote herself to South Africa's children—using her stories to "replant" pride in African cultures and history. In an interview in 1994, talking of the transition from resistance art to new arenas of "struggle," she declares: "I've got to work with young people every day of my life. If I can inspire young people to believe in themselves.... I want to do it every day" (Solberg 1996, 29).

Some years later in 2008, on receiving an honorary doctorate degree from the University of Pretoria, she affirmed her earlier statement, saying that she was "born at the right time so I could also play my role in society, especially with young people" (Magome 2008, 7). She goes on to say that she grew up to realize that "telling stories of my people would be my identity" (7).

Beginnings of Storytelling

In various interviews and in the prefaces to two collections of stories (2004; 2006), Gcina Mhlophe has paid tribute to her paternal grandmother's storytelling, which introduced her to the "magic" power of words to open up new worlds. The stories encouraged her imagination to "run wild." If the story animals could be in two places at once, why couldn't she go to school *and* stay at home to play? Why shouldn't she find a clever bird to do her household chores? Later on, words provided companionship to her as a lonely teenager in the Eastern Cape, homesick for her grandmother and Kwazulu-Natal home. She was a voracious reader and an academic achiever, working hard to please her sister in Johannesburg who was paying for her schooling. In *Love Child*, a retrospective collection of intimate biographical writing, she describes herself as a "Miss Ugly-Top-of-the-Class" outsider. In her description of two "transforming moments," she tells of finding her voice. One was an encounter with an imbongi, a praise singer. After describing his flamboyant dress, she goes on:

> His use of language was pure and flowing—and so were his movements. He leapt forward and hit the ground with his oxtail stick, hardly making a sound. I saw some people unconsciously imitating him. One minute, he would be praising, the next he was reflective and critical. ...I simply sat there, and in my dreamy mind, saw myself in similar attire, doing what I had just seen the man do. I made my decision there and then that I was also a praise poet [7].

Soon afterwards she wrote her first poem, lying alone in her favorite spot under some wattle trees. She felt like a new mother and then read it aloud: "My voice sounded like it was a special voice, made specially to perform poems with dignity. That's the day I fell in love with myself" (8). In describing the imbongi's performance and her discovery of the power of her own voice, Mhlophe could be describing her later self. On the stage her presence is larger than life. Her voice is her musical instrument, and she mesmerizes her audiences of all ages.

Mhlophe arrived in Johannesburg in 1980 and, with no possibility of a university place, took a job as a domestic worker, looking after a family of four children. A daily ritual of games, rhymes and storytelling began and soon she found herself spending her evenings planning the next day's story. She reports that she had to be careful at first as she was not sure how the family would respond to her African folktales (Sithole 1989). It would be interesting to know which of the thirty-six stories she recorded and wrote in this time became part of her repertoire.

Mhlophe is impatient with attempts to draw lines between conventional literary genres; thus, as mentioned earlier, personal memoir and fiction are interwoven in several of the stories in the *Love Child* collection. Several "stories" and poems record her frustrating situation as domestic servant and factory worker. She acknowledges, though, that her unhappiness led her to hone her writing skills: in the story "The Toilet" she hides away in a public toilet after sneaking out of her sister's backyard room at dawn. The stories are poignant and, at times, darkly funny. In "My Dear Madam" she pokes bitter fun at her racist employer in the saga of mishaps in a delivery of coal. It is interesting to speculate what her employer has made of her several honorary doctorates and international renown, having warned her departing "maid": "Actually you will die with a broom in your hands. Blacks will never rule this country.... Do you understand?" (44).

An article in the *Star* newspaper quotes Mhlophe on her breakthrough to theatre in 1980:

> I'd never recited my poetry before. I'd never even heard of a woman being a praise poet. When I'd heard of it in the Transkei, it was a man who was doing it. One day I was invited to a writers' gathering in Soweto and I told them I wanted to read. People were standing up with their papers and their books, but when I started, I began by singing and dancing and came on with my poetry.... People who were in drama saw me and they thought I might be all right for stage work but it was 1982 before I appeared in Maishe Maponya's "The Nurse" ... [MacLiam 1987, 13].

As Imbongi

An imbongi comments and criticizes, as well as praises. Oral performance has always interwoven politics and poetry (Kaschula 2001, xv). The 1980s were cruel times and Mhlophe used the "drum" of her writing to protest. Her stark poem "Say No," included in *Love Child*, might well have been addressed to suburban madams:

> Say No, Black Woman
> Say No
> When they call your husband at the age of 60 a boy
> Say No [45].

Although consciously using her art to build solidarity and to tell the world what was going on in apartheid South Africa, interviews reveal her open-mindedness. Thus in 1989, in defending Gibson Kente's crowd-pulling musicals, she claims that his "social themes" like "wife-bashing, teenage pregnancy … are no less important than blacks taking over the country" (August 2002, 280).

She always insisted on her right to write on a personal level, as in this comment when she regrets that she cannot share her love poems on public platforms: "No-one can dictate what you should write…. I fall in love. That is a very real part of my life as well. I don't spend every minute fighting the system" (Sithole 1989, 20).

Her award-winning play—*Have You Seen Zandile?*—tells the story of her disrupted childhood and her complicated relationship with her mother. It was written in the midst of the 1986 State of Emergency, but she says it "had to be written because there was something that mattered inside me that needed to be told" (Solberg 1996, 26). The play drew large audiences to Johannesburg's Market Theatre and won awards in Edinburgh and Chicago. But it was criticized in some political circles as "irrelevant" (Sithole 1989, 20).

Perhaps it is the deft mixing of personal and political in Mhlophe's work that makes it so appealing and timeless. An example is the story "Love Child" that gives her collection its name. It came out of the violence between different political camps in the early 1990s and her own experience as the "love child" of a Zulu father and a Xhosa mother (Mhlophe 2002, xi). Two villages are engaged in a bitter war and a young man, Mthunzi, is led by a mysterious young woman, Nomlambo, to a cave where he meets five old women playing wonderful music on a large drum. They teach him to play the drum and send him out with the words: "Take it with you to the battlefield tonight—Go and stop that war!" (105). On hearing the music, the warriors drop their weapons and begin to mingle. In a comic scene, they discover surprising family connections, which teach them the folly of their animosity:

> "Mfowthu, I do not know you; I am Zondo, who are you?"
> "Dlamini? You don't say! My wife is Madlamini."
> "And you look so much like the Thabethe people; am I right? He-he, I knew it!" [105].

Another example of the power in Mhlophe's mix of personal and social comment is the deceptively lyrical poem "Sometimes When It Rains." The early verses are happy memories of watching goats running from the rain; then she breaks into nostalgia with the comment that rain meant, "We didn't have to fetch water / From the river for a day or two." Then the lens widens:

> Sometimes when it rains
> And rains for days without a break
> I think of mothers
> Who give birth in squatter camps
> Under plastic shelters
> At the mercy of cold and angry winds [*Love Child,* 62].

Between 1989 and 1993 Mhlophe shifted from theatre to storytelling (August 2002). In 1989 the bug had clearly bitten: "When I do storytelling, I'm alone on stage. I go to town. It's my stuff; I can close my eyes and eat it" (August 2002, 280). Her storytelling always involved more than her individual performances; she organized the first of a series of storytelling festivals at the Market Theatre in Johannesburg in 1989 and by 1993 had set up the Zanendaba (Bring Me A Story) group of women storytellers. Of course, the line between theatre and Mhlophe's brand of storytelling is blurred. Thus, Zakes Mda (1997) describes her storytelling performances as a "highly participatory form of theatre" (143). In 1993 Mhlophe recounts how she had thought storytelling "would be a part-time thing but when I got inside I saw how vast it was" (August 2002, 280). Her audience was "ripe," and her phone would not stop ringing with invitations to perform for people of all ages and political persuasions:

> One of the frustrations of theatre is that the bright lights can make you unable to see your audience. And I love to see my audience, I gain strength from that.... But something else was happening in South Africa. I was feeling the glaring demand to do specific kinds of theatre. And I don't know if I was in the minority, but I felt that political messages could also be put across through storytelling, without being party political [280].

She was sending political messages in merely telling the stories from her childhood. "Our stories lay under [the white people's imported stories] and were presented as something to be ashamed of ... something not good enough" (Sithole 1989, 18).

However, as someone who "likes things that last," on the publication of her first book, *The Snake with Seven Heads,* she declares, "I am essentially a writer" (Sealey 1988, 12). This title tells the story of a loyal wife Manjuza, a famous wedding dancer. Her husband has been turned into a snake, but she hides him away in a pot and cares for him lovingly. One night her grandmother appears to her in a dream to give her the task of dancing at seven weddings to break the spell. Yet, as the academic and author Njabulo Ndebele (2011) comments, it is often impossible to read her writing without hearing her voice, as in this extract from the story as published in the collection *Madiba Magic* (2002):

> A wedding without Manjuza to stand up at the right time—when the bride was about to come out, looking her best, smelling of beautiful herbs and her face glowing like the morning sun—that wedding was no wedding at all. Indeed, a wedding without Manjuza was a wedding soon forgotten [66].

From the start, Mhlophe's story performances were always interspersed with poems and rhymes. And, although always entertaining, her stories are didactic. However, her taking on the mantle of an imbongi in the 1990s, as, for example, at the Truth and Reconciliation Commission (TRC) hearings in 1997, broke new ground. In his essay on the "de-oracisation" of African women, Bukenya quotes the African proverb, "The hen knows that the dawn has come but it watches the mouth of the rooster" (2001, 33). Looking back from the vantage point of post-apartheid 2014, it is easy to underestimate Mhlophe's courage.

In an interview in 1989, on being asked about her identity as a woman artist, she asserts her independence, using again the phrase "falling in love with myself":

> I started after I had fallen in love with myself. I had accepted myself. I had accepted the kind of person I am. So I see things whatever way I see them and I don't feel: Am I female? Am I male? Am I black? [August 2002, 276].

Despite this disclaimer, she is clearly a women's activist. Four years later in 1994, her role as a black woman in theater comes under the spotlight. She claims that "black women know they've got to get in there and do it themselves rather than criticising that the man didn't do it this way or that" (August 2002, 283). In "Sitting Alone Thinking," a poem she performed in 1997 at the TRC and included in *Love Child*, she considers how gender might affect politics with a series of questions like:

> Would Mr President be a better man
> If he had a womb and breasts full of milk? [85].

Mhlophe opened the women's hearings at the TRC by quoting Bessie Head's words on the two key functions of storytelling: firstly, telling or recording the realities, and then dreaming the future (Oboe 2007). In her poem "A Brighter Dawn for African Women," included in *Love Child*, she first talks of the indignities women have endured for centuries but then she goes on:

> But you would not say so by the smile she bears
> To kiss the sunrise each morning ...
> The woman of Africa wants to sing a song of love
> To bring back old wisdoms that will shine a new light [107].

Into Books for Young Readers

Her writing for children is all about bringing back "old wisdoms." She has written three major children's collections of African stories, *Stories of Africa*, *Our Story Magic* and *African Tales: A Barefoot Collection*, which was published in the United Kingdom. All received warm praise, in spite of the rather pedestrian illustrations in the two South African books. The Barefoot Books collection leaves a satisfying sense of wholeness—largely due to Rachel Griffin's intricate designs and collages, which connect the separate stories. In recent years, there have been some entrancing collaborations between a writer and an illustrator in South African folktale collections, like that between Linda Rode and Fiona Moodie in *In Die Nimmer-Immer Bos* (*In the Never-Ever Wood*) (2009). One might hope that, in the next few years, Mhlophe's publishers will team her with a brilliant artist to produce a landmark book.

The preoccupations that have emerged in this essay can be traced through Mhlophe's children's stories, both traditional and contemporary. Themes like the wonder of stories and music, loyalty, humility, and the triumph of an underdog are common. Her valuing of children is clear in stories like "Moonlight Magic," where a child is a mysterious gift. Her joy in hard work and the thrill of performance might be reflected in *Molo Zoleka!* In *The Singing Chameleon*, her chameleon, ostracized as an ugly nonentity, becomes a symbol of good luck after overcoming the dangerous python with his song.

Men often come out rather badly in her stories. The most despicable must be the father in "Dad Is Eating Ashes" (from *Our Story Magic*). In the midst of a terrible famine, he hides away pots of honey to eat in secret and at meal times insists on eating ashes, saying to his wife, "There is so little food in the pot. You can eat with the children; I will eat ashes" (47).

Mhlophe's shrewd humor runs through many of her stories. Her workshopped modern fable *Horns Only* (Dada et al.) tells the story of an exclusive party, which only animals with horns may attend. Monkey and Zebra manufacture some horns, only to have them fall off in the heat of the dancing. They are about to slink away when the other animals come to their senses:

> "Why must they have horns anyway?" asked Duiker.
> The animals thought and thought. Nobody had an answer [n.p.].

Could she be poking fun at high-flying politicians in her *Queen of the Tortoises*? Desperate to be a leader, brown Tortoise soaks herself in the river and declares herself the cleanest animal—and therefore "Leader." But, to her disappointment, she finds that the next day's leaders' meeting is to be held across the river. Two kind ducks offer to take her across the river if she promises to hold on tightly with her mouth. She is now so pleased with herself that

"Leader" is too lowly a title; only "Queen" is good enough. Once up in the sky, she persuades the ducks to take a detour over the forest so she might show off her flying to the other animals. But foolishly she cannot resist shouting down, "I am the Queen …" She falls and smashes her shell. Having learned humility, Queen Tortoise comes to love her new segmented shell.

Conclusion

Surely, Mhlophe is writing about herself and her mold-breaking work in her story co-created with Jeannie Kinsler, *Queen of the Imbira*. In this extract she might well be giving her creed on the power of art. Against all traditions, Khethiwe has secretly learned to play the imbira. The king is dying and Khetiwe slips in to play him her healing music:

> The king opened his eyes. …he saw his grandparents and their grandparents looking at him. They were smiling at him and they were all saying the same thing.
> "Qhubeka uphile! Keep on living!"
> But more than that …he heard the music, he heard the splash of the waterfall in the secret cave …He understood the hiss of the fire beside his home in the evening, and the laughter of the children who lived in his village. He remembered the sound of the old people talking and smiling while he fell asleep on his sleeping mat and the fire played with the shadows.
> He stood up—then he saw Khetiwe, playing her imbira. … "Let it be known" the king said, and even as he spoke, his voice grew stronger. "Let it be known that in THIS land ALL girls may play the music of our ancestors. Play the Imbira. Do not stop! Qubeka udlale!" [29].

In commenting on Mhlophe's oral poetry today, Njabulo Ndebele (2011) argues that, while sustaining the passion of her 1980s theater and storytelling work, she has matured into "a tested and accomplished artist" (n.p.). She uses the time-tested mnemonics and rich verbal techniques of African oral poetry; but Ndebele argues that she is "pushing the limits" to create an art form for contemporary South Africa.

Note

1. See Gcina Mhlophe's web site for an impressive list of her awards. http://www.gcinamhlophe.co.za/

Children's Books

Gordon, Marguerite, Nelson Mandela and Teresa Williams. 2002. *Madiba Magic: Nelson Mandela's Favourite Stories for Children*. Cape Town, SA: Tafelberg.

Mhlophe, Gcina. 1988. *Have You Seen Zandile?* Johannesburg, SA: Skotaville.
_____. 1989. *The Snake with Seven Heads.* Illustrated by Hargreaves Ntukwana. Johannesburg, SA: Skotaville Publishers.
_____. 2002. *Love Child.* Pietermaritzburg, SA: University of Natal Press.
_____. 2004. *Stories of Africa.* Scottsville, SA: University of KwaZulu-Natal Press.
_____. 2006. *Our Story Magic.* Scottsville, SA: University of KwaZulu-Natal Press.
Mhlophe, Gcina, and Hargreaves Ntukwana. 1990. *Queen of the Tortoises.* Braamfontein, SA: Skotaville.
Mhlophe, Gcina, and Jeannie Kinsler. 2003. *Queen of Imbira.* Cape Town, SA: Maskew Miller Longman.
Mhlophe, Gcina, and K. Becker. 2008. *The Singing Chameleon: A Traditional Story from Malawi.* Pietermaritzburg, SA: Songololo.
Mhlophe, Gcina, and Rachel Griffin. 2009. *African Tales: A Barefoot Collection.* Bath, UK: Barefoot Books.
Mhlophe, Gcina, and Elizabeth Pulles. 1994. *Molo Zoleka!/Hi, Zoleka!* Johannesburg, SA: David Philip, Songololo Books.

An Odyssey Through Fantasy: Fiona Moodie's Long Journey Home

Anne Hill

The multiple award-winning anthology *In the Never-Ever Wood* brought together three mature talents in a seamless collaboration: Linda Rode, anthologist and storyteller; Fiona Moodie, illustrator and author; and Elsa Silke, translator. Rode and Moodie won the Via Afrika M.E.R. Prize for Illustrated Children's Literature in 2010, and Silke won the South African Translators' Institute (SATI) 2012 award for outstanding translation.

Several significant strands in the evolution of Moodie's oeuvre[1] come together in this publication: an acute sense of the particular details that define a setting; mastery of the elements of her own visual language; and her ability to tune into a writer's literary quality, especially when it is elegantly economical, and translate it into visual language that complements a refined text.

Fiona Moodie's illustrations for the collection were a major feature of her 2010 solo exhibition at the Irma Stern Museum in Cape Town. In her address at the opening, Ingrid de Kok (2010) drew attention to Moodie's ability to create a compelling sense of place:

> And then there is something strange, both robust and refined—I can only call it respect—for the forms of and relations between animals and people and landscape. A sort of severe kindness, or kind severity, in the way Fiona depicts mountains and earth, trees and cottages, holes in the ground, stars and skies and plants, as well as small frightened creatures and large misunderstood ones [n.p.].

Moodie's progress towards the deceptively simple and elegant integration of imagination, feeling, landscape and literary sophistication that de Kok describes has been an odyssey that started in early childhood, took her far from home, and returned her to her native roots richly endowed with intercultural experience and knowledge of her craft.

Genesis of the Journey

Moodie wanted to write and illustrate books since the age of seven. She describes her childhood on an apple farm in the mountainous Overberg region of the Western Cape, the southernmost province of South Africa, as "solitary but happy" (pers.comm.). While her older brother and sister were away from home, attending boarding schools in Cape Town, she lived in her imagination, primed by plenty of literature familiar to British children, including Beatrix Potter's (1902-1911) tales, A.A.Milne's (1926) *Winnie the Pooh*, and English versions of Astrid Lindgren's (1950) *Pippi Longstocking* stories and Selma Lagerlof's (1922) *The Wonderful Adventures of Nils*. In addition, "there were few toys and I played with flowers and so on ... I wasn't really interested in reality; reality was in my head" (pers.comm.). The effects of this isolation were alienating:

> There were hardly any books in English that had a South African feel in those days and because books are so powerful, or were then, before TV arrived in 1972, I grew up thinking that what surrounded me wasn't quite real—that reality was in England where Mrs Tiggywinkle[2] [sic] was. I kept on looking for hedgehogs and badgers and foxes in the dusty veldt[3] on the farm [Moodie 2011, n.p.].

Moodie's sense of being outside the reality of everyday life was exacerbated when at eight years old, she went to boarding school in Cape Town. The relaxed and intimate routines of the small farm school of twenty-four scholars that she had attended for the first two grades was replaced by an often baffling, authoritarian regime of rules, structure and restrictions:

> There were so many rules; I was always in trouble. We had chapel every day; were only allowed out for a restricted time on two Sundays a term. It was education for life. It was intense, full of drama, and wildly close friendships. We sang a lot—we would lie on the lawn and sing in three part harmony, make up plays. All our energy went into making things up. I got very thin, probably because I was miserable [pers. comm.].

Moodie was sent home to recover her health. After a tonsillectomy and a period of time at home "everything came right" at school. She regards this experience as significant because it gave her a sense of the permanence of home no matter where she might be physically, at any particular time, and confidence in the support of her parents. This groundedness enabled her as a young woman traveling alone in Europe, to take risks that were important later in her development as an artist. The discovery of a sense of "home" also later drew her, after an extended sojourn in Europe, to refine the hues and tones of her palette in terms of the landscape, light and heat of her birth place in Africa.

After a story she had written was chosen to be broadcast on radio, the eight-year-old Moodie found her niche at school, and a circle of friends, as the dormitory storyteller and dramatist after dark. Her experience of overcoming ostracism and bullying as the "new girl" was echoed in her illustrations for Eva Bernatová's *The Wonder Shoes*. In this story, a lonely child, new in town, overcomes her loneliness by persuading her former tormentors to join her in staging a circus performance. In a rare departure from the fantasy genre, Moodie sets the story in a real Welsh village where she and her husband had lived in a forbidding stone Victorian era asylum building.

In her illustrations, the grey drabness of the stone buildings echoes the cold loneliness of Emma, the protagonist, until the village is transformed by the arrival of a circus. The performance ring is flooded with warm yellow light. The performers frolic in lively patterned brilliant red, blue and green costumes. The dominant motif is the circle, which comes to symbolize friendship, joy and energy in the final illustration.

After completing her schooling, Moodie studied English, French and Drama (non-performing) at the University of Cape Town (UCT), followed by a secondary school teaching qualification. At the time that she would have gone to Michaelis, the Faculty of Fine Art at UCT, illustration was not really taken seriously as "Art." In retrospect, Moodie is glad she did not have a formal art education at university straight after school as she believes that at that stage, striving for a sophisticated visual language may well have undermined her personal, emotional and possibly childlike approach to making art for picture books. She feels close to her own childhood and this is reflected in her books (pers.comm.). The emphases of her degree in literature, French and drama turned out to provide essential leverage in her development during the next, most formative period of her emergence as illustrator and author.

A Wandering Apprentice

Prompted by a sense of unease about the way things were in South Africa, Moodie set off to explore "other ways of being" (pers.comm.) in Europe, seeking out situations that challenged the comfortable assumptions of her privileged milieu at home. She returned home restless; her experiences of various kinds of employment in Europe and Cape Town had confirmed her desire to write and illustrate children's books for a living, but she was unsure of how to realize her passion. In 1975 she enrolled at the École Nationale Superieure des Arts Decoratifs in Paris, France, but recalls this as a less significant learning experience than the time she spent observing and drawing in the city, in between her studies and working as a psychiatrist's receptionist to support herself.

Following a chance meeting with an Austrian illustrator she took her portfolio to the Bologna (Italy) Children's Book Fair in 1976:

> At the fair I met a young Italian illustrator called Fulvio Testa and the next thing I knew I was being taken to the Bohem Press stand, where a small, lively bear of a man 20 years my senior, with a beard and mischievous shiny brown eyes was talking animatedly, surrounded by people. This was Stepan Zavrel, the art editor. Around him were illustrators, editors, friends, passers-by—he seemed to know everybody and even if he didn't, he behaved as if he knew them well. There was a lot of laughter and drinking of wine and the stand was like none other at the fair—decorated with potted palms and big round stones and wicker chairs. It seemed to be attracting the most amazing crowd—artists mostly. In amongst the laughter and chaos, book deals were being done, rights were being sold, illustrators discovered and commissioned. Fulvio introduced me to Stepan and he took the time to carefully go through my portfolio of work, which he said was not very good. Somehow I didn't mind at all—perhaps because he liked the last thing he looked at, a story I'd written and illustrated in Paris. He told me this was the direction I should go in, that my technical ability would improve with work and time. The most important thing was that I was a promising artist with imagination and Bohem Press would surely end up publishing my work! [Moodie 2009, n.p.].

Zavrel lived in both Paris and Italy, and for the next four years Moodie became part of an intensely creative and itinerant "family" of artists, learning her craft by observing a succession of European illustrators, including Polish Józef Wilkoń and British David McKee, who passed through or worked with Zavrel in his "rugged" (Moodie 2009) farmhouse in Rugolo, Italy.

Zavrel was an immensely encouraging, if exacting, mentor and editor who influenced the shaping of Moodie's approach in her first five books, all fantasy that included fairytale, folklore and myth, and published by Bohem Press. Although her work during this period is Euro-centric, Moodie regards folk genres as universal and freely available for ownership and adaptation across cultural boundaries to reflect differing points of view.

In her etchings for *Schaukelpferd* by Paula Geldenhuys,[4] Moodie draws the reader into Benjamin rocking-horse's emotional quest for belonging and self-confidence. She describes the style of her work in this, her first book, as "in between the Anglo-Saxon way which is very realistic and the stylisation of the Czech influence. [It] falls between two stools" (pers. comm.).

The style of Moodie's version of Jeanne-Marie LePrince de Beaumont's *La Belle et la Bête*[5] echoes the elegance of late Renaissance Italy and Paris. To enhance the fairytale ambience of the book, she introduces conventions of medieval illuminated manuscripts. Miniatures complement the stylized full-page illustrations and the text. The images are densely patterned; human forms are mostly static and flattened, although movement is suggested in the shapes of the patterning: flowing hair; billowing clothes. Formal arrangements of architectural elements create an impression of neo-classical perspective. The story world is theatrical; one of elegant artifice, mannerist gestures and the use of framing proscenium devices—arches, trees and columns. The effects of ochres, greens and burgundies are reminiscent of English, French and Flemish tapestries of the period; no natural light is attempted. In the illustration of the flight of the two jealous sisters from their pastoral home, the lines become fluid, there is more form and movement in the landscape, tree forms are more organic, flows of moonlit color more free—elements that hint at the rhythms of Moodie's later style. The book represents a milestone in Moodie's development; there is unity in its visual language that is a particular strength of her mature work.

The gentle humor of a version of an obscure fairy story, *Der Zuckerprinz*,[6] printed on the back of a breakfast cereal box, caught Moodie's attention. She rewrote it, but it is in the illustrations that she finds her own voice. Although there are recognizable visual elements from *La Belle et la Bête* (use of pattern, Italianate architecture and landscape), they are infused with vitality, humor and characterization, particularly in playful cartoons of people she knows in the crowd scenes and, notably, of Zavrel as the exasperated king. It is as if she expresses her desire to escape Zavrel's direct influence in Geraldine the protagonist's quest to fashion her own prince. Moodie animates the fairy tale world with a spirit of independence and mischief, traits strongly realized later in *Fynbos Fairies* (Krog, 2007). She is no longer constrained by stylization, but uses it flexibly with humor and grace to draw readers into a fairy tale world they can inhabit, rather than observe.

In *A Mermaid's Tale* Moodie reprises some of the theatrical features of *Beauty and the Beast* in the illustrations' spatial architecture, gestures, patterning and use of miniatures. Forms and figures appear to be choreographed to create the illusion of an underwater dance-drama.

Back at home, during the 1980s the political tensions in South Africa intensified. Violence bloomed all over the country. The apartheid regime responded to resistance to its divisive 1983 constitutional reforms with increased repression, militarization, and states of emergency. The future looked bleak, and Moodie, who had married fellow South African, Sean Baumann in 1981, left South Africa for the United Kingdom where she and her husband lived and worked for the next eight years and where their twin daughters were born in 1986.

... Where the Heart Is

According to Moodie, the idea for *The Unicorn and the Sea*[7] was generated over a meal in an encounter with Gianfranco Ogliani, professor of medieval literature at Venice University. He challenged her to give him a set of specifications and he would generate a story for her in twenty-four hours! She gave him a list: a quest, a unicorn, and the sea. The next day a story outline about the unicorn's quest to overcome his fear of water and to find meaning for his life was delivered to her lodgings. Ogliani tossed in a bonus; a fanciful myth suggesting the origin of the highly endangered horned whale, the *narwhal*, whose existence is threatened by hunters who believe its horn has magical powers.

In the illustrations for *The Unicorn and the Sea*, color moves south. Deephued watercolor washes flow in forms representing a relaxed, sun-washed landscape. Moodie (pers. comm.) ascribes this to her nostalgia at the time for her home near Cape Town: the distant Helderberg Mountains, the generous sweep of False Bay, the brilliant quality of natural light. At this point, late Gothic painters such as the Italian Paolo Ucello influenced Moodie. The red foxes in the forest are an echo of the red dogs in Ucello's *The Hunt in the Forest* (1397–1475). In Moodie's version of Uccello's pastoral Italian landscapes and mysterious forests, small details resemble African elements; a fleeing figure pursued by a fire-breathing dragon that resembles a crocodile; ostrich-like birds chasing a dog; a black-faced sheep familiar to South African farmers, stone pines and palm trees common in Cape Town. These illustrations point to a turning point in Moodie's personal sense of place in a deeply felt attachment to her home environment.

A growing spirit of independence in the last three books for Bohem Press—*A Mermaid's Tale; The Sugar Prince* and *The Unicorn and the Sea*—marks the end of Moodie's apprenticeship as an illustrator, and the beginning of her artistic journey back to Africa. In February 1990 the impossible happened:

> Mandela[8] was released, [husband] Sean wanted to work as a doctor in South Africa—we returned to Cape Town with our two small girls in December 1991 and have been living here since then [pers. comm.].

All at Sea

With her illustrations for Eva Bernatová's *The Wonder Shoes*, Moodie had slipped her moorings at Bohem Press. Her experiences with new publishers of *The Wonder Shoes, The Boy and the Giants,* and *Haddock* were happy; her editors were sensitive to her artistic decisions, and she demonstrated her ability to respond to the particular traits of a text in commissions. In Jan Mark's *Haddock*, a humorous spoof of a fairy tale with rather adult themes of temptation, jealousy, betrayal and true love, Moodie's illustrations are a light-hearted pastiche of the original style of her underwater quest stories, in keeping with the writer's gently ironic tone. On the other hand, the effects of insensitive management of a project on the artistic integrity of a book are evident in the uncomfortable way an "epic" text—wordy and metrically flawed, and in a font that tends to disappear into the backgrounds of illustrations—is superimposed on Moodie's precise and delicately rhythmic illustrations in *Atlantis Rises,* for which she was nevertheless awarded a SAPPI prize in 2000.

Moodie has an ancestral link with the setting of *The Boy and the Giants,* a retelling of a Hebridean folktale. The first Moodie in South Africa came from the remote Orkney Islands off Scotland in the wake of the Napoleonic wars. He eventually settled at Grootvadersbosch (pers. comm.), to this day an unspoiled area of indigenous forest, and a World Heritage site. A profound sense of stewardship of the natural environment is a central theme in Moodie's version of the tale.

On Home Ground

Nabulela, Moodie's re-telling of a Zulu folk tale from Phyllis Savory's (1988) collection, is the first of five books set unequivocally in a southern African landscape. Moodie depicts Nabulela, a ghostly giant river monster that enjoys eating humans, as a dragon-like *leguaan* or water monitor, commonly seen in South African rivers. The mountains recall the familiar ramparts of the dramatic Drakensberg range of the KwaZulu-Natal Province, and the detailed cultural references, including the Zulu princess's fondness for her faithful dog, create a warm emotional context for this scary story, published in seven South African languages.

A sense of mischief, so evident in *The Sugar Prince* and *Haddock,* and her enchantment with the flora and small animals of her childhood permeate Moodie's meticulous watercolor paintings for *Fynbos Fairies,* which won the 2007 Exclusive Books IBBY South Africa Award and is based on an idea from Cicely Mary Barker's (1923) *A World of Flower Fairies.*

Moodie acknowledges her intention to reconcile the world of books and the world of South African children: "It was a delight to be painting flowers and I hope that my pictures may help to awaken in children an interest in the natural beauty that surrounds us in South Africa" (Rabinowitz 2007, n.p.). For Moodie, the *Noko* stories about a group of friends that include a porcupine, warthog, pangolin, bat-eared fox, vervet monkey and a guineafowl, represent a homecoming and consciously embrace the values expressed in the post–1994 South African constitution's logo: "Unity in Diversity."

...The story [of Noko] has at its heart the African concept of Ubuntu, which is essentially the idea that people are interdependent and need to trust and help each other—everyone is family.

So the fact that Noko [the porcupine] and Takadu [the pangolin] are friends, not family members, is intentional and underlines the idea of Ubuntu in which we are all responsible for each other whether there are blood ties or not [Moodie 2011, n.p.].

The integrity of Moodie's vision and her art has not been easily achieved; she has stated that "I take great delight in doing the initial rough drawings for a book but producing the final art work is sometimes a struggle that may involve discarding many finished pictures that I subsequently reject. Writing comes more easily" (pers. comm.). She set herself a formidable challenge in the techniques she chose for *In the Never-Ever Wood*. Not wanting the illustrations to intrude on a finely honed text, she aimed to produce a softly burred line that nevertheless had strength and clarity, by etching on plastic. Color was then applied in subtly modulated watercolor washes to the resulting prints on Fabriano paper. She enhanced the text by introducing miniature vignettes as chapter headings, a feature she had first practiced in her illustrations for *La Belle et La Bête*. The choice of a soft buff paper underscores the importance of the production team's sensitivity to the intentions of the illustrator and writer, in defining the overall quality of the reader's experience of the book. All the fruits of Moodie's experiences of travel, art, and experimentation coalesce in her illustrations for this collection, in which "stories from the enchanting folklore of Africa converse with those from Europe, the East and elsewhere" (Rode, 2009, vi). Southern African imagery becomes mainstream.

In Moodie's post 1992 imagery, fantasy is enacted in real settings for South African children; the familiar becomes magical. Her great contribution to South African children's literature is to banish the alienation she experienced as a child, and to affirm the centrality of an African child's imagination in fantasy's enchanted multicultural world.

Notes

1. Fiona Moodie has exhibited in major venues: Zurich, Galerie Maag, 1979; Munich, International Youth Library, 1981; New York, Metropolitan Museum of Modern Art, 1983; Madrid, Museum of Modern Art, 1984; Japan: Tokyo, Habashi Museum of Art and Nishinomiya City, Otari Museum, 1984; Venice, Centro Culturale di Esposizione, 1991; Aix-en-Provence, Biblioteque Mejanes, 1992; Paris, Centre Georges Pompidou, 1993; Cape Town, Irma Stern Museum, 2010. She is represented in the Chihiro Art Museum collection, Japan, and in private collections internationally.

2. A character in Beatrix Potter's (1905) *The Tale of Mrs Tiggy-Winkle* (London: F. Warne & Co., 1905).

3. *Veldt (also, veld)*: open, uncultivated land

4. English: *Benjamin Rocking-Horse*, 1980.
5. Published in English as *Beauty and the Beast* (1980) by MacDonald, UK. Source: *The Young Misses Magazine, Containing Dialogues between a Governess and Several Young Ladies of Quality Her Scholars*, by Madam Prince de Beaumont, 4th edition, volume 1 (London: C. Nourse, 1783), 45–67. First published in 1756 in France under the title *Magasin des enfans, ou dialogues entre une sage gouvernante et plusieure de ses élèves*. The first English translation appeared in 1757. http://www.pitt.edu/~dash/beauty.html
6. Published in English as *The Sugar Prince* (1982) by Hutchinson U.K.; also by Hwa Books, China; and Le Cerf, Paris.
7. Also published in France (Le Cerf, Paris); Norway (Altera, Oslo); the Faroe Islands; Spain; China (translation, Hwa 1 Books Co.); and South Australia (Era Publications).
8. Nelson Mandela, jailed for 27 years for leading the banned African National Congress.

CHILDREN'S BOOKS

Bernatová, Eva. 1990. *The Wonder Shoes*. Illustrated by Fiona Moodie. New York: Farrar, Straus & Giroux.
Curtis-Setchell, Deborah. 2000. *Atlantis Rises*. Illustrated by Fiona Moodie. Cape Town, SA: Trident Press.
Geldenhuys, Paula. 1979. *Schaukelpferd*. Illustrated by Fiona Moodie. Zurich, Switzerland: Bohem Press.
Geldenhuys, Paula. 1980. *Benjamin Rocking-Horse*. Illustrated by Fiona Moodie. London: MacDonald General Books.
Krog, Antjie. 2007. *Fynbos Fairies*. English poems by Gus Ferguson. Illustrated by Fiona Moodie. Cape Town, SA: Struik Random House Umuzi.
Mark, Jan. 1994. *Haddock*. Illustrated by Fiona Moodie. London: Simon & Schuster.
Moodie, Fiona. 1980. *La Belle et la Bête*. Zurich, Switzerland: Bohem Press.
_____. 1982. *A Mermaid's Tale*. Zurich, Switzerland: Bohem Press.
_____. 1982. *Der Zuckerprinz*. Zurich, Switzerland: Bohem Press.
_____. 1986. *The Unicorn and the Sea*. Zurich, Switzerland: Bohem Press.
_____. 1993. *The Boy and the Giants*. New York: Farrar, Straus & Giroux.
_____. 1996. *Nabulela*. Cape Town, SA: Tafelberg.
_____. 2001. *Noko and the Night Monster*. London: Frances Lincoln.
_____. 2007. *Noko's Surprise Party*. London: Frances Lincoln.
Rode, Linda. 2009. *In the Never-Ever Wood*. Illustrated by Fiona Moodie. Translated by Elsa Silke. Cape Town, SA: Tafelberg.

Martie Preller: Empowering Readers Through Stories

MARITHA SNYMAN

Martie Preller is one of the best known and most prolific Afrikaans children's and youth book writers. Her last novel *Onderwater* is her thirty-seventh book, not including the books she has translated. Many Afrikaans speaking children grew up and still do with The Balkie and Babalela, the two central characters in *Die Balkie-boek* and *Babalela* respectively. The Balkie character in *Die Balkie-boek* is so popular that he receives fan mail from Afrikaans children living abroad in Australia, Canada, Germany and Namibia. Preller's youth books are also widely read and prescribed in schools.

Not only is Preller a popular author, but she has received numerous awards: Silver Sanlam youth book awards for *Anderkantland* (Land on the Other Side) and *In die Tyd van die Esob* (In the Reign of the Ilev); Afrikaans Language and Cultural Association (ATKV) awards for children's books *Jy en Toetenkat* (You and Toetenkat), *Daar's 'n Spook in My Kas* (My Cupboard Is Haunted), and *Die Balkie-boek*; the C.P. Hoogenhout medal for *Anderkantland*, the prestigious Alba Bouwer award for *Die Balkie-boek* (The Balkie Book) as well as the Tienie Holloway medal for *Babalela, Lisa het 'n Plan* (Lisa Has a Plan) and *Diep, Diep in die Donker Bos* (Deep, Deep in the Dark Wood)—the sequel to *Babalela*, and lastly the M.E.R. prize for *Ek Is Simon* (I Am Simon). Most of her books have, unfortunately, not been translated into English with the consequence that most English speakers in South Africa cannot enjoy her specific brand of creativity.

The following of her award-winning books were translated into English: *Daar's 'n Spook in My Kas* translated after the Afrikaans book had gone out of print as an educational publication with the title *My Cupboard Is Haunted*; the well-known Balkie character also appears in three educational books with the titles, *Balkie and the Sun's Resting Place*, *Balkie and the Vicious Virus*, and

Balkie and the Pirates of the Sea; the first book in her choose-your-own-adventure series of three books, *Jy en die Draakakkedis / You and the Dinosaur* were simultaneously published in English and Afrikaans but not the award-winning *Jy en Toetenkat*. *Ek Is Simon* was also simultaneously published as *I Am Simon*. *In die Tyd van die Esob* was rewritten in English and published by the author herself as *In the Reign of the Ilev* in a "Kindle book" format. In this case, Preller used the pseudonym Mary Meddlemore, a "writer" who wrote the book "on her behalf." The only other youth book that was published in English and Afrikaans is *Dreamcatchers/Droomvangers*.

We can only speculate about why her highly acclaimed and most popular books were not published in Afrikaans. One factor might be that children's and youth literature is not valued highly by the hegemonic Afrikaans literary system—mainly male and white (Kleyn 2013). Children and youth books are, as a rule, not reviewed or discussed in the media, they are merely announced. It is, in addition, expensive to produce books for the small Afrikaans population that has access to and is interested in books. Jaco Jacobs, an extremely popular and gifted Afrikaans children's and youth book author describes the situation as follows (my translation): "It is a miracle that publishers are still prepared to publish original Afrikaans picture flats, notwithstanding the fact that it is a good deal cheaper to translate foreign books as co-productions with big international publishing houses" (Jacobs, 2011, n.p.). A third problem is that the local English children and youth book market—as shown in existing sales figures—is inclined not to buy books translated from Afrikaans, but rather opts for internationally produced best sellers and classic English books.

This essay describes Preller's oeuvre by referring to the few translated works and related books that were published as extensions of the initial successful Afrikaans publications. In some cases, Afrikaans books are added to do justice to Preller's work.

Preller's charm and skill as an author for children lies in her ability "to climb into the minds of the children" (Van Wyk 1996, 9) for whom she is writing. There is something distinctively "childlike" in Preller's way of seeing the world and life, and she is not afraid of trying something new and often outrageous. "I often don't know what exactly to do. Then the magic happens spontaneously. [...] My writing has reawakened the wantoness of youth in me. I refuse to write 'down' to children. They know and understand all adult emotions" (my translation) (Preller 2000b, n.p.).

She was married, had three children, and got divorced. She started writing when she was forty. She followed "the way of her heart" and made a life out of writing—not an easy feat when writing in Afrikaans. She sees the births of her children and her grandchildren as the most meaningful moments in her life. "Augustinus said that love is like a stone: it anchors you to the ground.

Children are like stones: they keep you on firm ground. They are your anchors in life itself" (Preller 2000b, n.p.).

When Fantasy and Reality Converge

Perhaps the most discerning quality in Preller's work is her ability to create a fantasy world that her readers find completely credible. This is evident in both her books for younger and older children. She explicitly sets out to assimilate reality and fantasy into one seamless whole. "The magical qualities of the African continent fascinate me. We [Afrikaans speakers in South Africa] inherited the distinction between reality and fantasy from Europe. In Africa the two concepts intermingle. The day that I can successfully demonstrate this African characteristic in my work, I can die in peace" (Van Wyk 1996, 9).

That she manages what she sets out to do is evident in her work. In the famous *Die Balkie-boek* there is no distinction between fantasy and reality: not in the way in which the stories are written, not in the way both the author and the illustrator, Elizabeth Pulles, talk about The Balkie. He is real as can be and is at the same time not real at all. It is common knowledge that The Balkie himself told the stories to Preller who made sure that they got published. The borders between fantasy and reality further fade when The Balkie is described by his creators as follows: "The Balkie is a Balkie. This means that he is not a dog, a bear or even a camel. He is a Balkie, and a very cute one" (my translation) (Preller 2000b, n.p.). Pulles, the illustrator also confesses: "It is like he is really there" (my translation) (Grobler 2000, 6).

The convergence between fantasy and reality is also evident in the details of The Balkie's life. He is woolly, has a long nose and is terribly curious. And he loves biscuits. He became part of a regular family in a very prosaic way. His story begins when the children Isak, Bert and Karien discover him one morning under a heap of leaves where he is snugly lying asleep. Of course they want to take him home, and when they start telling Balkie about the biscuits at home, Balkie (who doesn't know anything about people and who keeps asking questions about them) is easily convinced. Since then The Balkie has been living with the three children and the father and the mother (using "the" before every noun is part of Balkie's language) and Roelf the dog and Miaaukatjie the cat on a smallholding somewhere near Johannesburg—not in fantasyland but near the biggest city in South Africa.

Kotzé (2013) contends that The Balkie is so popular because he is the young curious child who reads about him and for whom everything is still fresh and new and different. He drives the parents mad with all his questions, although he has already realized that he does that. When they start becoming red in the face, he stops. Children who hear his stories learn valuable lessons about life. The Balkie, for instance, has to make friends with the ghost in his cupboard and learns in this way to overcome his fear of the dark.[1] Balkie as first person narrator inspires trust in his readers by acknowledging to them that he, a fantasy character, is also afraid of things and sometimes becomes irritated with adults—just like them.

The publishers of *Die Balkie-boek* decided not to translate any of the existing *The Balkie* books but to use The Balkie character in an educational reading book series. Three books were published in this series that was developed in accordance with the revised *National Curriculum Statement* (South Africa 2002). Every title comprises a Learner's Book and Teacher's Guide. Creative reading, learning and language activities are used in an integrated approach to facilitate language learning and help foster and nurture a love of reading among children. Preller provided the creative input while a reading specialist, Mart Meij, was responsible for the educational content. The three titles relate three adventures of Balkie: *Balkie and the Sun's Resting Place*, *Balkie and the Vicious Virus*, and *Balkie and the Pirates of the Sky*. In *Balkie and the Sun's Resting Place*, The Balkie and the Stikisaurus embark on a hazardous journey to find the sun's resting place. Along the way they are confronted by strange perils: desert dust devils, mighty zzzzingers, a riverrabble rouser and a mountainous moose. In *Balkie and the Pirates of the Sky*, The Balkie saves the world when the pirates of the sky abuse computer technology for personal gain. Unlike Ben-Hackie, The Balkie does not underestimate the powers of Polly the parrot. In *Balkie and the Vicious Virus*, The Balkie must climb right into the father's computer to conquer the vicious virus that wants to destroy the computer. The Balkie is helped by F1, alias Felp, and a mouse that has a lot to say. In the process he meets a knight, a weird guard and the slimy, cunning Urvis.

At first sight, these books look like the original *The Balkie* books: the same quirky comments by The Balkie, the merging of fantasy and reality and the familiar illustrations. However, the outrageous adventures of The Balkie create the impression that he (or Preller) is trying too hard to amuse the reader. The original charm is missing because the mundane familiarity of the initial stories, when changed to fantasy, is lost. Superficially it is The Balkie, but not really. These books are, unfortunately, the means for English speakers to meet The Balkie. The Balkie still reserves his charm mainly for Afrikaans readers.

A convergence of fantasy and reality is present in most of Preller's books. In *The Haunted Cupboard,* the main character meets the ghost he has blamed all along for his lost clothes. The ghost and Bertus's stories develop alongside each other until they merge and each character find solutions to their problems (Eiselen 2005).

Anderkantland (Land on the Other Side) is another book that features a dual reality, but has never been translated into English. The first person narrator, who is unnamed, loves the pine forest near her home. When she opens a door in this space it becomes a big forest inhabited by all the fairy tale characters she knows (Steenberg 1995). She becomes part of Snow White's tale and comes to terms with her father's plans to remarry and that she will then have a step-mother. The fantasy world fades after she has learnt to deal with reality. Fantasy is the key to Preller's work, but it is fantasy that is firmly grounded in reality.

More Than Words

As if two worlds are not enough, Preller also draws on extra-lingual elements to help portray the fantasies she creates. The Balkie continuously refers to the illustrations in the story so that the illustrations become an organic part of the story and not mere decorations. It is Preller's use of strong story concepts that allows her to play with extra-fictional techniques in order to create more "real" fantasy worlds. The creative game with the paratext[2] causes the borders between text and paratext to fade. For instance, Preller uses the paratext to establish the character of The Balkie as a fictional author. The "legend" about how The Balkie was born, is a good example.

Elizabeth Pulles, *The Balkie*'s illustrator, was on her way to the post office one day in 1993 when she saw something sitting under a tree in Westdene, Johannesburg. "It was not a dog, but something doglike with a biggish head—a bit like a donkey's and a lovable face like that of teddy bear" (my translation) (Grobler 2000, 6). She ran home to quickly draw it and then phoned Preller who pasted the drawing on her wall and waited for him to start talking to her. Preller told the story to the editor of an Afrikaans magazine for women. "Then The Balkie started to talk and since that day he has never stopped talking ... [...] He still flips in and out of the lives of Preller and Pulles—like a woolly child" (my translation) (Grobler 2000, 6). Be assured that Preller and Pulles are sane women—as sane as a writer and an illustrator of children's books can be. These stories created around and about The Balkie bring him from fantasyland into reality. The Balkie's web page plays the same role.[3] There readers can learn about his physical dimensions, his diet, etc.

To allow the paratext to play such a big role in a book, excellent collaboration with all parties involved in the production of a book is needed. This includes author, illustrator, designer, and publisher. In the case of Babalela, the publisher's agreement to produce and sell merchandising items like a Babalela doll and t-shirts also contributes to expanding Babalela's magic.

Let's Love Reading

Preller explicitly states that books are preferable to her than human beings. Books are an escape from life. Books are her life (Preller 2000b). It is therefore understandable that she specifically aims to make reading an experience that her readers will enjoy. She is always conscious of who the intended readers are and tries to engage them in the books she writes, using a variety of techniques.

In her choose-your-own adventure books, she explicitly states that she chose to write this type of book for the following reasons: the reader will be actively engaged in the reading process being both the central character and dictating the course of the story; the reader is forced to follow accurately the instructions to create the story; and the books do not at all resemble school books so that the reader's antipathy towards reading doesn't come into play (Preller 2000a). Reviews, sales and reprints are evidence that her deliberate attempts to promote reading and making it fun are successful. These books are described by reviewers as "exceptionally suited for slow readers ... contemporary and refreshlingy new [...] Highly comendable for young readers" (my translation) (Gericke 2008, n.p.).

By using a wide variety of references—such as in *Die Balkie-boek* to fairy tales and Greek legends—she stimulates readers to recognize familiar patterns and activates a form of "textual self-reflection." Preller also engages her readers actively by creating characters with whom her readers can identify. When Babalela says, "Leave me alone," to the adults who take him from the bush where he lives, the words resonate in all children who have been told by grownups what to do and what not to do. "Leave me alone" ("Los my uit" in Afrikaans) has become a slogan that toddlers who know the book, shout at the merest hint of adult interference. And adds Jaco Jacobs (2011), "A whole generation Afrikaans children have grown up with Babalela and learnt that is fine to say 'Leave me alone' if people keep on bothering you" (my translation, n.p.). No wonder that sales of the *Babalela* series currently amount to 75,000 books.

Preller's children's books are described as innovative and postmodern (Le Roux 1998), books that challenge young people and never underestimate them (Eiselen 2005). A very effective way to stimulate reading is by writing books in which readers can identify with the characters. This Preller does well in *Dreamcatchers*, the only youth book that has been translated into English. A dream catcher is an object used in an old Native American legend. It is a circle made of twigs or wire to which feathers are attached. By hanging this in front of the window good dreams are allowed to go through but bad dreams are caught and prevented from entering the room. Such a dream catcher becomes the metaphor for the different ways in which each character in this book makes their dreams come true (Hough 1997). The story is "predictable" (Van der Walt 1998, 6), but because it is character-driven it engages the reader. This moving story containing wise advice about the value of good life management is never moralistic (Hough 1997; Van der Walt 1998). Freddie and his mother live in a poor community, but one where everybody knows and helps each other. Freddie feels helpless because he cannot change their dire financial circumstances. Robbie is the catalyst who helps Freddie to earn money. With the money comes a new friend, Bill, "one of the most evil and cunning characters ever in Afrikaans youth literature" (my translation) (Hough 1997, 16). He causes Freddie to nearly lose all, even his soul.

I Am Who I Am

In conclusion, one aspect is prominent in Preller's own life as well as in her books: she wants to empower her readers with the insight she has gained in life, namely that everybody must be who she/he wants to be and can be. To Preller stories are safe places "where you can do what you wish" (my translation), "[...] where people will leave you alone and when they don't, you can shout like Babalela 'leave me alone!' [...] When you are a child you are so afraid to be yourself that you easily become what other people want you to become ...[...] ...actually you must just be yourself" (Preller 2000b, n.p.). In *I Am Simon*, the best time of day is when Simon gets into bed at night accompanied by his favorite animal book. Then the animals start to talk to him. In the ensuing adventures with the animals Simon has to admit that he is weaker, slower, less clever, less agile and uglier that the elephant, the duiker (a kind of antelope), the spider, the ape and the warthog. In the end he realizes that he is like he is: unique and worthy (Eiselen 2005). In *Maar My Magtig, Moesak!*, a book that is not translated into English, Aron finds that all people wear masks and that people are not always who they appear to be.

Preller openly says that she translated and wrote two books under the name of her alter ego, Mary Meddlemore, because she needs to disguise herself sometimes. This need is the focus of many of her youth books. *In the Reign of the Ilev* is one example. This story of four young people who are the chosen ones in an ideal city somewhere in future is again told against the background of varying realities. The orderly community in which they live, is ruled by sophisticated technology. Competition and winning are the central themes in this novel (Snyman 1997) that also explores the nature of relationships and the intricate union of good and evil in Ilev. In this existence where everybody is fighting for autonomy, Nina, as the central character, comments on the existing order: "People here are like that: they don't call things by their names..." (35). The masks are always there. To be true to oneself and shed the masks are the most important values that Preller portrays in her work in contrast to a world where mass appeal is the norm.

Notes

1. This story later developed into a book called *Daar's 'n Spook in My Kas* (1994) ("There's a Ghost in My Cupboard"—my translation) later reworked as *My Cupboard Is Haunted* (2003) as part of a series called Big Books/Small Books used in schools.
2. This refers to all elements outside the verbal text that refers to the verbal text, e.g., illustrations, cover, what the author says about the book, marketing material as well as technological expansions of the text.
3. http://www.martiepreller.co.za/balkie.html.

Children's Books

Preller, Martie. 1992. *Jy en die Draakakkedis / You and the Dinosour*. Pretoria, SA: Van Schaik.
―――. 1994. *Anderkantland*. Cape Town, SA: Tafelberg.
―――. 1994. *Daar's 'n Spook in My Kas*. Cape Town, SA: Human & Rousseau.
―――. 1996. *In die Tyd van die Esob*. Cape Town, SA: Tafelberg.
―――. 1996. *Jy en Toetenkat*. Pretoria, SA: Van Schaik.
―――. 1997. *Droomvangers/Dreamcatchers*. Cape Town, SA: Human & Rousseau.
―――. 1998. *Maar My Magtig, Moesak!* Cape Town, SA: Tafelberg.
―――. 2000. *Babalela*. Pretoria, SA: LAPA.
―――. 2000. *Die Balkie-boek*. Cape Town, SA: Human & Rousseau.
―――. 2003. *Ek Is Simon/I Am Simon*. Cape Town, SA: Human & Rousseau.
―――. 2003. *Lisa het 'n Plan*. Pretoria, SA: LAPA.
―――. 2003. *My Cupboard Is Haunted*. Cape Town, SA: Human & Rousseau.
―――. 2004. *Balkie and the Pirates of the Sea*. Cape Town, SA: Best Books.
―――. 2004. *Balkie and the Sun's Resting Place*. Cape Town, SA: Best Books.
―――. 2004. *Balkie and the Vicious Virus*. Cape Town, SA: Best Books.
―――. 2004. *Diep Diep in die Donker Bos*. Pretoria, SA: LAPA.
―――. 2013. *Onderwater*. Pretoria, SA: LAPA.
Preller, Martie and "Mary Meddlemore." 2012. *In the Reign of the Ilev*. The Story Dimension Series: Kindle edition. http://marymeddlemore1.wordpress.com.

Changing the Colors of South Africa: Post-Apartheid Illustrations of Elizabeth Pulles

Erin F. Reilly-Sanders

At the end of apartheid in 1994, South Africa adopted a new flag for the newly unified country. By combining the black, green, and yellow of the African National Congress at the center of the anti-apartheid movement, with the red, white, and blue of the former Dutch and British colonial powers in South Africa, this symbol is intended to represent the history and diversity of the population. To educate and entertain upcoming generations, authors and illustrators of picture books also hoped to share this new inclusive spirit by depicting previously unseen diversity in their characters, actions, and settings. New hues spilled onto a previously tightly controlled palette, challenging illustrators like Elizabeth Pulles to change the colors of South Africa represented in their illustrations.

A white artist of Afrikaaner descent, Pulles's work exemplifies some of the challenges and opportunities facing picture book illustrators across South Africa. Her journey began by connecting with the art of the picture book and becoming settled as a professional illustrator before confronting the visual ramifications of political and social change. Even after stepping into a world of color, Pulles's style continued to evolve, incorporating not only new colors, but working toward addressing a more global audience and experimenting with different media in her work. Despite publishers' initial, if gradually waning, enthusiasm for diversity in South Africa, the market still metaphorically restricts illustrators to a standard palette, which Pulles confronts creatively through her art.

Finding the Art of the Picturebook

Pulles took an unexpected route to expressing her art through the picture book. She started in graphic design studies with a Bachelor of Fine Arts degree at the University of Pretoria. Going on to a Master of Fine Arts degree at the Potchefstroom University for Christian High Education (now a part of North-West University), Pulles found that "hard-core design" was not her passion (pers. comm.). In graphic design, visual presentations tend to concentrate on communication and often use very prescriptive and literally descriptive artistic techniques. Pulles instead turned to fine arts where she was able to take a more emotional and intellectual approach to visualization in her work. While there was little opportunity officially to specialize in picture book illustration, Pulles focused on the area in her Master's dissertation, translated as "An Experimental Exploration of Graphic Manipulation for the Sake of Effective Communication in the Picture Book" (1990). She had found a job in graphic design but in the process of finishing her dissertation, decided never to return to it. Instead, Pulles moved into the South African picture book world as a freelance illustrator (Van Zyl and Botes 1994, 15).

Like other notable artists in the picture book industry, Pulles goes beyond the practicality of graphic design and brings a particularly artistic flavor to her illustrations. Some of her past work has included textbooks and leveled readers but she avoids those when possible, despite their greater potential for making a livable income, finding them too prescriptive (pers. comm.). With the amount of text in a textbook and the emphasis on clear communication of story through illustrations in readers, the creativity of the illustrator is rather limited. Instead, Pulles describes her style as free and poetic, focusing on color, movement, and line rather than descriptive detail.

In critiquing *Thandiwe's Choice* (Grobler), Jay Heale (2010) comments that Pulles "is a skilled artist at creating atmosphere and using bold, unexpected [color]. But she's not so good at drawing animals. Some of the kittens look like stuffed toys; the cow and horse don't come off much better" (n.p.). Rather than lack of ability in such a trained artist, this is more likely a stylistic choice. Pulles seems to be avoiding realistic representation in favor of indicating the animals as "iconic" cartoons. McCloud (1999) suggests that iconic representation, wherein the artist moves away from resemblance to convey the same idea with more abstract simplification, is often a useful technique in that it can put emphasis on the scene rather than the figures. With more individualistically rendered people compared to the animals, Pulles may also be asking the viewer to concentrate on the humans who are actually the active part of the story.

Even Pulles's early works beginning in the mid–1980s exhibit thorough understanding of the picture book form. She places the two principal characters in *Johnny Later and His Hammer* (Van Rooyen) toward the outer edges of the page, leaving only trivial details of the setting to span the gutter dividing a two-page spread. This serves the double purpose of demonstrating the distance between lazy Johnny lounging sloppily across a chair on the right and his industrious mother hard at work with her sewing sitting neatly upright on the left. Pulles's work also complements the text as it helps frame the poetry of *Here We Are All Back Again* (Grobbelaar) with lively scenes, like a beach filled with generic children that stretch in between stanzas rather than the active participation in storytelling found in the more particular illustrations of *Johnny Later*'s characters and plot.

Stepping into a World of Color: Publishing Picture Books at the End of Apartheid

While Pulles's early books feature white characters in segregated settings like the European folktale-style story of *Johnny Later and His Hammer*, or the landscapes populated with white children and families of *Here We Are All Back Again*, her books begin to diversify along with the country in the early 1990s. In this time period, F.W. de Klerk's new presidential administration started negotiations with the anti-apartheid movement for a non-racist South Africa. In 1990, the ban on the African National Congress was lifted and Nelson Mandela was released from jail. Heale (2004) comments, "South Africa was reborn in 1994 as a black democracy—and then had to dismantle the prejudices of the past" (29). Correspondingly, publishing began to change with the recognition that not all children were being included in their books. Pulles remarks that illustrators were "challenged to start illustrating for [all] South Africa" rather than the previously limited audiences (pers.comm.). The result was that 70 percent of children's fiction now featured a black hero or heroine (Heale 2004, 18), approaching the 80 percent of South Africans identified as black in the latest census (Statistics South Africa 2012). With few black illustrators, white illustrators needed to expand their palettes to include people of all types with whom they may not have had much previous interaction or opportunity to depict.

As apartheid was ending, Pulles's work featured an unnamed black character in a desegregated urban setting in *What a Fuss on the Big Yellow Bus* (Ramsbottom). Another protagonist named Vusi welcomed the reader into the informal settlements that grew up in the margins of the city in *The Snuff Tin Bakkie* (Kühne). Pulles found the process of diversification in illustration to be an important personal education—especially considering the difficulty of opening up one's mind without being patronizing (pers. comm.). As one of Pulles's first forays into new frontiers, *What a Fuss on the Big Yellow Bus* has a hurried style with arching, exaggerated perspective that unfolds the interior of the bus across the pages. This move allows the reader to see the wide variety of people interacting amidst the amusingly lighthearted conflicts between different passengers. The soft, cartoony lines, messy hatches, and pale but saturated hues remind the viewer that the trouble caused is all in good fun.

In comparison, *The Snuff Tin Bakkie* has a solemnity to the illustration, perhaps as the setting and black characters are further outside Pulles's previous experiences and suggesting respectful gravity. The background of many of the pages is tinted with a pale but heavy sepia, and the general palette is one of earth tones. Soft paint spattered across the scenes suggests the roughness of chalk pastels but may actually just be watercolors. The lines also take a more gentle appearance here, using black to subtly emphasize the characters and the principal action but outlining the background in softer greys and browns. The hatching is also much less apparent than in *What a Fuss on the Big Yellow* as the colored pencil blends with the background color.

Despite new subjects and settings, it is common for illustrators still to draw upon their own backgrounds. Pulles however, had never been in a setting like a poor black child's house, so for both illustrators and authors, research became an important component of creating books like *The Snuff Tin Bakkie*. Pulles notes that authors like Mari Grobler, a teacher in a predominantly black school, could bypass some of these politics by writing books that would appeal to all South African youngsters rather than only a small group. Similarly, Pulles depicts iconic scenes with only a vague indication of the setting in her newer illustrations compared with the free but detailed scenes of *Here We Are All Back Again* with its happy white children frolicking across vacation spots before heading back to school at the end of the holidays.

Sharing the Spectrum Abroad

Most of South Africa's indigenous literature reaches a limited audience, even within South Africa. A *Bookchat* subscriber asserts, "This is predominantly a verbal society. Many parents are illiterate. Books are not a part of household equipment.... Our students simply do not develop an intimate, comfortable relationship with the book" (in Heale 2004, 20). South African bookstores carry a much larger selection of foreign titles, often comprising the bulk of their children's collection. Unfortunately it appears that the separate section of indigenous children's literature is meant mainly for tourists, whom bookstore managers claim are responsible for most of the purchases from this selection (Heale 2004).

With a limited market, few publishers produce for home use. Instead, an overseas run becomes one of the few opportunities for the sale of a picture book to expand. *Hi Zoleka!* (Mhlophe) was one such title that introduced Pulles to the international stage and can be found more easily in both the

United States as well as England. In addition, other books from the early 1990s show an expansion toward global mainstream markets. *Lizo's Song* (Hodson) and *Thandi's Birthday Lion* (Kühne) mark a definite stage of development in Pulles's style that would appeal to a variety of children. Translucent, saturated watercolors, loosely curved forms, and very light application of line and hatch keep the images bright and cheerful, even when depicting some of the realism behind the stories. For example, Lizo is a street boy in an urban setting, happily accepting coins from people in line at an ATM one moment, and being chased away from singing at a hotel the next, and grumpy Thandi is too sick to go to the zoo for her birthday so her classmates bring an imaginary zoo to her. All of these books include more color, both in the illustration style and in the people depicted.

Pulles does a particularly good job of avoiding stereotypes by portraying people of different races involved in a variety of occupations and pastimes and not demarcating people with stereotypical articles like native dress (Kiefer 2010). Unlike the typical images of South Africa in souvenirs created for the tourist trade, Pulles's illustrations present simplified versions of what everyday people in South Africa might wear. Although the majority of characters are in clothes that might easily be seen in Europe or America, there are also typical school uniforms for children and more dresses and skirts for women, especially those going to church as in *Hi, Zoleka*, than is common abroad. Pulles's principal technique has been to keep the background simple and typically rural, unless otherwise specified, in order to include children who may not have been previously depicted (pers. comm.). The circumstances her characters live in may be best described as simple since Pulles avoids showing the lives of her characters as destitute. This representation comes across as authentic: children living in townships and informal settlements may appear deprived from an outsider's view but typically have resources like attractive furnishings and clothing, in addition to valuable family and community support that should not be patronized.

On the other hand, Pulles appears to avoid depicting particular physical characteristics of South African population groups beyond rounded faces and pale pink or soft shades of brown skin. Here Pulles's intentional vagueness suggests a representation of "people of different cultures as interchangeable," a common practice in South African illustration that focuses on "harmonizing cultural and ethnic differences" (Khorana 1998, 152). Khorana notes that "an emphasis on ... difference has been viewed with some suspicion as a legacy of apartheid ideology" (152), supporting Pulles's choice to portray diversity and equality at the same time.

At the same time, these books are unquestionably set in South Africa and, in some cases, require cultural information. *Thandi's Birthday Lion* shows a mixed race group of friends from her class cheering Thandi up at her party, which Pulles notes would be a "normal thing to find" with the development of integrated classrooms. *Lizo's Song* draws heavily on the Kaapse Klopse minstrel festival in Cape Town practiced by Cape Coloureds (who are people from a variety of mixed races).

Mixing Media and Widening Styles

Beginning around 1997, Pulles extends inclusivity to new materials in her illustration as well as diversity in the characters presented. *Lulama's Magic Blanket* (Grobler) and *Musa's Journey* (Grobler) mark the beginning of Pulles's classic collage style as she aims to appeal to even broader audiences. In these books she pulls back from the denser and more detailed illustrations of *Hi, Zoleka!* to leave more white space. On the other hand, torn strips of colored tissue paper create brighter colors than in previous books completed mainly in watercolor. Rich textures are created by layering strips over each other, the torn edges of the strips, and even the subtle wrinkles in the application of the strips to paper. Details like facial features and outlines are added with mixed media like ink, paint, and colored pencil.

Continuing similar techniques with two more titles by Grobler—*Siyolo's Jersey* and *Thandiwe's Choice* —Pulles incorporates an even greater variety of materials. *Siyolo's Jersey* includes additional textile elements of "material, wool, thread, pastel, eyeliner, and lots of love and tears" (Rinkwest 2009, n.p.) with great effect. These ingredients serve to "[emphasize] how Siyolo gallantly gives away bits of wool to needy causes" (Heale 2008, n.p.). In the first two books, the color scheme is mainly an exuberance of generally primary colors, but in *Siyolo's Jersey* and *Thandiwe's Choice*, Pulles plays with less conventional collections of color. *Siyolo's Jersey* brims with oranges, yellows, and browns offset by deep carmine red and occasional pale blues. *Thandiwe's Choice* adds more pale blue, green, lavender, and light pink to the oranges and browns but avoids red except as an occasional accent to create a rich but innovative palette. Pulles notes that this new stylistic evolution was very freeing, allowing her to move further away from the descriptive illustration of her early years (pers. comm.). In the end, her experimentation was rewarded with further access to overseas markets and high praise from *Bookchat* (Heale 2013).

This collage style appears in other books as well but with different effects. In *Neo and Baby Ben* (Kimberley), the result is more solemn than exuberant. When the tissue is restrained to pale blues and combined with predominant soft yellows and browns on the cover, it gives the appearance of tenderness and baby-softness. *Midnight Cat* (Maartens) presents a different development of the technique following the trajectory of free expression. The addition of brusquely-applied swishes of paint adds an expressionist flair, and the more limited color palette of blues with yellow is reminiscent of *Neo and Baby Ben*, although darker in value to convey the nighttime feel.

A Standard Palette: Continued Restraints on Illustration

Despite the progress in revolutionizing South Africa's political system and the universal freedoms accorded to every race, economic disparity continues to thwart true equality. Similarly, South African children's literature is still confined by inherent restraints. These books are highly dependent upon the market for financial support and even illustration is limited by a picture book author's text. However, Pulles still strives to bring all the colors of South Africa into her work.

Rather than being free to paint the ideal portrait of South Africa through children's books, publishers are dependent upon the income from selling their books. Most of this money comes from adoption for classroom use and carries with it restrictions on subject and presentation (Heale 2004). Since these books are geared toward educational use, they typically incorporate literal descriptive illustrations that directly replicate the text rather than fine art pictures like Pulles's daring mixed media work. This focus on prescription of art rather than exploration and innovation not only strikes a chord with Pulles's past frustrations with graphic design, but seems to privilege efferent readings for information (Rosenblatt 1978) at the expense of the affective, a place where the unification of South Africa and cooperation among its peoples may be most at home.

After apartheid ended, books were initially published in a wide array of languages reflecting South Africa's diverse populations (pers. comm.). However, English and Afrikaans maintained their positions of power by dominating the education system despite being the primary language of only 9% and 15% of the population respectively. While there are eleven official languages, most children's books today are only found in those two languages, and of those in the other nine languages, almost all are translations from English or Afrikaans (Heale 2004). Language limits the accessibility of a picture book's text, but because these books are primarily seen as instructional tools for print literacy, even art which might transcend barriers is withheld as well. Pulles laments the focus on verbal rather than visual skills, noting that children at around grades two and three are discouraged from visual communication and "stop using non-verbal language" (pers. comm.).

Despite Pulles's bold experimentation in the development of her illustration style in picture books, her work is still restrained by the author of the text with which she is working. For example, while *Midnight Cat* appears stylistically similar to Pulles's books done in conjunction with Grobler, the author's choices can have a significant impact on the cultural diversity of the illustrations. While Grobler deliberately chooses names for her characters that indicate to Pulles that they should be black, Terry and Teddy from *Midnight Cat* are most likely intended to be white, given Maartens's traditional white Afrikaans background (pers. comm.). It may seem that illustrators have some choice in how they depict characters in their stories, but Pulles comments that she would not have questioned this racial assignment, believing that Maartens's aim was more likely to use language in an imaginative way rather than to expose children to diversity.

Most recently, it is Pulles's work outside picture books that seems to be allowing her to promote rethinking race in South Africa. Since apartheid protected the disadvantaged rural and working-class whites who would be the most threatened by competition from coloured and black South Africans, Afrikaaners now seem to many to be the least respected cultural group in South Africa. Pulles comments that while growing up she wanted to be English as opposed to Afrikaans and rather than celebrate her own culture, she turned to others' cultural productions such as world music. By incorporating photographs from her parents' youth into a project that repurposes old wooden school chairs as art to raise funds for plastic replacements, Pulles hopes to bring new attention to Afrikaaner culture. Through her recent work as well as her sensitive, imaginative illustrations, Pulles continues to be part of changing the colors of South Africa to reflect the rich society that they depict.

CHILDREN'S BOOKS

Grobbelaar, Pieter W. 1988. *Here We Are All Back Again!* Illustrated by Elizabeth Pulles. Pretoria, SA: Daan Retief.
Grobler, Mari. 1997. *Lulama's Magic Blanket*. Illustrated by Elizabeth Pulles. Cape Town, SA: Tafelberg.
⎯⎯⎯. 1997. *Musa's Journey*. Illustrated by Elizabeth Pulles. Cape Town, SA: Tafelberg.
⎯⎯⎯. 2008. *Siyolo's Jersey*. Illustrated by Elizabeth Pulles. Cape Town, SA: Tafelberg.
⎯⎯⎯. 2010. *Thandiwe's Choice*. Illustrated by Elizabeth Pulles. Cape Town, SA: Tafelberg.
Hodson, Christopher. 1993. *Lizo's Song*. Illustrated by Elizabeth Pulles. Cape Town, SA: READ.
Kimberley, Agnes. 2007. *Neo and Baby Ben*. Illustrated by Elizabeth Pulles. Pietermaritzburg, SA: Shuter and Shooter.
Kühne, Klaus. 1992. *The Snuff Tin Bakkie*. Illustrated by Elizabeth Pulles. Cape Town, SA: Human & Rousseau.
⎯⎯⎯. 1993. *Thandi's Birthday Lion*. Illustrated by Elizabeth Pulles. Cape Town, SA: Human & Rousseau.

Maartens, Maretha. 1998. *Midnight Cat*. Translated by Darrel Bristow-Bovey. Illustrated by Elizabeth Pulles. Cape Town, SA: Tafelberg.

Mhlophe, Gcina. 1994. *Hi, Zoleka!* Illustrated by Elizabeth Pulles. Cape Town, SA: Songololo Books.

Ramsbottom, Margaret. 1990. *What a Fuss on the Big Yellow Bus!* Illustrated by Elizabeth Pulles. Cape Town, SA: Human & Rousseau.

Van Rooyen, Engela. 1988. *Johnny Later and His Hammer*. Illustrated by Elizabeth Pulles. Cape Town, SA: Human & Rousseau.

Joan Rankin:
Illustrator by Surprise

JAY HEALE

To decide on an artistic career at a time when there was a paper shortage was, perhaps, not a wise idea. But somewhere in that early determination came an acquaintance with *Peacock Pie*, a collection of poems by Walter de la Mare, newly illustrated by Edward Ardizzone (1946). Joan Rankin still says, "His illustrations fascinated me: something that has lasted a lifetime" (pers. comm.).

Rankin's grandmother gave her a box of Crayola crayons and a drawing book when she was three. Her first effort was a row of circular birds on a straight tree branch. This apparently convinced her grandmother that Joan was going to be a famous artist. She spent long hours imbibing the pictures published weekly in *Punch* magazine. All her favorites were there: Ronald Searle, Hoffnung and Arnold Roth. Drawing became Joan's lifesaver through the tedious school years. She states, "I think the teachers were well aware of what I was doing, but they turned a blind eye because I was quietly occupied" (pers. comm.).

Still urged onward by her grandmother after "matric" (matriculation: an examination written as one of the qualifications for university entrance), she studied fine art at the Michaelis Art School in Cape Town. After a year, her teacher, Eleanor Esmonde-White, suggested that Joan should change to graphic art. At that time the only medium that really appealed to her was wood engraving, which was taught by the already famous Katrine Harries. So, for the next year she struggled with old-fashioned type-setting and presses, which she remembers as a dreadful experience; then she illustrated with wood engravings, which she really enjoyed. As a teenager, she had written and illustrated four-page booklets about family and pets, with many pictures about her Pekinese dog's human life. But even though Joan was introduced to the head of Tafelberg Publishers, becoming an illustrator had not yet occurred to her.

In those days, graphic art was not a recognized degree subject, so Joan tried commercial art at Johannesburg Technikon, which lasted about a month before she changed back to fine art. She explored the history of costume most enjoyably, as well as weaving and pottery. "It seemed to be a year when I just joined in where things interested me," Rankin explained (pers. comm.).

Towards Illustration

A friend then advised that if she wanted to do art, it would be wise to get married. After three torturous weeks of secretarial work, Joan gave up, took the advice and was married at the age of twenty-one. "It seemed a very bad idea. I did have my own flat but my newly acquired partner was a houseman[1] and only came home after long intervals to eat and sleep" (pers. comm.). Her mother had warned her not to marry a doctor, but gradually she realized it was the ideal situation for creativity. While she set about being a housewife, cooking, having (eventually) three daughters, and learning to cope on her own, Joan worked briefly for a small publishing company. She also took up weaving because she thought, "If I just sat and drew, my children thought I needed stimulating, whereas if I wove, they left me alone" (Heale 1994, 36). The loom also had a flying shuttle that could be arranged to rap them on the head if they became troublesome.

Rankin decided she needed to learn a bit more, so she started weekly art classes with the artist Sidney Goldblatt. With him, she studied composition, tonal values, color and use of oils and acrylics. That was 1970, and she became addicted to abstract painting. Goldblatt had studied in London and Paris and settled in Marbella, Spain, before setting up a successful art teaching-studio in Johannesburg in 1958. His wife Wendy was a potter and started an annual craft exhibition. Joan joined her and sold handwoven creatures and wildlife scraperboard calendars. The creatures later became adapted as puppets, used first in a shadow puppet show for the Marionette Company of the Johannesburg Civic Theatre. Part of this show was performed at the opening of the State Theatre.

"Then with Alida van Deventer, a well known marionette puppeteer, we put on *The Widlows Tale*, a full production using black theatre, shadows rod puppets and a life size giant," Rankin related (pers. comm.). Actress Bess Finney offered some constructive comment regarding rhythm and pacing—both relevant to illustration of a story. Puppets usually have one expressive face, and so they need subtle body language and movement; Joan saw how this could enrich illustrated characters. But a full puppet production is a complicated matter! In retrospect, Joan admitted, "One would need such a lot of technical skill to create a volcano in theatre … [w]hereas on paper I could really have fun." So the puppetry tailed off, and the pleasure in illustration grew.

The Illustrator Emerges

At this point—at last for the children of South Africa—Joan Rankin turned more seriously toward illustration. She had already created several books, handmade except for the printing, that were sold at craft markets. Some newly written books were exhibited at the Rand Afrikaans University. In 1986 she won a competition to illustrate *The Far Away Valley* by the well-established author Jenny Seed, published by HAUM-Daan Retief. Her illustrations were done on scraperboard, photocopied, then colored in with oil pastels. Scraperboard produced an effect very similar to wood carving, which was in keeping with African art traditions. It launched Joan as an illustrator, and she went on learning from there. The Daan Retief Children's Book Club, later finding new life as Mike Jacklin/Knowledge Unlimited, realized they had found a useful illustrator, and she did a further eight books for them.

It is significant that Joan Rankin was the first South African to have exhibited at the international Premi Catalonia d'il.lustració in Barcelona. She was invited to exhibit (with pictures from *Tselane* written by Moira Thatcher) at the 23rd Exhibition of Original Pictures of International Children's books, Japan, 1988. She also had illustrations chosen for exhibition at the International Exhibition in Sarmede, Italy, for five consecutive years, 1987–1991.

In 1992, Joan met the renowned Bohemian illustrator Stepan Zavrel from whom she received some most valuable advice at the Bologna International Children's Book Fair. So Joan started sending work for exhibition at Bologna as a result of this meeting. In 1994, Niki Daly took *The Little Cat & the Greedy Old Woman* to Bologna where the theme was The New South Africa. It was accepted by Margaret K. McElderry and by Niki's agent who got it accepted by The Bodley Head. The nicest thing for Joan was that Niki's agent was also the agent for her beloved Ardizonne!

At some stage she turned to Christmas cards which sold well and weren't such a storage hazard at home. She was not the first international illustrator to do so. British artist Quentin Blake also created Christmas cards (as well as many cartoons for *Punch*), and Anthony Browne (also from the U.K.) designed greetings cards and worked as a medical artist before ever illustrating a children's book.

South African Children's Book Illustration

Various words come to mind: immense *variety*, clear *quality*, and an appreciation of what is Africa. South Africa's books are part of the publishing of the western world. There is none of the gaunt, hard style that can come from Eastern Europe, not quite the exuberance of South America or the visual significance of the East. Perhaps South African illustrators share a sense of playfulness, which has been a constant element in Rankin's style.

Development has followed the increased opportunities offered by printing techniques and budget. Great names of the past include Katrine Harries and Cora Coetzee who were masters of line drawing, primarily because that was all South African publishers could afford to print. Four-color printing was widespread on the other side of the Atlantic when such local artists as Niki Daly and Marjorie van Heerden were painstakingly doing their own color separations for picture books where they were allowed black and one color. Daly eventually was able to use full color in the glowing enlarged 2000 edition of *Fly, Eagle, Fly!* by Christpher Gregorowski: "In 1982, when I first illustrated *Fly, Eagle, Fly!*, full color illustrations were a luxury seldom seen in South African children's books" (Daly in Gregorowski 2000, n.p.).

Joan Rankin has worked her way through pen and ink drawings and strong scraperboard technique with such books as *Tselane, a Legend of Lesotho* by Moira Thatcher and *The Little Wise One, African Tales of the Hare* by Phyllis Savory, to an increasing use of watercolor with such early books as Iain Macdonald's *The Dancing Elephant*—which won for Joan the Katrine Harries Award of 1991, jointly with *Ask for Patricia/Vra vir Frederika* by Rene Deetlefs and *The Twelve Days of Christmas* (Anon). Since then she has used an increasingly subtle use of line and color wash.

Joan agreed to provide line drawings for the collection *Storyland* compiled by Jay Heale in 1991, which included almost all of South Africa's major authors at that time: Dianne Stewart, Jenny Seed, Marguerite Poland, Klaus Kühne, Philip de Vos, Cicely van Straten, Lesley Beake, Es'kia Mphahlele, Nola Turkington, Dianne Hofmeyr, Brenda Munitich, Peter Slingsby and Christopher Gregorowski. Joan Rankin's drawings seemed to fit easily with all of them, including a meeting of Lesley Beake's three sisters with the dream of a dinosaur, somehow arising through the strata of archaeology (81). Just a touch of Rankin's abstract work here?

Joan was also involved with the Little Library reading project (which won the IBBY-Asahi Reading Promotion Award of 1994) and illustrated *Hic...Hic...Hiccups!*, written by Dianne Hofmeyr, and *Scary Footsteps,* a story workshopped by Lindi Mahlangu, Lungi Maseko and Joan Rankin.

Learning that illustrators needed to provide much of their own publicity, Joan became involved in school visits, helped by the indefatigable Audrey Hitchcock, currently director/owner of Hedgehog Books. She used her shadow puppet skills to entertain children and for workshops. Until 2000, Joan had worked very much in isolation. In that year she went to a Cambridge (England) Illustrators' conference, and later the South African branch of the

Society of Children's Book Writers and Illustrators (SCBWI) started in Gauteng Province.

From then on, the books started flowing. She concentrated mostly on a technique of watery purple-blue tones with crisp outlines, sometimes on mostly white pages, as in *Who's Afraid of the Dark?* by Dianne Stewart, sometimes more boldly expanding to double-spreads, as in *Theo and the Cat Burglar* by Wendy Hartmann. Always her infectious humor enhanced the story—and beloved cats often found their way into the action. Joan developed a valuable interaction with author Wendy Hartmann. Both would produce rough ideas and exchange suggestions, before further consultation with publisher Aldré Lategan at Human & Rousseau. Joan would then enlarge the drawings, by which time the story would have gained more focus and depth. She says, "It is always give and take on all sides" (pers. comm.), although she admits that the lack of face-to-face meetings with other publishers in the past had sometimes led to conflict situations where she felt compelled to withdraw her work.

Rapid increase in the use of technology aided established artistic techniques. Previously, a watercolor with a single mistake might have had to be scrapped! For many years, color printing involved the CMYK process (of making "grey-scale" plates by color filtered photography of the cyan, magenta, yellow and black components of a picture). These had to be balanced on the machine by the master printer. So the production technique took over from the original artist. Now, through computerization, stages of the creation process can be saved and multi-layered differing techniques used. Recently, Joan explained in outline how she works:

> There was a lot of preliminary experimenting for this book [*The Happy Prince*], some of which was used.
> Drawing in sketchbook quite small.
> Put drawings and writing onto Photoshop where I enlarge and position everything to my liking.
> This is printed out in black and then traced onto watercolour paper.
> I outline with a pen in watercolour, paint in the shadows, then start on the colour using inks, cokis,[2] oil pastels and some acrylics as well as watercolours. There is a little bit of collage [pers. comm.].

Computer techniques are still not a hundred percent reliable. Joan notes that two spreads in Bloch and Sixel's adaptation of Oscar Wilde's *The Happy Prince* were printed lighter than she intended.

It may also be noted that nearly all color printing for South African picture books is done overseas for cost-saving and greater skill. A quick look through ten of Joan Rankin's books dating from 2007 showed that six were printed in Singapore, three in China and only one in Cape Town.

The Artist as Illustrator

Parents and educators tend to forget that picture books can be a child's first art gallery. All illustrators first were trained as artists. Cora Coetzee was a landscape artist. Brian Wildsmith used to aim at spending six months of the year as an artist and six months as an illustrator. Tony Grogan is known as a cartoonist, but he is also an accomplished artist of South African scenes and people. The danger of the "art gallery" metaphor is that viewers may expect each picture to be a work of art on its own, instead of recognizing its place in the progression of the book in both words and pictures. Japanese illustrator Suekichi Akaba, who was awarded the Hans Christian Andersen Award medal for illustration in 1980, made this comment: "A picture book is not a picture gallery. Displaying good pictures one by one will not make a good picture book. What is important is the flow and the drama created by turning the pages" (Glistrop 2002, 64). Joan Rankin is an artist who increasingly has tuned her vision to the needs and restrictions of illustration. In her work, the flow is all-important. She and the author are telling a story together. Even without the words, the artwork lures you on from page to page.

In line with the steady import of English books, South African illustration has also developed from the early concept of portraying what is happening in the story to individual invention and characterization added by the artist. In this way, one can compare Joan Rankin's joyful embellishments to Wendy Hartmann's simple text in *Just Sisi,* to the runaway interpretive humor supplied by Maurice Sendak for the nursery rhymes in *I Saw Esau* (Opie 1992). In the words of Iona Opie: "...with Sendak illustrations, the book has a new strength and an extra dimension" (n.p.).

Joan's list of illustrated works (1968 to 2012) include a total of sixty-eight books of which ten were published overseas and seldom have been seen in South Africa. Thirteen of her books were both written and illustrated by herself, starting with *Peter's Dulcie Duck*.

A Closer Examination of Two Recent Titles

A more detailed appraisal of two of Joan's latest works, *Just Sisi* and *The Happy Prince*, provides a clearer picture of her talent.

Just Sisi (in Afrikaans *Net Sisi*) contains five deceptively simple stories by Wendy Hartmann. To international readers Sisi may seem to be a rabbit. But rabbits are rare in Africa: her long legs make her much more like an African hare. The first story (in easy, gentle prose) follows Sisi carrying a bundle on her head for delivery to Ma Tembo. All the way she is oblivious of the unseen

African dangers (malevolent goats, crocodile, lion, snake) although the reader can see them clearly. On the way back, the creatures spring into action, but each time some instinctive action by Sisi takes her safely home again. The text mentions no such dangers; they are all in the pictures. This is highly reminiscent of that great story of *Rosie's Walk* by Pat Hutchins (1968) though Rosie the hen makes only one strutting and oblivious journey. In both books, the tension lies in the artwork, anticipation of disaster that never happens.

Just Sisi could well have made a picture book on its own. So we are fortunate to have four more (one in prose, three in light rhyme): a surprise party, painting the wall of Gogo's house, welcoming Dad home, and saying goodnight. What makes the book extra delightful is that the fully dressed Sisi is clearly African. So are the animals, the trees, the cooking pot, the thatched rondavels, the decorations on the house wall. Because *Sisi* is clearly for very young book viewers or readers, Joan uses clearly defined characters mostly on a white page. Just occasionally the scene spreads across a double page: the crocodile missing Sisi and falling on his nose into the river, the welcome home party, the joy that "Daddy is home!" The positioning of text and artwork on each spread is masterful. The colors are warm and welcoming. Sisi is a small rabbit with floppy ears, but could be any and every small girl.

Publisher Human & Rousseau must have felt that this book was going to be a winner. So they went to the extra expense of spot lamination on the covers, which creates a glistening, near 3D effect. *Just Sisi* won the local MER Award for illustration in 2011 and was chosen as South Africa's Honour Book for illustration in the 2012 IBBY Honour Books list exhibited in London, and afterwards around the world.

The Happy Prince is a well-known, bittersweet "fairy story" originally written by Oscar Wilde in 1888. As adapted by Carole Bloch and Margaret Sixel, the text retains much of its original poetic writing—with its echoing song of "Swallow, swallow, little swallow …"—but is more easily readable. However, it remains a story for older readers, which has allowed Joan Rankin to use a very different illustrative technique. There are two clear ingredients: the tale of the Happy Prince set up as a statue and so able to see the poverty and unhappiness in his own town, from which he was shielded when alive, blended with the visiting swallow's dreams of the wondrous richness of Egypt, which he is longing to visit once more. It is a tale of increasing winter set against distant summer. Both the main characters, the prince and the swallow, die, and the prince does so twice: once in his human "happy" status and again as a sadder though more humane statue.

The publisher, Jacana, has allowed Joan Rankin large pages, and she returns to her palette of grey, blue, and purple for the city, which could be any medieval European city (until one notices modern touches like high heels).

In glorious contrast, we see bright yellow lotus flowers by the Nile, a rust-red god Memnon on his granite throne with obsequious golden lions, and bright green palm trees in front of an orange ruin with dark brown crocodiles slithering past and birds "woven" into fronded branches. (Oscar Wilde calls it the Temple of Baalbek, apparently oblivious that it is far north in Lebanon.) So we have chilly, almost faded architectural cityscapes contrasting with the richness of Egyptian Africa. Poetry in both words and pictures.

The final word comes from Joan Rankin herself:

> All children's book people are passionate about what they do. This is crucial. Fun, humour and top quality artwork. Being able to express oneself visually on paper is just as important, if not more so, than writing. Creativity is soul food for me. It keeps me sane and happy [pers. comm.].

Notes

1. Medical intern; newly qualified doctors were required to complete a year of internship in a state hospital.
2. "Cokis" or "koki's," derived from a brand name, is the common term in South Africa for felt-tipped colored ink markers.

Children's Books

Anon. 1989. *The Twelve Days of Christmas*. Illustrated by Joan Rankin. Johannesburg, SA: Daan Retief.

Bloch, Carole, and Margaret Sixel (adapted). 2012. Oscar Wilde's *The Happy Prince*. Illustrated by Joan Rankin. Auckland Park, SA: Jacana Media.

Deetlefs, Rene. 1988. *Ask for Patricia/Vra vir Frederika*. Illustrated by Joan Rankin. Cape Town, SA: Human & Rousseau.

Hartmann, Wendy. 2011. *Just Sisi/Net Sisi*. Illustrated by Joan Rankin. Cape Town, SA: Human & Rousseau.

_____. 2007. *Theo and the Cat Burglar*. Illustrated by Joan Rankin. Pretoria, SA: LAPA.

Heale, Jay. 1991. *Storyland*. Illustrated by Joan Rankin. Cape Town, SA: Tafelberg.

Hofmeyr, Dianne. 1993. *Hic...Hic...Hiccups!* Illustrated by Joan Rankin. Johannesburg, SA: READ.

Macdonald, Iain. 1990. *The Dancing Elephant*. Illustrated by Joan Rankin. Cape Town, SA: Human & Rousseau.

Mahlangu, Lindi, Lungi Maseko, and Joan Rankin. 1996. *Scary Footsteps*. Illustrated by Joan Rankin. Cape Town, SA: Cambridge University Press.

Rankin, Joan. 1993. *Peter's Dulcie Duck*. Cape Town, SA: Anansi.

_____. 1995. *The Little Cat and the Greedy Old Woman*. London: The Bodley Head.

Savory, Phyllis. 1990. *The Little Wise One, African Tales of the Hare*. Illustrated by Joan Rankin. Cape Town, SA: Tafelberg.

Seed, Jenny. 1968. *The Far-Away Valley*. Illustrated by Joan Rankin. Johannesburg, SA: Daan Retief.

Stewart, Dianne. 2011. *Who's Afraid of the Dark?* Illustrated by Joan Rankin. Auckland Park, SA: Jacana Media.

Thatcher, Moira. 1986. *Tselane, a Legend of Lesotho*. Illustrated by Joan Rankin. Cape Town, SA: Tafelberg.

Listening to Others: Jenny Robson's Books for Young South Africans

Judith Inggs

Jenny Robson is one of the most respected and well-known South African writers for children and young adults. Born and raised in Cape Town, she has been living for many years in Botswana, where she is a music teacher. Robson was the first author to win four consecutive Sanlam Prizes for Youth Literature from 1994 to 2000 with a fifth award in 2005. To date she has published ten novels, with a further two novels for young adults to be published in the near future, *Back to Villa Park*, and *Monday Evening, Thursday Afternoon*.

Information on the NB publishers' website states that the "favourite theme in her books is the utter uniqueness of the individual" and that Robson "hates any form of stereotyping" (NB publishers, n.d.). This approach to her writing comes through clearly in her protagonists, each of whom displays an individual and unique identity. There is no sense, when reading Robson's books, that characters have been flattened or manipulated to fit into a particular plot or storyline; rather the story develops around and through the characters she portrays. This resonates well with her response to questions about the source of her ideas:

> Where do my ideas come from? All around me. Everyone's life is a story. Amazing, powerful things happen to people every day. There is a line in Desiderata that says, "Listen to others, even the dull and ignorant. They too have their story." And that's what I do. I listen [pers. comm.].

Depicting the Other

Through listening to others Robson tells the stories of a variety of characters, male, female, child, young adult, black, white and coloured. The fact that her characters are so varied raises questions around the controversial issue of who writes for whom, particularly in the context of post-colonial literature.[1] However, Robson vehemently opposes the suggestion that a writer can only write from first-hand knowledge: "I grew up as a white child in Cape Town. Does that mean I am doomed to only write about white city children and young people?" (pers. comm.). Justifying her decision to write about children and events in Botswana, for example, as in *Because Pula Means Rain* and *Praise Song* she goes on:

> Because I am standing at a distance from, say, Botswana cultural life, I think it gives me perspective. I can see meanings and connections and undercurrents that someone in the middle of that society won't notice because they are just so used to things being that way [pers. comm.].

Her insistence on writing about a variety of characters is supported by the fact that English language and Afrikaans young adult fiction in South Africa has always been dominated by white writers, and there are only a very few active black authors writing in any of the country's official languages. If white writers confined their stories to white protagonists their works would give a distorted view of South African society. By using focalizing characters from other racial groups, the implied, often white, reader is obliged to reflect on continuing inequalities and cross into the space of other sections of the community—a crossing that has gradually been increasing in real life since 1994, the year of the first democratic elections when Robson's first book was published.

Robson does not draw specific attention to the race of her protagonists. Rather, this is revealed through the names of the characters, the language that they use, and the spaces they inhabit. This is true of most of her novels, beginning with the first two, *Mellow Yellow* and *Don't Panic Mechanic*. A further feature of Robson's novels is the frequent inclusion of protagonists with a physical or psychological flaw. Robson confirms that she is "fascinated by rejection, by people who don't fit in, who are stigmatized in some way" (pers. comm.). *Mellow Yellow* tells the story of street children in Cape Town, all of whom have a story of rejection and abandonment and who hide their identity behind humorous, or ironic, nicknames, such as Space Gun, Rambo-man and Cockroach. The protagonist, Mess, is referred to as Mellow Yellow, because of the yellow jersey that he refuses to relinquish because it reminds him of his mother. He does not know his real name although his identity is encapsulated in a mysterious document kept in a tobacco tin around his neck—a document he cannot read but which turns out to be his birth certificate. By unlocking the mystery of this document he eventually finds both his grandfather and his mother, "knowing that he could throw away his yellow jersey at last" (138). Mess thus moves from anonymity to identity and self-respect, just like Space

Gun, who by the end of the novel is Reginald Smith, reporter. There is no mention of the race of the street children, but the picture on the front cover depicts a young coloured boy in a yellow jersey, and the street children speak in English peppered with Afrikaans colloquialisms and slang words.

In *Don't Panic Mechanic,* Mackenzie de Jongh's name and his home background identify him as a coloured boy from a poor area in Cape Town. Mackenzie is a fourteen-year-old boy with a severe squint, consequently nicknamed Chameleon Eyes, who constantly fails at school because of his visual impairment. In desperation his family ask him to leave school to look after his sister's baby, freeing his sister and mother to earn "real" money. Mackenzie's already low level of self-esteem is reduced still further by his role as a baby-minder. However, he finds that his impairment is an advantage when he decides to try begging at the doors of homes in more affluent areas of the city, despite his mother's strongly expressed conviction that only money made through hard work is to be respected. Towards the end of the narrative Mackenzie unknowingly knocks on the door of the owner of a fleet of taxis, who, reinforcing Mackenzie's mother's words, gives Mackenzie the dignity he has longed for, offering him a job as a "hopper," a taxi-driver's assistant. Mackenzie thus acquires status and self-esteem, empowered as a wage-earner and a contributor to household expenses. The reward for honesty and perseverance even in adverse circumstances is stressed when we learn that Mr. Tema is black and deaf, and has overcome his own impairment to the extent of owning the "biggest, best taxi fleet in Cape Town!" When Mackenzie enthusiastically accepts his offer, Mr. Tema tells him: "That's the spirit, MacKenzie. That's the kind of spirit that can get you anywhere you want to go. Anywhere" (150).

After these two novels, Robson moved on to tackle other topics. *Dark Waters* deals with issues arising from the blurring of spatial boundaries as citizens of different races began to live side by side as well as social issues such as drugs and adolescent depression. It tells the story of Zack, a white boy, and Jeremy, a coloured boy, who find themselves neighbors during a time when city suburbs were in flux. Neither Jeremy nor Zack feel that anyone *listens* to them, and it is this disempowerment and inability to make their feelings or views known that lead them to experiment with drugs. The environment in which they live is central to the narrative. Zack's home on the *vlei* (lake) is synonymous with his sense of identity, security and belonging. The threat of being taken out of this haven and moved to a concrete suburb of rows of "houses squashed together like eggs in a carton" (25) fills him with horror. But equally, Jeremy, uprooted from his own safe environment, feels out of place and alien at the *vlei,* which he perceives as hostile. Both characters reflect the difficulties experienced in coping with change. Neither is ready to deal with the unfamiliar space of the Other, whoever or whatever that Other might be.

While Zack and Jeremy reflect the concerns of many adolescents living through times of change, the adult characters are flatter and less developed, resulting in a display of more stereotyped attitudes and emotions. Zack's father is particularly predictable, commenting on racial mixing through an unconvincing analogy with pelicans and flamingos: "they keep to themselves, don't they? You don't find them all flocking together and nesting together..." (20). By the end of the story, however, an equilibrium is reached. Zack's family decide to stay at the *vlei,* and both Jeremy and Zack are able to end their dependency on drugs as they receive renewed support from their families.

The year 1996 saw the publication of two more works that on the surface are very different from each other, *Where Shadows Fall* (winner of the 1996 Sanlam Prize for Youth Literature) and *One Magic Moment* (winner of the second prize in the Kwela, Engen and NNTV Writing Competition). Nevertheless, both stories continue the theme of lost and found identity. The latter work is fundamentally a mystery story, in which a group of young inhabitants of a block of flats seek to unravel the secret behind a new arrival, Sheralee, who is an outsider, her identity shrouded in unanswered questions and secrecy. The chief protagonist, Jo, eventually solves the mystery and discovers Sheralee's true identity as Heather Bellini, who was kidnapped from a hospital by Sheralee's parents when their daughter died.

In this work Robson succeeds in writing a young adult mystery set firmly against the backdrop of South African society, complete with amateur cricket matches. *Where Shadows Fall* is a more ambitious writing experiment. It is also a story about mistaken and lost identity: in this case the primary message is that beauty is only skin-deep and one needs to see other people for what they are rather than for what one hopes they might be. In this novel Robson tackles traditional beliefs and the practices of a medicine woman regarded as evil by many of the residents of the town. The plot revolves around the characters' perceptions of themselves and of those they love, or believe they love. Both Lesedi and Tips use a potion to allow them to swap bodies with Lesedi's sister, Boinelo, and Tip's friend, Samson, whom they believe are more attractive. Subterfuge, deceit and self-deception are ultimately revealed as foolish and short-sighted. After these works, Robson's writing reveals a greater sophistication and a willingness to tackle more controversial and taboo topics as described below.

Futuristic Dystopias

The genre of science fiction is almost completely absent in South African young adult fiction, but Jenny Robson's two novels in this genre are among her best works. *The Denials of Kow-Ten* describes a future society in which the privileged inhabitants live in enclaves, built by world industrial leaders at the end of the twentieth century ostensibly to eliminate increasing crime and violence. Those deemed unworthy of living inside the enclaves are classified as the Almosts or, even more lowly, the Dregs. Residents of the enclaves are kept ignorant of the outside world, in a controlled state of illusion in a society constructed and subverted through language and image. Their memories are systematically eliminated through drugs, depriving them of their identities, a process attributed to a disease called Alzimes. Shiyne, the third person focalizer and chief protagonist, is defined by his propensity for asking questions and wanting to know what words mean, making language itself a site for the struggle for power.

He eventually discovers that the world beyond the fence around the enclave is a "nitrogram," an illusion created by the Enhancers, or the keepers of the "truth." Shiyne asserts his own power by venturing outside the enclave where he finds a stark wilderness peopled by the Others. In this novel Robson documents the denials of a society forced to forget its past, a society based on selection and segregation in a clear analogy with South Africa's own history, and yet in striking contrast to the latter's willingness to remember and acknowledge the wrongs inherent in that history. Shiyne ultimately fails in his attempt to negotiate his own position of power as his memories, too, are eliminated, but there is a glimmer of hope at the end as he senses words "drifting quietly through his mind" (137). In presenting a rigid, totalitarian society as the *status quo*, Robson succeeds in strengthening the implied reader's belief in democracy and freedom, along with the rejection of totalitarianism.

Robson returns to the theme of a futuristic dystopia in *Savannah 2116 AD,* a novel that has attracted attention from academics (for example, Cloete 2009; Steenkamp 2011). Society is divided into two main groups: the Cons— an ambiguous abbreviation of "conservationists" mingled with the idea of deliberate deception—are the ruling elite living in towns and cities while the Rurals live in primitive and remote enclosed villages. The GEDs (Genetically Enhanced Donors) have no individual identity and are referred to by numbers according to their date of birth; at the age of eighteen their organs are harvested in a sacrifice purported to be for the benefit of threatened species of wildlife.

Robson again uses language in this novel both as a means of empowerment and disempowerment and as a tool through which she demonstrates how reality is manipulated. Lucy, the endangered gorilla that is the supposed recipient of the GEDs' organs, is constantly renamed in the pretence that a gorilla is returned to the wild each time a GED is sacrificed. The species-to-species transplant programme had never worked, and the organs were instead used to prolong the lives of the Cons. The doctor describes his reports as "masterpieces of fiction" in which he "cons the Cons" (133) who never suspect that the gorilla is always the same Lucy, or, if they do, are "supporting the lie, because some things were best left unconsidered" (134).

Unlike *The Denials of Kow-Ten*, in this novel Robson's protagonists succeed in challenging the status quo when D-nineteen escapes his fate in a popular rebellion led by the Rurals, to whom his girlfriend, Savannah, belongs. Steenkamp (2011) comments that the "central theme of the novel remains the triumph of romantic love and redemption in the face of seemingly insurmountable odds" (114), highlighting Savannah's role in saving her people and giving D-Nineteen a new life. But such a reading of Robson's novel is superficial and does it an injustice. Their future life is left blank and far from secure; the reader learns that Savannah chooses a new name for D-nineteen—Adam— symbolizing a new identity and a new beginning but Savannah remembers her aunt's friend, Mrs. Vosloo, talking about freedom, about how the Rurals would one day live again on the land, warning "That's how it all started last time round!" (137). Both of Robson's science fiction novels develop new themes and a new genre in South African young adult fiction in order to reinforce principles of democracy and freedom and to push young readers to question certain attitudes and assumptions.[2] As Elsie Cloete (2009) remarks: "Without being prescriptive, Robson's *Savannah 2116 AD* quietly critiques more than two centuries of conservation practices in southern Africa (and most of Africa for that matter) that could lead to the dark ecofuture depicted in the novel" (47). The novel calls into question Western assumptions regarding the relationship between indigenous people, wildlife and wilderness areas by depicting the devastating consequences of "separating wild animals and landscapes from debilitating outside influences" (Cloete 2008, 51).

Silence and Discrimination

In 2000 the winner of the Sanlam Gold Prize for Youth Literature was Robson's *Because Pula Means Rain,* a sensitive novel which seeks to dispel the prejudices surrounding albinism in Southern Africa and which received the 2003 UNESCO Prize for Children's and Young People's Literature in the Service of Tolerance. In 2005 the Sanlam Gold Prize was awarded to *Praise Song*, a novel which narrates the murder of a young female teacher following her public disclosure of her HIV-positive status, focalized through an adolescent school girl, Gaone. In these works, as in her earlier novels, rejection and a search for identity are central. In *Because Pula Means Rain,* Emmanuel is rejected because of his pink skin, while his friend Keshia (called *Le-point-five* because she is half Motswana and half German) is equally rejected because her skin is paler than that of her friends. Similarly, and more devastatingly, Thozama Diko in *Praise Song* is rejected and ultimately murdered because of her honesty in disclosing the reality surrounding HIV/AIDs. Robson also hints at the silence surrounding HIV/AIDs in *Pula*, when one of the characters tells the young people of the village not to be afraid to speak about the disease because it "thrives on secrecy and silence" (58).

Because Pula Means Rain is written in the first person focalized through Emmanuel, the chief protagonist, an albino child living in a Botswana village. At the start of the novel he grieves his lost friend, Masego, killed at Kotsi Corner, a dangerous section of road just outside the village, which is the focus of the novel in that Emmanuel plays a role in removing the perceived curse from the corner. Just as *Where Shadows Fall* highlights the importance of seeing beyond the surface of a person's appearance, in this novel Masego was "the only one in the Village who saw past the way I looked, who saw me from the inside, the way I saw myself" (6).

One night Emmanuel hears the story of a young woman who accidentally suffocated her baby to silence him during a battle between warriors of different tribes. The baby's body was abandoned near Kotsi Corner and never found. Emmanuel believes, having spoken to Masego, that the accidents are caused by her chasing goats into the road, prompted by a crying baby. When he finds the skull of the missing baby's body he buries it under the home of the baby's uncle, Rre Pitlo, following which he believes he hears Masego laughing, finally allowed into the light and able to find peace. At the same time he learns the story of Mercy, a girl who had been attacked because of her HIV status, and whose life had been saved by a priest, Father Francis. In a scene where he believes that his pale skin means nothing to Mercy and hopes that a new time predicted for him by the Ngaka (the medicine woman who threw the bones for him) has come, he is dismayed to understand that he is merely a reflection of another albino, Father Francis. It is only when he realizes that the dreadful accidents have come to an end that he knows that his time has indeed come. Emmanuel is overjoyed at the idea that he is responsible: "I knew without any doubt that this miracle was because of me! Because of me!" (131).

The novel ends with Emmanuel experiencing a strong sense of achievement and of belonging: "Yes, *my* village. Home of *my* people" (133). Ultimately, however, although Emmanuel has attained a state of peace and acceptance of the things he cannot change, in reality only he has changed. The village goes on as before, with small children shouting and teasing him. The message is that change can only come from within and that to change the attitudes of others is a much longer and more difficult struggle.

In *Praise Song* Robson also promotes tolerance and pushes her readers to question their assumptions. The story is that of Gaone's teacher and takes place in Meriting, which means *place of shade* and which is therefore a fitting place for secrets and silence. The story generally focuses on the dangers of casual relationships and unprotected sex, but ultimately the message is the importance of honesty and the danger of hypocrisy and prejudice.

As the story progresses the reader is given clues, through Gaone's eyes, as to the perpetrator of the crime, Gaone's aunt, whose deep-seated prejudices become more and more apparent. Halfway through the novel, Gaone admits that she has known the identity of the murderer from the start, although the reader is kept in suspense. The teacher's crime is one of words in that she uses a public forum "to explain in clear and precise language exactly how AIDs was transmitted. She used words that had never been heard before in that hall, words that had never before been broadcast through loudspeakers in our town" (82). Gaone's aunt is filled with hate and unbridled anger when Miss Diko announces that she is HIV-positive. Her anger is so irrational, and so violent that she is the one who attacks and kills the teacher. Despite her knowledge of the identity of the murderer, Gaone decides to remain silent, believing that her aunt's true punishment is the constant fear that she may have been infected with HIV during the murder, through an accidental wound on her hand. She concludes: "There are punishments both more unbearable and more fitting than the laws and the judges and the courts and the prisons of our country can offer" (126). The decision to end the story in this way, however, seems in itself a form of silence, an unwillingness to speak out, equally damaging and as detrimental to society as the silence around HIV/AIDs.

There are clear and identifiable themes and threads which run through all of Robson's novels. She deals with questions of identity, alienation and belonging through the depiction of characters of all races in a variety of settings and in a way that avoids moralizing, didacticism and stereotyping. There are good reasons for her reputation as one of the most successful South African writers for children and young adults, and her two forthcoming novels are awaited with pleasure and expectation. Over the years her ability to listen to others and depict rounded and believable characters has been honed and polished to the extent that she can be regarded as one of the most skillful and sophisticated novelists writing today in Southern Africa.

Notes

1. For a detailed discussion of children's literature in post-colonial societies such as Canada, the United States, Australia and New Zealand, especially on the depiction of indigenous people by non-indigenous writers, see Bradford 2007. For a recent work on South African white writers writing black characters, see Sibanda 2012.

2. Part of this section appeared previously in Inggs 2006.

CHILDREN'S BOOKS

Robson, Jenny. 1994. *Don't Panic Mechanic*. Cape Town, SA: Tafelberg.
_____. 1994. *Mellow Yellow*. Cape Town, SA: Tafelberg.
_____. 1995. *Dark Waters*. Cape Town, SA: Tafelberg.
_____. 1996. *One Magic Moment*. Cape Town, SA: Tafelberg.
_____. 1996. *Where Shadows Fall*. Cape Town, SA: Kwela Books.
_____. 1998. *The Denials of Kow-Ten*. Cape Town, SA: Tafelberg.
_____. 2000. *Because Pula Means Rain*. Cape Town, SA: Tafelberg.
_____. 2004. *Savannah 2116 AD*. Cape Town, SA: Tafelberg.
_____. 2006. *Praise Song*. Cape Town, SA: Tafelberg.

Breaking New Ground with Reviva Schermbrucker

RUTH STONE *and* BARBARA A. LEHMAN

Reviva Schermbrucker, author, illustrator, and materials developer for children's literacy projects in South Africa, was born in Israel and immigrated to South Africa with her parents when she was five years old. Because the family moved several times during their first year in South Africa, she attended four different schools that year. This traumatic beginning—as a foreign child placed in an English medium, grade one class and only able to speak Hebrew—profoundly affected her whole life. She still vividly remembers those early years of alienation and describes herself at the time as a very insecure, tearful child, frightened of school, which was "nothing like home" (pers. comm.).

By the end of grade one, Reviva had learned to speak English and never spoke Hebrew again, not even to her parents. "I had to kill one language off to survive in the next," and English soon became her friend. She describes herself as a prolific writer of stories. "All through my life I have had this urge to write; I become swamped with ideas—it is almost a problem—stories rain down on me as I lie in bed at night like small stones" (pers. comm.). During creative periods as many as thirty ideas for stories were jotted on paper and stored in boxes and drawers. These notes provided inspiration and material for future projects.

Becoming an Author

An important opportunity arose when Reviva participated in a series of workshops presented by Niki Daly, designed for prospective authors who wanted to learn how to write for children. One of the exercises was to write stories about childhood experiences. She duly wrote three prose "poems" based on her childhood in Johannesburg. Niki Daly's comments were encouraging, and he asked for other stories that she had written. Charlie, the young son of a domestic worker, inspired one of the stories she showed him. Charlie lived with his mother in a shack in one of the informal settlements that mushroomed in townships around Cape Town during the 1980s. In the story, Reviva projected into the plot Charlie's desire to live in a "real" house and ride in his own car, and Daly agreed to illustrate the text of *Charlie's House*. Songololo Books, a division of David Philip, published the book in 1989, and an overseas edition, published by Walker Books, soon followed.

This publication marked a turning point in the genre of children's picture books written and illustrated for the South African market. For the first time, a book appeared in print with a plot featuring a contemporary black child in which the illustrations' setting reflected the reality of contemporary black townships. At the same time, it also celebrates the power of creativity to overcome bleak circumstances. In spite of his poverty, Charlie uses his rich imagination to escape those surroundings. The success of *Charlie's House* gave Reviva the confidence to believe that she could make writing for children her life's work, but the reality was that she needed to earn a living.

Merging Creativity and Social Responsibility

An advertisement for a materials developer for the Early Learning Resource Unit (ELRU) in Cape Town began her long, productive association with this organization. Reviva describes her work with ELRU as "a huge part of my life" with a team of "creative and dedicated educators." For ELRU she has produced, in collaboration with colleagues, over seventy separate materials as books, posters, games, picture packs, magazines, and teachers' guides.

Reviva's own experiences in grade one made her particularly sensitive to the plight of children who do not fit in at school. In the 1990s when she began to work for ELRU, she sensed that she had an inkling of what the majority of schoolchildren in South Africa experienced in their alienating, under-resourced, and ill-serviced classrooms. She relates hearing a quote at ELRU describing the education system that resonated deeply with her: "It was as if black children were foreigners in their own country" (pers. comm.).

In 1996, ELRU set aside funding for the "Anti-Bias Project" aimed at creating a body of children's materials that reflected diversity, addressed racism, ageism, and sexism, and boosted the status of indigenous languages. Reviva accepted the challenge and harnessed all her creative energies, well aware that, despite the underlying mission's seriousness, the most important qualities she needed to capture were authenticity and complete child-friendliness.

In addition, her early experience with learning English as a second language echoed with her work at ELRU, where in collaboration with a committed team she spearheaded the process to produce simple multilingual readers. The Anti-Bias Project acknowledged the reality of the majority of South African classrooms filled with children who speak different languages, and gave equal status to a child's mother tongue in the face of dominant-language instruction. Reviva conceived, wrote the text, and designed all these books, employing photography or artwork illustrations with color-coded texts in four of South Africa's official languages.

Three of the readers stand-alone:

- *String Together* is a simple counting book where stringing a necklace with various beads is subtly transformed into images reflecting the diversity of South Africans.
- *Knock! Knock!* is a play on the game Knock-knock, who's there? Behind each door is an illustration of a child within a family unit in a particular cultural context with the transliterated sound-words for knocking, ranging from the isiXhosa clicks of " Nkqo! Nkqo!" to the Afrikaans "Tok! Tok! Tok!"
- *Uthini?*—translated as "What do you say?"—unlike the other two, is illustrated with amusing artwork rather than photographs. The book exposes children to the imagery of common sayings in four languages, English, Afrikaans, isiXhosa, and South Sotho, while explaining their meaning, for example, the isiXhosa, "I feel like I'm being kicked by a monkey," when hungry.

ELRU's five "Keteka Series" books have been their most successful readers. Each book tells about a child from a different community. Once the children and families for the photographic illustrations were identified, Reviva developed a rough storyline with them. After the shoot, Reviva edited the photographs, wrote text, and designed the layout. Glossy paper, color-coded texts, and photographs combine to give readers verbally and visually contextualized experiences of how different South African children live. The texts are simple, straightforward, and informative—a far cry from the "bland and homogenized" readers of Reviva's childhood.

Titles in the Keteka Series include:

- *Antjie,* based on a child living in Genadendal village in the Western Cape;
- *Mhlanguli,* based on a child living in Khayelitsha township in Cape Town;
- *Azhar,* a story about a Muslim child living in University Estate, Cape Town;
- *Zimkhitha,* describing the lifestyle of a child living in Gobozana village, a rural settlement outside King William's Town in the Eastern Cape; and
- *Cindy,* describing a black urban family living in an apartment in a Johannesburg suburb.

The next series with ELRU, the "Mielie Books," combines commissioned photographs with Reviva's own painted illustrations. The first title, *At School,*

What If? focuses on inclusive education and the needs of physically disabled children. The series' second book, *They Were Wrong* encourages children to think critically about what they hear and to avoid prejudice and stereotyping.

Another book in the series with the unusual title *Am I a Lion That Eats People?* focuses on the stigma associated with people who reveal their HIV positive status. Readers are challenged to think about important social issues and to analyze their responses to those who are HIV-positive or sick with AIDS.

The last book, *Waiting, Waiting, Always Waiting*, relates the real life story of Lihle who, together with her family, is being housed with hundreds of others in a communal hall in Gugulethu after a devastating fire in the informal settlement where she lived. Her family's predicament highlights a wider socio-economic picture of poverty and the need for material assistance.

Reviva emphasizes that she is extremely grateful for the opportunity to work with ELRU. Throughout their long association she gained access to a wider range of communities, which she would never have reached had she been writing freelance. ELRU's strong social responsibility has reinforced the social awareness in her personal work and life philosophy.

Independent Work as an Artist and Writer

Despite her artistic background, Reviva initially did not consider herself the right kind of artist to illustrate children's books. Her career as a children's book illustrator started with a surge of energy after a major operation, and she was delighted when she finally managed to bring together her two sides—"the art training and her word-smithing"—in several self-illustrated picture books and readers published commercially. Each book's format is varied, and techniques used include artwork or photographs of people in uniquely South African contexts. The advent of digital photography gave Reviva the confidence to start taking her own photographs, so recent photographic works are also by her hand.

Reviva has always rejected the strict delineation of works for children according to the age of the "target group." She knows that many adults love picture books and that young children can be read some pretty challenging texts. When she begins a project she allows the idea to dictate the form, be it picture book, stories for young children, nonfiction, or youth novel. As a result, her work ranges widely.

A Child's Garden, a nonfiction gardening guide aimed at families, is a compilation of imaginative outdoor activities, some of which Reviva investigated with her own children in the garden. One of the activities involved pressing star-shaped fruits of succulent dune plants or "vygies" into clay or play dough. The impressions left in the clay highlighted their star-shaped form. The activity provided the inspiration for a reader, *Stars on the Dunes*, an imaginative story that links the origin of the brilliant color of the flowers of these indigenous plants to the different colors of the stars.

The Jam Tin and the Teacup is a pun-laced story about a humble jam tin orangutan that falls in love with a green-haired, snobby teacup missy and is repulsed by her superior attitude. The watercolor illustrations include a rendition of Nelson Mandela drinking a cup of tea alongside text in which the teacup boasts, "I am drunk with tiny sips by the most important lips..." (n.p.).

As her own children approached puberty, Reviva decided to try writing a novel for young teenage readers. A story about life in Johannesburg during the 1960s, a period when apartheid restrictions began to impinge on all South Africans, had been "simmering on the backburner" for many years. Incidents in the story were based on the real-life experiences of close family members. Armed with bundles of letters hoarded in files and boxes for more than thirty years, and with her family's blessing, she began writing *Lucky Fish!* The novel describes what it was like to be the child of white political activists imprisoned during the apartheid regime. It is also a story about the "coming of age" of thirteen-year-old Steven who, despite the absence of his parents, manages to navigate successfully through the vagaries and hardships he encounters in very unusual circumstances. There is gentle irony in the title, as Steven was both unlucky with his parents in jail and envied by his friends who coveted his luck in the freedom from parental authority their absence afforded him.

In the novel, Reviva interprets Steven's feelings and frustrations with real empathy and love that could only be expressed by someone with intimate understanding of teenage behavior and firsthand knowledge about the experiences of the central character depicted in the novel. Several political incidents described in the novel resonated strongly with similar experiences of many South Africans in different settings and contexts in the 1960s. This is an authentic account of the difficulties experienced by white activists, who made important contributions to the struggle for democracy and freedom for all citizens of South Africa. The text is raw and real and does not sanitize events and incidents to make them more palatable. It is an important story of that time period that deserves to be shared with today's youth.

Reviva considers *An African Christmas Cloth* her most innovative and daring production. "You have to be more than a bit crazy to spend two and a half years on a single picture book," she says, "but I'd start again tomorrow if I could" (pers. comm.). Reviva meticulously embroidered eighteen tapestry friezes that depict a countdown toward Christmas Day, and the double-page spreads were scanned from the tapestries. The plot that links the tapestries together revolves around the eccentric Aunty Apples as she putters through the South African landscape on her bright red scooter. This story involves humorous but gentle and respectful contrasts between European Christmas traditions and South African cultural interpretations.

Exploring Different Genres of Children's Books

In 2006, following her work at ELRU, Reviva accepted an invitation from Cambridge University Press to contribute as an author-illustrator in the development of the Rainbow Reader Series. The project offered opportunities to work with authors, illustrators and design artists, and to experiment with different genres involved in the production of books for children. A sample of readers written and illustrated by Reviva includes:

- *Taste*, a grade two reader that explores the elements of taste using photographic collages of the facial expression of real children as they sample different foods;
- *The World in There*, a delightfully quirky set of paintings and graphic text that illustrate and describe the squeamish world inside a dustbin. There is an assortment of human detritus, not to mention an interesting array of the creepy crawlies that inhabit the world within a rubbish bin; and
- *The Red Skedonk* that evolved out of the lived experiences of family and friends in a dilapidated but much loved red car. The story's line drawings were executed by a teenage budding artist. This title encapsulates the way the author combines the facets of her work and weaves them into cameos reflecting a South African way of life.

Reviva continues to explore pressing social issues in her private and commissioned work. The Highlighters series published by Shuter and Shooter is an ongoing photographically illustrated series of readers that focus on the human rights and values of individuals and families living in different South African communities. The text for these books emerged from the photographic collages and interviews collected on site in homes, communities, schools, and institutions. The topics Reviva has explored include bullying, cultural diversity, learning difficulties, albinism, and dwarfism.

- *Nobody's Doll* is a studiously unsentimental yet sensitive and poignant account of the issues and problems children with Albinism face at home, at school, and in the community. The text is accompanied by intimate, beautifully photographed illustrations that encapsulate the central message of the book: "We are all the same on the inside and the difference on the outside makes us all the more interesting."

- *Bringing Bullying into the Open* involved a collaboration of several individuals and groups of children, including a teenage victim of bullying, the Cape Town drama group Kidz Take Over, and a Waldorf school in Cape Town. The graphic photographs and text depict various scenarios involving bullying, followed by classroom activities that address general ways of coping with bullying.
- *Learning Our Way* explores the way children with learning difficulties cope with and manage the challenges they face at Khanysa School in Plumstead, Cape Town, and highlights how they solve the everyday problems they encounter.
- *My Home in Walmer Road* explores a day in the life of Siraaj Raciet and his Moslem family as they interact with the eclectic lifestyles of a multiracial community living in Woodstock, Cape Town.

Working on the Highlighter Series was a challenge in terms of approaching the themes "authentically and honorably without resorting to sermons or judgments," and to "develop simple storybook solutions," according to Reviva. She further stated that it has been "a balancing act that keeps me on my toes" and that the issues she addresses and the stories she writes about

> reflect segments of the reality of the lives of many of South African children. They are based on my philosophy that views children as complex, savvy and capable of a whole lot more than people expect, and perfectly able to sniff out the sentimental and the false. There is an urge in me to break new ground, mix genres, explore hybrid illustrations, tackle difficult subjects, and to draw into the world of children's books, people and places that have not previously featured as fiction or non-fiction [pers. comm.].

A New Approach

In 2011, Reviva decided to put her stories and illustrations onto a new format and try to retain creative control over her own work. This was a response to the frustrations created by the limited publishing opportunities available in the South African market and the creative urge to continue writing. The digital revolution incorporating the availability of new technologies and software including Photoshop and InDesign gave birth to the possibility of compiling written materials in DVD format.

An African Suitcase is an extraordinary visual and textual treat that includes a compendium of twenty-seven separate items including picture books, short stories, novels, poems, fiction, and non-fiction. The texts are uniquely illustrated with photographs, drawings, paintings, embroideries, or illustrations from long forgotten favorite childhood books collected over many years. The level of reading varies from simple to challenging and includes general and local content.

- *Green Tongue* incorporates spectacular photographs of the intricate shapes and structural form of the leaves of different South African indigenous plants. The text combines two textual formats: single vividly descriptive and tongue-twisting words for younger readers and scientific names and formal anecdotes for aspiring botanists.
- *Mmpundulu, the Lightning Bird* is an imaginative twist on the origin of lightning based on African folklore.

Reviva's latest venture, "Children of Southern Africa," a series of what will eventually consist of eight books, builds on an abiding concern:

> There is a real need to write reading materials that reflect genuine and current lifestyles that are not stereotyped, unrealistic or romanticized, but give a balanced and authentic depiction of how aspects of everyday life are influenced by cultural traditions and the ever changing infusions of modern pop culture [pers. comm.].

Recent travels to destinations in southern Africa confirmed that communities are connected to their past through ancient traditions and historical influences. At the same time they are not locked in a time warp, but as members of a global society their current lifestyles and ways of thinking are affected by the influences of the twenty-first century. In towns, cities and villages there is evidence of the ubiquitous fashion of jeans, t-shirts and sneakers, and the pervasive use of cell phone technology.

Armed with cameras and a laptop, and travelling in a Toyota Cruiser fitted out as a camper, Reviva and her husband Peter embarked on trips to selected southern African countries and locations within South Africa itself. The modus operandi at each destination was uniquely localized and involved first identifying two children, a boy and a girl, who would be willing to tell their story and be photographed. A potential storyline would emerge from the initial interaction with the chosen subjects in time, place, and space. Numerous photographs taken in different settings and locations created the background and stimulus from which suitable text could be linked and crafted into storybook form. The books about Children of Southern Africa are about real children, their names are not fictional. The format of the text is 90 percent nonfiction, tweaked here and there to conform to the storyline. The photographic images and artistic design provide a visually rich background that captures the lifestyles of children in African communities and highlight the ambience of their unique locations. Six books in the series are currently in DVD format, to be published in book form once the series is completed:

- *Mauro and Adelaide, Their Life in Quelimane, Mozambique.*
- *Kero and Beeby, Their Life in Great Zimbabwe, Zimbabwe.*
- *Lindeka and Vuyane, Their Life in Malkerns, Swaziland.*
- *Thobeka and Samukelo, Their Life in Yeoville, South Africa.*
- *Myrtle and Daneco, Their Life in Kassiesbaai, South Africa.*
- *Lebohang and Polo, Their Life in Ha Lesala, Lesotho.*

Conclusion

The real value of Reviva's body of work to date is embedded in her versatility and her capacity to be a creative author, a vibrant illustrator, and an imaginative developer of educational materials. Her ability to collaborate with people from all walks of life and stakeholders in the publishing business has resulted in books and educational resources that have made significant progress towards promoting multilingualism, anti-bias attitudes, and inclusive education in South African schools. Her fluid, easy-to-read style of writing and the intriguing combinations of artistic techniques used to illustrate the books she writes make her one of the more unique authors and illustrators of South African children's literature. Reviva Schermbrucker's work is authentic, subtle, naturally inclusive, never sanitized or overtly politically correct. She tells a good story as it really is, and she is still going strong.

CHILDREN'S BOOKS

Schermbrucker, Reviva. 1989. *Charlie's House*. Illustrated by Niki Daly. Cape Town, SA: David Philips.
———. 1992. *A Child's Garden*. Cape Town, SA: Tafelberg.
———. 1996. *Knock! Knock!* Photographs by Sue Hillyard. Cape Town, SA: Early Learning Resource Unit.
———. 1996. *String Together*. Photographs by Lynne Stuart. Cape Town, SA: Early Learning Resource Unit.
———. 1997. *Antjie*. Photographs by Sue Kramer. Cape Town, SA: Early Learning Resource Unit.
———. 1997. *Uthini?* Illustrated by Trish de Villiers. Cape Town, SA: Early Learning Resource Unit.
———. 1998. *Mhlanguli*. Photographs by Sue Kramer. Cape Town, SA: Early Learning Resource Unit.
———. 1999. *Azhar*. Photographs by Sue Hillyard. Cape Town, SA: Early Learning Resource Unit.
———. 2000. *Zimkhitha*. Photographs by Rob Pollock. Cape Town, SA: Early Learning Resource Unit.
———. 2001. *Cindy*. Photographs by Motlhalefi Mahlabe. Cape Town, SA: Early Learning Resource Unit.
———. 2002. *The Jam Tin and the Teacup*. Pietermaritzburg, SA: Shuter and Shooter.

_____. 2002. *Stars on the Dunes*. Cape Town, SA: New Africa.
_____. 2003. *Lucky Fish!* Bellevue, SA: Jacana.
_____. 2003. *At School, What If?* Photographs by Wayne Conradie. Illustrated by Reviva Schermbrucker. Cape Town, SA: Early Learning Resource Unit.
_____. 2003. *They Were Wrong!* Photographs by Wayne Conradie. Illustrated by Reviva Schermbrucker. Cape Town, SA: Early Learning Resource Unit.
_____. 2005. *Am I a Lion That Eats People?* Photographs by Enver Essop. Cape Town, SA: Early Learning Resource Unit.
_____. 2005. *An African Christmas Cloth*. Johannesburg, SA: Jacana Media.
_____. 2006. *Waiting, Waiting, Always Waiting*. Photographs by Enver Essop. Cape Town, SA: Early Learning Resource Unit.
_____. 2008. *Bringing Bullying into the Open*. Pietermaritzburg/Cape Town, SA: Shuter & Shooter.
_____. 2008. *Learning Our Way*. Pietermaritzburg/Cape Town, SA: Shuter & Shooter.
_____. 2008. *My Home in Walmer Road*. Pietermaritzburg/Cape Town, SA: Shuter & Shooter.
_____. 2008. *Nobody's Doll*. Pietermaritzburg/Cape Town, SA: Shuter & Shooter.
_____. 2009. *The Red Skedonk*. Illustrated by Dylan Birkett. Cape Town, SA: Cambridge University Press.
_____. 2009. *The World in There*. Cape Town, SA: Cambridge University Press.
_____. 2012. *An African Suitcase*. (DVD format). Self-published.
_____. 2014. *Kero and Beeby, Their Life in Great Zimbabwe, Zimbabwe*. Pietermaritzburg, SA: Duzi Publishing.
_____. 2014. *Lebohang and Polo, Their Life in Ha Lesala, Lesotho*. Pietermaritzburg, SA: Duzi Publishing.
_____. 2014. *Lindeka and Vuyane, Their Life in Malkerns, Swaziland*. Pietermaritzburg, SA: Duzi Publishing.
_____. 2014. *Mauro and Adelaide, Their Life in Quelimane, Mozambique*. Pietermaritzburg, SA: Duzi Publishing.
_____. 2014. *Myrtle and Daneco, Their Life in Kassiesbaai, South Africa*. Pietermaritzburg, SA: Duzi Publishing.
_____. 2014. *Thobeka and Samukelo, Their Life in Yeoville, South Africa*. Pietermaritzburg, SA: Duzi Publishing.
Schernbrucker, Reviva, and Thomas Rose. 2009. *Taste*. Cape Town, SA: Cambridge University Press.

This essay is adapted and updated from an article first published in 2011 in *Bookbird: A Journal of International Children's Literature* 49.1: 9–16.

Dianne Stewart: Writer with a Sense of Purpose

Jay Heale

At the first ever World Congress in Africa of the International Board on Books for Young People (IBBY) in September 2004, Professor Elwyn Jenkins (2012) started his plenary lecture with these words:

> South Africa has three great contributions to make to world children's literature: the folktales of its peoples; books about its magnificent animals, plant kingdoms and landscapes; and stories which document, grieve over, and celebrate our history [5].

Dianne Stewart's contribution is largely in the spheres of folktales and of our animal-filled landscape, though many of her reality stories also bear witness to both the grief and the joy of our social history.

Dianne's early writing was based on the foundation of a Bachelor of Arts degree in Psychology and isiXhosa at Rhodes University in 1973, followed in 1974 by an Honours degree in African languages through the University of South Africa (UNISA) while she was teaching isiXhosa part-time. Part of the motivation for this came from her mother, Leslie, who was a fluent speaker of isiXhosa. Dianne is also very much aware of the influence of a brilliant English teacher, Mrs. Shipley, under whom she studied as an American Field Service Scholar in the United States after graduating from high school at the Collegiate College for Girls in Port Elizabeth. She spent that "gap year" at Chatham, New Jersey, where she was taught by Mrs. Shipley who "stretched us in our critical analysis of texts and our creative output" (pers. comm.). Mrs. Shipley must have been a fine teacher, for her son, David Shipley, went on to win the 1987 Pulitzer Prize for General Non-Fiction for *Arab and Jew: Wounded Spirits in a Promised Land* (1986).

Responding to *Bookchat* magazine's call for indigenous stories in 1985, Dianne submitted two short tales that were accepted for inclusion in *Storytime* (Heale 1987). "Thekwane and Frog" (*uThekwane* is the isiZulu name of the *hamerkop* or *scopus umbretta* bird) has two differing species helping each other, much in the style of Aesop's fable "The Lion and the Mouse" and is set on the family farm on the north coast of KwaZulu-Natal. "The Orange Tree" is a tale of drought and conservation, as well as the reward of generosity. Both contain lucid descriptive passages about their African settings. Supplying personal details for a later issue of *Bookchat*, Dianne said:

> In my writing I am influenced by the landscape and I endeavor to create a strong sense of place in my stories. My academic studies in African Languages have enriched and enlarged my personal vision, providing insight into some of the cultures around me [Stewart 1996, 12].

All her writing carries a sense of purpose, as well as warm, deliberate descriptions of Africa, often of the east coast region where she lives.

From a childhood of being read to aloud, then of reading for herself such favorites as the tales of Hans Christian Andersen, as a teenager Dianne came to realize, partly through studying Jane Austen's *Pride and Prejudice* (1813), that literature reflects society. In her writing, she has developed a straightforward, positive prose style, telling a good story well. The key to the passages of description in her books is her appreciation for and love of Africa, its people, places and traditional literature.

Dianne Stewart's writing can be regarded under three headings: picture books, collections of traditional folktales, and a widening diversity of genres.

Picture Books

Having accepted the constraints imposed by picture books on vocabulary, length, and arrangement of text, Dianne Stewart was fortunate to work with a number of South Africa's leading illustrators. In *The Runaway Hen* Kathy Pienaar uses rich reds and yellows which give a glow to the story of Delani who wants a hen of his own, gets one, loses it and then finds himself looking after four chicks. A child's life is full of such momentous occasions. *Mondi, the Music Maker* benefits from imaginative blocks of color devised by the late Ian Lusted.

> *Mondi* is an uplifting tale of a crippled boy who could not "dance or play soccer as his friends did" though he could make music for them on his recorder. He earns money playing for the crowds outside Durban's 'Workshop' shopping centre, but has to choose whether to spend it on his sister's college fees or on replacing the recorder which he has lost on the train [Heale 1996, 40].

This well-produced book was published by Garamond who deliberately risked money by creating versions in English, Afrikaans, isiXhosa and isiZulu at a time when black South African-language children's books were very scarce. *Mondi* was included in the annual Honours List of the South African Children's

Book Forum. Among her other picture books was an advantageous author-illustrator collaboration with Jude Daly in creating *The Dove* and *The Gift of the Sun*. Both books were published internationally and won commendations. *The Gift of the Sun* was included in the prestigious *White Ravens* International Youth Library list of 1997.

The Dove, first published by Greenwillow Books in New York, is based on the harsh living and a freak flood of the Valley of a Thousand Hills inland from Durban in the KwaZulu-Natal Province. Grandmother Maloko needs to sell beadwork to earn money. It is the dove, a visitor after the local floods and symbol of peace, as in the Noah story, which brings the required inspiration. Both text and pictures portray poverty and accept it, without sentiment, creating a reassuring story based on the result of honest toil.

A similar theme appears in *The Gift of the Sun*, though this is far more in the folktale genre. Its name is based on the isiZulu proverb: *"woth' omabili,"* which means "He basks in both suns," referring to an elderly person who sits in the morning and afternoon sun in order to keep warm. Thulani, the farmer in the story, does exactly this. In fact, he loves to bask in the sun all day. Every afternoon when the sun begins to sink, he stands up, straightens his stiff back and goes to milk the cow. Then, becoming lazy, he sells first his cow, then the goat, the sheep, the geese and finally plants a field of sunflowers. With each transaction he assures himself, "Dora will be pleased." But she isn't. However, their abundant seeds encourage the chickens to lay more eggs, so Thulani can buy some sheep and a cow and happiness returns. Even Dora is delighted. Such is "the gift" of the sun. Increasing foolishness is replaced by increasing good sense. Thulani has built on his knowledge and his graph of good fortune climbs until the sunflower seeds prove a true "Gift of the Sun."

The Gift of the Sun is one of Dianne Stewart's most successful stories, with translations into Danish, Norwegian, Swedish, French, Spanish, isiXhosa, isiZulu, Afrikaans and South Korean. Jude Daly's artwork, precisely effective in *The Dove*, here creates a spacious, airy African horizon full of accurate observation of genuine rural life in South Africa presented with dignity and affection. *The Gift of the Sun* won the Katrine Harries Award for Illustration in 1997, was chosen as the South African IBBY Honour Book for illustration and was on exhibition at the 1998 IBBY Congress in New Delhi.

Citing Stewart's *The Mealie-Cob Children,* Jennifer Whyte, a teacher for seven years in KwaZulu-Natal, staunchly supports picture books' practical application in the classroom:

> *The Mealie-Cob Children* was THE book to read. The children LOVE this book. Every child in the school knew about *The Mealie-Cob Children* and how to make them. That story is a real hit with Zulu home-language children, learning English as their First Additional language [pers. comm.].

Traditional Folktales

Dianne's studies in African literature had brought her into close contact with the oral tradition of Africa. As she points out in her introduction to *Daughter of the Moonlight and Other African Tales* these oral tales "were not only entertaining, but also a means of education, and reinforcing cultural and social standards" (3). She has published four collections of folktales, each one a little more ambitious.

Daughter of the Moonlight and Other African Tales contains eleven retold stories, gathered from the Southern African region including Lesotho and Swaziland. The first two are from San and Khoi traditions, the original hunter-gatherer and pastoral-herder peoples. The others come from Xhosa, Zulu, Sotho and Swazi oral traditions. In an essay entitled "San Tales—Again," Elwyn Jenkins (2012) comments: "Stewart's story 'The sun and moon of the San people' is clearly based on Bleek and Lloyd material" (28).[1]

In their early-recorded versions, African folktales can be dry and basic, relying on the individual storyteller for dramatic technique. Dianne adds more visual description, as well as expands the dialogue and characters. Her opening sentence for "The Hungry Jackal" reads: "A wind appeared from nowhere and set the landscape in motion, gathering up the dry red dust which caked the sparsely scattered bushes and tufts of bristly grass" (8).

She is word-painting the African landscape. In "The Cattle Herder's Song" she provides extra cultural detail from Swaziland:

> One year, at the First Fruits Festival, the king's son saw that beer had been prepared by the women and had been placed in a row of calabashes outside the kraal. All the men, women and children had gone to the fields with their baskets to gather the first ripe produce of the harvests: maize, millet, ground-nuts, sugar cane, and pumpkins [21].

Exactly ten years later, Dianne Stewart produced a far more extensive collection, *The Zebra's Stripes and other African Animal Tales*. This contains thirty-three animal stories culled from sources as far-spread as Ethiopia, Togo, Nigeria, Namibia, Zambia, as well as plenty from South Africa itself. Stories of different animals are grouped together, followed by a page of "Interesting Facts" about that particular animal. So the book offers young readers African folklore together with snippets of factual knowledge. This collection was followed by a wider selection entitled *Folktales from Africa*, superbly illustrated by Marjorie van Heerden.

Building on her research for these animal stories, Dianne created a similar collection of stories based on birds. *The Guinea-Fowl's Spots and other African Bird Tales* has annotations of factual knowledge as well as many examples of proverbs mentioning birds. Proverbs are an integral part of the African oral tradition, as captured in her compilation of African proverbs, *Wisdom from Africa,* now in its sixth reprint. Stewart's unique collection of bird folktales is additionally enhanced with superbly characterful illustrations by Richard Mackintosh. With a strengthened storytelling technique and less florid descriptive passages, this is one of Dianne's most successful additions to the storytelling wealth of Africa.

A Widening Diversity of Genres

The first ever fully democratic elections took place in South Africa in April 1994, and *Chasing the Wind* is a book of that auspicious year. Books do not get published overnight—no matter how much would-be authors dream of such a thing. A manuscript has to be read, assessed, considered, edited, the book designed and printed, marketing planned, before a book is ever actually published. This means that Dianne Stewart was busy creating this book before those elections took place, certainly before the effects on South Africa could be known.

In *Chasing the Wind*, the young heroine's cousin, Tammy, writes letters from America. She says, *"They cannot believe that apartheid is dead and that South Africa actually has a democratically elected government at last"* (52). That was true. The world could not believe it.

During the plenary session of the IBBY Congress held in September 1994 in Seville, "Reports from National Sections," South Africa was given time to speak. Delight in this country's new-found democracy was shared with the 700-strong Congress. As a result, members of the South African delegation were overwhelmed. People they had never met from countries they hardly knew existed were hugging them for joy.

Dianne Stewart did not try to write about that overwhelming joy. She set out to write a story about ordinary people living in an ordinary South Africa, but one in which racism, prejudice and skin color did not need to be mentioned. Such an idea was overwhelming in its pure simplicity. There is a clue to the skin color of Oom Piet who grumbles, after being retrenched from his job at the fish factory, "I wonder how many whiteys got fired? Probably none" (37). That is all.

The plot is well summarized by teacher Christine Cozien (1996) who wrote in *Molo Songololo* magazine:

> This story is about a girl called Jodie whose mother died soon after she was born. Her father cannot manage her, so she lives with her Oom (Uncle) Piet and Tant (Aunt) Marie who both take very good care of her and love her a lot. She wants to meet her real father but her uncle and aunt are scared that she will be hurt to

see what he is really like. When she eventually meets him, all her dreams of the perfect father are shattered [17].

The action takes place mostly in Plettenberg Bay on the southeastern shore of South Africa, the area near where Dianne herself grew up and had her own schooling in Port Elizabeth, a little way up the coast. There must be echoes of her school days in the opening chapters where Jodie and her friends talk about passing final exams, about their boy-friend hopes, about what to do after schooling finishes. She finds relationships difficult at times because her mother is long dead, her father is who-knows-where, and she lives with her aunt and uncle. To Jodie's surprise, her chosen boy, Grant, reveals that both his parents are dead. Yet he seems so normal. Jodie becomes determined to trace her living father. In the book's climax she does so, but he has already found another wife and family: he is coldly uninterested in his visiting daughter. So her desire for family was indeed "chasing the wind."

Chasing the Wind is concerned with personal and emotional development, though the social sphere is not ignored. It stresses the problem of job losses and of youngsters without parents—both all too common features in the South Africa of today. It is ideal reading for students as a bridge between the format of a short story and that of a full-length, complex novel. That is one explanation why *Chasing the Wind* is today in its fourteenth reprint. But all credit to the author. This is a smoothly-written, competent character study, full of sympathetic understanding. A refreshingly moral story in which teenagers manage to survive quite well without recourse to any of the vices that clutter so many youth novels.

Also for teenage readers is Dianne's "The Crash" which won the 1995 Maskew Miller Longman's (MML) Young Africa Award in the short story category and was included in *Short Stories, Southern Africa and Beyond* (Stephenson 2008) in company with stories by such eminent authors as Ahmed Essop, Nadine Gordimer, Njabulo Ndebele and Chinua Achebe. It is a vigorous story told at a fast pace, concerning a boy's anguish at being involved in a traffic accident, with accurate hospital procedures to make it more convincing. Guilt brings no easy answers, but understanding and forgiveness make the burden more bearable.

Another short story published in *New Contrast* magazine is "Bread for the Journey." This is a skillfully woven tale, using food as the connecting link, especially the Zulu pot-bread *ujeqe* of mother's home cooking. Jabu, a young Zulu woman, has left home to take a lecturing job in Kampala, Uganda. But in what seems a typical case of professional jealousy, her head of department hires another teacher who takes a large slice of Jabu's teaching. Indignant, she travels back to Durban where she finds her mother too weak to bake any more, so Jabu starts cooking; and from now on there will be Ugandan food as well as Zulu. It all gives truth to a traditional Zulu story that, returning home, one can never expect things to be the same again.

In both these compact, realistic short stories, Dianne Stewart creates fully-rounded main characters and uses details from modern Africa to paint the scene and hold the reader's attention.

As evidence of her growing diversity, Dianne Stewart compiled and edited *Durban in a Word*, a collection of essays about the east coast city-port Durban, which helped to raise funds for the organization "Noah" (Nurturing Orphans of Aids for Humanity). She worked with Professor Lindy Stiebel on a north coast writers' trail that followed authors in the coastal area north of Durban. She has also given much time to presenting workshops on creative writing in schools and for adult groups, as well as having added to her studies a Master of Arts degree in creative writing at the University of Cape Town in 2008. All clear evidence of her growing versatility.

Dianne's most recent picture book, *Who's Afraid of the Dark?*, is almost surprisingly light and frisky, emphasizing how important (and comforting) animals are to children as pets. A memory of early childhood, perhaps, but also linked to the arrival of her second granddaughter Olivia (to whom the book is dedicated). Of this story, Dianne said in a newspaper interview:

> Although I sometimes place my stories within a particular culture or social setting and I need to be familiar with that context, I try to go beyond that and touch on universals that are part of the human condition. For example, fear of the dark is an emotion that is experienced universally [Stewart 2012, 12].

It may be a coincidence that Dianne's first published stories appeared in the same year (1987) as the first international symposium on children's literature in South Africa, "Towards Understanding." But it is certainly true that her writing has grown in strength and structure along with the indigenous children's literature with which she has identified herself.

It was at this symposium that the idea of a national body on children's books was launched: the South African Children's Book Forum (SACBF), later to become IBBY SA. Dianne Stewart supported their aims and, for some years, ran a regional branch of the SACBF in Stanger, KwaDukuza. Dianne has every right to be regarded as a major contributor to the national children's literature of South Africa, supporting such a cause not only with her varied writing but also in her continuing personal involvement.

Note

1. In the 1870s, Wilhelm Bleek and Lucy Lloyd meticulously set down San language and traditions as related to them by surviving San who had been released from labor gangs for this purpose.

Children's Books

Heale, Jay, comp. 1987. *Storyland.* Illustrated by Alida Bothma. Cape Town, SA: Tafelberg.
Stephenson, Arlene, ed. 2008. *Short Stories: Southern Africa and Beyond.* Cape Town, SA: Oxford University Press, Southern Africa.
Stewart, Dianne. 1988. *The Mealie-Cob Children.* Pietermaritzburg, SA: Shuter & Shooter.
_____. 1989. *The Runaway Hen.* Illustrated by Kathie Pienaar. Cape Town, SA: Human & Rousseau.
_____. 1990. *Mondi, the Music Maker.* Illustrated by Ian Lusted. Durbanville, SA: Garamond.
_____. 1992. *The Dove.* Illustrated by Jude Daly. New York: Greenwillow. Cape Town, SA: David Philip.
_____. 1994. *Chasing the Wind.* Cape Town, SA: Oxford University Press.
_____. 1994. *Daughter of the Moonlight and Other African Tales.* Cape Town, SA: Struik.
_____. 1996. *The Gift of the Sun.* Illustrated by Jude Daly. London: Frances Lincoln. Cape Town, SA: Tafelberg.
_____. 2004. *The Zebra's Stripes and Other African Animal Tales.* Cape Town, SA: Struik.
_____. 2005. *Wisdom from Africa.* Cape Town, SA: Struik.
_____. 2006. *Folktales of Africa.* Illustrated by Marjorie van Heerden. Cape Town, SA: Struik.
_____. 2007. *The Guinea-Fowl's Spots and Other African Bird Tales.* Cape Town, SA: Struik.
_____. 2008. *Durban in a Word.* Johannesburg, SA: Penguin Books.
_____. 2010. "Bread for the Journey." *New Contrast* No. 149, Vol. 38 No.1: Autumn 2010.
_____. 2011. *Who's Afraid of the Dark?* Illustrated by Joan Rankin. Johannesburg, SA: Jacana Media.

The author would like to acknowledge the great assistance of the National English Library archives (NELM) in the research required for this essay.

Ann Walton: Families and Fables

Anne Hill

Ann Walton's first love was visual art and design, but after thirty years of close engagement with writing, mainly for young children, she defines herself as writer and artist. However, she also has played a major, multi-dimensional role in driving a number of creative projects for various publishers, as art director, author, and illustrator. In the mid–1990s she was designer and art director for a particularly significant series of over one hundred titles for the publisher Juta Gariep's "Star Stories" series. In collaboration with Lesley Beake as commissioning editor, she was art director for forty-eight titles of Kagiso's "Zebra Books." When Maskew Miller Longman bought Kagiso, the Zebra titles formed the first group of the longer-lived "Stars of Africa" series. Walton was also writer and art director of nine books for Juta's "Read and Learn" series about southern African wildlife, the content of which was verified by three botanists: Connie Krug, Eugene Moll and Sue Milton. The literary qualities of characterization and plot and the empathy that her narratives bring to these books lifts them out of a literal information genre to provide the reader with engaging aesthetic experiences.

Walton began to write at school, but after graduating from high school completed studies in commercial and fine art. In her early working life, there are indications of her drive to be involved in projects from conception to production. She began her working career in the State Library in Pretoria, South Africa, and then as a proofreader in the provincial library in Cape Town. She later moved on to qualify as a dress designer and worked in a clothing factory. Then the acting editor of *Contrast,* a literary journal, asked her to produce illustrations for the publication. Commissions for books and magazines followed. These projects, however, stirred unease in her because "I didn't always like what I was reading, especially sentimental, patronizing stories" (pers. comm.). While humor and lightness characterize her texts, she treats children's gaze on the world with respect, never trivializing or infantilizing their worlds, qualities that indicate what she was looking for in the texts she illustrated. Over time, she has written mainly for picture books in genres of nonfiction, realism, and fantasy, in a lively narrative mode complemented by a loyal team of gifted illustrators.

Realism: Families First

The synergy between Walton and her illustrators, particularly the more frequent collaborators Natalie and Tamsin Hinrichsen, Marna Hattingh, and Piet and Diek Grobler, has been key to fulfilling the meaning of many of her books, and needs to be acknowledged in discussing her work.

Walton's first solo text, *We Shouldn't Keep It!*, complemented by Jo Harvey's dynamic and colorful illustrations, sets the tone for many subsequent books. Spirited, affectionate, quirky and imaginative, it explores the dark resentments of a first-born child who feels displaced by the arrival of a new sibling.

Empathy with her characters undergoing the universal vicissitudes of family life infuses *Don't Scratch!*, illustrated in appropriately agitated mark-making[1] by Trish de Villiers. An energetic pair of siblings, bored and irritable, afflicted by chicken pox, exasperate their mother by venting their frustrations on each other in mischievous horseplay. Furthermore, they seek their own messy solutions to alleviate their itches, in spite of their mother's anxious efforts to treat their malady appropriately, and her repeated injunction: "Don't scratch!" Walton often embraces episodes in life that families would rather forget, helping young readers to transcend these experiences through the empathy and humor of her language.

Walton is comfortable writing for a range of young readers, from primary through elementary stages. In *Big Fat Lies* tardy Sam misses the school bus and spends the day sheltering from the rain—and hiding from his mother passing by in her car—in the local library with an elderly stranger and former biology teacher who helps him to find information on DNA for a hastily invented school "project." His new mentor informs him that he shares fifty per cent of his DNA with a banana! When Sam confesses the misdemeanors and deceptions of his day to his mother, she does not believe him. Walton slips in a humorous aside on the mother's scientific knowledge: "I said don't tell lies, Sam!" she retorts when he announces that she shares her DNA with a banana. Nikki Jones' mixed media illustrations in collaged blocked primary colors overlaid with gestural mark-making, capture the messy progress of Sam's chaotic day, enhancing readers' access to the dramatic irony underpinning his final exchange with his mother.

Something to Do, told in under a hundred words, is a masterpiece of economy and skill in constructing a meaningful reading experience for a novice reader. In spite of its use of conventions of rhyme, repetition and an almost completely monosyllabic vocabulary pitched at beginner readers, it resonates with a child's concern for her friend "in bed with flu and she has nothing to do" (16). The emotional warmth of the text builds from page to page in a series of rhythmic waves to affirm the bond of compassion between the friends. Incidentally, it also affirms the consoling power of literature.

For many decades since the onset of apartheid repression and consequent permanent separation due to exile and emigration, the heartbreak of families of the diaspora has been a common reality for South Africans of every hue. In the fantasy *Here I Am* Walton addresses the longing of a South African grandmother to be present at the arrival of her first grandchild in "another land" (30). Determined Gran enlists the services of a series of iconic African birds and animals to transport her from zone to zone of the African continent, until she parachutes triumphantly to her waiting children's front door to meet June, her grandchild:

"I've come to tell you that I love you, sweetheart."

"I know," said June [32].

Piet Grobler's vibrant illustrations propel the reader through the text at a cracking pace and provide a rich sub-text. The images are loaded with humorous past and present cultural references, including the "hippy" style of the young parents, which for South African readers generally denotes a liberal anti-apartheid Establishment orientation; and a black angel floating past the window with a vuvusela, a single-note trumpet that produces a deafening drone when sounded by a crowd. Much loved by South African sports fans, it often causes alarm and irritation among foreigners. A mixed-race pair of hikers pass a Cape Dutch manor; ubiquitous windmills feature in the arid interior of South Africa; a white colonial explorer and his bearers cross Africa's central savannah, oblivious to the dramatic passage of Gran borne on an ostrich in her ostrich-feather-era nineteenth century finery and observed by a heavily armed contemporary black ranger in camouflage fatigues. Tea is provided for film star Meryl Streep on the set of "Out of Africa"; even surrealist artists Salvador Dali's melting clocks and Henri Rousseau's jungle feature in the odyssey. As Gran mounts a white goose to complete her journey over the Mediterranean Sea, a whimsical reference to Don Quixote's fantastical quest can be spotted in the landscape far below. Walton and Grobler collaborate to produce a book that is a transcendently joyous affirmation of the intimate ties that bind families separated by their times, chosen spaces and a globalizing environment.

In *The Great Big Fish,* young Joe emulates his fisherman father and catches an enormous fish for supper. On his way home, the catch in his bag becomes increasingly remarkable as his friends identify it first as a guinea fowl, then a goat that winks knowingly at the reader. When he presents his "goat" to his mother, she affirms the boy's pride in his accomplishment, while restoring him to reality with a loving gesture and praise for providing the family with a fish for supper. Finally, Joe shares a wry reflection on his imaginary exploit with his good-humored father. Natalie Hinrichsen's simplified, rhythmic dreamscapes in her illustrations signal that the story is set in the psychic world of the child's imagination. Hinrichsen's sensitivity to Walton's intentions is shown in the way she supports Walton's shifts between genres of realism and fantasy, depending on Walton's vision of what is happening in the child protagonist's psyche. In contrast, her illustrations for the straight forward adventure, *A Fine Day for Flying,* suggest that the jungle landscapes of protagonist Ben's imagination are as real to him as the interiors of his home and neighborhood chimneys, unlike Joe's dreamscapes in *The Great Big Fish,* in which Walton's narrative style approaches the archetypal rhythms of fable, signaling the child's deeper need to be seen as heroic.

For Walton, family life includes the companionship of animals. The animals in *A Fine Day for Flying* and *Have You Seen My Donkey?* remain located in their animal personae, oblivious to their roles in the dramas their human handlers are undergoing. In *A Fine Day for Flying,* illustrated by Natalie Hinrichsen, Honey-Bun, a dog resembling a brown Staffordshire bull terrier, unwittingly accompanies Ben in an imaginary hair-raising flight and crash landing in the cockpit of his "aeroplane," a cardboard box equipped with improvised "flying" paraphernalia. Sparky's beloved donkey, Chunky, is lost, suspected stolen, and found in *Have You Seen My Donkey?*, illustrated in dramatic naive style by Marna Hattingh. Expressive use of livid color, flattened shapes and bold patterns both accentuate the emotional intensity of Sparky's anxiety and universalize the situation.

Pets in *We Must Go Shopping Now Samson,* illustrated by Diek Grobler, *I Don't Belong to You* and *Tiger and Louise* both illustrated by Marna Hattingh, shift into anthropomorphic mode. Mrs. Manchip's wily dog, Samson, depicted by Grobler as an engagingly calculating cartoon character with a mind of his own, deliberately sabotages her shopping expedition to subvert his travel arrangements in a bicycle basket and satisfy his appetite in *We Must Go Shopping Now Samson.* On the other hand, *I Don't Belong to You* strikes a warning note against attempts to domesticate a wild creature. Sam is mortified when his captive, a wood pigeon, goes into decline and reveals her desire to escape to freedom in a heart-rending song. As in *Have You Seen My Donkey?*, Hattingh uses expressive techniques to underscore a universal message, this time resisting humans' assumption of dominance over nature. Again her liberal use of livid blue deepens the reader's emotional response to the wood pigeon's suffering. Tiger, the canine partner in *Tiger and Louise* suffers impaired self-esteem and remorse after he instinctively bites Louise when she falls on top of him during a boisterous dancing game at her birthday party. He takes action to express his concern for the injured Louise who forgives him, and their relationship of mutual love is restored. Notably, Hattingh's doll-like figures depict a postracial circle of birthday guests in natural color, a more gently modulated palette, and perspective that lends spatial depth to her illustrations, elements that enhance humane ideals of belonging, forgiveness and restitution.

Fantasy: Walton as Fabulist

Walton's love of fable is a thread that runs through her oeuvre from the mid–1990s to her most recent text published in 2009. She prefers to invent her own fables rather than retell or imitate existing tales (pers. comm.). The tales, all of which are anthropomorphic in that animals speak, can be categorized as those that feature only animals and those that include humans.

Although some of the motifs in Walton's stories are familiar, the forms they take are original. While they demonstrate her understanding and control of the conventions of the genre, she tends to subvert culturally bound expectations. For example, readers may be familiar with the helpful trickster who betrays his weaker victim's trust but gets his comeuppance when the victim turns trickster. *Lying Toad*, illustrated in mixed media by Nikki Jones, has some affinity with many versions of this scenario, but upsets the predictable cautionary motif by transforming the snake, perceived generally as deceitful and malevolent, into the trusting victim of the soft-bodied toad, who then flips back to its natural position in the food chain when he is eaten by the snake.

There are cautionary elements in *We Want Tails!*, a creation story of how the dutiful tortoise, by being polite and conscientious, secured from Kudu fit-for-purpose tails for the self-important elephant and eland tormented by troublesome flies, as well as a little tail for his humble self. Tamsin Hinrichsen's illustrations succeed in striking a balance between the "folksy" nature of the tortoise's mission and the grander mythic tone of a creation story. The sculptural quality of the forms, their weight and scale on the pages, rich harmonious hues and graceful movement, as well as the lustre of the book's production add up to a thoroughly satisfying sensory and aesthetic experience. Tamsin Hinrichsen is also the illustrator of *The Tale of Sun and Moon*, an optimistic tale of trial, error and compromise in arriving at a distribution of heavenly bodies that suits all the animals on the planet. Visually, Hinrichsen's fresh and open vistas and serene animals invite a perception that the story may serve as a metaphor for more gentle human relations with the natural ecology of the planet.

Mythic fables featuring human protagonists include *The Girl and the Golden Amulet*; *The Red Man*; and *Tell the Moon*. The role of the crocodile in *The Girl and the Golden Amulet* is ambiguous. The crocodile decides to cure a young girl of her grief so that her bitter tears will no longer render her unpalatable. Having freed her from grief, the crocodile becomes increasingly reluctant to consume her. He gives her a golden amulet to protect her from harm, even from himself, and returns her to her father. Although the crocodile allows her to bury the golden amulet rather than return it to him, so that she will be protected by being afraid of him, "... his hungry eyes gazed steadily at Miriam, never letting her out of his sight. Miriam shivered" (15). Tamsin Hinrichsen's static, stylized images, suspended in a deep green world dominated by the thorn-like patterns of the crocodile's scales and teeth, create a visual context full of mystery and menace for the text.

In southern African culture, the *tokoloshe* is a much-feared sprite that can wreak havoc amongst communities. He is unpredictable, spiteful, and indestructible. The tokoloshe is the *The Red Man* who threatens two children, Vusi and Sias, with starvation and death for disturbing his diseased pool. The whole community rallies to trap, defy, and burn the sprite, who never returns to their village. Nevertheless, they never again visit the lifeless grey pond of the tokoloshe. Walton illustrated the story herself in warm earth colors and African patterns in a landscape of stylized iconic baobab trees, conical clay and thatched homes, and figures reminiscent of the technique used by Zulu artist John Muafangelo in his woodcuts.

Finally, *Tell the Moon* brings Ben, a farmer and symbolic Everyman, into a relationship of potential conflict with nature, represented by Francolin on behalf of the birds. Ben shows his respect for nature by sparing the tree where they nest, and the birds respond by helping him to harvest his crops. With the moon as arbiter, Ben and Francolin strike a mutually beneficial deal to share the harvest. Natalie Hinrichsen won the Vivian Wilkes award in 2005 for her images of a perfectly ordered world, elegantly constructed from regular patterns of shapes and forms that extend and deepen the perspective of the landscapes, creating a futuristic atmosphere. The massive moon accepting the bowed farmer's promise gives the accord between the human and the birds cosmic significance.

The world Walton and her illustrators create for children is deep and wide, familiar and mysterious. It forges both cosmic and local connections for her readers. The element that is missing in many of them is the quality of production that publishers need to bring to the realization of projects to do justice to the written and visual texts. Perhaps local publishers need to look beyond the constraints of the South African market to the global audiences that expect the quality that the work deserves. Too many enchanting stories that could enrich succeeding generations have an ephemeral existence, or are limited to distribution via local education institutions as components of reading schemes. The sad consequence of this limited view of literature for South Africa's children is that they are deprived of the rich heritage that could build a literate nation.

Note

1. Mark-making refers to a technique used by an artist to create textural effects on a surface, for example, dots, scratches or swirls.

Children's Books

Walton, Ann. 1991. *We Shouldn't Keep It!* Illustrated by Jo Harvey. Cape Town, SA: David Philip Songololo.
———. 1995. *Lying Toad.* Illustrated by Nikki Jones. Cape Town, SA: Kagiso Zebra.
———. 1997. *Don't Scratch!* Illustrated by Trish de Villiers. Cape Town, SA: Kagiso.
———. 1998. *Here I Am.* Illustrated by Piet Grobler. Cape Town, SA: JUTA.
———. 1999. *The Girl and the Golden Amulet.* Illustrated by Tamsin Hinrichsen. Cape Town, SA: JUTA.
———. 2002. *A Fine Day for Flying.* Illustrated by Natalie Hinrichsen. Cape Town, SA: Juta Gariep.
———. 2002. *The Great Big Fish.* Illustrated by Natalie Hinrichsen. Cape Town, SA: Juta Gariep.
———. 2002. *Have You Seen My Donkey?* Illustrated by Marna Hattingh. Cape Town, SA: Juta Gariep.
———. 2002. *I Don't Belong to You.* Illustrated by Marna Hattingh. Cape Town, SA: Juta Gariep.
———. 2002. *We Must Go Shopping Now Samson.* Illustrated by Diek Grobler. Cape Town, SA: Juta Gariep.
———. 2002. *Where Shall We Go?* Illustrated by Piet Grobler. Cape Town, SA: Juta Gariep.
———. 2003. *The Red Man.* Illustrated by Jean Fullalove. Cape Town, SA: Juta Gariep.
———, with Connie Krug. 2004. *Peanut and the Puff Adder.* Illustrated by Ian Lusted. Cape Town, SA: JUTA.
———, with Eugene Moll. 2004. *A Fine Family of Warthogs.* Illustrated by Tamsin and Natalie Hinrichsen. Cape Town, SA: JUTA.
———, with Eugene Moll. 2004. *Hera and Harry, Spotted Hyenas of the Bushveld.* Illustrated by Chip Snaddon. Cape Town, SA: JUTA.
———, with Eugene Moll. 2004. *Pincushions in Peril!* Illustrated by Elizabeth Andrew. Cape Town, SA: JUTA.
———, with Eugene Moll. 2004. *Takalani and the Great Big Fire.* Illustrated by Lyn Gilbert. Cape Town, SA: JUTA.
———, with Sue Milton. 2004. *A Very Busy World.* Illustrated by Natalie Hinrichsen. Cape Town, SA: JUTA.
Walton, Ann. 2005. *How Many?* Illustrated by Marna Hattingh. Cape Town, SA: Tafelberg.
———. 2005. *Tell the Moon.* Illustrated by Natalie Hinrichsen. Cape Town, SA: Tafelberg.
———. 2005. *We Want Tails!* Illustrated by Tamsin Hinrichsen. Cape Town, SA: Tafelberg.
———. 2005. *Working for Louis Pasteur.* Durban, SA: Solo Collective.
———. 2007. *Tiger and Louise.* Illustrated by Marna Hattingh. Cape Town, SA: Tafelberg.
———. 2009. *Big Fat Lies.* Illustrated by Nikki Jones. Cape Town, SA. Cambridge University Press.
———. 2009. *Something to Do.* Illustrated by Natalie Hinrichsen. Johannesburg, SA: Jacana.
———. 2009. *The Tale of Sun and Moon.* Illustrated by Tamsin Hinrichsen. Johannesburg, SA: Jacana.

Part 3. Noteworthy New Talent

Introduction

In literary arenas, it is far easier to identify established creators than to recognize clearly new talent. Often, limited productivity makes it harder to judge what their lasting contribution to the field may be. However, it would be shortsighted to overlook promising names that may have a significant impact on the future shape of South African children's and young adult literature. We also have echoed multiple times in this book what other South African scholars of children's and young adult literature have noted regarding the dearth of published writers and illustrators of color. These new talents signal promising directions that may eventually rectify that situation.

Twenty years after the change in government, the publishing situation in South Africa is shifting as formerly suppressed and silenced voices emerge. Storytellers like Gcina Mhlophe helped to pave the way earlier with her passion for reinvigorating pride in black South African cultures and history. Her work since the end of apartheid has unearthed many of the stories that were marginalized for so many decades. Now others are following her example and portraying the diverse, authentic experiences of contemporary young people, particularly in the new millennium. In this section, we present critical analyses of the work of three individuals, whose writing has already garnered critical acclaim in South Africa and abroad.

  KAGISO LESEGO MOLOPE
  NOKUTHULA K. MSIMANG
  SALLY (S. A.) PARTRIDGE

One thing that these three authors share in common is their focus on issues relevant to contemporary young adults' lives, including sex, pregnancy, living with HIV, interracial friendships, economic disparities, and personal and cultural identity. Both Msimang and Molope also feature past struggles in settings from the 1980s when young people faced choices about whether to join the movement at the expense of their own schooling and personal safety. These accounts create the context for more recent experiences adolescents face with the unpredictability and possibility of a rapidly changing, but still evolving country in which roles and realities are being completely redefined even as youth negotiate their way toward maturity. In her dark, school friendship-based scenarios, Partridge reminds readers that young South Africans' post-racial milieu, signaled in the names of her characters, is not without hazards that threaten adolescents everywhere. Cyberspace, a competitive consumerist teenage sub-culture and the burgeoning drug trade lure her characters into crises that are ahistorical from a South African point of view, but depicted with unflinching realism in the details of their contemporary settings.

Collectively, the work of these individuals has received important awards, such as the M.E.R. awards and the Bessie Head writing fellowship sponsored by the *Sunday Times*. It also has garnered critical recognition from selection for the prestigious International Board on Books for Young People's biennial Honours List and by positive literary reviews. This acclaim demonstrates that these authors already are having an impact beyond national borders and likely will continue to expand with a global audience.

In highlighting these new talents, we celebrate the development of book creators whose work may not have been possible twenty years ago and who are pushing the boundaries of literature for South African adolescents today. However, this admittedly is a very limited group, and we also note the lack of representation in literature for younger children or among illustrators. No doubt their absence is partially due to our oversight, but it also highlights a real gap in the literature particularly for readers in the middle age range of nine to twelve. Finally, as always, when it comes to literature for children, the dominance of women in its creation among this group is persistent and consistent with many places around the world.

More diversity in the types of literature and its creators needs continued encouragement, but these individuals are ones to emulate. They give hope for others whose voices and images need to be shared, for it is this group who represents the future. Like the eagle in *Fly, Eagle, Fly* (Gregorowski 2000), South African literature for children and adolescents can soar ahead, unlimited by the past.

Kagiso Lesego Molope: The Caged Bird Flies and Sings

Rajendra Chetty

Born into the heart of apartheid South Africa, Kasigo Lesego Molope has become the voice she felt was denied to her as a child and those of other oppressed African women. Molope was born in 1976 in a township north of Pretoria in a place that was then called Bophuthatswana; an area demarcated by the white South African government as one of the "homelands" created to allow black South Africans permanent residence outside of "white areas." Molope grew up in a time of political violence—intensified by the ever present possibility of police brutality and violence against women both on the streets and even with people you knew.[1]

Molope expresses an ever-present sense of the difficulty of being a black girl during the apartheid era, pre–1994. Ironically the oppression she felt was not only the physical oppression of a repressive state but also the mental oppression suffered by activist women. She refers to the constant message that the struggle was led by men, which resulted in boys feeling they had a more legitimate claim to the country than girls. She describes her experience as being at the bottom of the pyramid while growing up thinking that even within an oppressed group she belonged to the most oppressed, the ones with no voice. It is with this voice that Molope speaks as an African feminist writer who embraces the inspiration of women's issues arising from conflict: of apartheid, of societal expectations and representation in popular culture, of sexual assault and of imposed silence. Molope extends this focus to include the survivor as the witness to atrocity. In an email interview in April 2013 with Cheryl Logan, a lecturer at Ohio State University, she asked, "What do we do when we've been allowed, somehow, to live when so many have perished... am I to write what I witnessed?" (pers. comm.). As a writer, Molope states that you can choose to ignore them or you can let them live in books and short stories. It is these echoes of Molope's childhood and growing years of experience that we hear in her writings—providing platform and voice for women of all ages, hence the imagery of the caged birds that fly free and sing.

Educated in a private multiracial school in South Africa, Molope recognizes her father's concern that to have allowed his children to be educated by the Department of Education and Training set up specifically for black people would have restricted their choice of quality tertiary education. She describes her choice to attend the University of Cape Town as a need to keep moving because writers grow when they move. This, together with her interest in the UCT Literary Theory course, provided Molope with the opportunity to graduate in English Literature and Literary Theory from the University of Cape Town and to work with eminent writers like Andre Brink and Dorothy Driver.

Molope's nomadic drive to experience places different from those she has become accustomed to took her to Canada in 1997, where she still resides. In Canada, Molope completed a diploma in Assaulted Women and Children Counselling. In rape crisis and community centers she experienced the constant battle of people in dire and immediate need to receive government grants, leaving Molopo discouraged and disillusioned. Her extensive work in public education met with resistance from many teachers who were not interested in speaking to boys about sexual assault. Molope has embraced this theme of a woman "speaking out" in her writing.

Three Strongly South African Novels

Molope's first novel, *Dancing in the Dust,* appeared as the South African representative on the International Board on Books for Young Peoples' Honours List for 2006, making her the first black South African to achieve this recognition. Her novels are written for adolescents and young adults, creating a previously stifled voice for the children of apartheid. *Dancing in the Dust* is a novel about growing up in a society filled with fear and oppression. The story is set against the background of apartheid South Africa in the 1980s, a time of oppressive politics and daily fear among the majority of South Africans. Tihelo is a thirteen-year-old girl on the brink of young womanhood. She lives with her older sister, Keitumetse and their mother Kgomotso. The family of women live in a township near the political capital of South Africa, Pretoria. This is significant as their proximity to the heart of the oppressive government highlights the constant oppression in which they exist. This juxtaposition of political dominance and township life is echoed by the two streams which Molope creates: that of a male dominated white political structure and the township life of the independent black women in Tihelo's home.

The constant risk and adversity experienced as part of apartheid's day to day reality is emphasized in the simple storytelling of Molope's novel, not allowing the reader to escape the reality of the hardship of apartheid on the lives of black South Africans. The novel raises questions which seek answers: the absent father in Tihelo's home and the fact that Tihelo herself is a lighter color than her female relatives. These questions allude to Molope's determination to face questions regarding the role men play in the lives of women. Tihelo shoulders responsibility and brutal experience—the kind a child should not be burdened with. She witnesses murder, beatings, comrades exiled and lost opportunities. Her own near rape and torture by white policemen provides a context for exploring how abuse impacts on her growing sexual identity. The loss of control over one's own body is a major theme in Molope's writing. Tihelo's search for her missing mother sees her become aware of community responsibility though witnessing other families who are anxious and afraid and seeking those they love. The start of this community responsibility as part of one's own identity is an integral aspect of Tihelo's growth and distinctive independence. As Tihelo's heritage unfolds, she resolves to write a letter to her birth mother. It is in this letter that we see the full formation of Tihelo's identity take place. Tihelo signs the letter off by claiming her real name and her place in life: "My name is Tihelo Masimo—revolutionary!" (187). As she asserts her name and her identity, we see the young woman merge with all that she has been faced. The assertions of this salutation symbolizes Tihelo's coming of age.

 Set in the political turbulence of the 1980s-1990s, *The Mending Season* reflects the political and personal turmoil of the changing social and political world of South Africa. The possibility of apartheid ending and South Africa embracing a multicultural society is echoed in the movement of Tshidiso, a teenage girl, into a multicultural school. The challenges and opportunities inherent in the political scene of the time are mirrored by those faced by this young woman.

 Tshidiso lives in a home with four sisters: Tumane, Malesedi, Malebone and Mabatho. The sisters lost their parents as young girls and a constant sense of their mourning is present. Malebone, Tshidiso's mother passes away, leaving her in the care of her aunts. The household of women is viewed with judgment as these women, having fended for themselves from a young age, rewrite the rules by which a woman should live. Their assertive views regarding the role of women create a distance in the community between their home and the other township folk. The sisters reject the ideals of marriage, domesticity and motherhood which legitimize the domination of men over women. They fiercely guard their own world, cocooning themselves from the suspicion and allegations from outside.

 The netball courts provide a setting for a racial incident at school, offering opportunity for the reality of racial incidences in a multicultural and changing society to be unpacked. The incident revolves around Tshidiso being called a "kaffir" (similar to being called "nigger" in the U.S.). She feels the on-going pressure to be accepted in her new context and realizes that by telling the truth when the media seeks answers, she will, in fact, face the possibility of being rejected. The role of language in forging identity becomes apparent. Tshidiso asserts herself by voicing the unmentionable, "she called me a 'kaffir'" (107). By saying the "unsayable" in Setswana, which is forbidden by the school's English-only policy, Tshidiso reasserts herself, claiming pride in her own language and her own person, her identity. *The Mending Season* captures a time of transition in the private and public world of Tshidiso and South Africa—the phases of reconciliation. The novel echoes the title: where no whole is mended without some form of "messiness"—to mend that which is broken takes effort, trial and error, and persistence.

The primary focus of Molope's third novel, *This Book Betrays My Brother,* deals with the coming of age of young women grappling with their emerging sexual identity and sexual development. This novel serves to mark the end of a place of innocence for the narrator, Naledi, as she is faced with loyalties and judgments against the abuse of women. The need to be attractive to the opposite sex and to conform to social expectations is overwhelming, allowing Molope the space to explore this expectation of women to conform as opposed to redefine their own social expectations.

Naledi is the daughter of a well-off family who has moved to an upscale suburb that is an extension of the township. Naledi and her brother find that while they benefit from the financial fruits of their father's business, they yearn to be part of the social group of their township peers. Their separateness is not only geographical but also reflected in their use of English as their language of choice and the private schools they attend. Molope grapples with the power of language and its duality—in the way language has the ability to both isolate and bring together.

The novel explores the relationship and loyalties between Naledi and her brother, Basimane. He is described as a boy who is adored by his family and the community. The crux of Naledi's anguish resides in a point where she sees Basi rape his girlfriend, Moipone. Naledi is faced with the reality of life: a complicated truth, in which the family rally to protect Basi's future and one where Moipone's story is viewed with suspicion. Molope forces readers to focus on issues such as the ability for protection of those in a socially superior position. Naledi is faced with a choice between her loyalty to her sibling and the need to speak out against sexual violence. There is a poignant truth in Molope's execution of the loss of innocence through which this young woman begins to understand her own growing sexual identity while at the same time she is exposed to rape, discrimination against homosexuality, and the harsh reality of the world of gender and class discrimination.

Gender Issues Examined

Molope refuses complicity and opens up gender equality issues that remain pressing in South Africa today. She turns up the volume and fills the silences of those voices which are not heard—those who speak out against sexual violence. That nothing has been written about the black female child during apartheid is a revealing statement she made during a 2004 interview (Williams 2008). Identifying the very different experience of the black female child as opposed to the young male, she embarked on writing novels which explore and probe the many facets of the childhood and adolescent experience of the black girl in the context of South Africa in the turbulent years of 1980–1990. These final years of the apartheid era provide the backdrop which echoes the turmoil of a child growing up.

Williams refers to "adolescents battling to come to terms with their own identities and with realizing their positions within the broader communities, their personal journeys are thrown into sharp relief by the changeable circumstances in which they find themselves" (Williams 2008, 39). The protagonists of Molope's novels are faced not only with the expected demands of adolescents, but also with the demands of a socio-political world defined by strict racist regulations. The male dominated political system, together with the patriarchal social milieu found within the South African townships, place Molope's protagonists in a particularly vulnerable space, a space explored in Molope's writings. The changing face of South African politics during the late 1980s provides a backdrop fraught with possibility and fear—a sense of not knowing what will emerge after the dissolution of the apartheid system. The potentially predictable world of the emerging adolescent became an unpredictable world of an emerging democracy in which people of all races and classes needed to redefine their identities to fit into the new found society. Mpho Lukoto observes that "these children were the product of a changing country" (cited in Williams 2008, 39). It is these children to whom Molope gives a voice.

Molope introduces the feminist *Bildungsroman*, generally understood as a coming of age exploration of primarily male protagonists. Stefan Helgesson emphasizes the role of the community in this process—a significant role used by Molope in her understanding of the girl child's maturation process; a process which cannot be separated from the socio-political climate nor the community influence in apartheid South Africa. Molope's probing of the role of men and the powerful female community members in her novels allows for the feminist discussion to be highlighted and questioned by protagonist and reader. Helgesson notes that the *Bildungsroman* "allowed self and society to merge. The fulfilled individual was, by definition, fully integrated with society" (cited in

Williams 2008, 40). It is this very society that Molope's characters engage with as they grapple to "merge" with societal gender and political roles established within the South African context.

The notion of female sexual agency is central to Molope's texts. The stigma associated with feminine sexuality as girls are taught to fear the consequences of submitting to their own desire: Sex = pregnancy = loss of dreams and opportunity. Space is denied for the development of an integrated sexual identity. Molope's characters demand that this space is interrogated.

Sorcha Gunne (2010) refers to Molope's use of strategic silence in Tihelo's refusal to remember her abuse which is motivated in part, by a desire to protect her family from the shame which is associated with sexual assault. Gunne recognizes a need to find "a language that can articulate the trauma of sexual violence" (164) and notes Molope's engagement with political and social connotations and consequences of rape in post-apartheid South Africa. Also noted is Molope's success in rewriting history to include the voices of those often left on the social and revolutionary margins while simultaneously using her narrative to place emphasis on the challenges of writing about rape.

The Power of Adolescence

The main characteristic differentiating adolescent literature from children's literature lies in the way in which social power is used in the narrative (Trites 2000). Children's literature often "affirms the child's sense of Self and her or his personal power" (3), and adolescent literature depicts protagonists negotiating a position for themselves within the many social institutions in which they have to function. This aligns itself with Molope's desire to seek identity for her protagonists as they negotiate their way through the various factors that influence this formation of identity. Power can be defined in many different ways. Inggs uses it as both an active and a passive concept. Adolescents are subject to the power exerted over them by society and its institutions, but they also possess individual power to act. They are both subjects and agents, and they are "both repressed and liberated by their own power and by the power of the social forces that surround them" (Inggs 2007, 37).

Exploring the role of mothering and being mothered in the forming of identity also is a common thread in Molope's writing. She reconstructs the notion of motherhood as she unpacks the "maternal" influence of the mothering role through many factors. *The Mending Season* provides a literary context to interrogate concepts of mothering and being mothered, illuminating this discourse in the formation of identity. The text probes various aspects of "mothering": motherhood from the daughter perspective offers a nourishing and limiting umbilical link to culture. The sisters' "house of mothers" allows a space for alternative views on mothering and being mothered.

Molope, like the American feminist poet Adrianne Rich, distinguishes between two aspects of motherhood: the experience—"the potential relationship of any woman to her powers of reproduction and to children; and the institution—which aims at ensuring that potential and all women shall remain under male control" (Spencer 2013, 56). Molope grapples with this concept of a patriarchal ideology defining and regulating "motherhood" on behalf of women. Spencer explores how the role of the sisters' own dynamics, in terms of mothering and taking on roles of mothering each other, allows for interrogation of family discourse and power relationships among sisters. Molope's texts explore the multi-dimensional aspect of mothering and the joys and sacrifices of motherhood in "complex individuals wrestling with the patriarchal institution of motherhood, or rejecting it entirely" (Spencer 2013, 56). It is the mother that nurtures the fledglings to take their first flight out of the nest, and as they soar to great heights, they also learn to use their voice to sing songs of their new freedom.

Note

1. The author would like to acknowledge with thanks Ms. Cheryl Logan of Ohio State University for sharing her notes on an email interview she conducted with Kasigo Lesego Molope. The biographical details included in the first part of this essay are from that interview.

Children's Books

Molope, Kasigo Lesego. 2002. *Dancing in the Dust: A Novel.* Toronto, Canada: Tsar.
———. 2005. *The Mending Season.* Oxford Southern African Fiction. Cape Town, SA: Oxford University Press.
———. 2012. *This Book Betrays My Brother.* Cape Town, SA: Oxford University Press.

Nokuthula K. Msimang: The Gentle Gender Warrior

ROBIN MALAN

Formerly known and published under her maiden name Nokuthula Mazibuko, this author now prefers to be known by her married writer-name Nokuthula K. Msimang. She was born in 1973 in Soweto, near Johannesburg. Her secondary school education was at St. Barnabas College in Johannesburg. Her undergraduate years were spent at the University of Cape Town; she achieved her Honours degree and her Master's degree at the University of the Western Cape. In 2007 she completed her Doctorate in African Literature at the University of the Witwatersrand.

She has worked as a documentary film director/producer: *Lady Was a Mshoza* (1999), *The Gift of Song* (2000), and *The Spirit of No Surrender* (2006). She has written extensively for South African television, notably for *Soulcity*, *Takalani Sesame*, and *Molo Fish II*. The *Soulcity IV* series focused on gender violence, sexual harassment and statutory rape; the writing team was nominated for an Avanti Award (granted by the Joseph and Frances Brucia Foundation to recognize excellence in the performing arts).

Her teaching work includes lecturing at the University of Cape Town's Academic Support Programme (1993–1994) and lecturing and tutoring at the Wits Schools of Performing Arts and African Literature (2003–2005). She has presented her academic work at various national and international conferences. In 2007 she lectured at the George Washington University (February–March 2007), where she presented her work on "Life Stories and Memory Making in South Africa" to various audiences. Her other academic passion is African Literatures (novels and film), particularly what she considers the ground-shifting work of Zakes Mda.

From 1994 to 2011 she served as an assistant editor of *English Alive*, the annual anthology of high school writing, published by the South African Council for English Education (SACEE), Western Cape branch. There were occasional years when she had to opt out as a result of juggling young motherhood, marriage, academic career and regular job.

In 2008 she was co-compiler of *South African Plays for TV, Radio and Stage*. She has recently been appointed the Overseer of the South African Broadcasting Corporation's (SABC) Children Unit, guiding the future content of that unit on South African national broadcasting.

Her Books

Msimang wrote two novels (under the name Nokuthula Mazibuko) in the "Siyagruva" series, comprised of twenty short novels for teens. There were eight characters who featured regularly in the novels, which were all centered on a dance studio. In most of the novels, two of the characters were foregrounded, while other characters took minor roles in the story.

In the Fast Lane

Brunette is a young girl currently living with her father, a TV producer and director, in Langa, one of Cape Town's oldest traditionally black townships (her parents' marriage having broken down some time before). Because of her father's irregular hours, Brunette has become somewhat ill-disciplined, frequenting older student parties and drinking to excess, and her parents agree that she should go to her mother's home in Soweto for a holiday. Her mother Thembi Khumalo is a famous TV and stage actress. The parents agree that she can take her friend Samantha with her. Samantha comes from a wealthy black family who live in the affluent Cape Town suburb of Pinelands. The two girls leave behind their friend Shelley, as they feel it would be too awkward to have a white girl tag along in the township of Soweto.

Another good reason for Brunette to move to Gauteng Province is that her latest boyfriend Thabang, a student at the university, is keen that they should have sex together, and she has had to be inventive in finding ways to put him off. However, he also lives in Soweto and will be going home for the vacation. Brunette believes she can go on seeing him there, and a solution to his entreaties will somehow present itself.

When they arrive in Johannesburg, the girls find that Brunette's cousin Kedibone—seventeen and in her final year at school—is staying with Brunette's mother, together with her new-born baby. The first surprise of the holiday! Kedibone's mother has thrown her out of the house on discovering that Kedibone was pregnant.

Thabang invites Brunette and Samantha to a twenty-first birthday party, and, on their return, they discover that Kedibone has attempted to commit suicide by drinking detergent. Thabang rushes them to the hospital in his mother's car. On recovering, Kedibone reveals that she is HIV-positive, and is anxiously waiting for the results of the baby's tests.

From this point on, the holiday is taken up with all four of them—Thembi Khumalo, Kedibone, and the two girls from Cape Town—learning about living with HIV. They discover that they all know very little about it, and so there is concerted research done and sensible sharing of information.

By the time the holiday is over and Brunette and Samantha return to Cape Town, Brunette has done some good, hard thinking. She is determined not to lose her virginity before she decides to. Her father notices:

> [H]is daughter was back to being the cheerful, respectful girl he was used to. Signs of the drinking, smoking party animal had disappeared. The holiday with his ex-wife had definitely done Brunette a world of good [67].

Nokuthula has written the story with a light touch and in an easy conversational style. There is no preaching in it, and the characters are confronted with a reality very much of their time. They are made to realize that they carry around with them prejudices and ignorant notions that are non-productive in caring for someone with HIV. For instance, they are embarrassed to find they are scared to use Kedibone's toothbrush and that they are separating her crockery and cutlery from theirs. Through this device the writer is able to get across the valuable lesson that information and knowledge are the only sensible base for compassionate caring of someone with HIV.

A Mozambican Summer

Again, it is Brunette who is the lead character in Msimang's second "Siyagruva" story (under the author name Nokuthula Mazibuko). Brunette's mother is doing a show in Mozambique, and she invites Brunette to bring two friends along with her for a short holiday; accommodation and living expenses are provided, but not airfares. This time her affluent family background allows white Shelley to join Samantha as the favored friends.

During the course of the novel, each of the girls has a particular issue to deal with. Samantha's is that her holiday romance with handsome Antonio starts looking fragile when the girls see him in a local mall accompanied by a female, when he had told them he had to do the grocery shopping for his mother. Shelley's issue is an ardent desire to run into a pop group very famous in South Africa and in the neighboring countries, called 340ml. Those concerns are peripheral to what happens to Brunette.

She is talent-scouted by a modelling agency and gets permission from her mother to do an ad for them. The offer is then upped to a permanent contract. To Brunette's distress, her mother says no. When they inform the agency of this decision, the alternative offer of intermittent modeling work in Cape Town while she completes her schooling sounds very appealing, and Brunette's mother agrees to it. However, she decides they have to consult Brunette's father. He flatly refuses.

All looks bleak, and there seems to be nothing to redeem the collapsed holiday for any of the three girls. Then Samantha discovers that the girl in Antonio's life is no more than a cousin who was helping him do the shopping for his mother; Shelley befriends 340ml and even joins them as a dancer onstage for a number; and Brunette's dad relents, with some firm restrictions put in place. Thus Brunette can launch herself into her limited modeling career. So, it proved to be a happy holiday for all, though each of them, in their different ways, had to learn to cope with disappointment.

There hangs over the novel the element of privilege, however, and the Siyagruvers left back home in Cape Town show no resentment in the face of their pleasure at Brunette's burgeoning career as "a mini-supermodel!"

Spring Offensive

This is Nokuthula's first nonfiction work. In 2003 she was awarded the Bessie Head writing fellowship (given by the Sunday Times of South Africa to promote excellence in nonfiction writing), which enabled her to complete *Spring Offensive* (under the name of Nokuthula Mazibuko). The following quote from the back-cover blurb of the Timbila edition provides an appropriate summary:

> *Spring Offensive* is the story of the young people of South Africa who in the 1980s formed military underground structures, rendering the apartheid state unworkable. They were part of the groundswell that caused chaos and confusion in the country, and literally set on fire the edifices of oppression. Often referred to as the 'lost generation,' the youth organised to sabotage the state from within the townships, in neighbouring states as well as in the rest of the world. The story is told through the experiences of friends who belonged to MK[1] units.

In this account, Nokuthula tells the story of two young men: she is able to draw on direct knowledge and research, as one of the protagonists, Nhlanhla Mabaso, was her second husband; and the other, Hlula Msimang, is the brother of her current, third husband, Ntsika Msimang (who also features in the book).

A shared childhood in Soweto, attending the same primary school, St. Matthew's Catholic School, leads the two friends to joint involvement in the student political structures of the time. Their involvement in the Young Christian Students (YCS) organization leads them to working for the United Democratic Front (UDF) as budding activists.

They meet Kgomotso Nkadimeng, one of the founders of the Congress of South African Students (COSAS), and their involvement becomes more active. Nhlanhla is arrested during a march on the mayor's house, but the case is dismissed because of insufficient evidence that the protesters intended any harm to the mayor.

The next step for the young friends is the move into the underground movement of MK. Soon their superiors in the movement decide that they should leave South Africa for further training. The World Council of Churches "Children of War" tour in the United States provides cover for their departure. While Nhlanhla is part of that initiative, Hlula travels to Lusaka and meets the ANC leadership. The leadership decides that the two young men would move to Australia to continue their schooling. They are, however, able to persuade the authorities to have them return to Africa, and they spend time in a safe house in Zimbabwe, where their connections to their cells within South Africa continue. Their return to South Africa comes, in fact, after the unbanning of the organizations and the return from exile of the political leaders.

Nokuthula concludes her account of these young activists: "Hlula is currently (2006) the Chief of Police in Tshwane. Nhlanhla works at an Open Source computer Centre" (77). The book could perhaps have had a stronger, more effective structure, and unfortunately, the text in the Timbila edition is poorly edited.

Freedom Song

This novel owes its genesis to the nonfiction title *Spring Offensive*, which was noticed at the Cape Town Book Fair by Glynis Lloyd of Maskew Miller Longman publishers. They suggested to the author that she recast it in the form of a novel for young people. Here are extracts from the publisher's summary of the novel:

> *Freedom Song* is the story of Ayanda Lwandle, an accountant who works for the Department of Environment and Tourism in Tshwane (Pretoria or ePitoli), and Thapelo Kuzwayo, an ex-fighter for Umkhonto we Sizwe (MK), the armed wing of the ANC [African National Congress] during apartheid. The Department is worried because a workers' union has gone on strike, refusing to remove the garbage—and there is a World Environment Conference coming up, hosted by the city. During the negotiations to end the strike, Ayanda meets Thapelo (TK), an old boyfriend of hers, and they uncover a plot by a corrupt official in the Department.
>
> As high-school students, twenty years before, Ayanda and TK find that their lives are more and more disrupted by the system of apartheid. [...] This doesn't stop them from behaving like ordinary teenagers, singing in their school choir, organising a concert—and falling in love.
>
> But one day they hear that the rent in the township is being increased yet

again by the councillors who are cooperating with the apartheid government against their own people. TK and some of his friends decide to petrol-bomb a councillor's house. [...] Their unit performs a few sabotage operations until the police discover their cache of weapons, and the members of the unit realise that they can no longer live safely in South Africa. MK sends TK to Tanzania, and Ayanda to Cuba. After many years apart, the two are reunited when they meet in 2008 [80].

Freed from the constraints of nonfiction, Nokuthula has constructed a convincing novel from the material that made up the research for *Spring Offensive*. It is a strong work about young people with aspirations and commitment.

Asked in the interview that accompanies *Freedom Song* what she found most difficult to write in this novel, Nokuthula answered:

> The book has two time periods, the 1980s and 2008, twenty years later. I found it difficult writing the characters as teenagers and then, twenty years later, as adults. How had they changed? How is the way they look today different to [*sic*] how they looked in 1988? Are they still freedom fighters today? What have they lost personally because of having to fight when they were so young? [76].

It is not entirely clear that she has answered all of her own questions in the novel.

The Short Stories

The rest of Msimang's output is to be found on her website. This contains a collection of twelve short stories. There is no need to deal with each and every one of these, as some are slight pieces, perhaps no more than writing exercises. Some, however, are undoubtedly among the writer's very best work.

"Love songs for Nheti" is an altogether charming story of persistent tubby suitor Vusi who decides that the only way to woo his beloved Nheti is to sing deliciously bad songs to her. Nokuthula has written delightfully off-center parodies, of which these are a few examples:

> You are like an engine [angel]
> I will call you hazel
> Your name is like music
> Oh my dear Nheti! [...]
>
> When I see birds fly
> I really ask why
> My love for you
> Is like a shoe [is so blue]
> Ohh Nheti! Nheti!!
> I want to say...
> Let's pie [fly] away!! [...]

> Don't leave me slowly [lonely]
> You are my baby
> Don't say to me wayweee [maybe]
> We belong together
> Like birds of a weather [feather]
> The sky is so blue
> That's what I feel for you!!!!! [n.p.].

Nheti and her friend Zaza dream up various ways of making Vusi stop his serenading, eventually throwing stones at him. His ardor undaunted, however, he devises ever more cunning ways to resist their disincentives: he appears encased in armor made of cardboard boxes, which simply deflect their stones without causing him any harm.

Even when Nheti is driven to running down the street after Vusi "to punch him," this backfires on her when she hears someone call out, "Look, Nheti is running after her sweetheart Vusi!" It is therefore suitably enchanting to read in the final section of the story:

> Twenty years later, Nheti and Vusi's wedding was attended by at least two hundred or so people. Friends, relatives, work colleagues, and gatecrashers! Nheti looked beautiful in a cream silk dress that her friend Zaza, now a famous dress designer, had made for her. Zaza was of course the best lady, and she looked stunning in her very own yellow design. There was plenty of stew, rice, and different coloured vegetables for a wedding feast. [...] When everyone had eaten, they sang and danced to their hearts' content, ululating "Hilililileeeee!!!" and laughing with joy [n.p.]

"The Doll" is an endearing story of generational miscommunication. Nheti's politically correct father has worked hard to find his eight-year-old darling just the right doll for her: a black doll, dressed in moSotho (of Lesotho) attire and with a distinctive moSotho hat woven of straw on her head. Poor Nheti, what she had been hoping and yearning for was a white doll with long straight blonde hair that she could brush and comb. She asks her father if he can return this doll and find a replacement that fits her requirements. Her father argues:

> "Hau, my precious, but this is a moSotho doll!!! I had to look all over for it! In this country, they don't make black dolls, you know! We have to be black and proud, Nkosazana!" Bab'Langa never missed an opportunity to instil pride in his daughter [n.p.].

Her mother will have none of Nheti's complaining:

> "Nheti, other children do not even have food to eat! And here you are with a whole birthday present, and you are not even grateful!" Mrs Langa never passed up the chance to let her children know just how lucky they were to have a mother

and a father who cared for them, by providing food every day, and saved up enough to buy small presents on birthdays and at Christmas. [...] "uBaba is not taking back that doll! Say thank you, and give your father a kiss!" [n.p.].

The adult reader may well make all sorts of assumptions about racism on Nheti's part, and it is difficult to resist those, so strong is her father's desire to raise a truly African daughter, a daughter of the soil. But, when all is said and done, Nheti's wish is in no way tainted by such considerations. She wants a doll whose hair is blonde and combable and brushable. Nothing else. By dint of some careful negotiating with her friends, she manages to swap her doll for a fire-damaged blonde-haired white doll.

Various other short stories follow: "In a Name," "Love Story," "Ghost," some of these suffering from a weak unconvincing ending, or, like "Mama's Recipes," being nothing more than an excuse to reproduce some recipes!

In "Nkgono," the ancestral spirit of her grandmother comes to Nheti's rescue when she offers the child ways and means to foil the bullies at school.

In "Happy Xmas!" Christmas day dawns bright and sunny. MaShezi has her children and grandchildren come to visit her in the township house she has lived in for fifty years. Only Veli, her last-born, is not present, but out drinking the day away, returning at night. The ending is full of tragic foreboding:

> MaShezi's old eyes looked on the bloody shirt worn by her last-born. She looked on with sadness and defeat. Her last-born continued to sob and to swear as he rinsed the red knife in the kitchen sink, muttering about being willing to kill any bastard who messed with his woman. MaShezi went to her bedroom and wished that it had rained that day. Maybe then her last-born would have stayed at home that Christmas day [n.p.].

Conclusion

Three novels, one nonfiction account and twelve short stories: that is the extent of Msimang's output to date. It is not clear when the short stories were written, but they may pre-date *Spring Offensive*, which is referred to on the website as "her latest book." For her work to have more substance, there needs to be more of it and, especially, more in print.

There is no doubt that she has considerable talent: she writes about strong characters, especially female characters. In the Foreword to *Spring Offensive*, Muff Anderson calls her "a gender warrior." Of the country in which she lives and writes, she says, in the interview that accompanies *Freedom Song*:

> "South Africans are survivors. We come from a terrible place, and we are here to tell our story. The struggle continues. We must fight poverty, and fight for our

children, and their children's children, to be healthy and to be the best they can be" [77].

Nokuthula K. Msimang is an author for young people who we hope develops and grows into an author to be reckoned with.

Note

1. MK is the abbreviation for the armed wing of the ANC, Umkhonto weSizwe, "the Spear of the Nation."

Children's Books

Mazibuko, Nokuthula. 2003. *In the Fast Lane*. Claremont, SA: New Africa Books, Siyagruva series.
———. 2005. *A Mozambican Summer*. Claremont, SA: New Africa Books, Siyagruva series.
———. 2006. *Spring Offensive*. Elim, SA: Timbila Publishing.
———, comp. 2008. *South African Plays for TV, Radio and Stage*. Cape Town, SA: Oxford University Press Southern Africa.
———. 2009. *Freedom Song*. Cape Town, SA: Maskew Miller Longman.

Sally Partridge: Transitions from Outside In and Inside Out

Anne Hill

Sally Partridge, born during the final turbulent decade of the apartheid regime in South Africa, was recognized by the newspaper, *Mail & Guardian*, as one of their Top 200 Young South Africans under age thirty-five in 2011. Her record of literary achievement is remarkable. By the time of this accolade, all three of her young adult (YA) novels had attracted awards. *The Goblet Club* won both the "I am a writer" competition for new authors—co-sponsored by the South African Broadcasting Corporation (SABC), publisher Human & Rousseau, *Huisgenoot*, *You*, and *Drum* magazines—as well as the M.E.R. prize for best youth novel. Her second novel, *Fuse*, was shortlisted for the Percy FitzPatrick Award in 2010 and was South Africa's nomination for the International Board on Books for Young People (IBBY) 2012 Honour Roll. *Dark Poppy's Demise* won the M.E.R. prize for best youth novel 2012, this time sponsored by Media24 Books. A short story, "Take Me Home United Road," has been shortlisted for a 2013 Commonwealth literary prize.

Sally's apparently instant success has actually been the result of a lifelong enthusiasm for storytelling. In personal email correspondence she explained:

> I have been writing my whole life, and before I could write, I used to make up stories to amuse my parents. I was an imaginative child and storytelling came naturally to me. Writing was a natural progression. Most of my characters were around my own age at the time. Strangely, this habit didn't extend into adulthood and stopped around my teenage years. I suppose you could say my heart settled on young adult fiction. I enjoy writing about young people.

Asked to name a book that inspired her to be a writer, Partridge frankly acknowledges her indebtedness since childhood to J.K. Rowling's *Goblet of Fire* (2000):

My favorite [book] was *The Goblet of Fire*, and every time I felt bad I'd turn to the part where Harry's name was called out of the goblet and feel better. I still do this twenty [sic] years later, so I can safely say that is the one book that's made the biggest impression on me, and as a writer I can only hope to one day make the same impression on my readers [It's a Book Thing 2012, n.p.].

In a recent review of Charlie Human's *Apocalypse Now Now* (2013), Niall Alexander places Sally Partridge in the company of South African authors Lauren Beukes, Sarah Lotz and Human, whose novels represent a "bout of excellent speculative and other genre fiction" (n.p.). Irreverent, edgy, largely dystopian and definitely post-apartheid, these disturbing stories skip lightly between conventional genre categories, but owe more than a hint of kinship to nineteenth century gothic roots and contemporary "steampunk" that has its origins in a fascination with the steam-driven behemoths of the industrial revolution and speculations about the seedier effects of technology on social behavior.

The remarkable difference between Partridge's novels and those of science fiction/fantasy writers Beukes, Lotz and Human, is that her gothic scenarios are all too plausible in real life. The technology that threatens, enchants and empowers her protagonists comes not from imagined contemporary derivatives of steam-powered engines, but via familiar digital devices in the intimacy of teenagers' bedrooms and pockets. It is as if gothic and punk traces drifting in her cultural milieu are drawn into the intimate lives of her characters who mirror the adolescents you could encounter just around the corner, in "normal" schools and shopping malls every day, although it is notable that her characters tend to define themselves as outsiders. The question put to Sally (pers. comm.) was: Why do you find these protagonists interesting?

> I think all teenagers secretly see themselves as outsiders. They're at a sensitive point in their lives where they want to fit in with their peers, but they have yet to learn the social niceties of conversation. It's an awkward stage to be at. Also, young people often feel alienated from their parents and other adults. They exist in a world of self-importance and discovery where adults don't play a role. This is another element of being "an outsider." On a personal note I am more inclined to write about young people that don't fall headfirst into peer pressure and the social hierarchy of high school. They are the free thinkers, the questioners, and that appeals to me.

It is significant that in this interview, Sally has identified the young adult's "sensitive point" of transition as her point of entry into the art of fiction. In her novels, these are critical moments from which there is no turning back, rendered with shocking power in her art.

In Partridge's first two novels, *The Goblet Club* and *Fuse*, malevolent forces converge on the protagonists from outside themselves. They are essentially lured into webs of intrigue spun by peers who take advantage of their curiosity and vulnerability as they are maneuvered into spaces of belonging in their schools' social relations. In the latter two novels, *Dark Poppy's Demise* and *Sharp Edges,* protagonists precipitate the action, choosing to enter situations that they know are inherently risky. The multiple protagonists of *Sharp Edges* all make decisions that precipitate fateful consequences. Whether the changes in the protagonists are from "outside in" or "inside out," both paradigms fundamentally disrupt and reconfigure lives in ways that make a return to childhood innocence unthinkable.

Outside In

According to Sally Partridge, school and cyberspace "are the natural habitats for teenagers, like the dark alley and roof tops for crime noir detectives" (pers. comm.). The setting of *The Goblet Club* is devoid of the magic of Harry Potter's school for wizards. Nevertheless, it shares an essential gothic characteristic, which is more significant to the structure of the novel than its unspecified location—"Nowheresville" (4)—in a recognizable South Africa. Walton (2009) suggests that "The essential moment every gothic must contain is the young protagonist standing alone in a strange house" (n.p.). Protagonist fifteen-year-old Mark Llewellyn Bryce, defiant and disaffected, is driven to the school that will tame his rebellious behavior:

> After taking one look at the place, I was ready to take my own life, it was that frightening. Our car drove through the front gates towards what looked like a haunted house. A monstrous face brick building loomed ahead with tall chimneys spewing forth foul black smoke [4].

The description of St. Matthew's College has powerful allusions to William Blake's (1808) images of the "dark satanic mills" of nineteenth century industrialism, with its connotations of exploitation, especially of children trapped in the toils of systemic repression, corruption and abuse.

In *The Goblet Club,* secretive experimentation with chemistry that leads to unimaginable horror, the consequence of a lethal brew of abandonment, rejection, abuse, revenge, conspiracy, betrayal, and vulnerability resonates with the themes of another of Partridge's mentor-texts, Mary Shelley's *Frankenstein* (1818), written when she was just nineteen. Partridge explains: "I thought to myself, if a young Victorian woman could write one of the world's greatest stories, then what's stopping me? The story really inspired me to finish a book and send it out into the world" (It's a Book Thing 2012, n.p.).

The justice achieved in the denouement of *The Goblet Club* is dubious: the protagonist is left bereft of friends and burdened with a terrible secret. Maria Nikolajeva (cited in Sell 2002) proposes that children's literature negotiates a three-stage process of "growing up," the last of which is an initiation from childhood to adulthood, a process that "creates anxiety, the dominant emotion in young adult novels, because the protagonist realizes that there is no way back, that this is no longer a dream, a game, or a fancy-dress ball...The security of a childhood paradise is about to be lost" (111). This sense of having made a profound transition is strongly present in the final chapter of *The Goblet Club*. The protagonist takes leave of the reader on a note of formality: "So there you have it: the single most extraordinary event in my young life was the experience I had with the Goblet Club. How for a brief moment in my life, I was truly happy. I belonged to a group of friends who enjoyed my company, and I theirs..." (137). For Mark the protagonist, the shocking moral ambiguity of the adult world into which he has been so violently initiated will haunt him for the rest of his life.

In *Fuse*, Partridge's gaze alights on an insidious threat to unsuspecting lives secure in the comfortable routines and often nasty hierarchies of middle class relations. The threat is a lethal nexus in cyberspace of marginalized individuals sitting at their computer terminals in the privacy of their homes; poisonous disaffection wrought by bullying; global media streaming concentrations of attention on incidents of violent revenge on streets and campuses on the other side of the world; and the potential to unleash death and destruction locally on an unimaginable scale thanks to knowledge available on the Internet.

Kendall, bullied protagonist of *Fuse*, and an orphan—lonely, timid, frail and physically unattractive compared to Justin, his handsome and popular adoptive older brother—is drawn into a dangerous plot by Craig, the friend for whom he had always longed. Kendall's unease grows as Craig's dangerous fantasy takes root in reality, drilling down inexorably to their very local environment. For Kendall, the game is suddenly over when he becomes a fugitive under Justin's protection, which shatters their family and plunges the brothers into a murky world of crime and poverty. Details that define the urban texture of the settings of the brothers' flight are hyper-realistic, so that the harsh facts of the potential effects on Kendall's personal life of playing with fire become inescapable. Unlike Mark in his transition to adulthood in *The Goblet Club*, however, Kendall discovers his agency, and that there is firm ground in the trustworthiness of his mother and brother. In this novel, the circle is closed, the moral universe to some extent restored for the protagonist.

Inside Out

"Inside out" describes both the origin in Partridge's later novels of the action in protagonists' motivations, as well as the traumatic changes wrought in their subsequent lives by these crises. In *Dark Poppy's Demise,* the protagonist, Jenna, is an initiator. Challenged by her confidante, Anisa, to admit that she has targeted the object of her affection, Eric, on the school campus, she responds: "'I don't stalk him.' This was a lie. I'd been shadowing him since the first day I'd seen him, walking through the front gate with his bag slung over his shoulder, the cutest guy I had ever seen" (2–3).

Driven by resentment when Eric seems to ignore her advances, Jenna, alias "Dark Poppy," pursues an online contact with a flattering stranger, Robert. Anisa shares a prescient warning: "If my mother caught me talking to strange men online, she'd kill me" (35), which Jenna dismisses. Even when Eric makes friendly overtures, she prefers to respond to her online suitor, and is skillfully lured into an addictive liaison that becomes a nightmare with significant hallmarks of gothic drama, as described by Walton (2009):

> What I really get out of [gothic dramas] is the girl and the house. The girl is innocent in a way that isn't possible for a more enlightened heroine.... She may scream, she is alone and unprotected, and she comes from a world where that isn't supposed to happen. Things are mysterious and frightening, she is threatened, and she's supposed to fold up under that threat, but she doesn't. There's a girl and a house and the girl has more agency than expected, and she doesn't fold in the face of intimidation, or you wouldn't have a plot.... The heroines of gothics discover inner resources they did not know they had and keep going to win through [n.p.].

A more significant element of the gothic in Partridge's novel, however, is the relationship of Jenna's experience of the sublime through the revelation of her sexuality, which precipitates a loss of control that almost extinguishes her life; and terror, pain, and threat of imminent death. In an essay on "Gothic Sublimity" David Morris (1985) describes the sublime as "a vertiginous and plunging—not soaring—sublime, which takes us deep within rather than far beyond the human sphere" (306). The moment of Jenna's message to Robert, "I think I love you" (102), reads as a fateful plunge that results in anxiety—"it was driving me crazy with worry"—and physical turbulence: loss of concentration, "a stupor," "I couldn't breathe. I wanted to cry out" (103). Despite her misgivings, at Robert's prompting, she breaks rules, changes her identity from blonde to black. In Freudian terms, her ego is in crisis.

Morris (1985) maintains that in Gothic texts, "Terror was a liberating—hence dangerous—force" (306). Terror propels Jenna's transition from helplessness in the face of the power of her newly discovered sexuality, to her violent recovery of agency and control. She also reaches a profound understanding of her responsibility for the effects of her choices on her dejected family: "And it was all because of me. I had done this" (179). Ultimately, in an online exchange, she is able to negotiate a relationship with Eric on her own terms:

SINDROME (Eric): So you want to maybe see a movie later?
EMOGRRL (Jenna): Maybe I should go out. I'm starting to get cabin fever. But to be clear, this isn't a date.
SINDROME: Got it. See you later, Jenna.
EMOGRRL: Bye, Eric [181].

The epilogue makes it chillingly clear however, that on a social level, the corruption of innocence persists, one victim at a time.

Sharp Edges explores the perspectives of a group of friends shattered by the drug-induced death during her birthday celebration of Demetria Crowley, "Demi," the group's exuberant lodestone. The group's world is in shards, and each character retraces the painful intersections of their piece of the tragedy with the progress of incidents that had made up the whole fateful event.

Bonang, narrator of the prologue to the novel, epitomizes the brittle, hedonistic, and competitive teenage culture that generates both a reckless taste for risk and miserable insecurity among friends. "I smile at the compliment. I had squeezed myself into the teeniest, sparkliest dress I own. I like looking good when I go out. Scratch that. I love looking better than everyone else" (2). In the novel's prologue, the Bonang vignette is the "before" picture of teenage certitude, and the mysterious wraithlike Ashley—"her face is pocked with holes from previous piercings as if she took all the metal jewellery out in one go"—represents the post-trauma survivors. The story behind Ashley's flight from Cape Town is told in a series of accounts from the survivors' various points of view.

The structure of *Sharp Edges* departs from the schema of her first three novels, which track the central characters' existential crises precipitated by their involvement in acts of violence in conventional linear narratives. In *Sharp Edges*, Partridge juxtaposes perspectives to reveal the complex webs of dependence, friction, attachments, jealousies and deceptions that hold the group of friends in tension together, while setting in motion a train of events that make them all unintentionally complicit in Demi's death. For each character, the experience of facing mortality ruptures their known world, and their place in it. Their reactions include psychotic rage, depression, change of identity, resort to drug abuse and attempted suicide, and flight.

In Conclusion: Looking ahead

Bonang's introduction to *Sharp Edges* sets a scene that chimes with the qualities of YA fiction that draw Partridge to the exuberance of the genre: "YA is like the kid sister of the other older, more serious genres that dyes its hair a million colours and pierces its bottom lip and sticks diamantes all over it's [*sic*] pink Blackberry" (It's a Book Thing 2012, n.p.).

For now, Partridge appears to remain committed to her genre: "I read a lot of South African fiction, and I'm quite proud of my collection, but my true love will always be YA" (It's a Book Thing 2012, n.p.). Her sources of inspiration are eclectic and unpredictable however:

> Many of my ideas occur out the blue. I'll be inspired by something arbitrary, then the story will fall into place as I write it down. Many times ideas, or even solutions to difficult plot problems, come to me in my sleep. Writer friends have described the process as dreamstorming [pers. comm.].

A trilogy is planned. Passion for her art drives her:

> I learn more about my craft with every book. I've been very privileged to have been mentored by incredible editors and publishers. Even now, when I complete a book the first thing I do is send it to a writer friend to read. I soak up their knowledge like a sponge. I am not precious about my writing. I want to improve [pers. comm.].

Sharp Edges is evidence of an evolving interest in form and the emergence of an interest in complexity. Whether or not her themes of radical "outside in" and "inside out" disruptions in characters' lives are superseded with the passage of time, the dreamstorming is bound to yield compelling results.

CHILDREN'S BOOKS

Partridge, Sally. 2007. *The Goblet Club*. Cape Town, SA: Human & Rousseau.
_____. 2009. *Fuse*. Cape Town, SA: Human & Rousseau.
_____. 2010. *Take Me Home United Road*. www.commonwealthfoundation.com/updates/shoists-announced-2013-literary-prizes#sthash.XftMyesy.dpuf.
_____. 2011. *Dark Poppy's Demise*. Cape Town, SA: Human & Rousseau.
_____. 2013. *Sharp Edges*. Cape Town, SA: Human & Rousseau.

Afterword

BEVERLEY NAIDOO

At IBBY's 2004 Congress in Cape Town—its first on the African continent—I was very conscious of our closeness to Kirstenbosch Gardens. It's here that you can see the remains of the 17th century bitter almond hedge planted by Jan van Riebeeck to mark the boundary between the nascent European colony and the rest of Africa. A hedge!

Our histories are inescapable. They run through us like underground streams. Our past, so scarred with struggles over physical boundaries, created deep boundaries in the mind. In 1994, when the parents, grandparents, aunties and uncles of all South Africa's children queued together to vote, hopes soared high that maybe, just maybe, it was possible to cross the old divides. Expectations differed depending on where one was situated, but how blessed we were with the voices of Nelson Mandela and Archbishop Desmond Tutu. Those long sinuous lines, with everyone waiting to enter through the *same* door, reflected an extraordinary moment in history.

Twenty years on from our landmark year, this book is a welcome stock-taking of how South African children's literature has fared. As these essays reveal, we can celebrate the loosening of boundaries around subject matter and the diversifying of places and communities in which stories are set. It's good to see acknowledgment of "transition movers" who were pushing the boundaries well before the 1990s, thanks also to a few radical publishers prepared to take risks. In exile, I first "met" Chris van Wyk as the author of the poem "In Detention" (1979): *"He fell from the ninth floor / He hanged himself / He slipped on a piece of soap while washing / He hanged himself..."* (45). The poem traveled widely, with sharp impact. It could not only be read out at anti-apartheid rallies but was a poem that grabbed the imaginations of older high school students, stirring many questions. When I learned that Chris also wrote books for children as well as adults, I was delighted. He clearly knew that our young generation mattered! How do you develop—and broaden—the next generation of writers if you don't begin by stimulating and encouraging young readers?

These essays allow us to infer how editorial knowledge and sensitivity advanced from the time when most publishers never questioned stereotyping, racial or other. Huge strides were made in disturbing old orthodoxies in the U.S. and U.K. during the 1970s and 1980s around issues of representation—often accompanied by heated discussions—as teachers, librarians, parents and publishers were challenged to consider racism and representations of gender, class, culture and disability when assessing books for young people. What had previously been taken for granted as "a good story" was now under scrutiny... and gradually we saw change towards a wider, less biased, literary experience.

While South Africans embarking on this road in the 1990s had the benefit of articles and books produced during these earlier struggles, they nevertheless had to face their own difficult journey. I recall how, on a post-exile trip back to South Africa, a specially-convened discussion with white and black teachers in Port Elizabeth in 1993 led to a mini-explosion of steam from a group of white teachers. They accused me of politicizing literature and literacy by introducing issues of racism. As the "outsider," I could say things and take the flak more easily. Later, I was quietly thanked by some teachers from a "coloured" school who had listened in silence. The shift to educational publishing and market dynamics post–1994 brought its own exigencies. Twenty years later, the expectation that characters in novels should be rounded and real, whoever they are, goes without saying.

We can also celebrate a vibrant sense of diverse landscapes, both rural and urban. Many books now exist in which young South Africans can recognize their own world. While books—especially picture books—in the nine official black South African home languages have slowly increased, there are not nearly enough and funding is a major issue. The challenges remain huge. We are reminded here about the ongoing lack of published writers and illustrators of color. Apartheid was full of so many silences. Kagiso Lesego Molope, born in the year of the Soweto uprising of 1976 and first black writer to represent South Africa on an IBBY Honours List in 2006 is quoted in Rajendra Chetty's profile, asking, "What do we do when we've been allowed, somehow, to live when so many have perished... am I to write what I have witnessed?" The terrain is vast and unmapped for writers who are survivors of a brutal past and who take on the responsibility of writing for a future generation.

It is not an easy career choice to be a writer. It is certainly not one made by someone looking for financial security. Nor would you begin unless you had been gripped by the power of storytelling. Think of Chris van Wyk's grandmother who imbued in him a love of books, while hiding from him her own illiteracy. Think of Gcina Mhlophe's grandmother who passed on her love of storytelling, leading Gcina to create her project *Nozincwadi* ("Mother of Books") taking storytelling and books to schools far and wide across South Africa. Both Chris and Gcina were fortunate to have an older generation behind them who were passionate about the power of stories and reading. In spite of apartheid's vicious designs, their grandparents valued education. Today's children live in a very different world where much of the storytelling culture has been lost.

Many schools are also badly failing children. Dr. Nick Taylor, head of the National Education and Development Unit (NEEDU), an independent body that reports to the Minister of Basic Education, was quoted in a South African newspaper, *The Witness*, on October 22, 2013, when he spoke of a "national catastrophe" and has called for reading to become a national priority (The Witness, 2013). NEEDU's 2012 summary report vividly outlines the significant problems with teaching and learning to read, in addition to the lack of books in classrooms.

Non-government organizations play an important role in highlighting the serious situation. Among these is Nal'ibali (isiXhosa for "Here's the story") a program driven by the Project for the Study of Alternative Education (PRAESA) in collaboration with Times Media. Nal'ibali is a national reading-for-enjoyment campaign aimed at parents, teachers, librarians and children themselves.

During term time (when schools are in session), stories in two languages—English and either isiXhosa, isiZulu, Sesotho or Afrikaans—are published in a weekly supplement to a number of regional newspapers. Alongside the stories, there are activities for young children and interviews with writers for middle school to older readers. These basic materials are supported by Nal'ibali's imaginative website with practical ideas and advice for running reading clubs.

South African children's literature needs readers if it is to be sustainable—and to grow. Yet my fear is that too many teachers are simply functional readers who never themselves experienced as learners the joy of engaging actively with stories and books. When children are encouraged to respond personally and creatively to stories in whichever language, the foundations are laid for learning to infer, to interpret and to evaluate—all higher cognitive skills.

Many of today's teachers need inspirational re-education to begin their own journeys in storytelling and books. These essays show that we have a wonderful resource in our literature and in its creators. It will be a tragedy if the promising directions signaled under "Noteworthy New Talent" are cut short by widespread failure to develop the reading potential of all our children in South Africa today.

Locked up on Robben Island, Nelson Mandela and fellow prisoners won their struggle for the right to have books and to study. They read, put on plays, discussed and debated. Literature opened windows across the water, across continents. At least their minds could be free. With such a "Madiba legacy," it is indeed time for reading to become a national priority.

Beverley Naidoo was born in South Africa and began writing in exile in England, with her first children's book *Journey to Jo'burg* banned in her home country until 1991. Her many awards include the Carnegie Medal for *The Other Side of Truth*. Her website is www.beverleynaidoo.com.

Appendix: Literary Awards and Prizes

Afrikaans Taal en Kultuurvereniging (ATKV): The Afrikaans Language and Culture Association (Afrikaanse Taal- en Kultuurvereniging), ATKV, aims to promote the Afrikaans language and culture. The ATKV prizes/awards are children's choice awards given annually in many different categories, including media and for the following age categories: three to five years; six to seven years; eight to nine years; ten to twelve years; and thirteen to fifteen years.

Alba Bouwer Prize: presented every three years by the Suid-Afrikaanse Akademie vir Wetenskap en Kuns (South African Academy for Science and Arts) for the most outstanding literary publication in Afrikaans for the seven to twelve age group.

Astrid Lindgren Memorial Award: awarded annually by the Swedish Arts Council to honor the Swedish children's author Astrid Lindgren. The Lindgren Award annually recognizes "authors, illustrators, oral storytellers and promoters of reading" whose "work is of the highest quality, and in the spirit of Astrid Lindgren" (http://www.alma.se/en/).

Bookchat Book of the Year: presented annually for the best children's book in English received by Bookchat—originally *Bookchat* magazine (1976–1997), now Bookchat website (from 2008).

Commonwealth Literary Prize: initiated in 1987 by the Commonwealth Foundation and awarded for established and new writers in four regions of the Commonwealth: Africa, Caribbean and Canada, South Asia and Europe, and South East Asia and Pacific. Renamed and altered in 2011 with two prizes: Commonwealth Book Prize and Commonwealth Short Story Prize.

C. P. Hoogenhout Medal: formerly awarded every two years by the SA Institute for Library and Information Science and then by Children's Literature Research Unit (CLRU) of the University of South Africa (UNISA) for Afrikaans children's books. No longer awarded.

Elsabe Steenberg Award: given by the South African Academy of Science and Arts. This award has been given since 2008 to children and youth literature (for ages five to twelve, teenagers and young adults) translated from any language into Afrikaans.

The Exclusive Books IBBY SA Award: awarded biennially to an illustrated literary work for children (picture book or illustrated children's story book or illustrated book of poems) published in South Africa.

Hans Christian Andersen Awards: awarded biennially by the International Board on Books for Young People (IBBY) to a writer and an illustrator whose complete work is judged to have made an outstanding contribution to children's literature.

International Board on Books for Young People (IBBY) Honour List: a biennial selection of outstanding, recently published books, honoring writers, illustrators and translators from IBBY member countries.

Kate Greenaway Medal: awarded annually by the (British) Chartered Institute of Library and Information Professionals for the most distinguished work in the illustration of children's books. The artist must be a British subject living in the United Kingdom.

Katrine Harries Award: originally awarded annually by the SA Institute of Librarianship and Information Science (SAILIS) and then by the Children's Literature Research Unit of the University of South Africa to the best illustrator of a South African children's book. No longer awarded.

Macmillan Writer's Prize for Africa: awarded by Macmillan Publishers, but discontinued in 2007. This was a bi-annual competition devoted to works of fiction by African writers, aiming to promote and celebrate story writing from all over the African continent. The Junior Award aimed at stories for children aged eight to twelve, and the senior award at readers between thirteen and seventeen.

Maskew Miller Longman Literature Awards: awarded annually, with a particular focus on literature suitable for a youth audience rotating each year between different genres: novels, drama and short stories. Prizes are offered in all official languages of South Africa. Since 2007, these have replaced the Young Africa Awards.

M.E.R. Prize for children's books: forms part of the Media24 Books literary awards. These prizes are awarded annually by Media24, the print-media arm of the South African media company Naspers. They are open to authors and illustrators whose books are published within the Media24 Books stable, which include the NB group and Jonathan Ball Publishers. The M.E.R. Prize is awarded in two categories: for illustrated children's books ages zero to eight, and for youth/young adults ages eight to sixteen.

M-Net Prize: established in 1991 by M-Net (Electronic Media Network), a commercial television station in South Africa. In the early years, young adult novels were judged alongside adult works. This has been replaced since 2001 by the **M-Net Literary Awards** for adult novels written in one of South Africa's official languages. The aim behind these awards is to encourage authors to write in their home language, thus contributing to the longevity of all indigenous languages.

NOMA Concours: a competition organized by the Asia/Pacific Cultural Centre for UNESCO (ACCU) and supported by the Noma International Book Development Fund from 1978 to 2008, set up to discover promising illustrators, graphic designers and artists in Asia (excluding Japan), the Pacific, Africa, Arab states, and Latin America and the Caribbean.

Percy FitzPatrick Awards: initially awarded by the SA Institute for Library and Information Science and now given biennially by the English Academy of South Africa to the best South African children's book in English.

Sanlam Awards: Since its inception in 1980, the Sanlam Prizes for Youth Literature have rewarded outstanding quality in youth books (for ages twelve to eighteen years). The prizes are now awarded biennially in six language groups: Afrikaans, English, Nguni languages, Sotho languages, Tshivenda and Xitsonga. Prize-winning books are published by NB Publishers.

SATI Prizes for Outstanding Translation: awarded tri-annually in different categories, but also for children's books and in all official languages in South Africa.

Scheepers Prize: awarded by the South African Academy of Science and Arts every three years.

Tienie Holloway Medal: awarded tri-annually by the South African Academy for Science and Art for books for children under age eight.

Vivian Wilkes Award: Awarded annually (until 2005) by the South African Children's Book Forum to the illustrator of a South African children's book.

W.B. Mkhize Award: given by the Usiba Writers' Guild, the Zulu Writers Association.

Bibliography

Abate, Michele A. 2010. "A Role for Children's Literature. "*The New York Times*, December 26. http://www.nytimes.com/roomfordebate/2010/12/26.
Abbott, Pamela, Claire Walace, and Melissa Tyler. 2005. *An Introduction to Sociology: Feminist Perspectives*. London: Routledge.
Adichie, Chimamanda. 2009. *Chimamanda Adichie: The Danger of a Single Story* (video). TED.com.TEDGlobal. http://www.ted.com/talks/chimamanda_adichie_the_danger_of_a_single_story.html.
Aiken, Joan. 1982. *The Way to Write for Children*. London: Elm Tree Books.
Alcott, Louisa May. 1868. *Little Women*. Boston: Roberts Brothers.
Alexander, Niall. 2013. "Supernatural South Africa." Review of *Apocalypse Now Now*, by Charlie Human. TOR.COM. http://www.tor.com/blogs/2013/08/book-review-apocalypse-now-now-charlie-human.
Allan, Brooke. 1996. "Fantasy Land." Review of *Childish Things*, by Marita van der Vyver. August 18. http://www.nytimes.com/1996/08/18/books/fantasy-land.html.
Altshuler, Anne. 1995. "Breastfeeding in Children's Books: Reflecting and Shaping Our Values." *Journal of Human Lactation* 11: 293–305.
Andrews, Loretta Kreider. 1993. "The Dove." Review of *The Dove*, by Dianne Stewart. *School Library Journal* 39.9: 220.
Angelou, Maya. 1969. *I Know Why the Caged Bird Sings*. New York: Random House.
Anon. 1992. Review of *Song of Be*, by Lesley Beake. *Upbeat* March: 16.
Ashliman, D.L. 1998–2013. "The Sleeping Beauty in the Wood." *The Grimm Brothers' Children's and Household Tales*. http://www.pitt.edu/~dash/grimmtales.html.
Astwood, Gail. 1989. Review of "Rainbow, Merino and Traveller," by Lesley Beake. *South* October—November 26: 12.
Attwell, David, and Derek Attridge, eds. 2012. *The Cambridge History of South African Literature*. Cambridge, UK: Cambridge University Press.
August, Tyrone. 2002. "Interviews with Gcina Mhlophe 1989, 1993." In *Politics and Performance: Theatre, Poetry and Song in Southern Africa,* edited by Liz Gunner, 273–284. Johannesburg, SA: Witwatersrand University Press.
Austen, Jane. 1813. *Pride and Prejudice*. London: Thomas Egerton.
Authors Voices. 2008. International Literature Festival Berlin. http://www.literaturfestival.com/teilnehmer/autoren/2008/piet-grobler.
Bachelard, Gaston. 1969. *The Poetics of Space*. Translated by Maria Jolas. Paris, France: Presses Universitaires de France.
Barker, Cicely Mary. 1923. *A World of Flower Fairies*. London: Blackie.
Barker, Jane. 1991. "Girl with a Bird's Voice." *Weekend Post*, May 4.
Barnard, Rita. 2012. "Rewriting the Nation." In *The Cambridge History of South African Literature,* edited by David Attwell and Derek Attridge, 652–675. Cambridge: Cambridge University Press.

Bateson, Mary C. 2004. *Willing to Learn: Passages of Personal Discovery.* New York. Pantheon Books.
Beake, Lesley. 1993. "Of This Place, of That Time." In *Towards More Understanding—The Making and Sharing of Children's Literature in Southern Africa*, edited by Isabel Cilliers, 24. Cape Town, SA: Juta & Co Ltd.
———. 2012. *Annual Report of Children's Book Network 2012* (CBN). Unpublished.
———. 2012. www.lesleybeake.co.za.
Bennett, Rosey. 1996. "A 25 Year Retrospective of South African Children's Reading of Other World's Books." In *Other Worlds Other Lives—Proceedings of the International Conference on Children's Literature 4–6 April 1995, Book Two*, edited by Myrna Machet and Sandra Olën and Thomas van der Walt, 84. Pretoria, SA: Unisa Press.
Bentley, Judith, and Peter Midgley. 2000. "Coming of Age in the New South Africa." *The Alan Review* 27.2: 52–58.
Bentley, Kin. 2004. "Fine Collection of Illustrations." *The Herald,* June 25.
Berger, Brigitte. 2002. *The Family in the Modern Age.* New Brunswick: Transaction.
Blackmore, Richard Doddridge. 1869. *Lorna Doone: A Romance of Exmoor.* London: Sampson Low, Son & Marston.
Blake, William. 1808/1998. *Milton, a Poem.* Princeton, NJ: Princeton University Press (reprint).
Bloom, Susan P. 2001. "The Star-Bearer: A Creation Myth from Ancient Egypt." Review of *The Star-Bearer: A Creation Myth from Ancient Egypt*, by Dianne Hofmeyr. *The Horn Book Magazine* 77: 219–220.
Blyton, Enid. 1942. *Five on a Treasure Island.* London: Hodder & Stoughton.
———. 1949. *The Secret Seven.* London: Brockhampton Press.
Borges, Jorge Luis. 1926. *The Oxford Dictionary of Literary Quotations*, edited by Peter Kemp, 138. Oxford, UK: Oxford University Press.
Bosman, Natalie. 2011. "Fiction and Fables." *The Citizen,* September 8: 1.
Botha, Marzahn. 2008. "Hi julle, daar's 'n nuwe taal—Jipiaans." *Die Beeld,* September 15.
Bothma, Alida. 2013. http://www.montagegallery.co.za.
Boyd, Carolyn. 2011. "Sivu's Six Wishes." Review of *Sivu's Six Wishes,* by Jude Daly. *The School Librarian* 59.1: 25.
Bradford, Clare. 2007. *Unsettling Narratives: Postcolonial Readings of Children's Literature.* Waterloo, Ontario, Canada: Wilfred Laurier University Press.
Brand, Gerrit. 2005. "Beste teks lê altyd nog voor." *Die Burger,* November 5: 12.
Brand, Lucia. 2005. "Monsters in perspektief." *Die Burger,* March 5: 8.
Brand, Marieke. 1988. "Illustreerder moet stories uit kind se oog sien." *Die Burger,* September 21.
Bredenkamp, Braam. 2006. "Kuier by Piet Grobler." *Storiewerf.* http://www.storiewerf.co.za/onderhoude/oh_pietgrobler.htm.
Breuer, Rosemarie. 2013. "Linda Rode: Author, Translator and Compiler of Children's Books." http://www.stellenboschwriters.com/rodel.html.
———. 2013. "Stellenbosch Writers." http://www.stellenboschwriters.com.
Britz, Elretha. 2009. "Bfn-skrywer een van SA se 'beste vertalers'." *Die Volksblad,* October 6.
Budin, Miriam Lang. 2000. "Fair, Brown, & Trembling: An Irish Cinderella Story." Review of *Fair, Brown, & Trembling: An Irish Cinderella Story*, by Jude Daly. *School Library Journal* 46.9: 214.
Bukenya, Austin. 2001. "Oracy and Female Empowerment in Africa." In *African Oral Literature: Functions in Contemporary Contexts*, edited by Russell H. Kaschula, 32–38. Claremont, SA: New Africa Books.
Burnett, Frances Hodgson. 1886. *Little Lord Fauntleroy.* New York: Scribner.
———. 1911. *The Secret Garden.* New York: Frederick A. Stokes.

Bush, Elizabeth. 2006. "To Everything There Is a Season." Review of *To Everything There Is a Season,* by Jude Daly. *The Bulletin of the Center for Children's Books* 59.60: 260.
Butler, Dorothy. 1980. *Babies Need Books.* London: The Bodley Head.
Buzzeo, Tony. 2012. *Inside the Books: Readers and Libraries Around the World.* Madison, WI: Upstart Books.
Cairney, Trevor. 2009. "Key Themes in Children's Literature: Humour." *The Trevor Cairney Blog,* April 5. http://trevorcairney.blogspot.com/2009/04/key-themes-in-childrens-literature.html.
Call, Nancy. 2001. "The Star-Bearer: A Creation Myth from Ancient Egypt." Review of *The Star-Bearer: A Creation Myth from Ancient Egypt,* by Dianne Hofmeyr. *School Library Journal* 47.4: 131.
Carroll, Lewis. 1949 edition. *Alice in Wonderland.* Illustrated by Philip Gough. London: The Heirloom Library.
Case, Dianne. 2012. "Dianne Case: The Home of Magic, Elves, and Talking Animals." *The Times,* September 11. http://nalibali.org/the-home-of-magic-elves-and-talking-animals/.
Cheal, David. 2008. *Families in Today's World.* London: Routledge.
Chiavetta, Eleonora. 2004. "A Modern Storyteller." In *SindiweMagona: The First Decade,* edited by Siphokazi Koyana, 167–173. Scottsville, SA: University of KwaZulu-Natal Press.
Cilliers, Isabel. 1988. *Towards Understanding—Children's Literature for Southern Africa.* Cape Town, SA: Maskew Miller Longman.
Cloete, Elsie. 2009. "Ecofutures in Africa: Jenny Robson's Savannah 2116 AD." *Children's Literature in Education* 40: 46–58.
Coetzer, Johan, L. 2009. "Wat het van Griet geword? (Sy't 'n ander naam, maar woon nog in 'n sprokie)." *Mousaion* 27.2: 129–138.
Collected writings from The Open School, Johannesburg. 1986. *Two Dogs and Freedom: Children of the Townships Speak Out.* Johannesburg, SA: Ravan/The Open School.
Commonwealth Writers. 2013. Commonwealth Short Story Prize 2013 Shortlist. www.commonwealthwriters.org.
Connor, C. J. 2010. Review of *Sivu's Six Wishes,* by Jude Daly. *School Library Journal* 56.12: 80.
Coolidge, Susan. 1872. *What Katy Did.* Boston, MA: Roberts Brothers.
Coughlan, Marjorie. 2008. "Colors!;Colores!" *PaperTigers Reviews.* September. http://www.papertigers.org/reviews/USA/papertigers/ColorsColores.html.
Cozien, Christine. 1996. Review in *Molo Songololo* 97: 17.
Dada, Fatima, Gcina Mhlophe, Leoni Hofmeyr, Heather Moore, and Jiggs Snaddon-Wood. 2002. *Horns Only.* Pinelands, SA: Centre for the Book; Maskew Miller Longman.
Daly, Niki. 1992. *Mary Malloy and the Baby Who Wouldn't Sleep.* New York: Golden/Western.
_____. 1996. "Niki Daly," *Something about the Author Autobiography Series* 21:75–102. Farmington Hills, MI: Gale.
_____. 2002. "Out of My Skin." *Sankofa* 1:35–44.
_____. 2006. *Welcome to Zanzibar Road.* New York: Clarion.
_____. 2007. "How to Travel Lightly (with 60 Years of Baggage?)" Speech delivered at International Reading Association's 52nd Annual Convention, Toronto, Canada, May 15.
_____. 2011. *No More Kisses for Bernard.* London: Frances Lincoln.
_____. 2013. Talk to Symposium of the Children's Book Network. Franschhoek, SA, May 15. Unpublished.
_____. n.d. "From Songololo to Jamela." Unpublished.
De Beer, Amanda. 2006. "Mia se ma toegang tot sprokieswêreld." *Litnet, May 9.* www.oulitnet.co.za/bazaar/mia_se_ma.asp_.
De Beer, Diane. 2011. "Drawing Children to Read More." *The Star,* May 5: 11.

De Kok, Ingrid. 2010. Address at the opening of Fiona Moodie's exhibition at the Irma Stern Museum, Cape Town, SA. August 30.

De la Mare, Walter. 1913/1946. *Peacock Pie*. Newly illustrated by Edward Ardizzone. London: Faber & Faber.

De Villiers, Leon. 2012. "Op vlerke van verbeelding." In *Afrikaanse Skryfgids*, edited by Riana Scheepers and Leti Kleyn, 89–93. Johannesburg, SA: Penguin.

De Vries, Izak. 2008. "Weessubversief." *LitNet*. http://www.litnet.co.za/Article/wees-sub-versief.

_____. 2013. http://www.izakdevries.co.za.

Deary, Terry. 2003. *The Horrible History of the World*. London: Scholastic.

Decandido, Graceanne. 2004. "The Star-Bearer: A Creation Myth from Ancient Egypt." Review of *The Star-Bearer: A Creation Myth from Ancient Egypt*, by Dianne Hofmeyr. *Teacher Librarian* 32.1: 22.

Del Vecchio, Stephen. 1994. "Review of *One Round Moon and a Star for Me*." *School Library Journal* 31.1: 190.

Dempers, Adele. 1998. "Jeugverhaal van Preller word sterk aanbeveel." *Volksblad*, October 12: 8.

Dickinson, Trevor. 2007. "Lila and the Secret of Rain." Review of *Lila and the Secret of Rain*, by David Conway. *The School Librarian* 55.4: 185.

Diedericks-Hugo, Carina. 2002. "Sulke boeke sal kinders lees." *Die Burger*, January 14.

_____. 2011. "Die wêreld van 'n kind." *Rapport*, February 5.

Dixon, Franklin D. in Marilyn S. Greenwald. 2005. *The Secret of the Hardy Boys*. Athens, OH: Ohio University & Swallow Press.

"Doctor Me Di Zin." 2001. *Kirkus Reviews*, September 1. https://www.kirkusreviews.com/book-reviews/roberto-piumini/doctor-me-di-cin/.

Dossier for the Hans Christian Andersen Illustrator Award. 2004. Cape Town, SA: SACBF.

Eccleshare, Julia, ed. 2009. *1001 Children's Books You Must Read Before You Grow Up*. London: Quintessence Editions Ltd.

Editorial Board of the University Society. 1927. *Fun and Thought for Little Folk (The Home University Bookshelf, Volume 01)*. New York: New York University Society.

Eiselen, Uca. 2005. "Martie Preller." In *Van Patrys-hulle tot Hanna Hoekom: 'n Gids tot die Afrikaanse Kinder -en Jeugboek*, edited by Gretel Wybenga and Maritha Snyman, 369–374. Pretoria, SA: LAPA.

Everall, Annie, and Viviana Quiñones, eds. 2012. *The World through Picture Books: Librarians' Favourite Books from Their Country*. http://www.ifla.org.http://www.ifla.org/files/assets/libraries-for-children-and-ya/publications/iflapicturebookscatalogue.pdf.

F., E. 1992. Review of *Somewhere in Africa*, by Ingrid Mennen and Niki Daly. *The Horn Book Magazine* 62.2: 193.

Fairer-Wessels, Felicité. A., and J.W. Wessels. 2007. "A Critical Discussion of the Art Styles Used by Selected Illustrators of South African Children's Books Since the 1950s." *Mousaion* 25.1: 117–140.

Fearnley, Jan. 2009. *Martha in the Middle*. London: Walker.

Flockemann, Miki. 1998. "Stories of Passage, Stories of Crossings: Trends in South African Literature, 1990–1995." In *Critical Perspectives on Postcolonial African Children's and Young Adult Literature*, edited by Meena Khorana, 143–158. Contributions in Afro-American and African Studies no. 187. Westport, Conn: Greenwood Press.

Forte, Maria. 2007. Review of *Sky Blue Accident/Accidente Celeste,* by Jorge Luján. Illustrated by Piet Grobler. *Papertigers* 12.5. www.papertigers.org.

Fouche, Lani. 2012. "Interview with Jaco Jacobs." *Bloemfontein Get It Free Magazine*, March 25.

Fourie, Elkarien. 2007. "Knap eksperimentlewerrobuustetaal op." *Die Beeld*, July 16: 15.

Frank, Anne. 1952. *Anne Frank: The Diary of a Young Girl.* Translated by B. M. Mooyaart. New York: Doubleday & Company.
Freeman, Evelyn B., Barbara A. Lehman, and Patricia L. Scharer. 1998."Crossing Borders." *The Reading Teacher* 51: 504–512.
Gericke, Lona. 2008. "Resensies van Suid-Afrikaansekinderboeke." http://sa-books.blogspot.ae/2008/02/resensies-van-afrikaanse-kinderboeke.html.
———. 2008. "A special tribute to Piet Grobler, Illustrator." *South African Children's Books Blog*, February 14. http://sa-books.blogspot.com/2008/02.
———. 2008. "Preller, Martie Jy en Toetenkat; Jy en Hercules; Jy en die Dinosourus (LAPA, 2007) Illustrasies deur Alistair Ackermann." http://sa-books.blogspot.com/2008/02/boekresensies-augustus-2007-preller.html.
Gerwel, Jakes, and Linda Rode. 1995. *Crossing Over.* Cape Town: Kwela.
"Gewilde kinderboeke word bekroon." 2009. *Ons Stad*, April 16.
Gibbs, Celia. 1995. Review of *Somewhere in Africa*, by Ingrid Mennen and Niki Daly. *The School Librarian* 40.5: 55.
Gibson, Robin L. 2005. Review of *Little Mouse. School Library Journal* 51.2: 96.
Glistrop, Eva. 2002. *The Hans Christian Andersen Awards, 1956–2002.* Basel, Switzerland: International Board on Books for Young People.
Goodreads. n.d. http://www.goodreads.com/quotes/tag/imagination?page=3.
Gouws, Tom. 1994. "So ongelooflik voorspelbaar ... gaap." *Beeld*, November 7: 8.
Granqvist, Raoul. 1997. "'Who Is Building the House?' Myth, Nation and Culture in African and Caribbean Children's Literature." In *Preserving the Landscape of Imagination in Children's Literature in Africa*, edited by Raoul Granqvist and Jürgen Martini, 23–41. Amsterdam, Netherlands; Atlanta, GA.: Rodopi.
Gray, Stephen. 2005. "Gcina Mhlophe." In *Indaba: Interviews with African writers*, edited by Stephen Gray, 148–152. Pretoria, SA: Protea Book House.
Gregorowski, Christopher. 1982, 2000. *Fly, Eagle, Fly!* Illustrated by Niki Daly. Cape Town, SA: Tafelberg.
Greyling, Cecile. 2004. "Reis opnuut deur woorde, Bloemlesing kan jong digters inspireer." *Die Burger*, October 21.
Greyling, Franci. 2004. "Leon de Villiers se voorgeslagte was boere—anders as hulle, boerhyegter met woorde en idees." http://www.storiewerf.co.za/cv's/cvleondevilliers.htm.
Grobler, Petrus (Piet). 2004. "'n Ondersoek na betekenis in prenteboeke vanuit 'n vertaalteoretiese perspektief met spesiale verwysing na illustrasies vir die werk van Annie M.G. Schmidt en ander herskrywings tussen Afrikaans en Nederlands." MA diss., Stellenbosch University, SA.
———. 2000. "'n Balkie onder 'n bos." *Volksblad*, June 14: 6.
Grobler, Piet. 2010. "Illustration: A Medium for Representing Minorities." Round table participant at International Board on Books for Young People 32nd World Congress, Santiago de Campostela, Spain, September 10.
———. 2013. http://www.pietgrobler.com/cv.htm.
Gunne, Sorcha. 2010. "Questioning Truth and Reconciliation: Writing Rape in Achmat Dangor's *Bitter Fruit* and Kagiso Lesego Molope's *Dancing in the Dust*." In *Feminism, Literature and Rape Narratives: Violence and Violation,* edited by Sorcha Gunne and Zoe Brigley Thompson, 164–182. New York: Routledge.
Handley, Trish. 1987. "Remember the Children." *Cape Argus*, August 26.
Hannavy, Sybil. 2006. "To Everything There Is a Season." Review of *To Everything There Is a Season*, by Jude Daly. *School Library Journal* 54.3: 26.
Harper, Susanne. 2008. "Tieners kan leer uit reis sonder 'n padkaart." *Die Beeld*, January 21.
Harries, Ann. 1980. *The Sound of the Gora.* London: Heinemann.
Heale, Jay. 1991, 2009. Reviews. *Bookchat.* www.bookchat.co.za

_____. 1994. *South African Authors & Illustrators*. Grabouw, South Africa: Bookchat.
_____. 1995. *SACBIP 95, South African Children's Books in Print 1995*. Grabouw, SA: Bookchat.
_____. 1996. *From the Bushveld to Biko*. Grabouw, SA: Bookchat.
_____. 2000. "The Gift of the Sun: A Tale from South Africa." Review of *The Gift of the Sun: A Tale from South Africa*, by Dianne Stewart. http://www.bookchat.co.za/reviews/reviews2000.html.
_____. 2004. *Adamastor: A View Over the Children's Literature of South Africa*. Kenilworth, SA: Bookchat.
_____. 2004. "Mr Humperdinck's Wonderful Whatsit." http://www.bookchat.co.za/reviews/reviews2004.html.
_____. 2005. "Uncle James and the Delicious Monster." http://www.bookchat.co.za/reviews/reviews2005.html.
_____. 2006. "SACBIP Reviews 2006." *Bookchat: South African Children's Books*. http://www.bookchat.co.za/reviews/reviews2006.html.
_____. 2006. "The Authentic, Unusually Alarming, Actual Factual Story Book." http://www.bookchat.co.za/reviews/reviews2006.html.
_____. 2008. "Lila and the Secret of Rain." Review of *Lila and the Secret of Rain*, by David Conway. http://www.bookchat.co.za/reviews/reviews2008.html.
_____. 2008. "SACBIP Reviews 2008." *Bookchat: South African Children's Books*. http://www.bookchat.co.za/reviews/reviews2008.html.
_____. 2009. Review of *Nelson Mandela: Long Walk to Freedom*, by Chris Van Wyk. *Cape Argus*, December 7: 9.
_____. 2009. "Let There be Peace." Review of *Let There Be Peace*, by Jeremy Brooks. http://www.bookchat.co.za/reviews/reviews2009.html.
_____. 2010. "SACBIP Reviews 2010." *Bookchat: South African Children's Books*. http://www.bookchat.co.za/reviews/reviews2010.html.
_____. 2011. "Goblin Diaries: Apprenticed to the Red Witch." http://www.bookchat.co.za/reviews/reviews2011.html.
_____. 2011. "SACBIP Reviews 2011." *Bookchat: South African Children's Books*. http://www.bookchat.co.za.
_____. 2012. "SACBIP Reviews 2012." *Bookchat: South African Children's Books*. http://www.bookchat.co.za/reviews/reviews2012.html.
_____. 2012."Vier Illustrators." http://www.bookchat.co.za/articles/article1210.html.
_____. 2013. "South African Children's Book Awards." *Bookchat*. http://www.bookchat.co.za/sacba.html.
_____. 2013. "Bookchat: South African Children's Books." *Bookchat*. http://www.bookchat.co.za/reviews/reviews2013.html.
_____. n.d. Reviews of Kagiso Lesego Molope's books. www.bookchat.co.za.
HIVSA. n.d. "HIV AIDS in South Africa." www.hivsa.com.
Hofmeyr, Dianne. 2008. "Beyond Borders: South African Illustration as a Visual Feast." *What Do You See? International Perspectives on Children's Book Illustration*, edited by Jennifer Harding and Pat Pinset, 116–124. Newcastle upon Tyne, UK: Cambridge Scholars Publishing.
_____. 2010. "The Sweet Smell of Sliced Watermelon and Swimming with Dolphins." *Dianne Hofmeyr: Children's Author*. January 15. http://www.diannehofmeyr.com/2010/01/15/the-sweet-smell-of-sliced-watermelon-and-swimming-with-dolphins/.
_____. n.d.a. "Dianne Hofmeyr: About Me." *Dianne Hofmeyr: Children's Author*. http://www.diannehofmeyr.com/about/.
_____. n.d.b. "Dianne Hofmeyr: The Waterbearer." *Dianne Hofmeyr: Children's Author*. http://www.diannehofmeyr.com/novels/the-waterbearer/.

Hough, Barrie. 1997. "Dapper seunnie bang omtewyshyrou." *Rapport,* December 14: 16.
_____. 1997. "Tiener tel skerwe van sy droom op." *Rapport,* December 14: 16.
Human, Charlie. 2013. *Apocalypse Now Now.* London, UK: Random House; Cape Town, SA: Struik.
Hutchins, Pat. 1968. *Rosie's Walk.* London: The Bodley Head.
IBBY. 2013. "IBBY Honour List 2010." http://www.ibby.org/index.php?id=270.
In die Tyd van die Esob. 2010. http://blogs.sun.ac.za/boekwurm/files/2010/09/Esob-Adri.pdf.
Inggs, Judith. 2006. "New Frontiers in English Language Young Adult Fiction in South Africa." *Bookbird* 44.2: 22–29.
_____. 2007. "Effacing Difference? The Multiple Images of South African Adolescents." *English in Africa,* 34.2: 35–49.
It's a Book Thing: Author's Pie: Sally Partridge. 2012. May 18. http://itsabookthingblog.blogspot.com/2012/05/authors-pie-sa-partridge.html.
Jacobs, Ihette. 2007. "Leon de Villiers." http://www.storiewerf.co.za/onderhoude/oh_leondevilliers2.htm.
Jaco Jacobs ryg pryse in vir eie en vertaalwerk. 2009. *Die Burger,* September 24.
"Jaco Jacobs." 2008. *Die Burger,* September 6: 13.
Jaco Jacobs. 2011. *Blogspot,* June 1. http://jacojacobs.blogspot.com/2011_06_01_archive.html.
_____. 2013. http://jacojacobs.co.za.
Jacobs, Marié. 2000. "Avontuur vir dié wat glo in helingskrag van woorde." *Die Volksblad,* July 24.
Jenkins, Elwyn.1993. *Children of the Sun: Selected Writers and Themes in South African Children's Literature.* Johannesburg, SA: Ravan.
_____. 2002. *South Africa in English-language Children's Literature, 1814–1912.* Jefferson, NC, and London: McFarland.
_____. 2006. *National Character in South African Children's Literature.* New York; London: Routledge.
_____. 2007. "Memories of Social Transition in Southern Africa." *Inozemna Philologia.* 119.2: 17–23.
_____. 2012. *Seedlings, English Children's Reading & Writers in South Africa.* Pretoria, SA: UNISA Press.
Johnson, David. 2012. "Literary and Cultural Criticism in South Africa." In *The Cambridge History of South African Literature,* edited by David Attwell and Derek Attridge, 818–837. Cambridge, UK: Cambridge University Press.
Johnson, Nancy J., and Cyndi Giorgis. 2001. "Fair, Brown, & Trembling: An Irish Cinderella Story." Review of *Fair, Brown, & Trembling: An Irish Cinderella Story,* by Jude Daly. *The Reading Teacher* 54: 539.
Jordan, Archibald Campbell. 1973. *Towards an African Literature: The Emergence of Literary Form in Xhosa.* Berkeley, CA: University of California Press.
Kaschula, Russell H. 2001. "Introduction: Oral Literature in Contemporary Contexts." In *African Oral Literature: Functions in Contemporary Contexts,* edited by Russell H. Kaschula, xi-xxvi. Claremont, SA: New Africa Books.
Khorana, Meena, ed. 1998. *Critical Perspectives on Postcolonial African Children's and Young Adult Literature. Contributions in Afro-American and African Studies no. 187.* Westport, CT: Greenwood Press.
_____. 2002. "Exploring the 'Dual Reality' of Children's Lives." *Sankofa* 1: 71–75.
Kiefer, Barbara. Z. 2010. *Charlotte Huck's Children's Literature,* 10th edition. New York: McGraw Hill.
Kirkus Review. 2001. "Imani's Music." Review of *Imani's Music,* by Sheron Williams. *Kirkus* 69: 1616.

_____. 2006. "To Everything There Is a Season." Review of *To Everything There Is a Season*, by Jude Daly. *Kirkus* 74: 129.
_____. 2007. "Sky Blue Accident." Review of *Sky Blue Accident*, by Jorge Luján, illustrated by Piet Grobler, translated by Elisa Amado. *Kirkus* 75: 227.
_____. 2010. "Sivu's Six Wishes." Review of *Sivu's Six Wishes*, by Jude Daly. *Kirkus* 78: 519.
_____. 2011. "Aesop's Fables." Review of *Aesop's Fables*, adapted by Beverly Naidoo, illustrated by Piet Grobler. *Kirkus* 79:1823.
Kleyn, A.J.T (Leti). 2013. "'n Sisteemteoretiese kartering van die Afrikaanse Literatuur vir die tydperk 2000–2009: Kanonisering in die Afrikaanse literatuur." PhD thesis, University of Pretoria, SA.
Kotzé, Suzette. 2013. "*Die Balkieboek* sal kleintjies vermaak." http://www.oulitnet.co.za/seminaar/balkie.asp.
Koyana, Siphokazi, ed. 2004. *SindiweMagona: The First Decade*. Scottsville, SA: University of KwaZulu-Natal Press.
Kruger, J.A. 1991. *Kinderkeur: 'n Gids tot Bekroonde Suid-Afrikaanse Kleuter-, Kinder- en Jeugboeke tot 1989*. Pretoria, SA: Universiteit van Suid-Afrika.
Kumagai, Clara. 2013. Review of *The Magic Bojabi Tree*. *INIS Magazine*. http://www.inismagazine.ie/reviews/book/the-magic-bojabi-tree.
Kumar, Lisa, ed. 2007. "Jude Daly." In *Something About the Author 177*, edited by Lisa Kumar, 42–44. Detroit, MI: Gale.
Kumar, Lisa, ed. 2011. "Jude Daly." In *Something About the Author 222*, edited by Lisa Kumar, 55–59. Detroit, MI: Gale.
Ladismith Tourism Bureau. 2013. "Klein Karoo, South Africa." http://www.ladismith.org.za/.
Lagerlöf, Selma. 1922. *The Wonderful Adventures of Nils*. New York: Doubleday, Page & Company.
Lakshaman, M. S. 2009. "Looking Beyond Global Literature as Bridges, Windows, Mirrors, and Sliding Glass Doors." *The Dragon Lode* 27: 11–17.
Le Roux, Marina. 1988. "Tafelberg-Uitgewers se 'Goue fluit, my storie is uit' gun en gee hierdie fluit vir elke SA kind." *Die Burger*, October 20.
_____. 1990. "Sprokies lofwaardig, maar ..." *Die Burger*, July 12.
_____. 1991. "Corlia Fourie sing soos 'n bottervoël." *Die Burger*, April 6.
_____. 1993. "Corlia Fourie skryf sprokies in die klassieke tradisie." *Die Burger*, June 22.
_____. 1993. "Religieuse en mitologiese toespelings in oortuigende verhaal uit Afrika." *Die Burger*, January 26.
_____. 1994. "Marita skryf 'n boek sonder leeftyd." *Insig* 8: 11.
_____. 1998. "Vyf wenners sluit die jaar af." *Die Burger*, December 12: 13.
_____. 2004. "Begin elke dag met 'n De Vos-versie." *Die Burger*, May 15: 6.
Leaf, Munro. 1936. *The Story of Ferdinand*. New York: The Viking Press.
Lehman, Barbara A. 2006. "Sense of Place and Displacement: Exploring International Places in the Writing of Dianne Case," *Journal of Children's Literature* 32. 2: 66–69.
_____. 2007. "Interview with Niki Daly, Children's Books Writer and Illustrator." *USBBY Newsletter* 32.1.
_____. 2013. "Masks in Storytelling, or How Pretty Salma Turned the 'Tale' on Mr. Dog." In *Fairy Tales with a Black Consciousness: Essays on Adaptations of Familiar Stories*, edited by Vivian S. Yenika-Agbaw, Ruth McKoy Lowery and Laretta Henderson, 159–172. Jefferson, NC: McFarland.
Lehman, Barbara A., Evelyn B. Freeman, and Patricia L. Scharer. 2010. *Reading Globally, K–8: Connecting Students to the World through Literature*. Thousand Oaks, CA: Corwin Press.
Lehman, Barbara, Kathy Short, Eun Hye Son, and Barbara Z. Kiefer. 2007. "Expanding Spaces in Children's Literature: International Books for Children." *Language Arts* 85: 84–91.

Lester, Julius. 2000. "Re-imagining the Possibilities." *The Horn Book Magazine* 76: 283–289.
Leuvennink, Jacqueline. 1992. "Vandag se vrou." *De Kat* 11: 56.
Lindgren, Astrid. 1950. *Pippi Longstocking.* New York: Viking.
Lodge, Katherine. 2012. *Let's Find Mimi.* London: Hodder Children's Books.
Lohann, Carl A. 1991. *Herfsblaar Gooi 'n Kaapse Draai: Hester Heese, Skrywer en Mens.* Cape Town, SA: Tafelberg.
Loots, Sonja. 2005. "De Villiers doenditweer." *Rapport*, October 2: 2.
Loubser, Henriëtte. 2009. "Die voorstelling van manlikheid in Afrikaanse prenteboeke." *Mousaion* 27.2: 77–93.
Maartens, Maretha. 1987. *Die Inkvoël (The Ink Bird, 1989).* Cape Town, SA: Tafelberg.
MacLiam, Geralt. 1987. "Poetry Opened the Doors to a Stage Career." *The Star Tonight,* July 17.
MacRobert, Marguerite. 2010. *How Creative Writers Write: Interviews with Successful Publishing Writers.* MA diss. Stellenbosch University, SA.
Magome, Mogomotsi. 2008. "UP Confers Honorary Doctorate on Mhlophe." *Pretoria News,* April 11: 7.
Magona, Sindiwe, David Attwell, Barbara Harlow, and Joan Attwell. 2000. "Interview with Sindiwe Magona." *Modern Fiction Studies* 46.1: 282–295.
_____. 2006. "Re: All That I Am." In *All That I Am... Because They Made a Difference in My Life,* edited by Leyla T. Haidarian and Mbulelo S. Plaatjie, 53. Claremont, SA: Spearhead.
_____. 2007. "Clawing at Stones." In *The Face of the Spirit: Illuminating a Century of Essays by South African Women,* coordinated by Beulah Thumbadoo, 131–133. Johannesburg, SA: Beulah Thumbadoo.
_____. 2009. Interview in *African Women Playwrights,* edited, with an introduction by Kathy A. Perkins, 1–11, 170–220. Urbana: University of Illinois Press.
Mail & Guardian. 2011. "Top 200 Young South Africans 2011." http://ysa2011.mg.co.za.
Mandela, Nelson. 1994. *Long Walk to Freedom.* Randburg, SA: MacDonald Purnell.
McCloud, Scott. 1999. *Understanding Comics: The Invisible Art.* Northampton, MA: Kitchen Sink Press Turtleback Books.
McDowell, Kate. 2000. "Fair, Brown, & Trembling: An Irish Cinderella Story." Review of *Fair, Brown, & Trembling: An Irish Cinderella Story,* by Jude Daly. *The Bulletin of the Center for Children's Books* 53: 395–396.
Mda, Zakes. 1997. "Theatre for Children in South Africa." In *Preserving the Landscape of Imagination: Children's Literature in Africa,* edited by Raoul Granqvist and Jürgen Martini, 137–144. Amsterdam: Rodopi.
Mears, Sarah. 2000. "Fair, Brown, & Trembling: An Irish Cinderella Story." Review of *Fair, Brown, & Trembling: An Irish Cinderella Story,* by Jude Daly. *The School Librarian* 48:135.
Meddlemore, Mary. 2010. *In the Reign of the Ilev.* http://www.amazon.com/dp/B009GXHI84.
Meiring, Andrelise. 2004. "Kinderboek propvol maagvashou-humor." *Die Volksblad,* January 19: 6.
Mennen, Ingrid. 2013. Interview by Naomi Meye. *Litnet,* April 4. http://www.litnet.co.za.
Meyer, Naomi. 2013. "Ingrid Mennen Vertel van Die Kinderboek *Ben en die Walvisse*—En van die Wonderbaarlike Reis." www.litnet.co.za
Mhlophe, Gcina. 2001. *Nozincwedi: Mother of Books.* www.gcinamhlophe.co.za.
Miles, John. 1980. *Stanley Bekker en die Boikot.* Johannesburg, SA: Taurus.
Milne, A.A. 1926. *Winnie-the-Pooh.* New York: E.P.Dutton & Co.
Montaigne, Michel de. 1923. *Essays of Montaigne.* London: Navarre Society.
Montgomery, Lucy Maud. 1908. *Anne of Green Gables.* Boston: L.C. Page & Co.
Moodie, Fiona. 2009. Contribution to a tribute to Zavrel for *Souvislosti* magazine to commemorate 10th anniversary of his death in 1999. Unpublished notes.

———. 2011. Address prepared for Umea Book Festival, Sweden, March 2011. Unpublished notes.
Morris, David B. 1985. "Gothic Sublimity." *New Literary History* 16.2: 299–319. http://www.jstor.org/stable/468749.
Morton, Kim. 2009. "Report on Room to Read in Zambia and South Africa." http://blog.roomtoread.org/room-to-read/2009/11/meet-dr-sindiwe-magona-one-of-our-local-authors-from-south-africa-and-top-10-best-african-women-writ.html.
Msimang, Nokuthula K. n.d. www.thulacreative.co.za.
Mtshali, Oswald Joseph. 1971. *Sounds of a Cowhide Drum*. Johannesburg, SA: Renoster Books.
Naidoo, Beverley. 1985. *Journey to Jo'burg*. London: Longman.
———. 2007. "South African Children's Literature: Lifting the Stones of Apartheid." *Bookbird* 45.4: 18–25.
Nal'ibali. 2013. October 28. http://nalibali.org.
NB Publishers. 2009. "Tafelberg." http://www.tafelberg.com/Books/6102.
———. "Jenny Robson: Biographical Info." http://www.nb.co.za/authors/1327.
Ngcobo, Gabisile. 2013. "13% of Pupils Can't Read a Word of English." *The Witness*. October 22. www.witness.co.za.
Ndebele, Njabulo S. 2011. "Gcina Mhlophe." *South Africa -Poetry International Web*. http://southafrica.poetryinternationalweb.org/piw-cms/cms-module/index.php?obj-id=19032.
NEEDU. 2013. "National Report 2012: Summary." http://www.saqa.org.za/docs/papers/needu.pdf.
Newman, David, M., and Elizabeth Grauerholz. 2002. *Sociology of Families*, 2nd edition. Thousand Oaks, CA: Pine Forge.
Nieuwoudt, Stephanie. 2002. "Grobler se prente laat kinders reis." *Die Burger*, August 26: 4.
———. 2007. "Absurde kat met die hoed bekoor steeds ná 50 jaar." *Die Burger*, September 24.
Nikita. 2008. "Goue Storie—Golden Story." Blog entry. September 16. http://chessaleein-london.wordpress.com/2008/09/16/goue-storie-golden-story/.
"Nog 'n wenner vir Tafelberg." 1986. *Die Burger*, September 16.
Norval, Roline. 2000. "Kinders kies self Alida se illustrasies as jaar se beste." *Die Burger*, March 16.
———. 2000. "Liefdeswerk vir illustreerder word deur ATKV bekroon." *Die Burger*, March 18.
Nuttall, Sarah. 1994. "Reading in the Lives and Writing of Black South African Women." *Journal of Southern African Studies*, 20.1: 85–98.
Oboe, Aanaklisa. 2007. "The TRC Women's Hearings As Performance and Protest in the New South Africa." *Research in African Literatures* 38.3: 60–76.
Odendaal, Gerda. 2008. "Suurlemoen! 'n Soete leeservaring." *Litnet* archives, October 15. http://www.givengain.com/cgibin/giga.cgi?cmd=cause_dir_news_item&news_id=54345&cause_id=1270.
Opie, Iona, and Peter Opie, eds. 1992. *I Saw Esau*. Illustrated by Maurice Sendak. London: Walker Books.
Pakendorf, Gunther. 1992. "'n Engel snel tot hulp." *Die Burger*, March 31.
Parker, Elize. 2010. "Kom ek skets jou 'n storie." *Leef*, December.
Parravano, Martha V. 1996. "The Gift of the Sun: A Tale from South Africa." Review of *The Gift of the Sun: A Tale from South Africa*, by Dianne Stewart. *The Horn Book Magazine* 72: 730.
———. 2011. "Sivu's Six Wishes." Review of *Sivu's Six Wishes*, by Jude Daly. *The Horn Book Guide* 22.1:135.
Paul, Korky. 1987. *Winnie the Witch*. Oxford: Oxford University Press.
Pople, Leatitia. 2008. "Prente vir die lekker." *Die Burger*, March 24: 6.
———. 2010. "Grimm met nuwe skop." *Die Burger*, November 6:10.

Posel, Deborah. 2001. "What's in a Name? Racial Categorisations Under Apartheid and Their Afterlife." *Transformation*: 47.
Potter, Beatrix. 1905. *The Tale of Mrs Tiggy-Winkle*. London: Frederick Warne & Co.
_____. 1907. *The Tale of Tom Kitten*. London: Frederick Warne & Co.
Preller, Martie. 2000a. Die maak van 'n kies-jou-eie-avontuur boek. *Literator* 21.2: 80–96.
_____. 2000b. Onderhoude. http://www.storiewerf.co.za/onderhoude/ohmartiepreller.htm.
_____. 2012. Personal web page. www.martiepreller.co.za/balkieboek.html.
Propp, Vladimir, A. 1975. *Morphology of the Folktale*, 2nd edition. Austin, TX: University of Texas Press.
Publishers Weekly. 1992. Review of *Somewhere in Africa*. January 1. http://www.publishersweekly.com.
_____. 1993. "The Dove." Review of *The Dove*, by Dianne Stewart. *Publishers Weekly* 240.20: 79.
_____. 1995. "Do the Whales Still Sing?" Review of *Do the Whales Still Sing?*, by Dianne Hofmeyr. *Publishers Weekly* 242.20: 72.
_____. 1996. "The Gift of the Sun: A Tale from South Africa." Review of *The Gift of the Sun: A Tale from South Africa*, by Dianne Stewart. *Publishers Weekly* 243.38: 83.
_____. 2000. "Fair, Brown, & Trembling: An Irish Cinderella Story." Review of *Fair, Brown, & Trembling: An Irish Cinderella Story*, by Jude Daly. *Publishers Weekly* 247.34: 71.
_____. 2004. "The Tale of Paradise Lost." Review of *The Tale of Paradise Lost*, by Nancy Willard. *Publishers Weekly* 251.43: 48.
_____. 2006. "To Everything There Is a Season." Review of *To Everything There Is a Season* by Jude Daly. *Publishers Weekly* 253.5: 72.
Pulles, Elizabeth. 1990. *'n Eksperimentele verkenning van grafiese manipulasie ter wille van doeltreffende kommunikasie in die prenteboek*. Potchefstroom, SA: Potchefstroom University for Christian High Education.
Quintero, Elizabeth P. 2009. *Critical Literacy in Early Childhood Education: Artful Story & the Integrated Curriculum*. New York: Peter Lang Publishing.
Rabinowitz, Daniel. 2007. Press release, June. Johannesburg: Random House Umuzi.
"Range of Pupil-Centred Schoolbooks Launched." 1998. *The Daily News*, September 21: 5.
Rautenbach, Elmarie. 2001. "Die uithou van skryf." *Insig*, December: 72.
Retief, Hanlie. 2002. "Ink & papier: woorde word sprokies." *Rapport*, November 16: 21.
_____. 2011. "Samestellers verskuif hiermee grense." *Die Rapport*, March 6.
Reynolds, Kimberley. 2007. *Radical Children's Literature: Future Visions and Aesthetic Transformations in Juvenile Fiction*. London: Palgrave Macmillan.
Riddell, Chris. 2008. *Ottoline and the Yellow Cat*. London: Harper Collins.
Rinkwest, Tarryn. 2009. "Siyolo's Jersey Takes the Cake at the Exclusive Books IBBY Awards." *LitNet*. November 24. http://www.argief.litnet.co.za.
Roback, Dianne, Jennifer M.Brown, Jason Britton, and Jeff Zaleski. 2001. "Imani's Music." Review of *Imani's Music* by Sheron Williams. *Publishers Weekly* 248.50: 70.
Rochman, Hazel. 1995. "Do the Whales Still Sing?" Review of *Do the Whales Still Sing*, by Dianne Hofmeyr. *Booklist* 91: 1652.
_____. 1996. "The Gift of the Sun: A Tale from South Africa." Review of *The Gift of the Sun: A Tale from South Africa*, by Dianne Stewart. *Booklist* 93: 145.
_____. 2000. "Fair, Brown, & Trembling: An Irish Cinderella Story." Review of *Fair, Brown, & Trembling: An Irish Cinderella Story*, by Jude Daly. *Booklist* 97: 120.
_____. 2010. "Sivu's Six Wishes." Review of *Sivu's Six Wishes*, by Jude Daly. *Booklist* 107: 114.
Rode, Linda. 2002. "*Die ongelooflike avonture van Hanna Hoekom*" deur Marita van der Vyver. *Storiewerf*. http://www.storiewerf.co.za/resenseer/hannahoekom.htm.
_____. 2001. "Actually More of a Bookmaker." Speech delivered at a Librarian's Course at University of the Western Cape, Cape Town, SA.

"Rooikappie nou slimmer Sprokies-heldinne te passief, sê feministe." 1991. *Die Burger*, January 17.
Rosenberg, Helen. 2008. "The Stone: A Persian Legend of the Magi." Review of *The Stone: A Persian Legend of the Magi*, by Dianne Hofmeyr. *Booklist* 95: 332.
Rosenblatt, Louise M.1978/1994. *The Reader, the Text, the Poem: The Transactional Theory of the Literary Work*. Carbondale, IL: Southern Illinois University Press.
Ross, Stewart. 2011. *Into the Unknown: How Great Explorers Found Their Way by Land and Air*. London: Walker Books.
Roux, Madeleine. 1997. "Juweel van debuut deur skrywer vir die jeug." *Die Burger*, February 26: 12.
Rowling, J.K. 2000. *Goblet of Fire*. London: Bloomsbury.
Saccardi, Marianne. 2002. "Imani's Music." Review of *Imani's Music*, by Sheron Williams. *School Library Journal* 48.1: 114.
Sanlam Prize for Youth Literature. http://www.sanlam.co.za/wps/wcm/connect/Sanlam_EN/sanlam/sponsorships/culture/sanlam+prize+for+youth+literature.
Savory, Phyllis. 1988. *The Best of African Folklore*. Cape Town, SA: Struik.
Schateman, Renée. 2007. "Interview with Sindiwe Magona." *Scrutiny2: Issues in English Studies in Southern Africa* 12.2: 154–164.
Scheepers, Riana. 2010. "Die Moderne Sprokiesboek is Uiteindelik Hier." *Die Burger*, February 7.
Scheepers, Riana, and Leti Kleyn. 2012. *Die Afrikaanse Skryfgids*. Cape Town, SA: Penguin.
Schuurman, Pieter. 2009. "Virus beland in jou bloed." *Volksblad*, September 21.
Sealey, Sally. 1988. "I Am Essentially a Writer." *The Star*, December 7: 12.
Sedgwick, Fred. 2011. *Inspiring Children to Read and Write for Pleasure: Using Literature to Inspire Literacy Learning for Ages 8–12*. London; New York: Routledge.
Sell, Roger. Ed. 2002.*Children's Literature as Communication*. Amsterdam, Netherlands; Philadelphia, PA: John Benjamins Publishing Company.
Sendak, Maurice. 1970. *In the Night Kitchen*. New York: Harper.
_____. 1981. *Outside Over There*. New York: Harper.
Sewell, Anna. 1877. *Black Beauty*. Norwich: UK: Jarrold & Sons.
Shelley, Mary. 1818. *Frankenstein*. London: Lackington, Hughes, Harding, Mavor, & Jones.
Shipler, David. 1986. *Arab and Jew: Wounded Spirits in a Promised Land*. New York: Times Books.
Shober, Dianne. 2013. *Sindiwe Magona: Climbing Higher*. Cape Town, SA: David Philip.
Sibanda, Silindiwe. 2012. *Through the Eyes of the Other: An Analysis of the Representations of Blackness in South African Youth Novels by White Writers from 1976 to 2006*. PhD diss., University of the Witwatersrand, Johannesburg, SA.
Sithole, Nokwanda. 1989. "Profile: Once Upon a Time." *Tribute*, November: 18–21.
Slingsby, Peter. 2002.*Jedro's Bane*. Cape Town, SA: Tafelberg.
Slippers, Bibi. 2012. "SA-Illustreerders: Alida Bothma." *Litnet*, April 24.
_____. 2013. "Tekeninge van die tye." *Rapport*, April 6. http://www.rapport.co.za/MyTyd/Nuus/Tekeninge-van-die-tye-20130405.
Snyman, Lydia. 1986. "Children's Book Illustrations: A Few Problematic Aspects of the Theory and Practice." In *Doer-Land-y / Far Far Away*, compiled and edited by Marianne Hölscher, 47. Cape Town, SA: South African National Gallery.
Snyman, Maritha. 1997. "Jeugboeke vertel iets van ons mededingende samelewing." *Beeld*, April 17: 8.
Solberg, Rolf. 1996. "Gcina Mhlophe: Interviewed on 7 December 1994." In *Reflections: Perspectives on Writing in Post-apartheid South Africa. NELM Interviews Series Number Seven*, edited by Rolf Solberg and Malcolm Hacksley, 26–36. Grahamstown, SA: National English Literary Museum.

Sophy. 2012. "Dianne Case: The Home of Magic, Elves and Talking Animals." *BooksLive*. September 11. www.bookslive.co.za.
South Africa. 2002. *Revised National Curriculum Statement Grades R-9*. Pretoria, SA: Department of Education.
South African Artlife. 2013. http://artlife.co.za/alidabothma.
Spencer, L. 2013. "The House of Mothers: Constructing Alternative Forms of Mothering in Kasigo Molope's *The Mending Season*. *English Academy Review* 30.1: 53–64.
Spender, Stephen. 1965. *Selected Poems*. London: Faber.
Spufford, Francis. 2003. *The Child That Books Built: A Life in Reading*. London: Picado.
Statistics South Africa. 2012. *2011 Census*. http://www.statssa.gov.za.
Steele, Liz, and Warren Kidd. 2001.*The Family*. Basingstoke, UK: Palgrave.
Steenberg, Elsabe. 1995. "Drie wenverhale is 'n geslaagde bydrae tot Afrikaanse jeuglektuur." *Beeld*, February 20: 6.
Steenkamp, Elzette. 2011. *Identity, Belonging and Ecological Crisis in South African Speculative Fiction*. PhD diss., Rhodes University, Grahamstown, SA.
Stein, Sara. 1994. "Book Reviews." *New York Times Book Review*, July 7.
Stevenson, Deborah. 2008. "Way Up and Over Everything." Review of *Way Up and Over Everything*, by Alice McGill. *The Bulletin* 61.11: 484.
Stewart, Dianne. 1996. *Bookchat* 127: 12.
_____. 2012. Interview in *Natal Witness*, May 30: 12.
Stewig, John. 2006. "To Everything There Is a Season." Review of *To Everything There Is a Season*, by Jude Daly. *Booklist* 102.16: 50.
Steyn, Tisha. 1995. "Ntataise: Opening Small Eyes to Wonders of Life." *City Press*, November 12: 28.
Stowe, Harriet Beecher. 1852. *Uncle Tom's Cabin*. Boston: John P. Jewett & Company.
Stretton, Hesba. 1867.*Jessica's First Prayer*. www.literaryheritage.org.uk.
Tan, Shaun. 2013. www.shauntan.net.
Telgen, Diane, ed. 1994. *Something About the Author*. Detroit: Gale.
Terreblanche, Christelle. 1991. "Die prinses moet nie in die kis lê en wag nie." *Vrye Weekblad* 12: 12.
Theron, Leentjie. 1993. "Mens kan Afrika voel en ruik." *Die Beeld*, July 19.
Thorne, Michael. 2006. "Interview with Niki Daly." http://www.illustrators.co.za/nikidaly.htm.
Thyssen, Candy Lynn. 2012. *The Representation of Masculinity in Children's Literature*. MA diss., University of Cape Town, SA.
Tötemeyer, Andrée-Jeanne. 1984. *The Racial Element in Afrikaans Children's and Youth Literature*. PhD diss., Stellenbosch University, SA.
"Toulopers—verse vir tieners." 2011. *Die Burger*, May 2.
Trites, R.S. 2000. *Disturbing the Universe: Power and Repression in Adolescent Literature*. Iowa City, IA: University of Iowa Press.
Tutu, Desmond. 1993. "Tutu's Moral Stature." *Sunday Times Heritage Project*. http://heritage.thetimes.co.za/memorials/ec/DesmondTutu/article.aspx?id=640998.
Uchima, Eileen. 2007. "The Power of Children's Literature in the Lives of Children." *LIS* 681, November 28. www.scribd.com/doc/145933716/Children-s-Literature-Essay.
University of Worcester. 2013."Piet Grobler." http://www.worcester.ac.uk/discover/pietgrobler.html.
Van Coller, Hennie, P. 1994. "Marita se trefkrag lê in goeie dialoog." *Volksblad*, December 5: 6.
_____. 2006. "Marita van der Vyver." In *Perspektief en Profiel: 'n Afrikaanse literatuurgeskiedenis*, edited by Hennie P. Van Coller, 481–506. Pretoria, SA: Van Schaik.
Van den Heever, Carla-Mari. 2006. "Stalmaats." *Storiewerf*, June.

Van der Walt, Derick. 2010. "Vinnige virus welkome toevoeging tot arm wetenskapfiksiegenre." *Litnet*, April 6.
van der Walt, Thomas. 1998. Lekker om weer 'n jeugboek te lees. *Beeld,* April 13: 6.
_____. 2005. "Afrikaanse kinder- en jeugprosa." In *Van Patrys-hulle tot Hanna Hoekom: 'n Gids tot die Afrikaanse Kinder -en Jeugboek,* edited by Gretel Wybenga and Maritha Snyman, 14–32. Pretoria, SA: Lapa.
_____. 2009. "Willemien en die geel kat." In *SATI Prizes for Outstanding Translation and Dictionaries: Judges' Comments on the Winners.* http://translators.org.za.
_____. 2013. "A National South African Children's Literature After 15 Years of Democracy?" Unpublished paper.
van der Walt, Thomas, B., and M.M. Nieman. 2009. "Die feministiese uitbeelding van die gesin in Van der Vyver se boeke vir volwassenes." *Mousaion* 27.2: 150–163.
Van Heerden, Marjorie. 1988. "An Illustrator Confides in Her Audience." In *Towards Understanding Children's Literature for Southern Africa,* edited by Isabel Cilliers, 235–241. Cape Town, SA: Maskew Miller Longman.
_____. 2003. "One Illustrator's Journey." Presentation given at South African Children's Book Forum annual meeting, Cape Town, SA.
_____. 2005. "The People and Things That Made Me a Writer and Illustrator of Children's Books." Talk given to Cape Librarians, Cape Town, SA.
_____. 2007. "Books for the Children of Southern Africa." http://www.marjorie-cv.blogspot.
_____. 2008. "The Mind of an Illustrator: Illustrating Nina and Little Duck." Paper presented at the Annual General Meeting of IBBY South Africa, August 7.
_____. 2009. "Were Adults Influenced by the Books They Read as Children?" Talk given at the Cape Town Book Fair, Cape Town, SA.
_____. 2011. "My Reis as 'n Kinderboekskrywer/Illustreerder." Presentation given at Afrikaanse Taal- en Kultuurvereniging (ATKV) Writers Workshop, Johannesburg, SA.
_____. 2012a. "Challenges in Developing Countries for Picture Book Authors and Illustrators." Presentation given at the Asian Children's Writers and Illustrators Conference, Singapore.
_____. 2012b. "Daai deurmekaar, ongepoetste tuin." In *Afrikaanse Skryfgids,* edited by Riana Scheepers and Leti Kleyn, 143–149. Johannesburg, SA: Penguin Books.
_____. 2012c. "Function of Illustrations in a Children's Book." Paper presented at the Asian Festival of Children's Content Conference, Singapore.
_____. 2013. "Marjorie's Curriculum Vitae." http://www.marjorie-cv.blogspot.
Van Niekerk, Raymond. 1986. Preface to *Doer-Land-y: Far Far Away,* compiled and edited by Marianne Hölscher. Cape Town, South Africa: South African National Gallery.
Van Rooy, Rikus. 2009. "Kyk uit en skrik gerus vir dié 'Harlekyn.'" *Die Burger,* August 15.
Van Taak, Marelize. 2003. "Ideaal vir vreeslose lesers." *Die Burger,* September, 27.
Van Vlimmeren, Dijlan. 2005. Interview for *Rotterdams Dagblad,* April 23. http://www.pietgrobler.com/testimonials.htm.
Van Wyk, Chris. 1979. *It Is Time to Go Home,* Johannesburg, SA: Ad Donker.
Van Wyk, Marguerite. 1996. "Sy skryf deur in kinders se koppe in te klim en woel." *Beeld,* September 25: 9.
Van Zyl, H. E., and M. M. Botes. 1994. *South African Children's Book Illustrators.* Pretoria, SA: Transvaal School Media Association.
Van Zyl, Pieter. 2002. "Verhale van Bybel in beeld." *Die Burger,* November 12.
Venter, Isabelle. 2005. "Vir die Jonges." *Die Beeld,* August 1.
Vermaak, Arnold. 2005. "Vonkel in kind se oog grootste lof." *Die Beeld,* October 19: 2.
Viljoen, Fanie. 2007. "Jeugromanvolgeheimesoos 'n stel van 'n Hollywood-fliek." *LitNet.* http://www.argief.litnet.co.za.
_____. 2008. "MML-letterkundepryswenners bied heerlike leesstof." *Die Burger,* April 14.

"Vindingryke skrywer skitter." 1998. *Die Burger*, October, 26.
"Vir slaaptyd of selflees—'n keur." 2012. *Die Beeld*, June 18.
Vorster, Magdel, and Thomas B. van der Walt. 2000. "Jonges verdien boeke wat hulle laat dink." *Die Beeld*, October 23: 4.
Vorster, Magdel. 2004. "Op pad na klassieke status?" *Die Beeld*, July 19: 11.
Wagener, Adie. 1996. "Multiculturalism in Children's Literature." In *Other Worlds Other Lives—Proceedings of the International Conference on Children's Literature 4–6 April1995. Book One*, edited by Myrna Machet, Sandra Olën, and Thomas van der Walt, 286–287. Pretoria, SA: Unisa Press.
Walkins, Linda L. 2006. "To Everything There Is a Season." Review of *To Everything There Is a Season*, by Jude Daly. *School Library Journal* 52.3: 216.
Walton, Jo. 2009. "A Girl and a House: The Gothic Novel." www.tor.com/blogs/2009/09/anatomy-of-the-gothic.
Watson, Victor, ed. 2001. *The Cambridge Guide to Children's Books in English*. Cambridge, UK: Cambridge University Press.
Wilder, Laura Ingalls. 1935. *Little House on the Prairie*. New York: Harper & Brothers.
Williams, J. 2008. "These Children Were the Product of a Changing Country: The Feminist Bildungsroman and the Issue of Community in the Novels of Kasigo Molope." *Sankofa* 7: 39–48.
Woodward, Cathy. 1987. Review of *One More Time* by Louis Baum. *School Library Journal* 33.11: 76.
Woolf, Virgina. 1945. *A Room of One's Own*. Harmondsworth, UK: Penguin Books.
Wybenga, Gretel, and Maritha Snyman. 2005. *Van Patrys-hulle tot Hanna Hoekom*. Pretoria, SA: LAPA.
Yenika-Agbaw, Vivian, Ruth McKoy Lowery, and Laretta Henderson, eds. 2013. *Fairy Tales with a Black Consciousness: Essays on Adaptations of Familiar Stories*. Jefferson, NC: McFarland.
Zaleski, Jeff, Dianne Roback, Jennifer M. Brown, and Jason Britton. 2001. "The Star-Bearer: A Creation Myth from Ancient Egypt." Review of *The Star-Bearer: A Creation Myth from Ancient Egypt*, by Dianne Hofmeyr. *Publishers Weekly* 248.9: 86.
Zipes, Jack. 2007. *When Dreams Come True: Classical Fairy Tales and Their Tradition*, 2nd edition. New York: Routledge.

About the Contributors

Tanya **Barben** is retired as the University of Cape Town Libraries' Rare Books Librarian and the curator, among others, of two children's literature collections. Her interest in children's books and their illustrations is strong, and she occasionally gives talks on the subject. She also spends time indexing, editing and researching, and teaching young students to read and write.

Bettie Parsons **Barger** completed her doctorate at Ohio State University. She has taught children's literature courses to both undergraduate and graduate students. Her research interests include children's literature and educational technology. She is an assistant professor of elementary and literacy education at Winthrop University, Rockville, South Carolina.

Rajendra **Chetty** is a professor and department head in the Faculty of Education and Social Sciences at the Cape Peninsula University of Technology and a National Research Foundation–rated social scientist. His research interests are language policy, postcolonial literature and teacher education. He is the author of *The Vintage Book of South African Indian Writing* (2010).

Genevieve **Hart** is an associate professor in the Department of Library and Information Science at the University of the Western Cape. She has also had many years' experience as a high school English teacher and librarian. She is a National Research Foundation–rated researcher; her research interests include literacy education, the role of libraries in social inclusion, and the reading and information needs of children and youth.

Jay **Heale** is the editor of *Bookchat*, South Africa's only periodical dedicated to children's literature. He served on the jury of the Hans Christian Andersen Award for the International Board on Books for Young People (IBBY). He is the author of many books for children and about children's literature, and has contributed to the *International Companion Encyclopedia of Children's Literature* (1996) and *The Cambridge Guide to Children's Books in English* (2001).

Anne **Hill** has been involved in initial and in-service teacher development since 1989, specializing in drama, art and literature-based approaches to literacy. She was a senior lecturer and head of the Department of General Education and Training programs at the Cape Peninsula University of Technology until her retirement in 2007, and has lectured at the University of Cape Town and Centre for Creative Education in Cape Town.

Judith **Inggs** is an associate professor at Wits University in Johannesburg. Her doctoral research focused on Soviet children's literature during perestroika, following which she developed an interest in South African young adult literature from the era of apartheid's end. Her interests include the translation of South African YA literature into European languages, censorship and translation and the development of Soviet young adult literature.

Lisa **Kimble**, a Pittsburgh, Pennsylvania, native, received her undergraduate degree in international studies at Ohio State University. After having taught English as a Second Language in Korea for three years, she continued her studies at OSU in 2013, earning her master's degree in early childhood education.

Barbara A. **Lehman** is a professor emerita of children's literature at Ohio State University. Her scholarly interests focus on multicultural and global children's literature and child-centered literary criticism. She was a Fulbright Scholar in South Africa and co-editor of *Bookbird: A Journal of International Children's Literature*. She lives in Columbus.

Marianne van **Loggerenberg** has had a passion for children's books since she can remember and is employed at Pan Macmillan SA, specializing in children's literature. She has translated several children's books into Afrikaans.

Robin **Malan** has spent his working life in education and the theatre. He has served as the artistic director of a theatre-in-education company and spent fifteen years teaching in Swaziland. For twenty years he was the editor of *English Alive*, an annual anthology of high school writing. He is the author of several books for teenaged readers and two gay-interest books and lives in Cape Town.

Andrés A. **Montañés-Lleras** is a Ph.D. student in the Literature for Children and Young Adults Program at Ohio State University, where he teaches undergraduate courses. He is also an author of children's literature in Spanish. His latest novel, *El dragón de vapor*, was published in Colombia in 2012.

Erin F. **Reilly-Sanders** received her Ph.D. from Ohio State University, where she teaches undergraduate courses. With a background in architecture and graphic design, her focus is often on the visual aspects of children's literature, including her dissertation work on the depictions of houses.

Maritha **Snyman** taught at the Department of Information Science at the University of Pretoria. Her research is focused on Afrikaans children's and youth literature, and she has published numerous articles on the subject. She was co-editor of the field's comprehensive guide, *Van Patrys-hulle tot Hanna Hoekom*, in 2005. She works as a freelance writer and publisher and is a research fellow at the University of South Africa.

Ruth **Stone** is retired from her position as a science lecturer in the teacher education program at the Cape Peninsula University of Technology. With her lifelong interest in African Indigenous Knowledge Systems, she is collaborating with colleagues at the University of the Western Cape on ways to integrate such knowledge into the school science curriculum.

Magdel **Vorster** is a recognized South African authority in children's literature who studied library science at Stellenbosch University. She has been a children's librarian and co-owner of a children's bookshop, Rapunzel, in Pretoria. She now lives in Abu Dhabi, from where she reads manuscripts for South African publishers and remains active in the literary community.

Thomas van der **Walt** is a professor in the Department of Information Science at the University of South Africa where he teaches children's literature, user studies and archival science. He lives in Pretoria, South Africa.

Index

Die Aarde Moet Vry Wees 28
Abate, Michele A. 125
Abbott, Pamela 84
Achebe, Chinua 231
acrylic 22, 26, 27, 114, 129, 203
Adamastor 5, 192, 193, 196
Adichie, Chimamanda 63
Aesop's Fables 75, 76, 130, 227
An African Christmas Cloth 220
African National Congress (ANC) 6, 105, 107, 190, 192
An African Suitcase 222
African Tales: A Barefoot Collection 170
Afrikaans literature 2, 3, 7, 9, 84, 90, 182–183, 197
Afrikaans Taal en Kultuurvereniging (ATKV) 23, 28, 82, 146, 147, 148, 149, 182, 271
Die Afrikaanse Skryfgids 96, 150
Ahrens, Kathleen: *Ears Hear* 96; *Numbers Do* 96
Aiken, Joan 139
Akaba, Suekichi 204
Al die Meisies Hou van Divan Louw 150
Al Everest se Voëls (All Everest's Birds) 22, 28
Alba Bouwer Prize 80, 123, 146, 182, 271
Albatross Winter 40
Alberto Berlusconi Award 135
albinism 212–213, 221
Alcott, Louisa: *Little Women* 56
Alexander, Niall 260
Alice in Wonderland 32, 97
Aliens en Engele 124
All Everest's Birds (Al Everest se Voëls) 22, 28
All the Magic in the World 137, 143
Allan, Brooke 85
Altshuler, Anne 160
Am I a Lion That Eats People? 219
Amabali maTshona kweLanga (Stories South of the Sun) 77
Amalungiselelo (Preparations) 70
American Library Association 19
Anderkantland 182, 185
Andersen, Hans Christian: *Eventyr* (Fairy Tales) 66, 75, 227; *The Ugly Duckling* 70

Andrews, Loretta Kreider 115, 116
Angelou, Maya: *I Know Why the Caged Bird Sings* 67
animal stories 9, 13, 70, 95, 122–123, 141, 179
Animals 117
Anne of Green Gables 56, 65
Anon.: *The Twelve Days of Christmas* 202
Another Kind of One Nation: Young South African Writings 1 78
Anti-Bias Project 217–218
Antjie 218
apartheid 1, 2, 6, 10, 12, 15, 38–39, 42, 47–48, 56, 65, 104, 106, 111, 112, 243, 244–245, 247, 254, 268
Apocalypse Now 260
Arab and Jew: Wounded Spirits in a Promised Land 226
The Arabian Nights 88–89
architecture 26, 177
Ardizzone, Edward 199, 201
Are We Nearly There? 32, 37
Ashliman, D.L. 89
Ashraf of Africa 156, 157–159
Ask for Patricia (Vra vir Frederika) 202
Astrid Lindgren Memorial Award 19, 271
Astwood, Gail 18
At School, What If? 219
Atlantis Rises 179
Attridge, Derek: *The Cambridge History of South African Literature* 101
Attwell, David 68; *The Cambridge History of South African Literature* 101
Attwell, Joan 68
August, Tyrone 167, 168, 169
Austen, Jane: *Pride and Prejudice* 227
The Authentic, Unusually Alarming, Actual Factual Story Book (Die Oorspronlike, Ongewoon Skrikaanjaende, Werklik Feitlike Storieboek) 97
Authors Voices 128–129, 130, 131, 135
Autumn Leaves in the Cape: Hester Heese, Author and Person (Herfsblaar Gooi 'n Kaapse Draai: Hester Heese, Skrywer en Mens) 26

Avanti Award 250
Die Avonture van Alice in Wonderland 97
Awareness Publishers 102
Azhar 218

Baartman, Sara 60, 62
Babalela 182, 187
Bachelard, Gaston: *The Poetics of Space* 56
Bacon, Francis 120–121
Balkie and the Pirates of the Sea 182, 185
Balkie and the Sun's Resting Place 182, 185
Balkie and the Vicious Virus 182, 185
Die Balkie-boek 182, 185, 187
Ballade van de Dood (in South Africa: *The Circle of Life*) 132–133
Barefoot Books 170
Barker, Cicely Mary: *A World of Flower Fairies* 179
Barker, Jane 24
Barnard, Rita 101
Barney Climbs a Mountain ('n Grot vir 'n Grootman) 156
Bateson, Mary C.: *Willing to Learn, Passages of Personal Discovery* 76
Bau and the Baobab Tree 16
Baum, Louis: *Are We Nearly There?* 32, 37
Baumann, Sean 177
The Bead Book 17
Beake, Lesley 5, 10, 12–20, 202, 234; *Bau and the Baobab Tree* 16; *The Bead Book* 17; *Café Thunderball* 13; *A Cageful of Butterflies* 13, 14, 15, 16, 18, 19; *Detained at Her Majesty's Pleasure, The Journal of Peter David Hadden* 12, 13, 14, 16; *Finding Dad* 18; *Grandfather Remembers* 13; *Home Now* 15, 19; *Jakey* 12, 14, 15, 16, 19; *Merino* 13, 15; *The Message* 18; *My Story, Our Stories* 19; *Puppery Magazine* 12; *Rainbow* 12; *Remembering Green* 14; *Rough Luck* 13, 16; *Song of Be* 13, 15, 18; *The Strollers* 9, 12, 14, 18, 106; "The Three Sisters of Three Sisters" 14; *Tjojo and the Wild Horses* 13; *Traveller* 14, 17, 18, 19; *Waiting for Rain* 13, 16
Beatrix Potter: *Tom Kitten* 139
Beauty's Gift 67
Because Pula Means Rain 208, 212–213
La Belle et la Bête 176–177, 180
Ben and the Whales: The Extraordinary Journey (Ben en die Walvisse: 'n Wonderlike Reis) 162–163
Ben en die Walvisse: 'n Wonderlike Reis (Ben and the Whales: The Extraordinary Journey) 162–13
Bennett, Rosey 18
Bentley, Judith 78, 110
Bentley, Kin 131

Berg, Irene 162–163
Berger, Brigitte 83
Bernatová, Eva: *The Wonder Shoes* 175, 178
Bertie at the Dentist (and series) 32
Bertie Blikbrein 147
Bertus Looking for a Book (Bertus Soek 'n Boek) 98
Bertus 'n Boek (Bertus Looking for a Book) 98
The Best Meal Ever 33, 35, 68–69
Betty's Braids 70
Beukes, Lauren 260
Bible for Children 27
Biehl, Amy 67
Biesele, Dr. Megan 16
Big Fat Lies 235
Biko, Steve 56
Bildungsroman 247–248; see also feminism
Black Beauty 76
Black Consciousness 101, 103–104
The Black Dog 141
Blackmore, R.D.: *Lorna Doone* 56
Blake, Quentin 201
Blake, William 261
Blakemore, Stella 151
Bleek, W.H.I. 77, 229, 232n1
Bloch, Carole: *The Happy Prince* 203, 205–206
Bloemhof, Francois 7, 151
Bloom, Susan P. 116
Blue Train to the Moon 57, 60
Blues, Tracy: *Betty's Braids* 70; *Paragon the Perfect Piglet* 70
Blyton, Enid 9, 11, 55, 65, 102, 112, 137
Bodenstein, Christel: *Stories South of the Sun* 25, 77
Bodenstein, Hans: *Another Kind of One Nation: Young South African Writings 1* 78; *I, A Living Arrow: Young South African Writing 2* 78; *Stories South of the Sun* 25, 77; *Up the Down Escalator: Young South African Writing 3* 78
The Bodley Head 32, 140, 160, 201
Bohem Press 176
Boikie, You Better Believe It 58, 59, 60, 61
Bologna International Children's Book Fair 159, 176, 201
Bookchat 3, 18, 22, 23, 24, 25, 26, 32, 34, 61, 68–69, 70, 97, 98, 114, 115, 117, 191, 193, 195, 226, 227; see also Heale, Jay
Bookchat Book of the Year (and Award) 143, 161, 163, 271
Die Boom Wat Wou Loop (The Wishful Walnut) 23
Boomklim (Climbing Trees) 83
Bophuthatswana 243
Borges, Jorge Luis 16

Bornoff, Emily 123
Borrels 150
Bosman, Natalie 130
Botes, M.M. 191
Botha, Marzahn 150
Bothma, Alida 9, 21–30, 76–77
Botswana 59, 207, 208, 213
Bouma, Paddy 5, 10, 97, 105, 107; *Bertie at the Dentist* (and series) 32; *The Mouseboat* 34
Bouma, Raymond 32
The Boy and the Giants 178
The Boy on the Beach 48, 52
Boyd, Carolyn 115
Bradford, Clare 214n1
Brandt, Marieke 26
Bratislava International Biennale for Illustration (BIB) 135
Bravo, Zan Angelo! 52, 53
"Bread for the Journey" 231
Bredenkamp, Braam 129, 131
Breuer, Rosemarie 134
Bright Books series 95
Bringing Bullying into the Open 222
Brink, André P. 244; *Die Avonture van Alice in Wonderland* 97
Brink, Tania (Jaco Jacobs): *Al die Meisies Hou van Divan Louw* (All the Girls Love Divan Louw) 150; *Liefde Laat Jou Rice Krispies Anders Proe* (Love Changes the Taste of Your Rice Krispies) 150; *My Hart Is Vol Graffiti* (My Heart Is All Graffiti) 150; *Ouens Is Nie Pizzas Nie* (Guys Are Not Pizzas) 150
Britton, Jason 115, 116
Britz, Elretha 152
Brooks, Jeremy: *Let There Be Peace: Prayers from Around the World* 115, 117
Brooks, Ron 32
Brown, Jennifer M. 115, 116
Browne, Anthony 201
Budin, Miriam Lang 116
Bugs 117
Bukenya, Austin 169
Burnett, Frances Hodgson: *Little Lord Fauntleroy* 65; *The Secret Garden* 65
Burningham, John 32
Bush, Elizabeth 116, 117
Butler, Dorothy 139
Buzzeo, Tony: *Inside the Books: Readers and Libraries Around the World* 115

Café Thunderball 13
A Cageful of Butterflies 13, 14, 15, 16, 18, 19
Cairney, Trevor 121, 147
Caldecott Medal 95
Call, Nancy 116

Calling the Sun (Sonroepertjies) 76
The Cambridge History of South African Literature 101
Cambridge University Press SA 17, 25, 221; *see also* Rainbow Reading series
Cameraman, Cameron 25
Cape Flats 41, 135; *see also* Gugulethu
Cape Technical College 113
Cape Technikon School of Art and Design 21
Cape Town 9, 14, 18, 19n1, 21, 26, 31, 32, 41, 42, 47, 55, 60, 65, 91, 92, 110, 112–113, 115, 143, 155–156, 159, 161–162, 164, 173, 174, 175, 178, 195, 199, 203, 207, 208, 209, 217, 218, 222, 234, 250, 252, 253, 264, 267; *see also* District Six; Table Mountain
Carnegie Medal 270
Carnival of the Animals 131
Carrick, Carol: *Valentine* 32
Carroll, Lewis: *Alice's Adventures in Wonderland* 32, 97
cartoon 35, 130, 131, 191, 237; *see also* comics
Case, Dianne 38–46; *Albatross Winter* 40; *Katy of Sky Road* 38, 43–45; *Love, David* 9, 38, 40–42, 45; *92 Queens Road* 38, 42–43; *What a Gentleman!* 45
"The Cattle Herder's Song" 229
Centre for the Book 71
Chaplin, Charlie 51
Charlie's House 109, 110, 216–217
Chasing the Wind 110, 230, 231
Cheal, David 83, 86
Cheeky (Parmant) 126
Chetty, Rajendra 268
Chiavetta, Eleonora 67
Childish Things (Dinge van 'n Kind) 83, 85–86
Children of God Storybook Bible 36, 97
Children of Southern Africa series 223
Children of the Sun: Selected Writers and Themes in South African Children's Literature 2–3
Children's Book Network 19
A Child's Garden 219
Chirchir Is Singing 115, 116
Cilliers, Isabel 22, 91, 93
Cinderella 52, 88–89
Cindy 218
Clacherty, Glynis: *Simon's Story* 33
Clarion 32
Cloete, Elsie 211, 212
Coetzee, Cora 76, 202, 204
Coetzer, Johan L. 87
Coetzer, Katrin 161
collage 9, 22, 24–25, 26, 129, 133, 195, 203, 221
Collected writings from The Open School,

Johannesburg: *Two Dogs and Freedom: Children of the Townships Speak Out* 10
Colors!; Colores! 134
coloured 6, 16, 38, 42, 43–45, 48, 50, 112, 268
Colours 117, 118
comics 35, 52, 65, 102; *see also* cartoon
Commonwealth Literary Prize 259, 271
Congress of South African Students (COSAS) 254
Connor, C.J. 115, 116
Contrast 234
Conway, David: *Lila and the Secret of Rain* 115, 117
Coolidge, Susan: *What Katy Did* 75
Coughlan, Marjorie 134
Cozien, Christine 230
C.P. Hoogenhout Medal 28, 77, 146, 182, 271
"The Crash" 231
Crossing Over 79, 110
Cunnane, Kelly: *Chirchir Is Singing* 115, 116
Curtis-Setchell, Deborah: *Atlantis Rises* 179

Daan Retief Children's Book Club 201
Daar 'n Spook in My Kas (My Cupboard Is Haunted) 182, 185
"Dad Is Eating Ashes" 170
Dada, Fatima: *Horns Only* 170
Dahl, Roald 11, 120, 149
Dali, Salvador 130, 140, 236
Daly, Jude 61, 111, 112–119, 137, 157, 228; *Animals* 117; *Bugs* 117; *Colours* 117, 118; *Fair, Brown & Trembling: An Irish Cinderella Story* 115, 116, 118; *Opposites* 117; *Seb & Hamish* 115; *Sivu's Six Wishes* 115, 116, 117; *Thank You, Jackson* 116; *To Everything There Is a Season* 115, 116, 117, 118
Daly, Niki 5, 10, 31, 32, 47–54, 109, 111, 113, 139–140, 157, 159, 201, 202, 216; *Ashraf of Africa* 156, 157–159; *The Boy on the Beach* 48, 52; *Bravo, Zan Angelo!* 52, 53; *Fly, Eagle, Fly!* 9; *Happy Birthday, Jamela!* 52, 53; *The Herd Boy* 52; *Jamela's Dress* 48, 52, 53; *Mama, Papa and Baby Joe* 51, 52; *My Dad* 49, 52; *Next Stop—Zanzibar Road!* 50, 52, 53, 153; *Not So Fast, Songololo* 6, 48; *Old Bob's Brown Bear* 49, 52; *Once Upon a Time* 49–50, 52; *Papa Lucky's Shadow* 48; *Pretty Salma* 51, 52, 53; *Ruby Sings the Blues* 51, 52; *A Song for Jamela* 48, 52, 53; *What's Cooking, Jamela?* 52; *Where's Jamela?* 48, 52; *Why the Sun and Moon Live in the Sky* 53; *Zanzibar Road* 50, 52, 153
The Dancing Elephant 202
Dancing in the Dust 244–245
D'Angelo, Alex: *Goblin Diaries: Apprenticed to the Red Witch* 98

Dark Poppy's Demise 259, 261, 263
Dark Waters 110, 209
Daughter of the Moonlight and Other African Tales 229
David Philip Publisher 157, 217; *see also* Songololo Books
Deary, Terry: *The Horrible History of the World* 152
death 18, 33, 69, 125, 132–133, 167, 205, 264
de Beaumont, Jeanne-Marie Le Prince: *La Belle et La Bête* 176–177
De Beer, Amanda 88
De Beer, Diane 132
Decandido, Graceanne 116
Deetlefs, Rene 155; *Ask for Patricia* (Vra vir Frederika) 202
de Klerk, F.W. 6, 192
De Kok, Ingrid 173
de la Mare, Walter 17, 199
de Lange, Johann 27
Del Vecchio, Stephen 160
democracy (in South Africa) 1, 12, 42, 157, 190, 192, 208, 230, 247, 267; *see also* freedom
de Montaigne, Michel 64
The Denials of Kow-Ten 111, 211, 212
Detained at Her Majesty's Pleasure, The Journal of Peter David Hadden 12, 13, 14, 16
de Villiers, Leon 120–127; *Aliens en Engele* 124; *Droomoog Diepgrawer* 123; *Ek en My Monster* 97, 121; *Elsie Soek 'n Strooihoed* 121; *Erik en die Kido-Dinges* 121; *Groete van die Hiëna* 124–125; *Die Klein Seuntjie en die Drake* 122; *My Sussie se Tande* 121; *Parmant* (Cheeky) 126; *Shorn* 111, 127; *Tales from the Marula Tree* (Maroelaboomstories) 122; *Wat Doen Jy Daniel?* 120, 125
de Villiers, Trish 235
de Vos, Philip 202; *Carnival of the Animals* 131; *Die Spree met Foete* 131
de Vries, Izak 125; *Special Days* 25
The Diary of Anne Frank 56
Dickinson, Trevor 114
Diedericks-Hugo, Carina 7, 146, 148, 151
Diep, Diep in die Donker Bos 182
digital techniques 52, 203, 222
Dijkstra, Lida: *Little Mouse* 132
Dinge van 'n Kind (Childish Things) 83
The Dinosaurs Are Back 143
Dipale tsa ka Borwa ho Letsatsia (Stories South of the Sun) 77
Disney, Walt 137
District Six 48; *see also* Group Areas Act
Dixon, Franklin W. 102, 108n1; *see also* Hardy Boys
Do the Whales Still Sing? 57, 61, 114, 118
Doctor Me Di Cin 133

Dr. Seuss 146–147
"The Doll" 256
Dolphin Day 141
Don Quixote 236
Don't Panic, Mechanic 109, 208–209
Don't Scratch! 235
Dossier for the Hans Christian Andersen Award 2004 277; *see also* Hans Christian Andersen Awards
The Dove 113, 114, 115, 117, 228
Drakensberg 179; *see also* KwaZulu-Natal
Dreamcatchers (Droomvangers) 183, 187
Driver, Dorothy 244
Droomoog Diepgrawer 123
Droomvangers (Dreamcatchers) 183, 187
drugs 40–42, 44–45, 242
Drum magazine 259
du Plessis, Daniël 149
Durban 39, 227, 228, 231, 232; *see also* KwaZulu-Natal
Durban in a Word 232
Duskant die Doodlyn 150
Dutton 140
dystopia 14, 211; *see also* science fiction

Early Learning Resource Unit (ELRU) 217, 219, 221
Ears Hear 96
Eastern Cape 13, 34, 195, 159, 165, 218, 228; *see also* Transkei
Eccleshare, Julia: *1001 Children's Books You Must Read Before You Grow Up* 18
École Nationale Supérieure des Beaux-Arts 32, 175
ecology/environment 2, 60, 221, 223, 227, 238
Editorial Board of the University Society: *Fun and Thought for Little Folk* 76
education 2, 8, 10, 16–17, 42, 50, 66, 70, 72n1, 94, 102, 108, 135, 156, 174, 185, 196, 199, 217–218, 244, 245, 251
Die Een Groot Bruin Beer (The One Big Brown Bear) 92
Eendag die Blou Voël (Someday the Blue Bird) 23
Eenkantkind (Aside Child) 9, 83
Die Eerste Keer (The First Time) 21
Eggs to Lay, Chickens to Hatch 101, 106
Einstein, Albert 155
Eiselen, Uca 73, 185, 187, 188
Ek en My Monster 97, 121
Ek Is Simon (I Am Simon) 182, 188
The Elephant's Pillow 115
Eliopoulos, Vangelis: *The Three Teapots* 96
Elsabe Steenberg Award 152, 272
Elsie Soek 'n Strooihoed 121
embroidery 220, 222

Ende, Michael 120
English Alive 250
Entertaining Angels (Griet Skryf 'n Sprokie) 82
Erik en die Kido-Dinges 121
Esmonde-White, Eleanor 199
Essop, Ahmed 231
etching 176, 180
Eugene Marais prize 82
Eventyr 66
Everall, Annie and Viviana Quiñones 68, 159
Every Precious Drop 25
The Exclusive Book IBBY SA Award 80, 179, 272
Exhibition of Original Pictures of International Children's Books 201
Eye of the Moon 57, 58, 59, 60, 61
Eye of the Sun 57, 60

F., E. 158
"The Face of a Killer" 59, 60
Fair, Brown & Trembling: An Irish Cinderella Story 115, 116, 118
Fairer-Wessels, Felicité A. 22, 26, 28, 95, 98, 129, 130
The Far Away Valley 201
The Faraway Island 57, 59, 61, 115, 118
Father Christmas Needs Help (Kersvader het hulp nodig) 93
Fearnly, Jan 152
feminism 82, 84, 169, 243, 246–248, 257; *see also* Bildungsroman
FIFA World Cup 2010 110, 161
Finding Dad 18
fine art 32, 36, 200
A Fine Day for Flying 237
Fine Music Radio 18
Finney, Bess 200
First, Ruth 104
The First Time (Die Eerste Keer) 21
Fish Notes and Star Songs 56, 57, 58–59, 60, 61–62
Fly, Eagle, Fly! 9, 202, 242
folk art 116, 129, 238
folktales 2, 24, 53, 61, 67–68, 73–75, 77–79, 80, 111, 113, 130, 140, 166, 168, 170, 176, 179, 202, 229–230, 238; *see also* Aesop's Fables; Grimm
Folktales from Africa 229
Foote, Robert 141
Fort Hare University 34
Forte, Maria 134
Fouche, Lani 146
Fourie, Corlia: *Die Meisie Wat Soos 'n Bottervoël Sing* (Tintinyane, the Girl Who Sang Like a Magic Bird) 24, 25; *Die Wit Flinder* (The White Butterfly) 24, 28

Fourie, Elkarien 126
Frank, Anne: *The Diary of Anne Frank* 56
Frankenstein 261
Freedom 1, 10, 161, 220, 243, 249, 263; *see also* democracy
Freedom Charter 105
Freedom Fighters 102, 104–105
Freedom Song 254–255, 257
Freeman, Evelyn B. 63, 116, 117
From Island to Bishopscourt 67
From the Heart of the Fire (Uit die Hart van die Vuur) 77
Fryer, Charles: *Steweltjies na Wonderland* (Little Boots to Wonderland) 26, 28
Fugard, Athol 61
Fun and Thought for Little Folk: Home University Series 76
Fuse 259, 260, 262
Fussy Freya 134
Fynbos Fairies (Fynbosfeetjies) 177, 179
Fynbosfeetjies (Fynbos Fairies) 177, 179

Garamond 227
Geldenhuys, Paula: *Schaukelpferd* 176
Gente, Gibson 167
George Washington University 250
Gericke, Lona 68, 128, 187
Gerwel, Jakes: *Crossing Over* 79, 110; *In the Rapids: Stories for a New South Africa* 79
"Gewilde kinderboeke word bekroon" 152
"Ghost" 257
Gibbs, Celia 158
Gibson, Robin L. 132
The Gift of Song 250
The Gift of the Sun: A Tall Tale from South Africa 114, 115, 116, 117, 228
Giorgis, Cyndi 116
The Girl and the Golden Amulet 238–239
Glistrop, Eva 204
The Goblet Club 259, 260, 261–262
Goblet of Fire 259–260
Goblin Diaries: Apprenticed to the Red Witch 98
Goldblatt, Sidney 200
Good Night, Grandpa 92
Goodreads 121
Gordimer, Nadine 231
Goue Fluit My Storie Is Uit (This Golden Flute Concludes My Story) 26, 28, 77
Goue Lint My Storie Begint (This Golden Ribbon Unties My Story) 26, 28, 76–77
Gough, Philip 32
Gouws, Tom 85
Grandfather Remembers 13
Grandpa Makes a Toy 24
Granqvist, Raoul 158
graphic design 21, 113, 191, 199

Grauerholz, Elizabeth 84
The Great Big Fish 236–237
Great Zimbabwe 59
Green Tongue 223
Greenwillow Books 113, 228
Gregorowski, Christopher 202; *All Everest's Birds* 22; *Fly, Eagle, Fly!* 9, 202, 242
Greyling, Cecile 27
Greyling, Franci 120
Griet Skryf 'n Sprokie (Entertaining Angels) 82
Griffin, Rachel 170
Grille en Goeters series 148
Grimm 73, 75, 82, 132; *see also* folktales
Grobbelaar, Pieter W.: *Die Aarde Moet Vry Wees* 28; *Here We Are All Back Again* 192
Grobler, Diek 235, 237
Grobler, Mari: *Lulama's Magic Blanket* 195; *Musa's Journey* 195; *Siyolo's Jersey* 195; *Thandiwe's Choice* 191, 195
Grobler, Petrus 184, 186
Grobler, Piet 5, 51, 88, 111, 128–136, 235, 236; *Little Bird's ABC* 128; *Makwelane and the Crocodile* 129; *Please Frog, Just One Sip* 130; *The Rainbow Birds* 128; *Rooi-Kiri Wordt Verliefd* 131
Groete van die Hiëna 124–125
Grogan, Tony 204
'n Grot vir 'n Grootman (Barney Climbs a Mountain) 156
Group Areas Act 6, 39, 41, 42, 48, 65; *see also* District Six
Die Gruwelike Geskiedenis van die Wêreld (The Horrible History of the World) 152
Gugulethu 47, 66, 69; *see also* Cape Flats
The Guinea-Fowl's Spots and Other African Bird Tales 229–230
Gunne, Sorcha 248

Haasmoles 147
Haddock 178–179
Hamilton, Tessa 76
hand-lettering 27, 130
Hannavy, Sybil 115, 117
Hans Christian Andersen Awards 5, 19, 48, 53, 135, 204, 272
Happy Birthday, Jamela! 52, 53
The Happy Prince 203, 205–206
"Happy Xmas!" 257
Hardy Boys 11, 102, 107, 108n1; *see also* Dixon, Franklin W.
Harlekyn 149
Harlow, Barbara 68
Harper, Susanne 151
Harries, Ann: *The Sound of the Gora* 6
Harries, Katrine 32, 199, 202
Harry Potter 88, 261
Hart, Yvonne: *Katy of Sky Road* 38, 43–45

INDEX

Hartmann, Wendy 137–144; *All the Magic in the World* 137, 140, 143; *The Black Dog* 141; *The Dinosaurs Are Back* 143; *Dolphin Day* 141; *In a House, in a House* 143; *Just Sisi* 137, 142, 143, 204; *The Key and the Casket* 141; "Ma Rosie's Pig" 143; *Marshmallows, Monsters and Mice* 139; *Nina and Little Duck* 98, 137, 139, 142; *One Sun Rises* 143; *The Short Cut* 141; *The Sun, the Moon and the Blanket of Night* 140; *Theo and the Cat Burglar* 141, 203; *Theo and the Circus Act* 141; *Theo the Library Cat* 140; *Voices in the Dark* 141; *We're Having a Party!* 138
Harvey, Jo 235
Hattingh, Marna 235, 237, 238
HAUM-Daan Retief 201
Have You Seen My Donkey? 237
Have You Seen Zandile? 167
Head, Bessie 169, 242, 253
Heale, Jay 3, 5, 48, 68, 80, 97, 161, 164; *Adamastor* 5, 192, 193, 196; *South African Authors & Illustrators* 200; *Storyland* 202; *Storytime* 25; see also Bookchat
Hedgehog Books 202
Heese, Hester: *Steweltjies na Wonderland* (Little Boots to Wonderland) 26, 28
Helgesson, Stefan 237
Henderson, Laretta 5
The Herd Boy 52, 53–54
Here I Am 111, 130, 236
Here We Are All Back Again 192
Herfsblaar Gooi 'n Kaapse Draai: Hester Heese, Skrywer en Mens (Autumn Leaves in the Cape: Hester Heese, Author and Person) 26
Hergé 152
Hic...Hic...Hiccups! 202
The Hidden Life of Hanna Why 83, 86–87, 88–90
Highlights Foundation 94
Hinrichsen, Natalie 70, 235, 236–237, 239
Hinrichsen, Tamsin 235, 238–239
history (of South Africa) 2, 5, 59–60, 104–105, 155, 190, 267
Hitchcock, Audrey 202
HIV/AIDS 15, 19n1, 34, 41, 55, 60, 213–214, 252
HIVSA: "HIV AIDS in South Africa" 19
Hodson, Christopher: *Lizo's Song* 194, 195
Hoffnung, Gerard 199
Hofmeyr, Dianne 5, 10, 55–63, 115, 118, 202; *Blue Train to the Moon* 57, 60; *Boikie, You Better Believe It* 58, 59, 60, 61; *Do the Whales Still Sing?* 57, 61, 114, 118; *Eye of the Moon* 57, 58, 59, 60, 61; *Eye of the Sun* 57, 60; "The Face of a Killer" 59, 60; *The Faraway Island* 57, 59, 61, 115, 118; *Fish Notes and Star Songs* 56, 57, 58–59, 60, 61–62; *Hic...Hic...Hiccups!* 202; *The Magic Bojabi Tree* (in South Africa: *The Name of the Tree Is Bojabi*) 59, 61, 130–131; "The Magic Man" 59, 60, 62; *Oliver Strange and the Journey to the Swamps* 61, 62; *A Red Kite in a Pale Sky* 9, 60, 61, 62; *The Star-Bearer: A Creation Myth from Ancient Egypt* 59, 61, 115, 116; *The Stone: A Persian Legend of the Magi* 61, 114, 115, 118; *A Sudden Summer* 60; *The Waterbearer* 58–60, 61–62; *When Whales Go Free* 58, 59, 61, 62; "Where the Dark Ocean Rolls" 59, 61
Hofmeyr, Leon: *Horns Only* 170
Home Now 15, 19
homelessness 6, 11, 15, 18, 41, 236; see also poverty; street children
Horns Only 170
The Horrible History of the World 152
Hough, Barrie 7, 125, 188
How High Can a Grasshopper Jump? 151
How Many Teeth Does a Crocodile Have? 151
How Wide Can a Hippo Open His Mouth? 151
Howes, Sally 32–33, 34, 36
Huang, Chu-Ren 96
Hughes, Shirley 160
Huisgenoot 259
Human, Charlie: *Apocalypse Now* 260
Human & Rousseau 142, 156, 160, 203, 205, 259; see also NB Publishers
humor (in art) 27, 129, 177, 203, 234
humor (in writing) 18, 50, 85, 97, 102, 107, 121–123, 146–148, 153, 170, 234
"The Hungry Jackal" 229
The Hungry Mind Review 114
Hutchins, Pat: *Rosie's Walk* 142, 205
Hy Bly My Broer 83

I, a Living Arrow: Young South African Writing 2 78
I Am Simon (Ek Is Simon) 182, 188
I Don't Belong to You 237
I Know Why the Caged Bird Sings 67
I Saw Esau 204
IBBY-Asahi Reading Promotion Award 5, 202
IBBY Honour List 11, 79, 114, 146, 150, 152, 205, 228, 242, 244, 259, 268, 272
IBBY SA 6
IBBY World Congress (Cape Town 2004) 135, 164, 226, 267
Imani's Music 115, 117, 118
In a House, in a House 143
"In a Name" 257
"In Detention" 267

In die Nimmer-Immer Bos (In the Never-Ever Wood) 73, 79–80, 170, 173, 180
In die Tyd van die Esob (In the Reign of the Ilev) 111, 182
In the Fast Lane 251–252
In the Never-Ever Wood (In Die Nimmer-Immer Bos) 73, 79–80, 170, 173, 180
In the Rapids: Stories for a New South Africa 79
In the Reign of the Ilev (In die Tyd van die Esob) 111, 182, 187, 188
Inggs, Judith 214n2, 248
The Ink Bird (Die Inkvoël) 6
Die Inkvoël (The Ink Bird) 6
Inside the Books: Readers and Libraries Around the World 115
International Board on Books for Young People (IBBY) 3, 5, 11, 31, 51, 68, 135, 159, 164, 230
The International Center for the Study of Children's Literature in France 131
International Exhibition in Sarmede 201
International Federation of Library Associations (IFLA) 68, 159
International Reading Association (IRA) 49, 143
International Society of Children's Book Writers and Illustrators 96
International Youth Library 34, 143, 228
Irma Stern Museum 173
It Is Time to Go Home 101
It's a Book Thing: 260, 261, 264–265

Jacana Media 205
Jackal and Wolf 74
"Jaco Jacobs ryg pryse in vir eie en vertaalwerk" 153
Jacobs, Ihette 120, 125, 126, 127
Jacobs, Jaco 145–154, 183, 187; *Bertie Blikbrein* 147; *Bertus Soek 'n Boek* (Bertus Looking for a Book) 98; *Borrels* 150; *Duskant die Doodlyn* 150; *Die Gruwelike Geskiedenis van die Wêreld* (The Horrible History of the World) 152; *Haasmoles* 147; *Harlekyn* 149; *How High Can a Grasshopper Jump?* 151; *How Many Teeth Does a Crocodile Have?* 151; *How Wide Can a Hippo Open His Mouth?* 151; *Kas Vol Monsters* 148–149; *Krieketpret/Gevaarlike Lopies* 150; *Liewe Land, 'n Oliphant* 147; *Madelief, Moenie!* 149; *Middernagfees* 149; *Moenie vir Bernard Soen Nie* (No More Kisses for Bernard) 153; *My Boetie Dink Hy's Batman en Ander Rympies* 146; *Net Aliens Eet Spinasie* 149; *Pretpark* 148; *Professor Fungus en die Zombie-Tamaties* 148; *Rugbypret* 150; *Slaaptyd, Matilda* 149; *Suurlemoen* 150; *Suzie se Superdoeper-Sjampoe* 147; *Toulopers—Verse vir Tieners* 151; *Troeteldrog* 148; *Verneukpan* 151; *Willemien en die Geel Kat* (Ottoline and the Yellow Cat) 152; *Wiskunde Gee My Maagpyn* 150; *Wurms met Tamatiesous en Ander Lawwe Rympies* 146; *Zackie Mostert en die Ongelooflike Kulkunsie* 148; *Zackie Mostert en die Super-Aaklige Soen* 148; *Zanzibarstraat, Hier Kom Ons!* (Next Stop—Zanzibar Road) 153; *Zanzstraat* (Zanzibar Road) 153; *see also* Brink, Tania; Roux, Lize
Jacobs, Marié 125
Jakey 12, 14, 15, 16, 19
The Jam Tin and the Teacup 220
Jamela's Dress 48, 52, 53
Jedro's Bane 1
Jekkers, Harrie: *Ballade van de Dood* (in South Africa: *The Circle of Life*) 132–133
Jenkins, Elwyn 1–4, 5, 158; *Children of the Sun: Selected Writers and Themes in South African Children's Literature* 2–3, 5; *Seedlings: English Children's Reading and Writers in South Africa* 3, 226, 229
Jenny Seed 2
Jesperson, Amand: *The Little Lost Goat* 25
Jessica's First Prayer 75
Joao, Zunica 150
Johannesburg 10, 41, 102, 106, 165, 167, 168, 184, 185, 199, 216, 218, 220, 250, 251
Johannesburg Civic Theatre 200
Johannesburg Technikon 199
Johennesse, Fhazel: *Wietie* 103
Johnny Later and His Hammer 191–192
Johnson, David 103
Johnson, Nancy J. 116
Jones, Nikki 235, 238
Jong, Erica 82
Die Jongspan 156
Jonker, Ingrid 27
Jordan, A.C. 67
Journey to Jo'burg 6, 270
Just Sisi 137, 142, 143, 204–205
Juta 234
Juta Gariep 234
Jy en die Draakakkedis (You and the Dinosaur) 183
Jy en Toetenkat 182

Kagiso 234; *see also* Maskew Miller Longman; "Zebra Books" series
Kariena Karyn (Katie Colly Wobbles) 23, 28
Karoo 2, 13, 15, 145
Kas Vol Monsters 148–149
Kaschula, Russel H. 166
Kate Greenaway Medal 32, 272
Katie Colly Wobbles (Kariena Karyn) 23, 28

Katrine Harries Award 28, 95, 114, 202, 228, 272
Katy of Sky Road 38
Kent, Graeme: *Aesop's Fables* 76
Kero and Beevy, Their Life in Great Zimbabwe, Zimbabwe 224
Kersvader het Hulp Nodig (Father Christmas Needs Help) 93
The Key and the Casket 141
Khoisan 1, 24, 60; *see also* San
Khorana, Meena 47, 194
Kidd, Warren 84
Kiefer, Barbara Z. 116, 194
Kimberley, Agnes: *Neo and Baby Ben* 195
Kinderkeur 3
King, Stephen 89
The King's Equal 96
Kinsler, Jeannie: *Queen of the Imbira* 171
Kirkus Review 115, 116, 117, 130
Kirkwood, Mike 103
Klee, Paul 131
Die Klein Seuntjie en die Drake 122
Kleinhans, Tertia 140
Kleyn, A.J.T. (Leti) 183; *Die Afrikaanse Skryfgids* 96, 150
Knock! Knock! 218
Kootjie Totjie 97, 98
Kotane, Moses 105
Kotzé, Suzette 184
Krieketpret/Gevaarlike Lopies 150
Krog, Antjie 71, 111; *Fynbos Fairies* (Fynbosfeetjies) 177, 179; *Sam, 'n Ware Verhaal van 'n Dogtertjie en Haar Olifant* (Sam, a True Story of a Little Girl and Her Elephant) 97
Krogh, Theunis 151
Krone, Bridget: *Tido's Bag* 33
Krug, Connie 234
Kruger, J.A.: *Kinderkeur* 3
Kühne, Klaus 202; *The Snuff Tin Bakkie* 192–193; *Thandi's Birthday Lion* 194–195
Kumagai, Clara 131
Kumar, Lisa 114
Kwagga 45
KwaZulu-Natal (previously Natal) 13, 14, 15, 60, 115, 165, 166, 179, 228; *see also* Drakensberg; Durban
Kwela, Engen and NNTV Writing Competition 210

Lady Was a Mshoza 250
Lagerlof, Selma: *The Wonderful Adventures of Nils* 174
Lakshaman, M.S. 63
Langenhoven, C.J. 76; *Kootjie Totjie* 97, 98
Lapa Publishers 148
Lategan, Aldré 142, 203
Leaf, Munro: *Ferdinand the Bull* 91–92

Learning Our Way 222
Lebohang and Polo, Their Life in Ha Lesala, Lesotho 224
Lehman, Barbara A. 52, 63, 116, 117, 129
Lemniscaat 130, 131
Le Roux, Marina 24, 25, 26, 83, 133, 187
Lesotho 105, 224, 228, 256
Lester, Julius 75
Let There Be Peace: Prayers from Around the World 115, 117
Leuvennink, Jacqueline 84
Lewis, Irene: *Grandpa Makes a Toy* 24
Liefde Laat Jou Rice Krispies Anders Proe 150
Liewe Land, 'n Oliphant 147
Life Is a Hard But Beautiful Thing 69
Lila and the Secret of Rain 115, 117
Limpopo Province 99n1
Linde, Freda 9
Lindeka and Vuyane, Their Life in Malkerns, Swaziland 224
Lindgren, Astrid: *Pippi Longstocking* 174
Lisa het 'n plan 182
Listen, Lefa (Luister, Lefa) 21
lithography 32
Little Bird's ABC 128
Little Boots to Wonderland (Steweltjies na Wonderland) 26, 28
The Little Cat & the Greedy Old Woman 201
Little House on the Prairie 75
Little Karoo 50, 74, 75
The Little Library 202
Little Lord Fauntleroy 65
The Little Lost Goat 25
Little Mouse 132
Little Red Riding Hood 24, 51, 53, 129
The Little Wise One, African Tales of the Hare 202
Little Women 56
Lizeka's Choice (ULizeka Wazikhethela) 70
Lizo's Song 194, 195
Lloyd, Glynis 254
Lloyd, Lucy 77, 229, 232n1
Lodge, Katherine 152
Logan, Cheryl 243, 249n1
Lohann, Carl 2; *Herfsblaar Gooi 'n Kaapse Draai: Hester Heese, Skrywer en Mens* (Autumn Leaves in the Cape: Hester Heese, Author and Person) 26
Long Juju Man 98
Loots, Sonja 120
Lorna Doone 56
Lotz, Sarah 260
Loubser, Henriëtte 85
Louw, Wynand: *Mr Humperdinck's Wonderful Whatsit* (Mnr. Humperdinck Se Wonderlike Watsenaam) 98
Love Child 164–167, 169

Love, David 9, 38, 40–42, 45
"Love Songs for Nheti" 255
"Love Story" 257
Lowery, Ruth McKoy 5
Luister, Lefa (Listen, Lefa) 21
Luján, Jorge: *Colors!;Colores!* 134; *Sky Blue Accident* 133–134
Lulama's Long Way Home 98
Lulama's Magic Blanket 195
Lusted, Ian 141, 227
Luthuli, Albert 104
Lying Toad 238

"Ma Rosie's Pig" 143
Maar My Magtig, Moesak! 188
Maartens, Maretha 7, 9; *The Ink Bird* (Die Inkvoël) 6; *Midnight Cat* 195–196
Maartens, Wendy: *Princess Sparrow* 23; *Three Cheers for Tyron* 23
Macdonald, Iain: *The Dancing Elephant* 202
Mackintosh, Richard 230
MacLiam, Geralt 166
Macmillan 34, 105
Macmillan Writer's Prize for Africa 98, 272
MacRobert, Marguerite 12
Madagascar 59
Madelief, Moenie! 149
Madiba Magic 78, 169
The Magic Bojabi Tree (in South Africa: *The Name of the Tree Is Bojabi*) 59, 61, 130–131
"The Magic Man" 59, 60, 62
Magome, Mogomotsi 165
Magona, Sindiwe 10, 19, 64–72, 68; *Amalungiselelo* 70; *Beauty's Gift* 67; *The Best Meal Ever* 33, 35, 68–69; *Betty's Braids* 70; *From Island to Bishopscourt* 67; *Life Is a Hard But Beautiful Thing* 69; *Mother to Mother* 67; *Nkanishe, the Stubborn Ogre* 70; *Paragon the Perfect Piglet* 70; *To My Children's Children* 65; *The Ugly Duckling* 70; *ULizeka Wazikhethela* (Lizeka's Choice) 70
Mahlangu, Lindi: *Scary Footsteps* 202
Mail & Guardian 259
Makwelane and the Crocodile 129
Malawi 14
Mama, Papa and Baby Joe 51, 52
Mandela, Nelson 6–7, 19, 32, 36, 45, 54, 78, 104, 105–106, 178, 181n8, 192, 220, 267, 270
The Mantis and the Moon 108n2
Maritz, Nicolaas 143, 157
Mark Jan: *Haddock* 178–179
Maroelaboomstories (Tales from the Marula Tree) 122
Marshmallows, Monsters and Mice 139
Maseka, Lungi: *Scary Footsteps* 202

Maskew Miller Longman 17, 23, 36, 71, 231, 254; *see also* Kagiso; "Stars of Africa" series; "Zebra Books" series
Maskew Miller Longman Literature Awards 151, 272
Mastori, Voula: *The Moon Story* 96
Mauro and Adelaide, Their Life in Quelimane, Mozambique 224
McCloud, Scott 191
McDowell, Kate 116
McElderry, Margaret K. 201
McFarlane, Leslie 108n1
McGill, Alice: *Way Up and Over Everything* 115, 117
McKee, David 176
Mda, Jakes 168, 250
The Mealie-Cob Children 228
Mears, Sarah 116
Meddlemore, Mary (Martie Preller): *In the Reign of the Ilev* (In die Tyd van die Esob) 183, 187
Meinderts, Koos: *Ballade van de Dood* (in South Africa: *The Circle of Life*) 132–133
Meiring, Andrelise 121
Die Meisie Wat Soos 'n Bottervoël Sing (Tintinyane, the Girl Who Sang Like a Magic Bird) 24, 25
Mejj, Mart 185
Mellow Yellow 110, 208
The Mending Season 245–246, 248
Mennen, Ingrid 110, 155–163; *Ashraf of Africa* (in United States: *Somewhere in Africa*) 110, 156, 157–159; *Ben and the Whales: The Extraordinary Journey* (Ben en die Walvisse: 'n Wonderlike Reis) 162–163; *'n Grot vir 'n Grootman* (Barney Climbs a Mountain) 156; *One Round Moon and a Star for Me* 159–160; *A Wish This Big* (Soos 'n Wens So Groot) 110, 160–161
M.E.R. Prize for children's books 28, 34, 77, 80, 83, 98, 125, 163, 173, 182, 205, 242, 259, 272–273
Merino 13, 15
A Mermaid's Tale 177
The Message 18
A Message in the Wind 6, 106
Meyer, Naomi 155, 162
Mhlanguli 218
Mhlophe, Gcina 5, 19, 69, 110, 164–172, 241, 268–269; *African Tales: A Barefoot Collection* 170; *Betty's Braids* 70; "Dad Is Eating Ashes" 170; *Have You Seen Zandile?* 167; *Horns Only* 170; *Love Child* 164–167, 169; *Molo Zoleka!* (Hi Zoleka!) 170, 193, 195; *Our Story Magic* 170; *Queen of the Imbira* 171; *Queen of the Tortoises* 170–171; *The*

Singing Chameleon 170; *The Snake with Seven Heads* 168; *Stories of Africa* 170
Mia's Mom 83, 84–85, 88, 129
Michaelis School of Fine Art 32, 175, 199
Middernagfees 149
Midgley, Peter 78, 110
Midnight Cat 195–196
Mike Jacklin/Knowledge Unlimited 201
Miles, John: *Stanley Bekker and the Boycott (Stanley Bekker en die Boikot)* 6
Milne, A.A.: *Winnie the Pooh* 174
Milton, Sue 234
"Mr Hare Meets Mr Mandela" 36, 107
Mr Humperdinck's Wonderful Whatsit (Mnr. Humperdinck Se Wonderlike Watsenaam) 98
mixed media 22, 23, 27, 129
Mmpundulu, the Lightning Bird 223
M-Net Prize/M-Net Literary Awards 18, 273
Mnr. Humperdinck Se Wonderlike Watsenaam (Mr Humperdinck's Wonderful Whatsit) 98
Moenie vir Bernard Soen Nie (No More Kisses for Bernard by Niki Daly) 153
Mofutsanyana, Thabo 105
Moll, Eugene 234
Molo Fish II 250
Molo Songololo magazine 230
Molo Zoleka! 170, 193, 195
Molope, Kagiso Lesego 241, 243–249, 268; *This Book Betrays My Brother* 246; *Dancing in the Dust* 244–245; *The Mending Season* 245–246, 248
Mompati, Ruth 105
Monde's Present 95
Mondi, the Music Maker 227
'n Monster in die Tuin (A Monster in the Garden) 93–94
A Monster in the Garden ('n Monster in die Tuin) 93–94
Monsters, Heroes and Sultan's Daughters: Cape Malay Folk Tales 25
Montgomery, Lucy Maud: *Anne of Green Gables* 56, 65
Moodie, Fiona 5, 80, 111, 173–181; *La Belle et la Bête* 176–177, 180; *The Boy and the Giants* 178; *A Mermaid's Tale* 177; *Nabulela* 111, 179; *Noko and the Night Monster* 179–180; *Noko's Surprise Party* 179–180; *The Sugar Prince* 178; *The Unicorn and the Sea* 177–178
The Moon Story 96
Die Mooiste Sprokies van Grimm 82, 132
Moore, Heather: *Horns Only* 170
Morris, David 263
Morris, Tertia: *No Thank You!* 24
Morton, Kim 69

Moshoeshoe, Chief 105
Mother to Mother 67
The Mouseboat 34
A Mozambican Summer 252–253
Mozambique 224, 252
Mphahlele, Es'kia 202
Msimang, Nokuthula K. (maiden name Nokuthula Mazibuko) 241, 250–258; "The Doll" 256; *Freedom Song* 254–255, 257; "Ghost" 257; "Happy Xmas!" 257; "In a Name" 257; *In the Fast Lane* 251–252; "Love Songs for Nheti" 255; "Love Story" 257; *A Mozambican Summer* 252–253; "Nkgono" 257; *South African Plays for TV, Radio and Stage* 251; *Spring Offensive* 253–255, 257
Mtshali, Oswald: *Sounds of a Cowhide Drum* 103
Muafangelo, John 239
Munitich, Brenda 202
Musa's Journey 195
music 13, 24, 43, 47, 51–52, 85, 150, 164, 166, 170, 195, 229
Mutloatse, Mothobi 103
My Boetie Dink Hy's Batman en Ander Rympies 146
My Cupboard Is Haunted (Daar's 'n Spook in My Kas) 182, 185
My Dad 49, 52
My Hart Is Vol Graffiti 150
My Home in Walmer Road 222
My Story, Our Stories 19
Myrtle and Daneco, Their Life in Kassiesbaai, South Africa 224

Nabulela 111, 179
Naidoo, Beverley 7, 109, 267–27; *Aesop's Fables* 130; *Journey to Jo'burg* 6, 270; *The Other Side of Truth* 270
Nal'ibali 36, 269
Namibia 13, 14, 15–16, 182, 228
Nasou Via Afrika 25, 68, 95
National Curriculum Statement 185
National Education and Development Unit (NEEDU) 269
National English Literary Museum (NELM) 233
National Library of South Africa: *Amandla ebali: The Power of the Story* 31
National Party 9, 65, 107–108
Naudé, Beyers 108n2
NB Publishers 77, 207; *see also* Human & Rousseau; Tafelberg
Ndebele, Njabulo 169, 171, 231
Ndungane, Njongonkule 67
Nelson Mandela: Long Walk to Freedom 32, 34, 35, 36, 105
Neo and Baby Ben 195

Index

Net Aliens Eet Spinasie 149
Neu-Ner, Michael 102
Nevin, Thomas A.: *The Zebra and the Baboon* (Sebra en die Bobbejaan)
A New Bed for Alexia ('n Nuwe Bed vir Alexia) 93
New Contrast magazine 231
Newman, David M. 84
Newman, John Henry 78
Next Stop—Zanzibar Road! 50, 52, 53
NGOs 3, 7, 18, 35
Nieman, M.M. 84, 85, 86
Nieuwoudt, Stephanie 131, 146
Night, Night, Sleep Tight 160
Nikita 28
Nikolajeva, Maria 261
Nina and Little Duck 98, 137, 139, 142
92 Queens Road 38, 42–43
Nkanishe, the Stubborn Ogre 70
"Nkgono" 257
No More Kisses for Bernard (Moenie vir Bernard Soen Nie) 153
No Thank You! 24
Nobody's Cat 26
Nobody's Doll 221
"Nog 'n wenner vir Tafelberg" 28
Noko and the Night Monster 179–180
Noko's Surprise Party 179–180
Noma Award for Publishing in Africa 2
Noma Concours for Picture Book Illustrations 28, 130, 273
Norval, Roline 26
Not So Fast, Songololo 6, 48
Ntataise Trust 94
Numbers Do 96
Nurturing Orphans of Aids for Humanity (NOAH) 232
Nuttall, Sarah 66
'n Nuwe Bed vir Alexia (A New Bed for Alexia) 93

Oboe, Aanaklisa 164, 169
Odendaal, Gerda 150
Oelke, Julius 77
Oelofsen, Vian 34
Ogliani, Gianfranco 177
Ohio State University 243, 249n1
oil pastels 22, 23, 26, 55, 201, 203
Okorafor, Nedei: *Long Juju Man* 98
Old Bob's Brown Bear 49, 52
Old Enough (Oud Genoeg) 93
Olinosters op die Dak (Rhinocephants on the Roof) 83, 129
Oliphant, Andries 103
Olive Schreiner Prize 101
Oliver Strange and the Journey to the Swamps 61, 62

Once Upon a Time 49–50, 52
Onderwater 182
The One Big Brown Bear (Die Een Groot Bruin Beer) 92
One Hundred Great Lives 103
One Magic Moment 210
One More Time 32, 37
One Round Moon and a Star for Me 159–160
One Sun Rises 143
1001 Children's Books You Must Read Before You Grow Up 18
Oom Japie en die Monsterplant (Uncle James and the Delicious Monster) 97
Die Oorspronklike, Ongewoon Skrikaanjaende, Werklik Feitlike Storieboek (The Authentic, Unusually Alarming, Actual Factual Story Book) 97
Oosthuizen, Janie 151
Open School in Soweto 10
Opie, Iona: *I Saw Esau* 204
Opie, Peter: *I Saw Esau* 204
Opposites 117
"The Orange Tree" 227
Orchard Books 160
The Other Side of Truth 270
Ottoline and the Yellow Cat (Willemien en die Geel Kat) 152
Oud Genoeg (Old Enough) 93
Ouens Is Nie Pizzas Nie 150
Ouma Ruby's Secret 106–107
Our Story Magic 170
"Out of Africa" 236
Oxenbury, Helen 32
Oxford University Press SA 68, 69

page design 7, 33, 203
Papa Lucky's Shadow 48
Paragon the Perfect Piglet 70
Parker, Elize 93
Parliament of the Republic of South Africa 19
Parmant (Cheeky) 126
Parravano, Martha V. 115, 116, 117
Partridge, Sally (S.A.) 242, 259–265; *Dark Poppy's Demise* 259, 261, 263; *Fuse* 259, 260, 262; *The Goblet Club* 259, 260, 261–262; *Sharp Edges* 261, 264–265; "Take Me Home United Road" 259
Paterson, Katherine: *The King's Equal* 96
Paul, Korky: *Winnie the Witch* 141
Paul, Nick: *Uncle James and the Delicious Monster* (Oom Japie en die Monsterplant) 97
Peace on Earth (Vrede op Aarde) 28
pen and ink 21, 26, 33, 48, 97, 221
Peppy 'n Them 106
Percy FitzPatrick Awards 18, 42, 77, 259, 273
Perrault, Charles 79

Peter Pan Prize 135
Peter's Dulcie Duck 204
Petroleum and the Orphaned Ostrich 106
Philip, David 10
photography 218, 221, 222–223
physical handicaps 17–18, 22, 102, 209, 219; *see also* albinism
Picasso, Pablo 51
Pienaar, Andries Albertus (Sangiro) 76
Pienaar, Kathy 227
Pippi Longstocking 174
Piumini, Roberto: *Doctor Me Di Cin* 133
Please Frog, Just One Sip 130
The Poetics of Space 56
poetry 27, 57, 71, 76, 78, 103, 107, 138–139, 146–147, 151, 164–168, 255–256, 267
Poland, Marguerite 2, 7, 202; *The Mantis and the Moon* 108n2
Pople, Leatitia 132, 135
Posel, Deborah 38
Potchefstroom University for Christian Higher Education (now part of North-West University) 191
Potter, Beatrix 32, 112, 139, 173
poverty 2, 10, 11, 15, 33–34, 41, 42, 60, 64, 69, 102, 209; *see also* homelessness; street children
Praise Song 208, 212, 213–214
Preller, Martie 182–189; *Anderkantland* 182, 185; *Babalela* 182, 187; *Balkie and the Pirates of the Sea* 182, 185; *Balkie and the Sun's Resting Place* 182, 185; *Balkie and the Vicious Virus* 182, 185; *Die Balkie-boek* (The Balkie Book)182, 185, 187; *Daar's 'n Spook in My Kas* (My Cupboard Is Haunted) 182, 185; *Diep, Diep in die Donker Bos* 182; *Droomvangers* (Dreamcatchers) 183, 187; *Ek Is Simon* (I Am Simon) 182, 188; *In die Tyd van die Esob* (In the Reign of the Ilev) 111, 182, 187, 188; *Jy en die Draakakkedis* (You and the Dinosaur) 183; *Jy en Toetenkat* 182; *Lisa het 'n Plan* 182; *Maar My Magtig, Moesak!* 188; *Onderwater* 182; *see also* Meddlemore, Mary
Premi Catalonia d'il.lustració 201
Preparations (Amalungiselelo) 70
Pretoria (Tshwane) 21, 120, 234, 254
Pretpark 148
Pretty Salma 51, 52, 53
Priddy Bicknell 152
Pride and Prejudice 227
Primo Alpi Apuane Award 135
Princess Sparrow 23
Prins, Alzette 126, 138
Prix Octogones de Chêne 131
Professor Fossilus and the Dinosaurs (Professor Fossilus en die Dinosourusse) 97

Professor Fossilus en die Dinosourusse (Professor Fossilus and the Dinosaurs) 97
Professor Fungus en die Zombie-Tamaties 148
Project for the Study of Alternative Education (PRAESA) 269
Propp, Vladimir, A. 87
Publishers Weekly 114, 115, 116, 117, 118, 158
Pulitzer Prize for General Non-Fiction 226
Pulles, Elizabeth 111, 186, 190–198
Punch magazine 199
puppets 200

Quarmby, Katherine: *Fussy Freya* 134
Queen of the Imbira 171
Queen of the Tortoises 170–171
Quevauvilliers, Sebastien 150
Quiñones, Viviana 68, 159
Quintero, Elizabeth P. 76

Rabinowitz, Daniel 179
The Racial Element in Afrikaans Children's and Youth Literature 5
racism 2, 6, 42, 60, 64, 110, 166, 192, 209, 245, 257
Rainbow 12
The Rainbow Birds 128
Rainbow Reading series 221; *see also* Cambridge University Press SA
Ramsbottom, Margaret: *What a Fuss on the Big Yellow Bus* 192, 193
Rand Afrikaans University (RAU) 201
Randall, Peter 108n2
"Range of Pupil-Centred Schoolbooks Launched" 95
Rankin, Joan 5, 111, 137, 140–141, 142, 143, 199–206; *The Little Cat & the Greedy Old Woman* 201; *Peter's Dulcie Duck* 204; *Scary Footsteps* 202
Rautenbach, Elmarie 87
Ravan Press 2, 10, 108n2
Ravishankar, Anushka: *Today Is My Day* 133
"Read and Learn" series 234
realistic style 24, 35, 115–116
Red Fox 160
A Red Kite in a Pale Sky 9, 60, 61, 62
The Red Man 238–239
The Red Skedonk 221
Reitzel, C.A. 72n1
religion 45, 69, 86, 156, 254; *see also* World Council of Churches
Remembering Green 14
Retief, Hanlie 27, 131, 135
Reynolds, Kimberley 75
Rhinocephants on the Roof (Olinosters op die Dak) 83, 85
Rhodes University 13, 226
Rhyme Journeys (Rymreise) 27

Rich, Adianne 249
Riddell, Chris: *Ottoline and the Yellow Cat* 152
Rinkwest, Tarryn 195
Rive, Richard 106
The Road to Democracy 1652 to 1994 104
Roback, Dianne 115, 116
Robben Island 161, 270
Robson, Jenny 110, 207–215; *Because Pula Means Rain* 208, 212–213; *Dark Waters* 110, 209; *The Denials of Kow-Ten* 111, 211, 212; *Don't Panic, Mechanic* 109, 208–209; *Mellow Yellow* 110, 208; *One Magic Moment* 210; *Praise Song* 208, 212, 213–214; *Savannah 2116* 111, 211–212; *When Bad Things Happen* 33; *Where Shadows Fall* 210
Rochman, Hazel 115, 116, 118
Rode, Linda 73–81, 86; *Another Kind of One Nation: Young South African Writings 1* 78; *Crossing Over* 79, 110; *Goue Fluit My Storie Is Uit* (This Golden Flute Concludes My Story) 26, 28, 77; *Goue Lint My Storie Begint* (This Golden Ribbon Unties My Story) 26, 28, 76–77; *I, a Living Arrow: Young South African Writing 2* 78; *In the Never-Ever Wood* (In Die Nimmer-Immer Bos) 73, 79–80, 170, 180; *In the Rapids: Stories for a New South Africa* 79; *Madiba Magic* 78; *Sonroepertjies* (Calling the Sun) 76; *Stories South of the Sun* (Dipale tsa ka Borwa ho Letsatsia) (Amabali maTshona kweLanga) 25, 77; *Tick Tock Story Clock* 76; *Uit die Hart van die Vuur* (From the Heart of the Fire) 77; *Up the Down Escalator: Young South African Writing 3* 78; *Vrede op Aarde* (Peace on Earth) 28
Rooi-Kiri Wordt Verliefd 131
"Rooikappie nou slimmer Sprokies-heldinne te passief, sê feministe" 24
Room to Read 69, 70
Roome, Diana Reynolds: *The Elephant's Pillow* 115
Rosenberg, Helen 114
Rosenblatt, Louise M. 196
Rosie's Walk 142
Ross, Stewart 80
Roth, Arnold 199
Rothman, Maria Elizabeth (M.E.R.) 76
Rough Luck 13, 16
Rousseau, Henri 236
Roux, Lize (Jaco Jacobs): *Stalmaats* (Stable Mates) 151
Roux, Madeleine 124
Rowling, J.K.: *Goblet of Fire* 259–260
Ruby Sings the Blues 51, 52
Rugbypret 150

The Runaway Hen 227
Rupert, Rona: *Al Everest se Voëls* (All Everest's Birds) 22, 28; *Die Eerste Keer* (The First Time) 21; *Luister, Lefa* (Listen, Lefa) 21; *Wat Maak Jy Hektor?* (What Are You Doing, Hektor?) 9, 21
Rymreise (Rhyme Journeys) 27

Saccardi, Marianne 117, 118
St. Barnabas College 250
Saint-Saëns, Camille 131
Sam, a True Story of a Little Girl and Her Elephant (Sam, 'n Ware Verhaalvan 'n Dogtertjieen Haar Olifant) 97
Sam, 'n Ware Verhaalvan 'n Dogtertjieen Haar Olifant (Sam, a True Story of a Little Girl and Her Elephant) 97
San (Bushmen) 2, 15–16, 62; *see also* Khoisan
Sankofa: A Journal of African Children's and Young Adult Literature 54
Sanlam Prizes for Youth Literature 83, 86, 182, 207, 210, 212, 273
SAPPI Prize 179
SATI Prizes for Outstanding Translation (South African Translators Institute) 152, 173, 273
Savannah 2116 AD 211–212
Savory, Phyllis 179; *The Little Wise One, African Tales of the Hare* 202
Scary Footsteps 202
Scharer, Patricia L. 63, 116, 117
Schateman, Renée 68
Schaukelpferd 176
Scheepers, Riana 80; *Die Afrikaanse Skryfgids* 96, 150
Scheepers Prize 125, 273
Schermbrucker, Reviva 216–225; *An African Christmas Cloth* 220; *An African Suitcase* 222; *Am I a Lion That Eats People?* 219; *Antjie* 218; *At School, What If?* 219; *Azhar* 218; *Bringing Bullying into the Open* 222; *Charlie's House* 109, 110, 216–217; *A Child's Garden* 219; *Cindy* 218; *Green Tongue* 223; *The Jam Tin and the Teacup* 220; *Kero and Beevy, Their Life in Great Zimbabwe, Zimbabwe* 224; *Knock! Knock!* 218; *Learning Our Way* 222; *Lebohang and Polo, Their Life in Ha Lesala, Lesotho* 224; *Lindeka and Vuyane, Their Life in Malkerns, Swaziland* 224; *Mauro and Adelaide, Their Life in Quelimane, Mozambique* 224; *Mhlanguli* 218; *Mmpundulu, the Lightning Bird* 223; *My Home in Walmer Road* 222; *Myrtle and Daneco, Their Life in Kassiesbaai, South Africa* 224; *Nobody's Doll* 221; *The Red Skedonk* 221; *Stars on the Dunes* 220; *String Together* 218; *Taste*

221; *They Were Wrong* 219; *Thobeka and Samukelo, Their Life in Yeoville, South Africa* 224; *Uthini?* 218; *Waiting, Waiting, Always Waiting* 219; *The World in There* 221; *Zimkhitha* 218
Schmidt, Annie M.G. 131
School Library Journal 37, 132
Schuurman, Pieter 149
Schwartz, Joseph 93, 96
science fiction 14, 111, 188, 211–212; *see also* dystopia
scraperboard 200, 201, 202
Sealey, Sally 168
Searle, Ronald 199
Seb & Hamish 115
Sebra en die Bobbejaan (The Zebra and the Baboon) 95
The Secret Garden 65
Sedgwick, Fred. 78
Seed, Jenny 202; *The Far Away Valley* 201; *Nobody's Cat* 26
Seedlings: English Children's Reading and Writers in South Africa 3, 226, 229
Sell, Roger 261
Sendak, Maurice 32, 91, 93, 204
Sereda, Maja 147
Sewell, Anna: *Black Beauty* 76
Sharp Edges 261, 264–265
Shelley, Mary: *Frankenstein* 261
Shipley, David: *Arab and Jew: Wounded Spirits in a Promised Land* 226
Shipley, Mrs. 226
Shirley, Goodness & Mercy 101, 103, 106–107
Shober, Dianne 67
Shorn 111, 127
Short, Kathy 116
The Short Cut 141
Short Stories: Southern Africa and Beyond 231
Shuter & Shooter 221
Sibanda, Silindiwe 214n1
Sikhakhane, Nomthandazo: *Every Precious Drop* 25
Silke, Elsa 80, 173
Simon's Story 33
Die Simpel Dinge Wat Mens Mis 83
The Singing Chameleon 170
Sirkus Toe Saam met 'n Tier (A Tiger Took Me to the Circus) 10, 92
Sisulu, Walter 104
Sithole, Nokwanda 167
Sivu's Six Wishes 115, 116, 117
Sixel, Margaret: *The Happy Prince* 203, 205–206
"Siyagruva" series 251
Siyolo's Jersey 195
Sky Blue Accident 133–134

Slaaptyd, Matilda 149
Sleeping Beauty 88–89
Slingsby, Peter 202; *Jedro's Bane* 1
Slippers, Bibi 129, 131
Smit, Louise: *Bible for Children* 27; *Professor Fossilus en die Dinosourusse* (Professor Fossilus and the Dinosaurs) 97
Smithsonian 114
Snaddon-Wood, Jiggs: *Horns Only* 170
The Snake with Seven Heads 168
Snow White and the Seven Dwarfs 88, 186
The Snuff Tin Bakkie 192–193
Snyman, Lydia 137
Snyman, Maritha 188
Sobukwe, Robert 104
Society for Children's Book Writers & Illustrators (SCBWI) 35, 203
Solberg, Rolf 164–165, 167
Someday the Blue Bird (Eendag die Blou Voël) 23
Something to Do 235–236
Somewhere in Africa 110
Son, Eun Hye 116
A Song for Jamela 48, 52, 53
Song of Be 13, 15, 18
Songololo Books 10, 109, 113, 140, 157, 159–160, 217; *see also* David Philip Publisher
Sonroepertjies (Calling the Sun) 76
Sonto, Sive: *The Little Lost Goat* 25
Soos 'n Wens So Groot (A Wish This Big) 110, 160–161
Sophy 40
Soulcity 250
The Sound of the Gora 6
Sounds of a Cowhide Drum 103
South African Artlife 24
South African Authors & Illustrators 200
South African Broadcasting Corporation (SABC) 14, 251, 259
South African Children's Book Forum (SACBF) 6, 35, 227, 232
South African Council for English Education (SACEE) 250
South African National Gallery 31
South African Plays for TV, Radio and Stage 251
Soweto 10, 85, 166, 250, 251, 253, 268
Soweto uprising 268
Special Days 25
Spencer, L. 249
Spender, Stephen 103
The Spirit of No Surrender 250
Die Spree met Foete 131
Spring Offensive 253–255, 257
Spufford, Francis 76
Staffrider 103
Stalmaats 151

Stanley Bekker and the Boycott (Stanley Bekker en die Boikot) 6
Stanley Bekker en die Boikot (Stanley Bekker and the Boycott) 6
The Star-Bearer: A Creation Myth from Ancient Egypt 59, 61, 115, 116
"Star Stories" series 234
"Stars of Africa" series 17, 234; *see also* Maskew Miller Longman
Stars on the Dunes 220
State of Emergency 167, 177
Steele, Liz 84
Steenberg, Elsabe 186; *Die Boom Wat Wou Loop* (The Wishful Walnut) 23; *Eendag die Blou Voël* (Someday the Blue Bird) 23; *Kariena Karyn* (Katie Colly Wobbles) 23, 28; *Stippe Stappe Stories* 28
Steenkamp, Elzette 211
Stein, Sarah 160
Stellenbosch 26, 93, 134
Stephenson, Arlene: *Short Stories: Southern Africa and Beyond* 231
Stevenson, Deborah 117
Stewart, Dianne 110, 202; "Bread for the Journey" 231; "The Cattle Herder's Song" 229; *Chasing the Wind* 110, 230, 231; "The Crash" 231; *Daughter of the Moonlight and Other African Tales* 229; *The Dove* 113, 114, 115, 117, 228; *Durban in a Word* 232; *Folktales from Africa* 229; *The Gift of the Sun: A Tall Tale from South Africa* 114, 115, 116, 117, 228; *The Guinea-Fowl's Spots and Other African Bird Tales* 229–230; "The Hungry Jackal" 229; *The Mealie-Cob Children* 228; *Mondi, the Music Maker* 227; "The Orange Tree" 227; *The Runaway Hen* 227; "Thekwane and Frog" 226; *Who's Afraid of the Dark?* 203, 232; *Wisdom from Africa* 230; *The Zebra's Stripes and Other African Animal Tales* 229
Steweltjies na Wonderland (Little Boots to Wonderland) 26, 28
Stewig, John 117
Steyn, Tisha 94
Stiepel, Lindy 232
Stillwell, Valerie: *Monsters, Heroes and Sultan's Daughters: Cape Malay Folk Tales* 25
Stippe Stappe Stories 28
The Stone: A Persian Legend of the Magi 61, 114, 115, 118
Stories of Africa 170
Stories South of the Sun 25, 77
The Story of Ferdinand 91–92
Storyland 202
Storytime (Jay Heale) 25, 226–227
Storytime (Sunday Times/Nal'ibali collection) 36, 107, 143

Stowe, Harriet Beecher: *Uncle Tom's Cabin* 76
Streep, Meryl 236
street children 9, 41, 194, 208–209; *see also* homelessness; poverty
Stretton, Hesba: *Jessica's First Prayer* 75
String Together 218
The Strollers 9, 12, 14, 18
A Sudden Summer 60
The Sugar Prince 178–179
The Sun, the Moon and the Blanket of Night 140
Sunday Times 19, 36, 107, 143, 242, 253
Suurlemoen 150
Suzie se Superdoeper-Sjampoe 147
Swaziland 224, 228

Table Mountain 14, 143, 155
Tafelberg Publishers 12, 21, 28, 76, 149, 199; *see also* NB Publishers
Takalani Sesame 250
"Take Me Home United Road" 259
The Tale of Paradise Lost 117
The Tale of Sun and Moon 238
Tales from the Marula Tree (Maroelaboomstories) 122
Tan, Shaun 140
Tanzania 78, 255
Taste 221
Taylor, Nick 269
teenage literature 58, 69, 82–83, 125, 149–150, 210–213, 220, 241–242, 243–249, 251–255, 260–261
Tell the Moon 238–239
Tenniel, John 32
Terreblanche, Christelle 82–83, 84
Testa, Fulvio 176
Thatcher, Moira: *Tselane, a Legend of Lesotho* 201, 202
"Thekwane and Frog" 226
Theo and the Cat Burglar 141, 203
Theo and the Circus Act 141
Theo the Library Cat 140
Theron, Leentjie 25
They Were Wrong 219
This Book Betrays My Brother 246
This Golden Flute Concludes My Story (Goue Fluit My Storie Is Uit) 26, 28
This Golden Ribbon Unties My Story (Goue Lint My Storie Begint) 26, 28
Thobeka and Samukelo, Their Life in Yeoville, South Africa 224
Thomson, Emma 152
Thorne, Michael 53
Three Cheers for Tyron 23

"The Three Sisters of Three Sisters" 14
The Three Teapots 96
Thyssen, Candy Lynn 158
Tick Tock Story Clock 76
Tido's Bag 33
Tien vir 'n Vriend 9, 83
Tienie Holloway Medal 129, 182, 273
Tiger and Louise 237
A Tiger Took Me to the Circus (Sirkus Toe Saam met 'n Tier) 10, 92
The Times 40
Tintinyane, the Girl Who Sang Like a Magic Bird (Die Meisie Wat Soos 'n Bottervoël Sing) 24, 25
Tjojo and the Wild Horses 13
To Everything There Is a Season 115, 116, 117, 118
To My Children's Children 65
Today Is My Day 133
Todd, Mel 156
Tolkien, J.R.R. 120
Tom Kitten 139
Torit of the Strong Right Arm 25
Tötemeyer, Andrée-Jeanne 2, 5; *The Racial Element in Afrikaans Children's and Youth Literature* 5
Toulopers—Verse vir Tieners 151
Towards Understanding 6, 10, 93, 156, 232
township 10, 47, 48, 65, 104, 194, 218, 243–244, 246, 251
traditional Africa 25, 115, 160, 179, 228
Transkei 65, 66, 69, 105, 159, 166; *see also* Eastern Cape
Traveller 14, 17, 18, 19
Trites, R.S. 248
Troeteldrog 148
Truth and Reconciliation Commission (TRC) 169
Tselane, a Legend of Lesotho 201, 202
Turkington, Nola 202
Tutu, Desmond 267; *Children of God Storybook Bible* 36, 97
The Twelve Days of Christmas 202
Two Dogs and Freedom 10
Tyler, Melissa 84

Ucello, Paolo 178
Uchima, Eileen 80
The Ugly Duckling 70
Uit die Hart van die Vuur (From the Heart of the Fire) 77
ULizeka Wazikhethela (Lizeka's Choice) 70
Umkhonto we Sizwe (MK) 254, 258n1
Uncle James and the Delicious Monster (Oom Japie en die Monsterplant) 97
Uncle Tom's Cabin 76
unemployment 2, 42

UNESCO Prize for Children's and Young People's Literature in the Service of Tolerance 212
The Unicorn and the Sea 177–178
United Nations 66
U.S. Parents' Choice Award 143
University of Cape Town 32, 160, 175, 232, 244, 250
University of Pretoria 120, 156, 165, 191
University of South Africa (UNISA) 226
University of Stellenbosch 31, 32, 34, 35, 74, 155
University of the Free State 145
University of the Western Cape 71, 156, 250
University of the Witwatersrand (WITS) 250
University of Worcester 134
Up the Down Escalator: Young South African Writing 3 78
Usborne 152
Uthini? 218

Valentine 32
Van Coller, Hennie 82, 85, 86, 87
Van den Heever, Carla-Mari 151
Van der Merwe, Meg 71
Van der Veken, Ingrid 97
van der Vyver, Marita 82–90; *The Authentic, Unusually Alarming, Actual Factual Story Book* (Die Oorspronlike, Ongewoon Skrikaanjaende, Werklik Feitlike Storieboek) 97; *Boomklim* 83; *Dinge van 'n Kind* (Childish Things) 83, 85–86; *Eenkantkind* 9, 83, 84; *Entertaining Angels* (Griet Skryf 'n Sprokie) 82; *The Hidden Life of Hanna Why* 83, 86–87, 88–90; *Hy Bly My Broer* 83; *Mia's Mom* 83, 84–85, 88, 129; *Die Mooiste Sprokies van Grimm* 82, 132; *Olinosters op die Dak* (Rhinocephants on the Roof) 83, 85, 129; *Die Simpel Dinge Wat Mens Mis* 83; *Tien vir 'n Vriend* 9, 83, 84; *Van Jou Jas* 83, 84
Van der Walt, Derick 149
Van der Walt, Thomas B. 5, 84, 85, 86, 110, 111, 124, 152, 188
van der Walt, Willem 7
van Deventer, Alida 200
van Heerden, Marjorie 5, 35, 91–100, 122, 137, 142, 202, 229; *Die Een Groot Bruin Beer* (The One Big Brown Bear) 92; *Father Christmas Needs Help* (Kersvader het Hulp Nodig) 93; *Good Night, Grandpa* 92; *Lulama's Long Way Home* 98; *Monde's Present* 95; *A Monster in the Garden* ('n Monster in die tuin) 93–94; *A New Bed for Alexia* ('n Nuwe Bed vir Alexia) 93; *Old Enough* (Oud Genoeg) 93; *A Tiger Took Me to the Circus* (Sirkus Toe Saam met 'n Tier) 10, 92

Van Jou Jas 83
van Niekerk, Raymond 31
Van Patrys-hulle tot Hanne Hoekom: 'Gids tot die Afrikaanse Kinder- en Jeugboek 3, 5, 22, 23, 28, 73, 120, 125, 152
van Riebeeck, Jan 267
van Riet, Samantha 126
Van Rooy, Rikus 149
van Rooyen, Engela: *Johnny Later and His Hammer* 191–192
van Straten, Cecily 202; *Torit of the Strong Right Arm* 25
Van Taak, Marelize 148
Van Vlimmeren, Dijlan 128
van Wyk, Chris 10, 101–108, 267, 269; *Eggs to Lay, Chickens to Hatch* 101, 106; *Freedom Fighters* (Sets 1, 2 & 3) 101, 104–105; "In Detention" 267; *It Is Time to Go Home* 101; *A Message in the Wind* 6, 106; "Mr Hare Meets Mr Mandela" 36, 107; *Nelson Mandela: Long Walk to Freedom* 32, 34, 35, 36, 105; *Ouma Ruby's Secret* 106; *Peppy 'n Them* 106; *Petroleum and the Orphaned Ostrich* 106; *The Road to Democracy 1652 to 1994* 104; *Shirley, Goodness & Mercy* 101, 103, 106–107; *Wietie* 103; *The Year of the Tapeworm* 101
Van Wyk, Marguerite 183, 184
van Zyl, Danie 108*n*2
Van Zyl, H.E. 191
Van Zyl, Pieter 27
Venice University 178
Venter, Isabelle 149
Vermaak, Adinda: *Rymreise* (Rhyme Journeys) 27; *Woordreise* (Word Journeys) 27, 28
Vermaak, Arnold 26, 120
Verneukpan 151
Viljoen, Fanie 126, 151, 152
Village Schools Project 16
violence 6, 60, 167, 213–214, 243, 244–245, 248, 253, 261–262
Vivian Wilkes Award 239
Voices in the Dark 141
Vorster, Magdel 123, 124
Vra vir Frederika (Ask for Patricia) 202
Vrede op Aarde (Peace on Earth) 28

Wagener, Adie 16
Waiting for Rain 13, 16
Waiting, Waiting, Always Waiting 219
Walace, Claire 84
Walkins, Linda L. 115, 116
Walton, Ann 17, 111, 234–240; *Big Fat Lies* 235; *Don't Scratch!* 235; *A Fine Day for Flying* 237; *The Girl and the Golden Amulet* 238–239; *The Great Big Fish* 236–237; *Have You Seen My Donkey?* 237; *Here I Am* 111, 130, 236; *I Don't Belong to You* 237; *Lying Toad* 238; *The Red Man* 238–239; *Something to Do* 235–236; *The Tale of Sun and Moon* 238; *Tell the Moon* 238–239; *Tiger and Louise* 237; *We Must Go Shopping Now Samson* 237; *We Shouldn't Keep It!* 235; *We Want Tails!* 238
Walton, Jo 261, 263
Warhol, Andy 51
Wat Doen Jy Daniel? 120, 125
Wat Maak Jy Hektor? (What Are You Doing, Hektor?) 9, 21
The Waterbearer 58–60, 61–62
watercolor 21–22, 23, 35, 48, 129, 130, 179, 180, 203, 220
Watermark Publishing 32
Watson, Victor 102
Way Up and Over Everything 115, 117
W.B. Mkhize Award 98, 273
We Must Go Shopping Now Samson 237
We Shouldn't Keep It! 235
We Want Tails! 238
Weideman, George 7
We're Having a Party! 138
Wessel, J.W. 22, 26, 28, 95, 98, 129, 130
west coast (of South Africa) 14, 19*n*2, 40
Western Cape 13, 14, 18, 74, 86, 91, 96, 162, 174, 218
What a Fuss on the Big Yellow Bus 192, 193
What a Gentleman! 45
What Are You Doing, Hektor? (Wat Maak Jy Hektor?) 9, 21
What Katy Did 75
What's Cooking, Jamela? 52
When Bad Things Happen 33
When Whales Go Free 58, 59, 61, 62
Where Shadows Fall 210
"Where the Dark Ocean Rolls" 59, 61
Where's Jamela? 48, 52
The White Butterfly (Die Wit Flinder) 24, 28
White Ravens 34, 143, 228
Who's Afraid of the Dark? 203, 232
Why the Sun and Moon Live in the Sky 53
Whyte, Jennifer 228
The Widlows Tale 200
Wietie 103
Wilde, Oscar: *The Happy Prince* 203, 205–206
Wilder, Laura Ingalls: *Little House on the Prairie* 75
Wildsmith, Brian 204
Wilko, Józef 176
Willard, Nancy: *The Tale of Paradise Lost* 117
Willemien en die Geel Kat (Ottoline and the Yellow Cat) 152
Williams, J. 247
Williams, Sheron: *Imani's Music* 115, 117

Williams, Teresa 142
Willing to Learn, Passages of Personal Discovery 76
Winnie the Pooh 174
Winnie the Witch 141
Wisdom from Africa 230
A Wish This Big (Soos 'n Wens So Groot) 110, 160–161
The Wishful Walnut (Die Boom Wat Wou Loop) 23
Wiskunde Gee My Maagpyn 150
Die Wit Flinder (The White Butterfly) 24, 28
The Witness 269
The Wonder Shoes 175, 178
The Wonderful Adventures of Nils 174
Woodward, Cathy 37
Woolf, Virginia 64
Woordreise (Word Journeys) 27, 28
Word Journeys (Woordreise) 27, 28
World Council of Churches 254; *see also* religion
The World in There 221
A World of Flower Fairies 179
The World Through Picture Books: Librarians' Favourite Books from Their Country 68, 159
Wurms met Tamatiesous en Ander Lawwe Rympies 146
Wybenga, Gretel: *Van Patrys-hulle tot Hanne Hoekom: 'Gids tot die Afrikaanse Kinder- en Jeugboek* 3, 5, 22, 23, 28, 73, 120, 125, 152

The Year of the Tapeworm 101
Yenika-Agbaw, Vivian 5
You and the Dinosaur (Jy en die Draakakkedis) 183
You magazine 259
Young, Ed 94
Young Africa Award 12, 42, 106, 231, 272

Zackie Mostert en die Ongelooflike Kulkunsie 148
Zackie Mostert en die Super-Aaklige Soen 148
Zaleski, Jeff 116
Zambia 56, 228
Zanendaba 168
Zanzibar Road (Zanzibarstraat) 50, 52
Zanzibarstraat (Zanzibar Road) 153
Zanzibarstraat, Hier Kom Ons! (Next Stop—Zanzibar Road) 153
Zavrel, Stepan 176, 201
The Zebra and the Baboon (Sebra en die Bobbejaan) 95
"Zebra Books" series 17, 234; *see also* Kagiso; Maskew Miller Longman
The Zebra's Stripes and Other African Animal Tales 229
Zimbabwe 56, 59, 224, 254
Zimkhitha 218
Zipes, Jack 87
Zuma, Jacob 104

www.ingramcontent.com/pod-product-compliance
Ingram Content Group UK Ltd.
Pitfield, Milton Keynes, MK11 3LW, UK
UKHW041924140426
5217IPUK00014B/304